The Landings at Suvla Bay, 1915

The Landings at Suvla Bay, 1915

An Analysis of British Failure During the Gallipoli Campaign

MICHAEL J. MORTLOCK

McFarland & Company, Inc., Publishers
Jefferson, North Carolina, and London

LIBRARY OF CONGRESS CATALOGUING-IN-PUBLICATION DATA

Mortlock, Michael J., 1933–
 The landings at Suvla Bay, 1915 : an analysis of British failure during the Gallipoli Campaign / Michael J. Mortlock.
 p.   cm.
 Includes bibliographical references and index.

 ISBN-13: 978-0-7864-3035-2
 softcover : 50# alkaline paper ∞

 1. World War, 1914–1918 — Amphibious operations.   2. World War, 1914–1918 — Naval operations, British.   3. World War, 1914–1918 — Campaigns — Turkey — Suvla Bay.   4. World War, 1914–1918 — Campaigns — Turkey — Gallipoli Peninsula.   5. Suvla Bay (Turkey) — History, Military.   I. Title.
 D582.S8M67   2007
 940.4'26 — dc22   2007018496

British Library cataloguing data are available

©2007 Michael J. Mortlock. All rights reserved

No part of this book may be reproduced or transmitted in any form or by any means, electronic or mechanical, including photocopying or recording, or by any information storage and retrieval system, without permission in writing from the publisher.

On the cover: *foreground* Suvla Bay shortly after the landing (*Courtesy of the Imperial War Museum*); *background* map of Dardanelles and star compass ©2006 Clipart

Manufactured in the United States of America

McFarland & Company, Inc., Publishers
 Box 611, Jefferson, North Carolina 28640
 www.mcfarlandpub.com

The author wishes to dedicate this history to all service personnel, English, Irish, Scottish, Welch, Dominican, Imperial, who dutifully served King, or Queen, and Country.

Acknowledgments

First and foremost I acknowledge my deep indebtedness to Dr. John L. Gordon, Jr., Professor of History at the University of Richmond, for his scholarly criticism and kindly encouragement. Professor Gordon gave me much wise counsel, an abundance of sound advice, and a wealth of constructive suggestions. Without Dr. Gordon's support, I seriously doubt whether I would have brought the project to a successful conclusion. Dr. Emory C. Bogle, Associate Professor of History, University of Richmond, lent me his considerable expertise in the fields of format and layout which proved invaluable, and for which I wish to express my gratitude. To the late Dr. David C. Evans, Professor of History, University of Richmond, I owe an acknowledgment for much help in the field of naval gunnery, and other nautical aspects appertaining to the Dardanelles theater of war, plus his kindly conversations on associated subjects. The present Chair of the Department of History, Dr. Hugh West, permitted me privileges which greatly helped me in securing permissions. Much is also owed to the delightful Debbie Govoruhk, secretary at the Department of History, who perfected, polished, and produced a properly finished manuscript on disk and hard-drive, following a lot of very hard work by Ms. Rebecca Shewman. I would also like to mention the kindness of Dr. Harry Ward, Professor Emeritus, who afforded me much help, advice, and encouragement.

Much of my research owes a great deal to the Boatwright Memorial Library of the University of Richmond and, in particular, its interlibrary loan service whose tireless staff, Mesdames Nancy Vick, Noreen Cullen, and Kit Davison, secured all the material I requested, much of it obscure. My gratitude is due also to certain reference librarians, specifically Nancy Woodall and Bill Sudduth, who helped me locate material invaluable to my researches. My especial thanks are due to a very sweet lady, Dean Judith L. Hunt, University Librarian at Montclair State University, who, while head of the University of Richmond Libraries, granted me every possible facility with which to further my investigations. In addition Dr. Hunt contributed a wealth of proofreading, expert advice, kindly insistence, and morale-boosting encouragement to this enterprise — not to mention long hours spent perfecting the layout of this, my major work to date. I am extremely indebted to Mr. James E. Gwin, Director of Collections Management, for permitting me to use his private office and personal computer on the weekends over a period of many years. I am also indebted to the Henrico County Public Library, Dumbarton Branch, the facilities of which I used over a period of some twenty years.

The ladies and gentlemen at the Technology Learning Center with monumental patience were responsible for conscientiously scanning maps and illustrations. These they not only inserted in the manuscript but also provided on CD. Melissa Foster and Sue McGinnis were the main technicians to aid me. In this same department Michael Frankson, Roberto Ritano, Ms. Robin Haskins and Robert Vendig contributed valuable expertise which enabled the finished product to display a high degree of professional perfection. I wish to thank one and all. Mr. Ernie Winters, of Action Graphics of Virginia, produced some fine maps to enhance the work. Messrs. Glenn and Thomas Walters, computer specialists, came to my aid on more than one occasion with technical, and technological expertise second to none. Gene Payne enhanced some old photographs. M. Julianne Roman is owed great thanks for creating the index.

I am also indebted to the United States Naval Academy at Annapolis and its Nimitz Library for lending me the microfilmed lectures, theses, reports, and recommendations entitled *The Gallipoli Campaign Studies*. This collection is specialized military and naval material, strategical and logistical in nature, and, from those perspectives, one of the most detailed appraisals of the Dardanelles operations. The Imperial War Museum, London, thanks to the kindness of the curator, Diana Condell, and two of her colleagues, furnished invaluable help. Many of the illustrations included in this work originated at the I.W.M. and I wish to pay tribute to the kindness of the keeper for allowing them to be used. The Alderman Library of the University of Virginia afforded much vital material. From there I obtained all I required in the way of British Cabinet papers, Hansard's records of Parliamentary debates, Ministerial replies, and Members' questions, plus one unique personal narrative, and the Virginia Military Institute kindly lent me microfilmed records of secret War Office, War Council, and Dardanelles Committee deliberations and directives. The Library of Congress provided helpful guidance to aid my researches. The Van Pelt Library of the University of Pennsylvania also deserves a mention for allowing me access to important insights with regard to my topic.

My sister, Patricia Anne Cobbold, furnished some vitally important information, for which I would like to express my gratitude. I also wish to acknowledge Richard Joseph Mortlock, my brother, who was responsible for photocopying the letter written by Private Jake Mortlock at Hill 60, and for contributing some remembered utterances of that former soldier. Owen A. Halliday supplied an intriguing vignette which I greatly appreciated. I also wish to thank Andrew Mackenzie for taking the trouble to ascertain facts about his great uncle, Private David Anderson Mackenzie of the Royal Scots, who was killed on Gallipoli. Former Suffolk soldier Victor C. Phillips, the Honorary Secretary of Suffolk Regiment's Old Comrades' Association, gave me every assistance, and I obtained valuable insights from the Suffolk Regimental Museum at Gibraltar Barracks, Bury St. Edmunds, and later at the Imperial War Museum, Duxford, Cambridgeshire—whence it had been transferred—and would like to record my gratitude for the assistance given by the respective curators and staff. I should also like to acknowledge the kindness of Major Nicholas Jenkinson, T.D., Officer Commanding, Battery-Sergeant-Major Terrence Smith, and the Battery Clerk Gunner Brian Hartington of the 202 (Suffolk Yeomanry) Battery, 100 Medium Regiment, Royal Artillery, T.A., in affording me much help over the years.

Finally I wish to state how much I owe to all of the sources I consulted over the many years my researches have occupied. Most of the authors of the primary source material—likewise the soldiers who provided the personal accounts—have passed on. In many instances the publishers have also—or have gone out of business, at any rate. I would particularly like to mention General Sir Ian Hamilton, the British C.-in-C.; his German-Turco counterpart, Marshal Otto Liman von Sanders—together with his subordinate Lt.-Colonel Hans Kannengiesser; Lt.-Colonel Thomas Gibbons, D.S.O., C.O. of the 1/5 Battalion, the Essex Regiment; Lt.-Colonel Frederic H.D. Bendall, of the 2/3rd Battalion, the London Regiment; Major John Gillam, of the Army Service Corps; Captains A. Fair and E.D. Wolton, of the 1/5 Battalion, the Suffolk Regiment; 2nd Lieutenant Edmund Priestman, of the 6th Battalion, the York & Lancaster Regiment; Sergeant John Hargrave, of the 32nd Field Ambulance; Captain Oskar Teichman, R.A.M.C., attached 1st Worcestershire Yeomanry; Henry Hanna, who chronicled the exploits of the 7th Royal Dublin Fusiliers, and war correspondents Messrs. Ellis Ashmead-Bartlett and Henry Nevinson—these military historians, together with the official historian, Brig.-General Cecil F. Aspinall-Oglander, are the ones who contributed the bulk of the backbone to the following work. I wish to fully acknowledge my indebtedness to these officers and gentlemen. I wish to express my thanks to all the other sources to which I have taken very great pains to cite on every occasion I have woven quotations from their texts into my account. I include those of my own comrades-in-arms who lent their very valuable knowledge—technical and otherwise—to assist my enterprise, and in some cases the related experiences of members of their own families in the Great War.

Contents

Acknowledgments	vii
Preface	1
Introduction	5
1. Plans and Prevarications	13
2. The Preparations for the Landings	32
3. The Landings	58
4. Failure	99
5. The End	123
6. The Conclusion	153
Appendix A: "Dead Men's Diaries Laud Turkish Foes"	163
Appendix B: "Why French Left Kum Kale"	167
Appendix C: Contemporary Views Expressed by Ministers and Members of Parliament	168
Appendix D: Private Mortlock's Letter from Hill 60	171
Appendix E: August 1915 Order of Battle	172
Notes	181
Bibliography	201
Index	219

Preface

The fatal shots at Sarajevo triggered an inexorable movement towards war as the interlocking cogwheels of intricate treaty commitments made the military mobilization of the major industrial nations of Europe probable, and an armed conflict extremely likely. The principal powers were already aligned via the Triple Alliance (Germany, Austria-Hungary, and Italy) and Triple Entente (Russia, France, and Britain); lesser countries were open to persuasion, or intimidation, as "the lamps were going out all over Europe."[1] At 11 P.M. Greenwich Mean Time on 4 August, Britain was at war with Germany over the violation of Belgian neutrality.

Contemporaries never described the war which began in the early days of August 1914 as "the First World War." Its origins were essentially European: a power struggle between Russia and Austria-Hungary in the Balkans, and the Franco-British fear of the German domination of western Europe.[2] Germany for its part had laid elaborate plans for a quick victory over France, formulated by General Count Alfred von Schlieffen, Chief of the German General Staff. According to the Schlieffen Plan, once France had been crushed the German armies could be entrained eastward to combine with those of Austria-Hungary to defeat the slower mobilizing Russian forces.[3]

Once the whirlwind events in northwestern Europe stabilized into the comparative security of siege warfare on a gargantuan scale, and those on the Eastern Front into a more fluid, but equally attritional slogging match, the Allied strategists sought alternatives. Their search for a means of breaking the stalemate eventually spawned a series of "side shows,"[4] possibly the most celebrated of which was the Gallipoli Campaign of 1915–16.

The Gallipoli Campaign was the progression of a strategy of forcing a passage through the Dardanelles, the southernmost neck of water separating Turkey-in-Europe from Turkey-in-Asia. The government of the Ottoman Empire,[5] although officially neutral until late October 1914, closed that international waterway at the outbreak of the war, much to the consternation of Russia and the other two Entente powers. There was, and is, unanimous agreement that Winston Churchill, then the British First Lord of the Admiralty, originally conceived the idea. Both Herbert Asquith and

MAP A
GEOGRAPHY OF THE DARDANELLES

David Lloyd George—the wartime British prime ministers—attributed credit for the scheme's initial conception to him.[6] With his "rugged fluency" and charismatic personality Churchill imposed his will upon his War Council colleagues at a meeting on 13 January 1915.[7] His objective was highly commendable, very unlike the attempts to accomplish it.

The plan was to force a passage through the Narrows of the Dardanelles that led to the Sea of Marmora, from which stretch of water the Royal Navy could bombard Constantinople. Sustained shelling would cause the capitulation of that capital, the fall of the government, and the exit of the Ottoman Empire from the war. This would open up the Black Sea lanes to shipping, thus freeing the Russians from their maritime isolation, and enabling them to be supplied with vitally needed arms and munitions. It also would release the huge surpluses of the Ukrainian granary for Anglo-French consumption, and greatly enhance the safety of the Suez Canal.

The attempts to realize the strategy fell into three phases: (1) a naval attack alone; (2) amphibious assaults by military forces with close naval support and succor; and (3) further landings with naval support and succor in conjunction with a determined offensive action by troops already ashore on the Gallipoli Peninsula. It is the third phase, the landings at Suvla Bay, which is the focus of this military history, for it is the author's contention that the idea was brilliant but its execution lamentable. Success eluded the operation for a great number of disparate reasons, and the blame for failure unfairly laid upon those whose voices could not be heard above the tumult of criticism and recrimination. The author's intention is to analyze the reasons for the failure. In particular he intends to highlight the role of the 54th (East Anglian) Territorial Division, most of whose volunteers came from the author's own area of eastern England, and whose personal accounts are featured throughout this text. These enthusiasts stand unjustly accused of implication in the cause of the *débâcle* which ensued. Likewise the author's argument is based on the contemporary consensus which maintained that inertia and inept leadership were two major factors which contributed to the defeat of the strategy. Furthermore, this same third phase, if prosecuted more vigorously, contained the ingredients for potential success sufficient to vindicate Churchill's faith in the enterprise.

The author has spent some 27 years on a work of three volumes, the only complete history of the 54th (East Anglian) Division in the Great War. This book is only a portion of that much larger work and history. The author obtained information on the Suvla Bay landings and the subsequent hostilities from official histories; military histories; regimental histories, military and naval documents; interviews with combatants; memoirs, autobiographies, diaries, and letters of soldiers, sailors, aviators, service chaplains, statesmen, ministers, and diplomats; cabinet papers, parliamentary proceedings, *communiqués*, and correspondence; newspaper accounts and war correspondents' assessments; and a wealth of secondary source material. The author also drew upon his not inconsiderable experiences with the British Regular Army, the British Territorial Army, and those experiences of his comrades-in-arms. Where apposite, they are included in the text, or in the endnotes.

Introduction

With the ratification of the Franco-Russian Dual Alliance in December 1893, the old Bismarckian security system collapsed and a new Continental balance of power came into being. Otto von Bismarck, the German Chancellor, knew his nation to be a military match for any single rival but feared the possibility of an anti-German coalition. From the end of the Franco-Prussian War in 1871 until 1893, he and his policy successfully kept France isolated and forged strong links with potential adversaries. The new configuration meant that the Triple Alliance of Germany, Austria-Hungary, and Italy confronted that of Russia and France, while Great Britain continued to retain its cherished freedom of action until it concluded the Anglo-French Entente Cordiale of 1904.[1] This became known as the Triple Entente after 1907 when Russia, already tied to France, signed a separate treaty with Britain.

For Germany this new development meant that in any future war the German army would have to fight on two fronts. As a result, the German General Staff, headed by Count Alfred von Schlieffen, drew up the plan that bore his name. Since the Franco-Russian agreement contained an automatic mobilization clause whereby those allies would mobilize if any one of the Triple Alliance should do so, the Schlieffen Plan's objective was a rapid victory over France. It entailed a curving massed attack thrusting south through Belgium aimed at the French capital. Paris once encircled, Schlieffen calculated, would induce the French to surrender. After this occurred the full force of the German military machine would hasten eastward to join their Austro-Hungarian comrades in the destruction of the slower mobilizing Russian armies.

> This strategy, which von Schlieffen worked out without consulting either the naval command or the architects of German foreign policy, had several disastrous features. The first was the automatic coupling that made war with France necessary from the outset if any military entanglement with the Russians should arise. A second was the intention of violating Belgian neutrality, which Great Britain had guaranteed; this would virtually force the British to enter the war against Germany as well.[2]

Thus, the order to mobilize initiated war. The promulgation of the fateful mobilization order activated ponderous metaphoric wheels of machinery which revolved relentlessly, bearing the European powers towards a conflict. The fatal attraction to strike before the opposition was fully prepared mesmerized the members of both alliances.[3] Mobilization entailed the ordering of all reservists to report to the ship or shore unit with which they had served, bringing battalions, batteries, squadrons, or boat crews up to full strength, or creating additional ones. Militiamen were called up for full-time service, and in most countries (Britain was one exception), conscription, once mobilization was effected, became universal for men between the ages of 18 and 35, even, in some instances, 45.

Once Austria-Hungary issued its ultimatum to Serbia on 23 July 1914, in retaliation for the assassinations of Archduke Francis Ferdinand and his wife at Sarajevo the previous month, it started a chain reaction which was to embroil all the European powers in the most horrific war in history. Less than two weeks later the British Foreign Secretary, Sir Edward Grey, made his famous remark that "the lamps were going out all over Europe"[4] in a dusk-gathering Whitehall room. The following evening Britain presented its own ultimatum to Germany.[5] It expired unanswered at midnight on 4 August. The next day mobilization orders went out as Britain declared war on Germany. In the tiny West Suffolk hamlet of Worlington, a telegram summoned Private S. Jacob P. Mortlock from a harvest field on the family farm.[6] *The History of the Norfolk Regiment,* however, states that:

> The order for mobilization reached both battalions [1/4th and 1/5th] on the evening of August 4, 1914, a few hours before the formal declaration of war. Next morning the 1/4th Battalion assembled at the Drill Hall in Chapel Street, Norwich, and was billeted in the City of Norwich Schools on Newmarket Road. The 1/5th Battalion mobilized at Dereham on the same day.[7]

Within days the British Expeditionary Force (BEF) embarked to aid the Belgians, and the Royal Navy's various fleets took up war stations and blockade duties. Throughout the world, Dominion and Imperial administrations made appropriate preparations. Australia, New Zealand, and Canada rallied behind the Mother Country; South Africa, after much soul-searching, did likewise. In northwestern Europe the celebrated Schlieffen Plan only just failed to give the German armies the speedy victory over the French that its conception had intended. The failure resulted from a watered-down version of the original Plan ordered by von Schlieffen's successor, Helmuth von Moltke; misinterpretation of its objectives by the field commanders[8]; and the magnificent fighting rearguard actions by the BEF, whom Kaiser Wilhelm II, in an order issued on 19 August, described as "General French's contemptible little army."[9] The Plan foundered at the Marne, and "the Race for the Sea" ensued.

Introduction

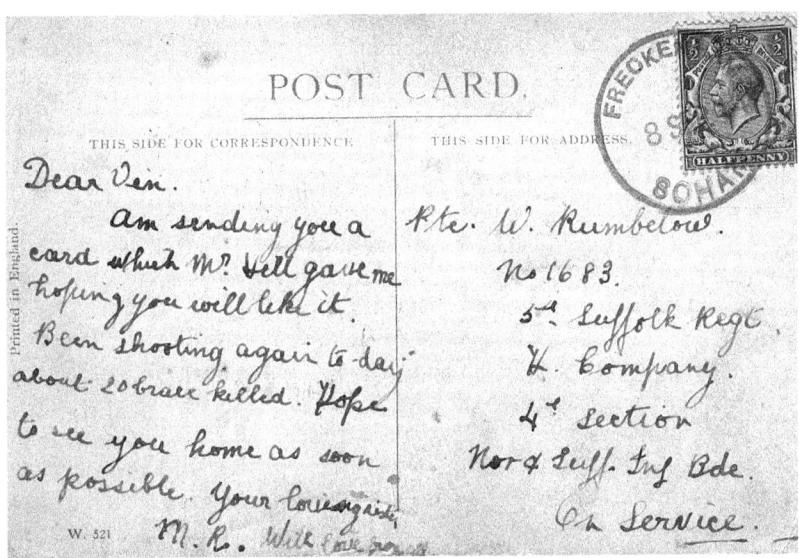

Postcard sent to Private Rumbelow, September 1914: front.

In the Sublime Porte, the seat of government of the Ottoman Empire in Constantinople, the leaders of the Turkish ruling faction, all-too-recently embroiled in the tinderbox of the Balkans, did not immediately commit themselves to either camp. In fact, in spite of a strong pro-German lobby on the ruling Young Turk Committee of Union and Progress, they professed neutrality, although pro-Russian sentiments were hard to detect.[10]

Before 1908, average Turks had minimal interest in their nationality. Religion was of far more importance, and Islam represented a concept greater than Ottoman nationality. Put simply, religion influenced them more than patriotism.

The year 1908 saw the emergence of a new political and largely nationalistic movement, the Young Turks. These zealots were animated by the aim of making their country a European power, and they were aggressive, inexperienced, and impatient. As is frequently the case with idealists, they were not taken seriously in their own land. Following the fall of Abdul Hamid in 1909, the Young Turks' ideology became more intensely nationalistic. These young firebrands included Jews and a high proportion of lax Moslems, so a robust patriotism grew up alongside diminishing religious fervor. The morale of Turkey was already high in 1914, notwithstanding the defeat by Bulgaria in the Balkan War of 1912–13, and the considerable military and naval support received from Germany strengthened it further. This support took the form of finance, *matériel*, officers of the armed services, experts, and instructors. Indeed, Germany's dream of realizing its projected Berlin-to-Baghdad rail link, and the possible need of force to establish and protect it, caused it to woo the Young Turks. It deliberately encouraged their aggressive attitude and adopted the position of a stronger and benevolently supervisory elder brother.

Private Jake Mortlock, D Company, 1/5th Battalion, the Suffolk Regiment, at age 19. Photograph taken in Colchester early March 1915. He had been a Territorial Force soldier in that unit for two years, and was called up for full time service upon declaration of war, 4th August, 1914. (Mortlock family photograph)

Private Mortlock had gone A.W.O.L. to attend what appears to have been some sort of party or celebration. The "Bernard" referred to was Bernard Powers — one of his best friends — shortly to be commissioned into the Middlesex Regiment, and subsequently seconded to the Royal Flying Corps. (Mortlock family photograph)

The several immediate victories for the Central Powers of Germany and Austria-Hungary which followed the outbreak of war in August 1914, Le Cateau and the Retreat from Mons in the west, and Tannenberg to the east, naturally convinced the Young Turks that their German patrons would win, but they decided to wait a bit rather than make a hasty commitment. Accordingly, Turkey remained "neutral" for almost two months—"but mobilized its troops."[11]

Two ultra-modern warships of the German navy, the *Breslau* and the *Goeben*, which cruised in the Mediterranean Sea during the fateful days of early August, eluded the British Royal Navy and, with Turkish connivance, slipped through the Dardanelles to anchor off Constantinople.

(See Map A.) At the same time resentment ran high in Turkey over the canceled contracts on two almost completed Turkish warships constructed in British shipyards. The fact that much of the money raised to finance these vessels was in the form of public subscription made the matter particularly sensitive.[12] Shortly thereafter came the announcement that Germany had "sold" the *Breslau* and the *Goeben* to Turkey. The furious British accused Turkey of a flagrant breach of neutrality. They were particularly incensed over the retention of the German crewmen, some of whom acted out the charade of wearing the fez! The sight of these two modern warships in the

Golden Horn, seen by the thousands of workers who crossed and recrossed the bridge every morning and evening, did much to stimulate war fever. Then, late in October, Turkish gunboats launched an unprovoked attack on Russian Black Sea naval installations which precipitated formal declarations of hostilities. Within a few weeks Turkish troops confronted British, Dominion, and Imperial forces in Mesopotamia and the Sinai, the Dardanelles were closed to Allied shipping, and minefields laid in that strategic waterway. Added to this the Turkish Army in the east launched an initially successful offensive against the Russians on the Caucasian front, and an appeal by the Grand Duke Nicholas to the Allies for help "came up for discussion" at a War Council meeting in London on 2 January 1915. The result: "The next day the Foreign Office despatched a telegram which assured the Grand Duke that something would be done."[13] Earlier, on 2 November, in a move designed to probe the vulnerability of the forts guarding the Dardanelles, the Admiralty in London ordered its Cruiser Squadron in the vicinity to bombard the Turkish forts. "The firing only lasted twenty minutes … but the mission had been accomplished … they had tested the forts and found them anything but impregnable. The lesson was read very carefully back in London."[14]

Once the struggle between the opposing armies in northwestern Europe stabilized into the static stalemate of siege warfare, Allied strategists started to search for alternatives, and Winston Churchill, the British First Lord of the Admiralty, was in the forefront. On 13 January 1915 his plan for forcing a passage through the Dardanelles, capturing Constantinople, and reopening access to the Black Sea obtained the sanction of the War Council. It was largely Churchill's personal magnetism and powers of persuasion that overcame the intense opposition of some of his colleagues.[15] Strangely enough some members of the War Council present did reflect upon the fate of Admiral Sir John Thomas Duckworth's daring Napoleonic Wars adventure of 1807. This, although initially successful, failed completely because the French encouraged Ottoman recalcitrance, and when the population of Constantinople took up arms, Duckworth's squadron suffered considerable damage which caused him to withdraw, and the British ships then had to run the gauntlet of the Dardanelles batteries in order to escape.[16] It was, in fact, an antique bombard dating from Mohammed II's siege of Constantinople in 1453, which projected "a 700 pound stone shot to cut the mainmast of Admiral Duckworth's flagship, and a second shot killed or wounded sixty men."[17]

The War Council instructed Vice-Admiral Sir Sackville Carden, who commanded the Mediterranean Fleet, to make an assessment of the possibilities of such a venture. Churchill and Carden exchanged telegrams in regard to the matter. Carden's assessment was cautiously optimistic, with the reservation that "he did not think Dardanelles could be rushed." In his

Introduction

MAP B
GALLIPOLI AND THE ISLANDS

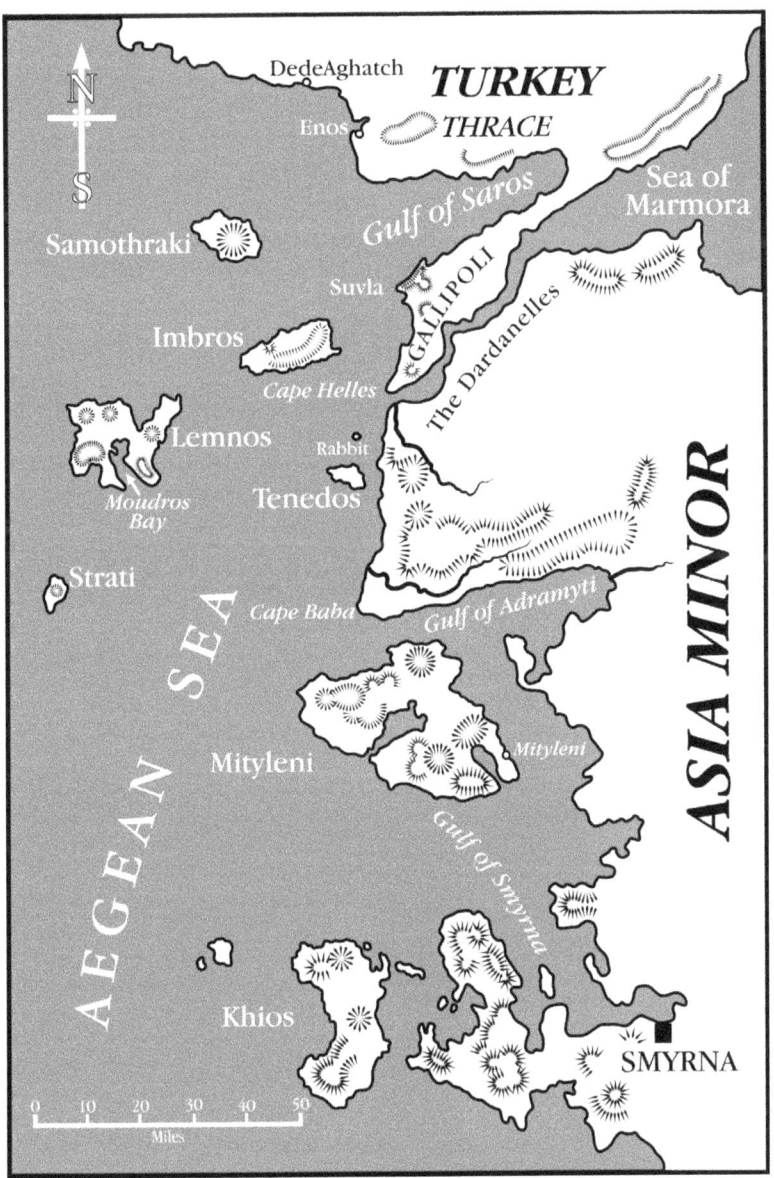

opinion "it might be possible to demolish the forts one by one." To this end Admiral Carden submitted a plan. His proposal was first to concentrate his fire on the entrance forts. When they were demolished he would proceed to deal with the inner forts, attacking them from the Straits and from the seaward side of the Gallipoli Peninsula.[18] Thus "largely on Carden's advice, the British War Council decided to mount an operation to force the Dardanelles by naval power alone."[19] Nonetheless as a precaution the War Council also decided to assemble a large body of troops in the area "to be available in case of necessity to support the naval attack on the Dardanelles.... The Admiralty was instructed to build special transports and lighters suitable for the conveyance and landing of a force of 50,000 men at any point where they may be required."[20]

Lieutenant Bernard Powers, R.F.C., in front of his airplane. He was one of Jake Mortlock's best friends — "a good lad." He was reported "missing" in the summer of 1917, and no trace of him, or his aircraft, was ever found. His poor mother, however, kept Bernard's bedroom ready for his return until the early 1920s. (Mortlock family photograph)

1

Plans and Prevarications

Accordingly, plans evolved which created an Anglo-French military expeditionary force. Its objective was to occupy the Gallipoli Peninsula in support of the fleet's attack on the Dardanelles fortifications and the clearance of that waterway of all obstructions. To that end, on 16 February 1915, the War Council decided to order the 29th Regular Army Division to sail for the Aegean within two weeks. Under item 1(a) the actual wording reads: "The XXIXth Division, hitherto intended to form part of Sir John French's army, to be dispatched to Lemnos at the earliest possible date. It is hoped it may be able to sail within nine or ten days."[1] But "this brought so sharp a protest from the generals in France" that two days later, on 18 February, Lord Horatio Kitchener, the Secretary of State for War, "revoked his decision."[2] This was a prime example of the haphazard way things were handled throughout the Gallipoli Campaign. On 12 March, Lord Kitchener appointed General Sir Ian Hamilton to command an expeditionary force.[3] Kitchener elaborated on the composition of the troops at Sir Ian's command, and, in the latter's own words:

> My troops were to be Australian and New Zealanders under Birdwood (a friend); strength, say, about 30,000. (A year ago I inspected them in their own Antipodes and no finer material exists); the 29th Division, strength, say 19,000 under Hunter-Weston — a slashing man of action; an acute theorist; the Royal Naval Division, 11,000 strong (an excellent type of Officer and man, under a solid commander — Paris); a French contingent, strength at present uncertain, say, about a Division, under my old war comrade the chivalrous d'Amade, now at Tunis. Say then grand total about 80,000 — probably panning out at some 50,000 rifles in the firing line. Of these the 29th Division are extras—*division de luxe.*[4]

Colonel Maurice Hankey recorded that on 12th March he saw the Prime Minister in the morning:

> Who told me the Government have decided to send Ian Hamilton to Dardanelles, as the Navy is rather stuck owing to howitzers concealed on shore. In afternoon saw Ian Hamilton to say goodbye.... Sir Ian asked me to go with him and said he would always keep a place on his Staff for me. Much tempted.... Sir Ian told me he is in an embarrassing position as Churchill

wants him to try to rush the Straits by a *coup de main* with such troops as are available in the Levant (30,000 Australasians and 10,000 Naval Division). Kitchener on the other hand wants him to go slow, to make the Navy continue pounding the Straits, and to wait for the 29th Division.

Hamilton, of course, was bound to act in accordance with Kitchener's instructions (dated 13 March), which begin as follows:

1. The fleet have undertaken to force the passage of the Dardanelles. The employment of military forces on any large scale for land operations at this juncture is only contemplated in the event of the fleet failing to get through after every effort has been exhausted.
2. Before any serious undertaking is carried out in the Gallipoli Peninsula all the British Military Forces detailed for the expedition should be assembled, so that their full weight can be thrown in.
3. Having entered on the project of forcing the Straits there can be no idea of abandoning the scheme. It will require time, patience, and methodical plans of co-operation between the naval and military commanders. The essential point is to avoid a check, which will jeopardize our chances of strategical and tactical success.[5]

Sir Ian was *en route* to the Dardanelles within a couple of days subsequent to his precipitate appointment. Hastening there on board a fast destroyer, he was still somewhat bewildered by the recent days' events.

The euphoria induced by the earlier huge gains of "the Russian steamroller" and the "it'll be over by Christmas"[6] thinking evaporated as the spring of 1915 approached. Defeated in several sectors of the Eastern Front, the Russian armies retreated nearly two hundred miles from their furthest point of advance. In the disorganized routs which resulted, the Russians lost vast amounts of ordnance, munitions, and equipment, much of it irreplaceable by home industry alone. Particularly crucial was the chronic shortage of rifles, which meant that not only were some soldiers in the front line unarmed, but also that reinforcements arrived without rifles or the knowledge of how to use them. Tsar Nicholas II, hitherto a popular figure allegedly endowed with spiritual powers in addition to his superior human qualities in the minds of many of his peasant soldiery, was no longer beheld as a semi-deity. The former patriarchal figure had not dismissed those generals the troops believed inefficient, incompetent, and responsible for the blunders which produced the catastrophic reverses. He had not arranged for arms, kit, clothing, and food in sufficient quantities. He had not ensured that they receive regular pay. No longer was he the para-human entity they once revered. As a consequence, the morale of the Russian forces sank gradually and steadily. This, coupled with the ineffective replacement of rifles, machine guns, artillery pieces, munitions, vehicles, and personal accoutrements, generally caused the leaders of

France and Britain gravely to fear the collapse of their ally Russia and its exit from the war. Something drastic had to be done to keep Russia in the field and raise the morale of the Russian common soldier. The idea of forcing passage through the Dardanelles to capture Constantinople and put Turkey out of the war, thereby unlocking the Black Sea, now really appealed to the minds of certain men in the Allied camp. Indeed the Tsar himself favored such a scheme, and his Foreign Minister, Serge Sazonov, urged Russia's Entente partners to take action.[7] Some of the British and French leaders believed that a steady supply of war *matériel* would not only supplement the output of inefficient Russian industry but also cheer the Russian frontline troops when they saw and handled arms made in British and French factories. Moreover, once the freighters carrying the vitally needed war supplies discharged their cargoes, they could then load their holds with the abundant surpluses of Ukrainian grain. Such an arrangement would enable the Entente Powers to plan against a deterioration in the food supply for their populations, particularly as the implications of submerged naval warfare were now fully appreciated. It would also provide the Russians with much-needed capital, which had virtually dried up with the closure of its only warm-water harbors and the consequent cessation of its major exports.

The engagement began on 23 February when the British Mediterranean Fleet bombarded the forts on either side of the entrance to the Dardanelles. The recently commissioned super-dreadnought,[8] HMS *Queen Elizabeth*, calibrated her mighty fifteen-inch guns and fired salvoes from the Gulf of Saros clear over the Gallipoli peninsula to pound the forts at Chanak on the Asiatic side of the Narrows. (See Map C.) During the first few days of March 1915:

> ... each day weather permitted, parties of English blue-jackets and marines went ashore on both headlands and blew up gun emplacements and magazines the fleet had not shattered.... On March 4th, the demolitions were completed, and Admiral Carden announced that the objectives of Step 1 had been attained.[9]

Churchill, impatient over delay and procrastination, ordered a more concerted attempt to force the Narrows with largely out-of-date warships which, in spite of their obsolescence, still possessed extremely destructive firepower. In August 1914 he had witnessed the massive German siege cannons devastate the Belgian frontier fortresses and had assumed a corollary with that of naval gunfire.[10] One enormous difference was, in the words of Captain Eric Wheler Bush, R.N., the large reliance on the "delayed action fuse" designed "to penetrate armour and burst in the ship's vitals."[11]

On the 18 March 1915, Rear-Admiral John de Robeck (successor to Car-

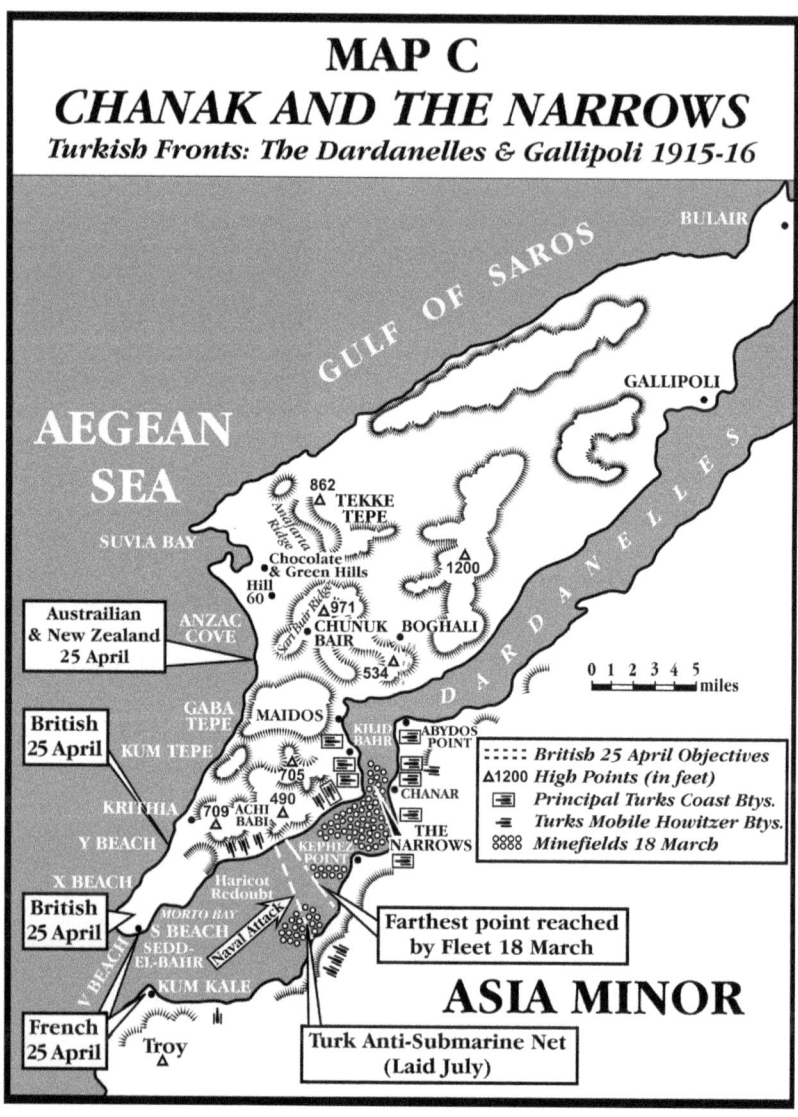

den, who had suffered a nervous breakdown) ordered the impressive fleet under his command into action. Led by his four hardest hitters, the *Queen Elizabeth*, *Lord Nelson*, *Inflexible*, and *Agamemnon*, with the backing of the French naval squadron of four warships, the task force moved in to pound the Dardanelles forts in the Narrows with broadside after broadside of large caliber high explosive shells. (See Map C.) Royal Naval Division personnel, including Sub-Lieutenant Rupert Brooke, observed the bombardment from

1—Plans and Prevarications

Left to Right: Commodore Roger Keyes, a distinct enthusiast for the Dardanelles operation; Vice-Admiral John de Robeck, commander of the naval task force; General Sir Ian M. Hamilton, G.C.B., Commander-in-Chief Mediterranean Expeditionary Force, and his Chief of Staff Major-General Walter P. Braithwaite, C.B. Taken on board the Vice-Admiral's yacht, *Triad*. (Imperial War Museum, Neg. No. Q13.560)

aboard ship. Their presence there was in case of the need for landing parties.

Initially the maneuvers proved successful, but sheer bad luck, in the form of a string of unswept mines borne southward on the strong Dardanelles currents, caused one French (*Bouvet*) and two British (*Irresistible*[12] and *Ocean*) capital ships to founder; a fourth warship (*Inflexible*) was so badly damaged she had to be towed to Malta for repairs.[13] HMS *Irresistible* was on the extreme right of Line C, close to the Asian shoreline; and, as she drifted closer, the Turkish gunners enthusiastically blasted her with shells, causing de Robeck to dispatch the destroyer *wear* to evacuate more than 600 men of the *Irresistible*'s crew, including dead and wounded. In spite of these setbacks, Step 2 of the strategy, to clear the mines, intensified. But the trawlers employed in the minesweeping came under sustained shellfire not only from the undamaged forts, but much more also from mobile field gun and howitzer batteries deployed along the coasts. The minesweeping went poorly, largely because the vessels assigned to the operation lacked the power to move swiftly against the current and thus presented easy targets for the Turkish gunners. Their civilian crews tended to abandon their efforts in the face of adversity even though sustaining no serious casualties. Eventually, however, as losses amongst the minesweepers began to mount, their merchant marine skippers and crews became extremely reluctant to continue such a hazardous task. Naval personnel were drafted in to stiffen the resolve of the trawlermen, and destroyers joined in the sweeping operations, but this still did not overcome the problem. As Commodore Roger Keyes observed:

> I did not think the fire from concealed howitzers and field guns would ever be a deciding factor. I was wrong. The *fear* of their fire was actually the deciding factor of the fortunes of that day. Two pairs of trawlers got out their sweeps immediately ahead of Line A and commenced to sweep upstream; they exploded three mines. A little later they turned and ran out of the Straits. The other pair left earlier in the proceedings without sweeping.[14]

These difficulties led Admiral de Robeck and his naval colleagues in the Aegean to report to the Admiralty that they could not force the Dardanelles unless one shore was in Allied hands.

Notwithstanding the Royal Navy's top brass's assessment, a consensus of neutral and opposition commentators maintained that the desired result only required a renewed onslaught by the Allied fleet. In Constantinople, the United States' Ambassador, Henry Morgenthau, voiced the opinion that if the British had pressed once more success would have rewarded them.[15] His view was openly available to all who cared to read the *New York Times* edition of 26 March 1915.[16] In his book, *Ambassador Morgenthau's Story*, he waxes most specific in his conviction — and that of all influential people in the Turkish capital — that the arrival of the British fleet was imminent.[17] From the same location, Dr. Harry Stuermer, a correspondent for a German newspaper *Kölnische Zeitung*, related the pessimistic views of the German gunners of the Chanak forts.[18] Even Enver Pasha, the Turkish Minister of War, expected the Allies to renew their attack and achieve the desired results.[19] Arrangements for the Sultan, his court, the treasury, civil and military authorities to vacate the capital to avoid capture appeared to General Otto Liman von Sanders sensible and justifiable precautions. "On the other hand those military preparations, which the Turkish headquarters had ordered between February 20 and March 1 to meet a successful passage of the allied fleet through the Dardanelles, might have been fatal ... because these orders exposed the Dardanelles to a hostile landing!"[20] They would, in fact, have abandoned the exterior coast of the Gallipoli Peninsula with its dominating heights, and done away with the defense of Asiatic headland at the mouth of the Dardanelles. "It was the feeblest imaginable defensive measure." Unfortunately for the Allies the Turkish authorities heeded Liman's strenuous remonstrations.[21]

It would seem reasonable to assume that much of the ordnance in the forts suffered severe damage or complete destruction from the sustained pounding delivered by the Allied navies' big guns. Of those which survived, some were antique relics of an earlier age of gunnery and were muzzle-loading cannon with no modern recoil system of hydraulic buffers and recuperators. This meant that they not only had a low rate of fire, but also had to be relaid after every round fired. Furthermore, thanks to the record of a German officer serving in that theater at the time, a catalogue of the total artillery deployed or installed along the entire length of the Dardanelles is available to the researcher. It was not nearly as intimidating as one might conclude: a total of 145 guns of various calibers for both sides of the Straits, and of these, only 43 were sited in the upper forts or on the crestlines.[22] Considering that British Admiral Algernon Limpus headed his country's naval mission at Constantinople for

Marshal Otto Liman von Sanders, Commander-in-Chief of the Turkish Fifth Army, and entrusted with the defense of the Gallipoli Peninsula. (Imperial War Museum, Neg. No. Q95.324)

several years there is no reason to suppose that this information was not available to British military and naval intelligence. Indeed, the First Lord of the Admiralty, Winston Churchill appeared to have specific knowledge with regard to the armament of the outer forts.

The very fact of the proportion of obsolete vessels used indicated that the strategy allowed for losses and required a greater degree of persistence than Admiral de Robeck was prepared to employ. All, apparently, that the Allies "needed was for the Nelson touch, but Nelson was not afloat where the narrows of the Dardanelles met the width of the Aegean. This was the disaster of the Dardanelles."[23]

Cape Helles, Anzac Cove, and Kum Kale

The Allies broke off their naval attack on 18 March, over five weeks before the first Allied troop landings occurred. "But the Turks were given two months' notice of the project by the premature bombardment of the Dardanelles in February, and the scheme was probably also betrayed through the Greek Court."[24] (King Constantine was well known for his pro-German sympathies—which were later to largely emasculate the Allied Salonika Expeditionary Force.) During this substantial period of grace the Turco-German military authorities fully prepared to combat the anticipated second assault.

Following the aborted naval assault of 18 March, an exceedingly desperate Ottoman government called in Marshal Otto Liman von Sanders, head of the German military mission at Constantinople, and offered him command of the Gallipoli army corps. Liman accepted the appointment on condition that every available field gun or howitzer was transferred to the Gallipoli peninsula, and an additional infantry division sent thence to reinforce the five already deployed there. For as he recounted in his *Five Years in Turkey*: "It was clear to me that they would not relinquish such a high prize without further effort. It would not have been in keeping with British tenacity or energy. Hence a large landing had to be counted upon."[25] He fully utilized the grace period that Lord Kitchener's vacillation regarding the assignation of the 29th Division bestowed upon him, together with the failure of the War Office to ensure that it was shipped fully battle-equipped. Liman "put his soldiers through a rigorous training regimen — including forced marches.... Behind all likely landing beaches [he] had troops dig inter-connected trench systems, protected with machine-gun posts and kilometers of barbed wire."[26]

The geography of the peninsula is not especially accommodating to a potential sea-borne invader. "The land is particularly irregular and broken, with many hills of crumbling stone, deeply gashed ridges and wooded hollows extending beyond the high sandstone ledges of the coast.... The few beaches are extremely narrow."[27]

The British planned to use the recently created Mediterranean Expeditionary Force (MEF) to land on and seize the Gallipoli peninsula. Its Commander-in-Chief, General Sir Ian Hamilton,[28] veteran of the Boer Wars (he had been at Majuba Hill in 1881), had at his disposal the British Regular Army's 29th Division (Lord Kitchener having relented), which consisted of units brought back from garrison duties in various parts of the Empire where Territorial Force contingents sent out from Britain replaced them. (The South Wales Borderers, for example, were just back from the successful siege of the East China German enclave of Tsing Tao

BASIC BRITISH ARMY STRUCTURE
(MODEL BASED ON INFANTRY ARM—
THAT OF CAVALRY DIFFERED CONSIDERABLY)

4 SECTIONS = 1 PLATOON; 4 PLATOONS = 1 COMPANY						
1 Section] 2 Section] = 3 Section] 4 Section]	1 PLATOON	2 PLATOON	3 PLATOON	4 PLATOON		COMPANY = 260 MEN
4 COMPANIES = 1 BATTALION; 4 BATTALIONS = 1 BRIGADE						
1 Company] 2 Company] = 3 Company] 4 Company]	1 BATTALION	2 BATTALION	3 BATTALION	4 BATTALION		BRIGADE = 4,960 MEN
3 BRIGADES = 1 DIVISION; 2 OR MORE DIVISIONS = 1 ARMY CORPS						
1 Brigade] 2 Brigade] = 3 Brigade]	1 DIVISION (A Division also included supporting & ancillary units, i.e.: Artillery, Engineers, Medical Corps, etc., making for a total of around 20,000 men.)	2 DIVISION		DIVISION (additional)	DIVISION (additional)	ARMY CORPS = (MINIMUM OF 38,000 MEN)

Adapted and expanded by the author from Wallace, *Kitchener's Army and the Territorial Forces*, 59.

in conjunction with the Japanese.)[29] Other bodies of troops drafted to Hamilton's command were the Australian and New Zealand Army Corps (ANZAC), the bulk of which was already in Egypt protecting the Suez Canal, and the 42nd (Territorial) Division, also in the Canal Zone. In addition, he had the Royal Naval Division (RND), a hybrid formation comprising of Royal Marine Light Infantry, members of the Royal Naval Volunteer Reserve, and sailors seconded for fighting on land (the poet Rupert Brooke served as a sub-lieutenant in the RND),[30] and a brigade of regular Indian Army infantry battalions. Since France elected to back the venture with military as well as naval might, Hamilton also had a French army corps of colonial and Foreign Legion troops under his overall command. In simple mathematical terms Sir Ian's attacking troops did not equal those of the defending ones, in a situation where every aspect promised to favor the latter. The unfortunate facts were that the number of Turkish Army divisions garrisoning the Straits had risen from only two in February, to double that number by the time of the March naval assault, and up to six when Hamilton was finally in a position to attempt his landings.[31] "For these he had only 4 British divisions and 1 French division — actually inferior in strength to an enemy in a situation where the inherent preponderance of defensive over offensive power was multiplied by the natural difficulties of terrain."[32] Surely not a good omen.

The Commander of the 29th Division, Major-General Sir Aylmer Hunter-Weston, submitted Sir Ian an "appreciation — ('a masterly piece of work,' the latter described it) written on his way out at Malta,"[33] which, in spite of his confidence, drew attention to the facts that:

> It is evident that land operations at this stage must be directed entirely towards assisting the Fleet; and no operations should be commenced unless it is clear that their result will be to enable our warships, with their necessary colliers, etc., to have use of the Straits.
> The Fleet, he holds, cannot do this without our help because of:
> (1). Improvement of the defenses.
> (2). The mobile howitzers.
> (3). The Leon floating mines.
> Things being so, he sets himself to consider how far the Army can help, in the light of the following premise:
> The Turkish army having been warned by our early bombardments and by the landings carried out some time ago has concentrated a large force in and near the Gallipoli Peninsula.[34]

From the outset the War Council/Dardanelles Committee[35] accorded the Gallipoli operations secondary treatment; priorities regarding troops, equipment, and artillery ammunition were invariably reserved for the Western Front. In fact those authorities, ever slow in accepting a new scheme, were equally sluggish when it came to sanctioning sufficient troops for its execution. "Worst of all, this fumbling dilatory policy had completely thrown away any chance of an element of surprise being enjoyed."[36]

The indecision at the War Office over the dispatch of the 29th Division created a dangerous postponement of the expected attack. This enabled the Turks, together with their German advisors, to greatly strengthen defenses and increase troop deployments in the region.[37] Hamilton experienced even more frustration and further delay when he discovered the 29th's divisional equipment incorrectly loaded. In order to sort the muddle out, he ordered the ships to sail from Mudros harbor on the Aegean island of Lemnos[38] to

The Russian cruiser *Askold*. Sole Russian warship supporting the operations. Nicknamed "the packet of Woodbines" by British soldiers and sailors, after a brand of cigarettes sold in fives. (Imperial War Museum, Neg. No. Q13.354)

Alexandria to rectify matters. The vessels then returned to Mudros, but invaluable time was lost.

> The really decisive factor in determining exactly when to start the landing operations was the weather. Whatever the size of the force landed, its seaborne lines of communication had to be kept open. Any Aegean fisherman could have told the planners that gales from the S.W. and N.E., mist, rain and heavy seas would persist, as in fact they did, until the end of April. This seemed obvious to those who knew the Aegean, but less so to the High Command, and it is not sufficiently emphasized in histories of the Campaign.[39]

Assembling in the large natural harbor of Mudros was one of the largest conglomerations of shipping the world had ever known. So, close to the site of Troy, and "the face that launched a thousand ships,"[40] fleets of a similar magnitude now congregated. All manner of craft, ranging from the Royal Navy's mighty super-dreadnought, the *Queen Elizabeth*, and other powerful warships of the British Fleet, to freighters, troopships, hospital ships, horseboats, watercarriers, right down to the humblest lighter and tugboat gathered there. The French Navy still had a squadron of warships to represent it, and the lone Russian cruiser, the *Askold*, which the British soldiers and sailors nicknamed "the packet o' Woodbines"[41] (because its five funnels resembled the formation of the similar number

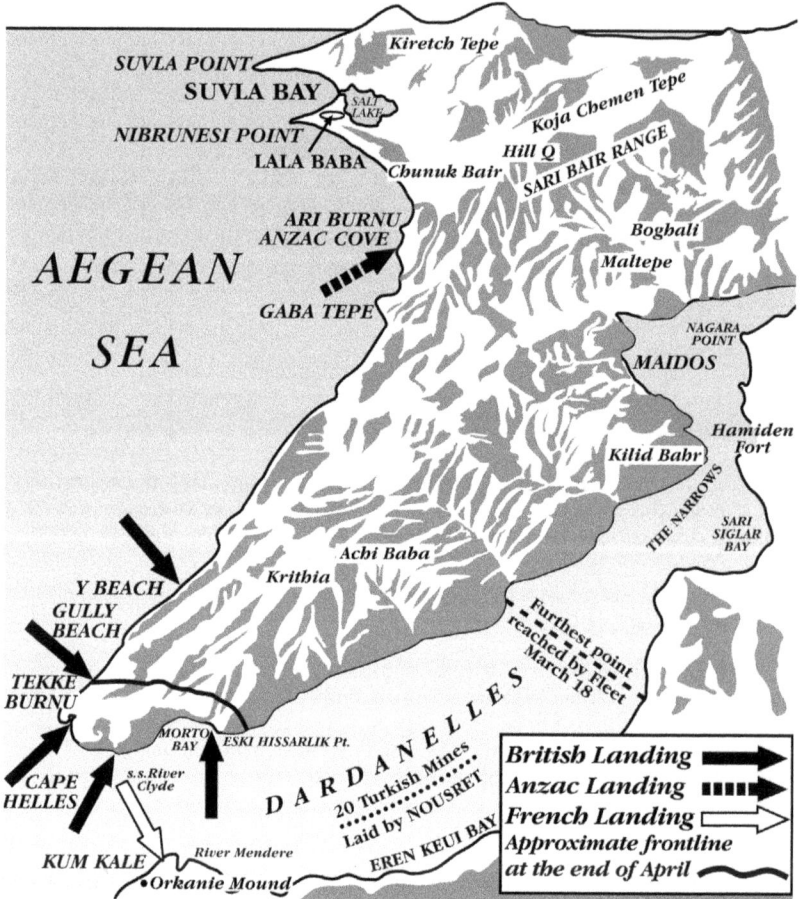

of cheap cigarettes sold in paper packets), continued in support. On shore miniature cities, camps of huts and tents to house the troops went up, plus hospital complexes, and huge amounts of stores accumulated. One photograph clearly reveals row upon row of hogsheads of wine in a French army compound; the *poilu* was not going to war without his *pinard*![42] Since space constriction precluded the massing of large numbers of troops on any one beach, Hamilton planned to make simultaneous landings at several points on the apex of the peninsula in the general area of Cape Helles and Sedd-el-Bahr. The Australian and New Zealand Army Corps' contingents were to go ashore at a cove near Gaba Tepe to the north. The French would launch a feint[43] attack at Kum Kale on the Asiatic side of the entrance to the Dardanelles, and the British another less forceful one on the Isthmus of Bulair. It was expected that together these would ensure a delay in the dispatch of enemy reinforcements to the real invasions' beachheads. Hamilton's objective was the Khilid Bahr Plateau which dominates the Narrows of the Dardanelles. He planned its seizure with a pincer movement that would cut across the Peninsula from the points mentioned above as the two forces worked towards each other until they met.[44] There are three principal commanding heights at the western end of the Gallipoli peninsula, Sari Bair, tall and high-peaked, lies between Suvla Point and Gaba Tepe. South of this, stretching inland from the Straits, is the plateau of Khilid Bahr. Farther southwest, nearer to Cape Helles, the hill of Achi Baba rises bare and rounded.[45] The eminence of Achi Baba, which confronted the Helles invasion forces, they were to take immediately; the Khilid Bahr plateau within 48 hours.[46] (See Maps C and D.)

Hamilton's careful examination of the coast from aboard ship convinced him that any landing upon the peninsula called for rapid accomplishment to produce surprise and success. Concerned that his troops might not enjoy the advantage of surprise, he sent a bluntly worded letter to the British High Commissioner in Egypt, Sir Henry MacMahon, remonstrating at the way he permitted the Egyptian press to betray troop strengths and their destinations, "making open references to the Gallipoli Peninsula."[47]

One does not have to be a military strategist to realize that speed was of the essence when in possession of the above information regarding Turkish troop dispositions, the depth-lacking beaches with barrier-like cliffs and the inhospitable countryside beyond them. It was crucial to the success of an amphibious operation of that nature to establish viable beachheads to ensure smooth and unendangered supply lines, and vital that strong contingents of combat troops advance immediately to seize, secure, and consolidate positions on the commanding high ground. Finally, the overall protection of the assaulting forces required the maintenance of vast naval superiority on the seas that almost encircled the theater of war.

Colonel Maurice Hankey, Secretary of the War Council/Dardanelles' Committee stated that: "The Allies had expected that Russia would help divide the Turkish forces by landing a considerable force from the Black Sea and seizing the northern outlet of the Bosphorus."[48] Another contemporary source, the distinguished German historian, Professor Hans Delbrück, maintained that " ... at the end of April the Russians assembled troops in Odessa to operate against Constantinople.... "[49] Yet another authority stated that: "It had been hoped that Russia would cooperate by landing 100,000 men on the northern coast of Thrace and seizing the northern outlet of the Bosphorus." Retired Russian Rear Admiral Prof. N.B. Pavlovich pronounced categorically that during May 1915:

> The Russian government and the high command were still waiting for the results of the operation by the English and French in the Dardanelles, but time did not stand still. The men of the 5th Caucasian Corps, earlier reserved for the landing in the Bosphorus region, were gradually replaced by home guards. As summer approached a troop landing became less and less probable. It was at this time that the officer in charge at the Headquarters of the Supreme Commander informed the commander of the 7th Army in Odessa that the plan to land forces in the Bosphorus region had been dropped altogether. The landing brigade newly formed out of the 2nd, 12th, and 38th home guard brigades was meant to occupy the region only if the Allies succeeded in opening the Dardanelles and Bosphorus, or alternatively for collective operations with Bulgaria.[50]

According to his former secretary, Sir George Arthur, Lord Kitchener himself fully expected a firm demonstration on the part of Russia to support the efforts of her allies. A force amounting to an Army Corps was mooted.[51] On the 4 March, 1915, the Secretary of State for War cabled Generals Maxwell and Birdwood:

> ... The concentration of troops at the entrance to the Dardanelles is not so much for operations on the Gallipoli Peninsula as for operations subsequently to be undertaken in the neighborhood of Constantinople. In these operations the co-operation of a Russian Corps of 40,000 men is contemplated.[52]

Later in the same month (March) Lord Kitchener, referred to the Russian promise of cooperation in his lengthy written instructions to General Sir Ian Hamilton.[53] The recipient of these instructions refers to the expected Russian contribution several times in his *Gallipoli Diary*. (See endnote 45 for an example.)

> The instructions bear the date of March 13, and three days earlier Kitchener had informed his colleagues that the forces to operate against Constantinople would consist of the Royal Naval Division, the Anzac Corps, the Twenty-Ninth Division, a French Division, and a Russian Army Corps—their strength being about 127,000 men and 298 guns.[54]

Such a substantial force would surely have made all the difference and one would expect that the Ally to whose aid the venture was intended to come would honor such a commitment. As it turned out, however, this proved illusory. "But no help came from the Power in whose interest the enterprise had been launched."[55] This very important factor in the Gallipoli equation is, for some inexplicable reason, virtually ignored by present-day analysts.

The die was cast and inexorably the day of the invasion, 25 April 1915, the so-called Battle of the Landing, drew closer. It opened with a *crescendo* of deafening sound of naval gunfire. "The tremendous bombardment from the men-of-war. They were demolishing forts and villages along the coast on either side, and through the glasses we could see them crumble away under the shells."[56] On the other side, the German leader of a naval machine gun detachment, Lieutenant Boltz, gives the following account of his impression on reaching the battlefield of Sedd el Bahr on the evening of May 3: "The battlefield presented a grand and awful spectacle. The point of the peninsula was surrounded by a circle of war ships and transports. The ships' guns, assisted by great searchlights, maintained a terrible fire against the Turkish lines."[57]

On that day the beaches of Gallipoli were to become scenes of hideous slaughter interspersed with imperishable acts of gallantry, courage, and daring. Major John Gillam, of the Army Service Corps, who served throughout the entire Gallipoli Campaign, and the war, witnessed some of them, and recorded his impressions in a diary.

> *April 22nd.* I am ordered to join another ship, the *Dongola,* in which are the Essex and the Royal Scots[58] [Territorials].... The harbour [Mudros] at night is a fine sight. A moon is shining and not a cloud in the sky, and the temperature about 50 degrees F.... It is interesting to note the confidence the Army and Navy have in each other....
>
> *April 23rd.* The first boat of the fleet leaves, named the River Clyde, an old tramp steamer, painted khaki. She contains the Dublin and Munster Fusiliers. Fore and aft on starboard and port the sides are cut away, but fastened like doors. She will be beached at "V" beach, and immediately that is over, her sides will be opened and the troops will swarm out on to the shore.... [Almost within sight of the plains of Troy, a twentieth century "Wooden Horse" to pour forth warriors from its belly.[59]] The strains of the Russian National Anthem float over the harbour from the Askold.... On the lower deck the Tommies give a concert, with an orchestra composed of a tin can, a few mouth-organs, and combs and paper—"Tipperary," "Who's Your Lady Friend," etc.... Feeling a bit lonely and homesick for the time when I can see my sisters again and punt up the river at dear old Guildford.
>
> But what about the Tommies on board?—they have just the same feeling, and yet keep playing their mouth-organs. Hear that Ian Hamilton feels a bit anxious over this job, but that Hunter-Weston, our Divisional General, is full of pluck and confidence.
>
> *April 24th.* Issue extra day's rations to troops on board, which makes four days' they will have to carry. Their packs and equipment now equal sixty pounds. How they will fight tomorrow beats me. I tried a pack on and was astonished at its weight.

Major Gillam muses about the time of their arrival at the fateful destination and the result of a successful outcome—the end of the war occurring soon thereafter.

We arrive at five in the morning, and the troops are to land at six.... If successful, the war here will soon be over, we think.

April 25th. Was awakened up at four by the noise of the distant rumbling of guns, and coming to my senses, I realized that the great effort had started. I dressed hastily and went on deck, and there found the Essex and the Royal Scots falling in on parade, with full packs on, two bags of iron rations (for they had breakfasted), and entrenching tools, two hundred rounds of ammunition, rifle and bayonet. I stood and watched — watched their faces, listened to what they had to say to each other, and could trace no sign of fear in their faces and no words of apprehension at forthcoming events in their conversation.... The booming of the guns grows louder. It is very misty, but on going forward I can see land, and the first officer points out to me the entrance through the Dardanelles. How narrow it seems; like the Thames at Gravesend almost. I can see the *Askold* distinctly. A Tommy said: "There's the old packet of Woodbines giving them what-ho!" She is firing broadsides, and columns of dust and smoke arise from the shore.... Seagulls are swooping over the calm sea above the din, and a thunderous roar breaks out now and again from *Queen Bess*. Her 15-inch guns are at work, and she is firing enormous shells — terrible shells, which seem to burst 30 feet from the ground....

8 A.M. The Essex are disembarking now, going down the rope ladders slowly and with difficulty.... They are landing in small open boats. A tug takes a string of them in tow, and slowly they steam away for "W" Beach. We hear the Lancashires have landed at "W" Beach, and are a hundred yards in-shore fighting for dear life. Tug after tug takes these strings of white open boats away from our ship towards land, with their overladen khaki freight. Slowly they wend their way towards the green shore in front of us, winding in and out of the transports, roaring battleships, and angry destroyers, towards the land of the Great Adventure. Never, surely, was Navy and Army so closely allied. I go below to get breakfast.... The steward calmly hands the menu round, just as he might on a peaceful voyage. What a contrast! Two boiled eggs, coffee, toast and marmalade. Here we are sitting down to a good meal and men are fighting up cliffs a few hundred yards away.

After breakfast Major Gillam went back on deck to continue his observation of the operations.

8.30 A.M. It is quite clear now, and I can see through my glasses the little khaki figures on shore at "W" Beach and on top of the cliff, while at "V" Beach where the *River Clyde* is lying beached, all seems hell and confusion.[60] Some fool near me says, "Look, they are bathing at 'V' Beach." I get my glasses on to it and see a hundred khaki figures crouching behind a sand dune close to the water's edge. On a hopper which somehow or other has been moored between the *River Clyde* and the shore I see khaki figures lying, many apparently dead. I also see the horrible sight of some little white boats drifting, with motionless khaki freight, helplessly out to sea on the strong current that is coming down the Straits. The battleships incessantly belch spurts of flame, followed by clouds of buff-coloured smoke, and above it all a deafening roar. It is ear-splitting.... Some pinnace comes alongside our ship with orders, and the midshipman in command says the Australians have landed, but with many casualties, and have got Johnny Turk on the run across the peninsula. I turned my glasses up the coast to see if I can see them, but they are too far away. I can only see brown hills and bursting shells, a dead calm sea, and a perfect day. The work of the Creator and the destroying hand of man in close intimacy.... This is war! and I am watching as from a box at the theatre.

10.30 A.M. Imbros is peaceful and beautiful, Gallipoli is beautiful and awful. We have moved closer to the beach and they are trying to hit us from the shore. Two shells have just dropped near us, twenty yards away; the din is ear-splitting, especially from the *Queen Bess.* I can hear the crackling of rifles on shore, which reminds me of Bulford.... [army rifle-ranges on Salisbury Plain]

11.30 A.M. We are going out to sea again. A tug comes alongside with wounded. They are the first wounded I have ever seen in my life, and I look over the side with curiosity and study their faces. They are mostly Lancashire Fusiliers from "W" Beach. Some look pale and stern, some are groaning now and again, while others are smoking and joking with the crew of the tug. I talk to one of the more slightly wounded, and he tells me that it was "fun" when once they got ashore, but they "copped it" from machine guns getting out of the boats into shallow water, where they found venomous barbed wire was thickly laid....

12 noon. We are going in closer again, and the Royal Scots[61] are leaving.[62]

Major Gillam's eye-witness account tallies with most others. The report he received, however, about the ANZAC landing was only half-accurate. Owing to a quirk current the Australian and New Zealanders landed at the wrong site, at a place with precipitous cliffs! They did indeed incur heavy casualties, but the chasing "Johnny Turk across the peninsula" was very short-lived, as the Turks under the command of Colonel Mustapha Kemal counterattacked in strength. Came nightfall General William Birdwood, their commanding officer, contacted Hamilton and recommended evacuation, to which the latter responded: "You have accomplished the first part. Now all you have to do is dig, dig, dig, until you are safe."[63]

However, newspaper reports published well after the event invariably described the landing at Anzac Cove as nothing short of a victory. The British accredited war correspondent Ellis Ashmead-Bartlett observed, in a dispatch highly imbued with romanticism, that: "The first Ottoman Turk since the last Crusade received an Anglo-Saxon bayonet in him at 5 minutes after 5 A.M. on April 25. It was over in a minute." In spite of the phrase's subsequent variations to avoid offending delicate sensibilities there can be no mistaking the imperial sentiment.[64]

"Y" Beach (see Maps C and D) was the one beach where success was surprisingly instant:

> The southbound *Queen Elizabeth* approached Beach Y, actually a mere landing path leading up a cliff. Hamilton was surprised to see British troops idling on the cliffs with no sign of any enemy. Clearly the main body [from V Beach as

per plan] had not arrived so far, and thus the Helles invasion was behind schedule. The general's chief of staff [Major-General Walter Pipon Braithwaite] urged him to order the Royal Naval Division down from its diversionary operation off Bulair and land them at this peaceful beach for a dash to the heights of Achi Baba, less than three miles away. Hamilton refused. It was far too early, he said, to commit his strategic reserve....[65]

Had others besides Hamilton's Chief of Staff appreciated the unbelievable opportunities for exploitation that "Y" Beach offered for transforming the whole Gallipoli situation, a different outcome could have transpired. For the troops at "Y" Beach, with no opposition confronting them, had Krithia, Achi Baba, and the severance of the enemy's lines of communication within their reach. Furthermore, they were fresh and of high morale, not confused and demoralized from a murderous reception as were many of their comrades at other invasion points. But the most promising of the landings was virtually ignored. No updated orders were sent or signals transmitted to the officers in charge, thus, disregarded and unreinforced, it was allowed to lose all its initial impetus. The more farsighted commanders of the Turkish defenders rushed in reserves, plugged the gap, and pressed forward against the enclave, forcing the evacuation of the beachhead in the late afternoon. Truly it was one of the campaign's many tragedies, and one may fairly say the first blots on the copybooks of General Hamilton and Major-General Sir Aylmer Hunter-Weston, the commander of the 29th Division. The former, because the gentlemanly code he adhered to would not permit him to interfere in matters he adjudged within the sacrosanct jurisdiction of a subordinate general[66]; the latter because, for whatever reason, he simply ignored "Y" Beach as if it did not even exist![67]

Thus, in spite of the huge naval bombardment and the bitter fighting on the beaches and cliff-tops, "once the momentary asset of tactical surprise had passed, and the Turks were able to bring up their reserves, the invaders could not expand their precarious footholds."[68] Ironically, the extremely successful French feint landing on the Asiatic headland offered a splendid opportunity. If the strategy allowed for upgraded status of a sector where success was apparent, and this landing given heavy reinforcements, such a revision could have produced positive results affecting the entire campaign.

The only one of the first day's objectives achieved was that of getting the troops ashore. The Khilid Bahr Plateau was never reached, and the sullen hill of Achi Baba was destined to frown down upon Australian, British, French (the composition of a Foreign Legion Division could encompass many foreign nationalities), Gurkhas, Irish, Newfoundlanders, New Zealanders (Maoris included), Punjabis, Senegalese, Sikhs and Welsh for over eight and a half bloody, disease-ridden months. It glowered triumphantly as their departing boats finally pulled out when they abandoned the struggle. Achi

Baba was to become the objective of the Helles armies, replacing the more grandiose one of Constantinople.

Gallipoli rapidly degenerated into a miniature Western Front, albeit without the horrors of poison gas and quagmires of mud. "Gallipoli was [also] unique in that there was no safe rear area — whether the soldier was in the front line, the rest camp dugout, or swimming at sea there was always a chance that he could be killed or maimed by enemy fire."[69] It possessed the same continuous lines of trenches, with barbed wire in front; the same sniping, bombing, and undermining; the same relentless shellfire, and the same horrendous casualties. But, unlike France and Flanders, there was rampant dysentery, heat, dust, chronic water shortages, and flies, flies, flies. Nor could the Allied troops look forward to the pleasant respite of home leave, or the chance to repair to *estaminet*, bar, beer-hall, or brothel to release some of the tensions of battle-weariness or provide a welcome break from the tedium of trench warfare.

On the other side the Turkish forces were now dug in deeply in mazes of intricate entrenchments, amply served by equally deep communication thoroughfares. An ardent "Westerner," Field Marshal Sir William Robertson, asked: "Has our success against the entrenchments in the Gallipoli peninsula been greater than in Flanders?"[70] The unpleasant truth was that "... when at last British and French forces were landed upon the Gallipoli peninsula they found the Turks well entrenched and better prepared for trench warfare than themselves for the Allies trusted for heavy artillery to the great guns of the ships, which were comparatively useless for battering down entrenchments."[71] Thus, because of these formidable lines of trench works coupled with the all-too-flat trajectories of the projectiles fired by the massive naval guns the defenders were secure from most of the detrimental effects of these high explosives. An *impasse* existed Hamilton begged and pleaded for replacement drafts and reinforcements for one more push to achieve victory. Eventually the reluctant members of the Dardanelles Committee relented, or were persuaded, and agreed to grant his request. He then formulated plans for the final offensive phase of the Gallipoli Campaign.

2

The Preparations for the Landings

The so-called Battle of the Landing, which commenced on 25 April 1915, succeeded in its initial objective; *i.e.,* the landing was effected. But it failed in its long-range objectives: to accomplish a juncture between the Australian and New Zealand Army Corps and the contingents to the south, to take Achi Baba, and to seize and occupy the Khilid Bahr Plateau along with the western shoreline of the Narrows. The primary cause of the failure was that General Sir Ian Hamilton delivered his attack with insufficient vigor; the secondary reason was that the forces available were unduly dispersed. Behind these lay others. The War Office displayed a lamentable ignorance of the geographical and topographical nature of the Gallipoli Peninsula as bicycles and trucks were allocated for the operation, although most of these remained at Alexandria thanks to the wisdom of less exalted beings. The chairbound generals at Whitehall also failed to obtain for issue to the officers of the Mediterranean Expeditionary Force (MEF) proper maps of the region they planned to invade.[1] "Not even an adequate staff map of the Peninsula existed at the War Office, an omission of very far-reaching consequences when the disembarkation was made."[2] Indeed, T.E. Lawrence recorded that "the expedition came out with two copies of some quarter inch maps of European Turkey as their sole supply."[3] To these reasons for the failure of the operation may be added the complete elimination of the element of surprise. This was due to the original decision of the War Council to rely on naval strength alone and the protracted efforts from the first salvoes at the beginning of November 1914, until 18 March 1915 when the Allies abandoned the naval attack. Such courses of action, the demolition of the forts by naval gunfire and parties sent ashore, together with the attempted minesweeping of the Narrows, left the Ottoman and German governments in no doubt that the Allies intended to force passage through the Dardanelles.[4] "No other first-class Power, except Great Britain, would ever have rushed bald-headed at the Dardanelles and Gallipoli, without months of reflection and silent preparation by a highly trained general staff, composed of the best brains in the army. Complete plans would have been found pigeon-holed long before the outbreak of war. But there were none in 1915."[5]

Marshal Liman von Sanders and his associates in the Turkish Army of Gallipoli expressed confidence in their ability to hold back the Anglo-French invasion. They enjoyed short lines of supply and communication, and could expect replacement drafts on a regular basis. Of equal importance, their soldiers possessed an abundance of water. Furthermore, they ensured their troops in the firing line a plentiful supply of bombs, an essential ingredient of trench warfare, although, like their opponents, they lacked the necessary field artillery ammunition to prepare the way for effective infantry advances. This made it impossible for them to eject the Allies from the peninsula. Thus, the situation lent itself to stalemate.

For the troops under Hamilton's command things did not improve at all. As May drew to a close, the sun climbed higher and higher each day, beating down mercilessly on the baked, barren earth and rock to seek out any sun-traps which it transformed into ovens. The corpses which lay unburied in no man's land (the Turks were seemingly indifferent about their dead) became bloated and blackened,[6] and, if punctured by a stray bullet, stank horribly.[7] Only the flies thrived on Gallipoli; they bred prolifically, and just increased and increased.

On the Cape Helles front, Major-General Sir Aylmer Hunter-Weston, in a series of bludgeoning frontal assaults, succeeded in pushing forward towards the strategically important village of Krithia and the key feature of the frowning fortress of Achi Baba. On his right the French fought bloody battles in the Kereches Dere for a redoubt figuratively named the Haricot. Captain Aubrey Herbert penned an epitaph to the Third Battle of Krithia, better known as the Battle of the Fourth of June. It is included for the power with which it tersely summarized the bitterness, frustration, and nausea which characterized much of the Gallipoli Campaign:

Half Hours at Helles
It is the Fourth of June.
Think not I never dream
The noise of that infernal noon,
The stretchers' endless stream,
The tales of triumph won,
The night that found them lies,
The wounded wailing in the sun,
The dead, the dust, the flies.
The flies! Oh God, the flies
That soiled the sacred dead.

> To see them swarm from dead men's eyes
> And share the soldiers' bread!
> Nor think I now forget
>   The filth and stench of war,
>   The corpses on the parapet,
>   The maggots in the floor.[8]

In the precipitous Anzac sector, where some of the gradients at the steepest parts "could not have been much less than 1 in 1,"[9] the two sides fought some particularly nasty engagements. The Turks attempted to drive the Australians and New Zealanders from their precarious footholds into the sea, and the latter desperately tried to improve dangerously enfiladed positions. No man's land and areas immediately in front of the trench parapets became so congested with corpses that the two sides arranged an armistice for each to bury its dead.[10]

On June 18 (the anniversary of a great historic victory, Waterloo), the British Ambassador to Russia, Sir G. Buchanan, in a cable to the British Foreign Secretary, Sir Edward Grey, alluded to the fact that: "... our operations in Gallipoli, which were at present making but very slow progress."[11] The brutal truth was that they were making absolutely no progress.

All the while, with the exception of the brief armistice mentioned above, the deadly sniping went on. Even men using a latrine, or shaving, fell victims to the fatal bullets from the unseen marksmen lying patiently in wait for such opportunities.[12] (The origin of the superstition that it is unlucky to accept a "third light" for a cigarette is actually reckoned to be a reality stemming from life in the First World War trenches.) An Australian sharpshooter, one Private Sing, allegedly accounted for over two hundred dead Turks! Colonel Maurice Hankey, Secretary of the Dardanelles Committee, while visiting the war zone in early August, reported the use of the periscopic rifle, invented by an Australian sergeant,[13] whose ingenuity enabled effective counter-sniping which greatly reduced this particular threat from the enemy.[14]

The engineers and their fatigue parties of infantrymen dug tunnels deep in the bowels of the earth which undermined enemy strongpoints or advanced their frontline jumping-off points closer to their Turkish counterparts. Sometimes these passed above or below the other's mining efforts, and if detected, a narrow excavation was directed thence at the end of which the sappers inserted a charge called a *camoufleche* and the enemy's tunnel was blown in. When they did not resort to this countermeasure, it became a war of nerves as to who could complete their undermining project first and detonate their charges before their rivals could do so.[15]

Light Horse Trooper Ernest Morton, who arrived at Anzac Cove after the initial landing, related what conditions were like:

We scratched little holes in the side of the hill, for protection. Then for three and a half months it never went out of my mind for one second, there was constantly shell-fire, rifle-fire, and machine-gun fire. Continuously for three and a half months. It was a terrible ordeal for a lad of nineteen to go into. We weren't on Gallipoli long before we were up in the front lines, of course, and used to throw what we called 'egg bombs' at one another [opposing armies]. One of these egg bombs landed on my cobber[16] that I enlisted with. Landed on his head and completely blew his head off. I was standing alongside him. That was a shock.[17]

The Members of the War Council[18] and the Dardanelles Committee[19] grew ever more restive at Hamilton's lack of progress, and his continual complaints about under-supply. Churchill, however, had much faith in Hamilton and remained confident that he, if given what he asked for, could accomplish the task. Lord Kitchener also moved to adopt a much stronger stance as the failure of the opening Western Front spring offensives became apparent, and, at the first meeting of the new Dardanelles Committee, advocated "prosecuting the campaign at the Dardanelles with the utmost vigour."[20]

Hamilton, for his part, constantly pleaded for the men and *matériel* for one more effort to tip the balance. Since, however, the so-called "Westerners" (i.e., those who opposed siphoning men and munitions away from the Western Front[21]) who sat on, or exercised influence upon, the decision-making bodies ensured the Western Front first priority in both, he had a difficult time securing either. One of the most ardent "Westerners," Chief of the Imperial General Staff, Field Marshal Sir William Robertson, wrote on May 16:

> "So long as we pay attention to Italy, the Balkan States and all such rubbish we shall never have contented minds. What we have got to do is to organize ourselves properly and realize that we have got to finish the job by our own exertions, in conjunction with Russia and France.... Our chief trouble lies in England and the War Office." In his opinion, the strength of the alliance would "increase only to the extent to which the British Army is increased" and concentrated in France.[22]

Fierce opposition such as this, coupled with the increased skepticism with which he was held by most of the people involved, further eroded his chances. Churchill and Kitchener did what they could to relieve his plight, but the Western Front's insatiable appetite for men, shells, and bombs continued to keep Gallipoli starved of all three, making the local manufacture of the unpredictable "jam-tin bomb" a necessary expedient.[23] Suffolk Regiment infantryman Private Mortlock did not rate these locally manufactured explosive devices very highly. Apparently the fuse lengths tended to err on the side of caution, enabling "… the ol' Turks to throw 'em back."[24]

Unfortunately the Commander-in-Chief of the MEF was himself one

"Jam-tin" bomb-making. Key weapons in trench warfare, grenades, mortar bombs, and hand-thrown explosives were almost totally unprovided for, leading to scenes such as above. While appearing to be a veritable hive of industry it gives an overall impression of being a somewhat primitive undertaking. (Imperial War Museum, Neg. No. Q13.282)

of the problems which occasioned the grudging release and dispatch of essential replacements, reinforcements, and war *materiél* to the Gallipoli war zone. Hamilton was far too nice a person, and too much the proper gentleman, to make a good general. Much of what he thought he needed to express bluntly, rather than inscribe on the pages of his diary. He needed to hector and bully to get what he wanted and impose his will upon others. His actions were always those of the perfect gentleman, even when occasion called for bluntness, if not rudeness. He sat back and grudgingly accepted second-best; he allowed subordinate generals with far less insight to run his show in their, all too often, incompetent or foolhardy way.[25] He needed to insist, upon threat of resignation, that the authorities in Whitehall grant all of which he knew was absolutely vital to the success of the operation — which they themselves appointed him to command. One of the few occasions when he put his view of matters across with a refreshing candor was in his cable to Lord Kitchener of 1 June 1915:

> On the 1st. instant I had said, "I still await the information promised in your x. 4773, A. 5, of the 19th. instant. In my opinion the supply of gun ammunition can hardly be considered adequate or safe until the following conditions can be filled:

(1) That the amounts with the units and on the Lines of Communication should be made up to the number of rounds per gun which is allowed in War Establishment figures of the 29th. Division.
(2) That these full amounts be maintained and dispatched automatically without any further application from us...."[26]

The response was negative because of the "Westerners" insistence that the demands of France made it impossible to concede such amounts.[27] Hamilton had asked only for the laid-down allowance for one division to meet the needs of the entire British, Dominion, and Imperial components of his expeditionary force!

The expedition, accorded secondary rank from the outset, received secondary treatment. The War Council, Dardanelles Committee, and the War Office did not respond to Hamilton's frequent appeals for sufficient new troops to replace the many dead, wounded, sick, and diseased who depleted the all-too-thin ranks of his army.

The battles of Neuve Chapelle, Aubers Ridge, Givenchy and Festubert, however, with their appalling losses, negligible gains, and profligate consumption of artillery ammunition, weighed heavily with the British Secretary of War, Earl Kitchener of Khartoum. He was, moreover, "by this time strongly opposed to any early resumption of the offensive on the Western Front." With brutal frankness he stated:

> Such an attack, before an adequate supply of guns and high-explosive shell can be provided, would only result in heavy casualties and the capture of another turnip field in France.[28]

Thus by mid-June Lord Kitchener no longer opposed, as was the case in May, the dispatch of large reinforcements to the Gallipoli theater. At the meeting held on 17 June, the War Council and Dardanelles Committee listened to a scheme which Kitchener and Churchill advocated of finding extra troops for Gallipoli without lessening the Western Front requirements. Finally, after meeting three days later, the opponents at last relented and agreed to grant Hamilton's request for replacements and reinforcements in order that he might make one more push and thereby retrieve the situation.[29] At that meeting the members unanimously agreed "to reinforce Sir Ian Hamilton with the three remaining divisions of the First New Army with the view to an assault in the second week of July."[30] Towards the end of this same month "the Government's offer of a fourth reinforcing division enabled Sir Ian Hamilton to amplify very considerably the scheme for the August offensive."[31] Transportation, however, was a real problem to be faced, considering the large numbers of troops involved. In the light of this the Dardanelles Committee "decided to accept the risks entailed and charter as transports the mammoth liners, *Aquitania*, *Mauretania* and *Olympic*, each of which could hold from six to seven battalions."[32]

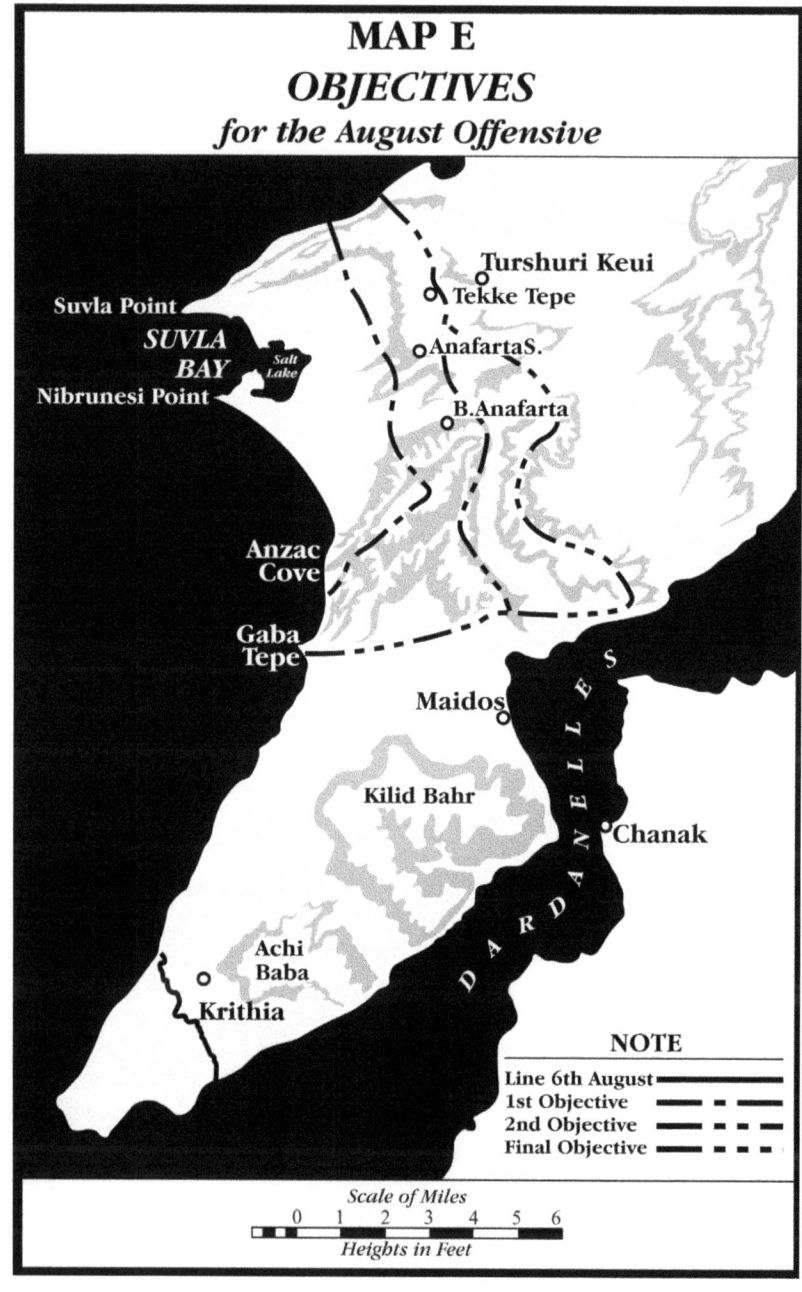

On 30 May the Commander at Anzac, Lieutenant-General William Birdwood, proposed that the first phase of any new operations should consist of an advance by night to seize Chunuk Bair, and within a day or two other nearby prominent topographical features of the Sari Bair range. While these attacks were in progress and more ground gained, it would make the feasibility of a large reinforcement of the ANZAC forces realistic. The second phase would entail an advance on a broad front to secure a dominant position astride the peninsula from Gaba Tepe to Maidos.[33]

Having adopted the Birdwood plan, Hamilton, for his part, decided to use the bulk of the fresh divisions at his disposal to strike at Suvla Bay which "was but one mile further from Mudros than Anzac Cove, and its possession would ensure a submarine-proof base and a harbor good against gales."[34] Success at Suvla against a reportedly small defending garrison would, after the taking of the strategic heights, protect and support the left flank of the ANZAC breakout.[35]

July was almost over before the bulk of Hamilton's new drafts reached the vicinity, and the fresh effort thereby possible. He received an additional 50,000 men, the vast majority of them Kitchener's New Army volunteers, or Territorial Force soldiers who volunteered for overseas service. They consisted of the 10th (Irish), 11th (Northern), 13th (Western), all New Army Divisions; and the 53rd (Welsh) and 54th (East Anglian) Territorial Force Divisions. As the latter is more the focus of this work its composition is of relevance. The 54th sailed from Britain minus its divisional artillery, a serious deficiency.[36] It also lacked any transport mules, which meant that later on everything "had to be humped."[37] Other important elements absent were divisional Royal Army Medical Corps Field Ambulance and Royal Signals detachments. The three brigades which the 54th Division comprised were the 161st, consisting of four battalions of the Essex Regiment, the 1/4th, 1/5th, 1/6th, and the 1/7th; the 162nd was composed of 1/5th battalion the Bedfordshire Regiment, the 1/4th battalion of the Northamptonshire Regiment, and two battalions of the London Regiment, 1/10th, and 1/11th; the 163rd comprised two battalions of the Norfolk Regiment, the 1/4th and 1/5th, the 1/5th of battalion of the Suffolk Regiment, and the 1/8th battalion of the Hampshire Regiment. Added to the foregoing were two companies of Royal Engineers, 1/2nd, and 2/1st East Anglian Field Companies, and the Divisional Cyclist Company, 3/1st East Anglian Cyclist Company.[38] The inclusion of the last-named was laughable as no roads existed at Suvla, and very few throughout the whole Gallipoli Peninsula!

At this juncture it may be helpful to differentiate between "New Army" and "Territorial Force." The former was composed almost entirely, apart from a few non-commissioned officer (NCO) instructors and some officers, of volunteers who responded in such overwhelming numbers to Lord Kitch-

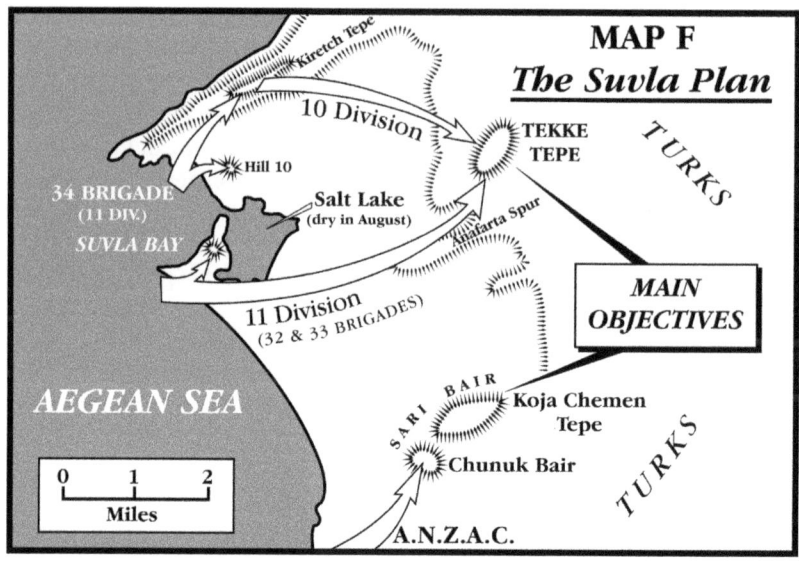

ener's unique poster appeal: "YOUR Country Needs YOU!" The bulk of these men, "the first 100,000," got posted to so-called Service Battalions of Regular Infantry Line Regiments to be equipped, drilled, and trained (frequently not in that order!—as they often awaited the arrival of uniforms, rifles, bayonets, webbing, and other kit).[39] It is obvious then that none of these enthusiasts, with the exception of those who failed to divulge a previous service record, had more than a year's exposure to army life. These contingents, together with their supporting, service, and complementary units, i.e., artillery, engineers, medical corps personnel, pioneers, etc., made up the New Army Divisions. On the other hand, the Territorial Force, which was the brainchild of the reforming Richard Burdon, Viscount Haldane, and created by the 1908 Act of Parliament, the Territorial and Reserve Forces Act,[40] consisted in the main of locally recruited county or city infantry battalions, with an appropriate complement of cavalry brigades, largely Yeomanry units. Because of the parochial nature of the formations a "magnificent 'Territorial' *esprit de corps* existed in 1914, an *esprit* that was never lost from 1914 to 1918, an *esprit* that in the first few months of the war exceeded that of the Regular divisions."[41] A main role of the Territorial Force in the event of war provided for home defense in the absence of the British Expeditionary Force (virtually all of the home-based regular army) which would be committed to the continent of Europe. Since its inception all Territorial Force battalions had Regular Army Permanent Staff Instructors (PSIs), NCOs and Warrant Officers; and a Regular Army Adjutant or Permanent Staff Officer (PSO), usually a captain, but occasionally a major.

2—The Preparations for the Landings

This was the site of the first Territorial Force Annual Training Camp for Privates How, Jaggard, Mortlock, Rumbelow, and other personnel of the 5th Battalion, the Suffolk Regiment. (Mortlock family papers)

Furthermore, in peacetime a Territorial Force battalion or brigade possessed at least a full-time colonel, quartermaster, armorer, farrier, and a clerk. The minimum requirements obliged all Territorial Force personnel to report for drill one evening a week, and attend a two-week annual training camp. As it was planned, legislated, and budgeted for in Parliament the Territorial Force never experienced the embarrassing kit and instructor shortages which plagued the hastily mobilized New Army contingents.[42] As the creation of the Territorial Force met home defense needs, there was no obligation on the part of its officers and men to volunteer for service overseas.[43] Following the outbreak of war, however, and the subsequent developments, the War Office called upon Territorial soldiers to volunteer to serve abroad,[44] and, in the case of the 5th Battalion the Suffolk Regiment,[45] those "72% who volunteered for foreign service became the 1st/5th Suffolks, while those who elected to remain for home service became a separate battalion, designated the 2nd/5th Suffolks."[46] The latter did not remain in Britain as the War Office expanded the terms of service which sent those lambs to the slaughter on the Western Front. (Incidentally, in the early part of the War, those Territorials who volunteered for overseas service wore the Imperial Service brooch above the right breast tunic pocket.[47])

The 1st/5th Suffolks trained full-time after mobilization on 5 August 1914, and as one of their first assignments they dug anti-invasion entrenchments which formed part of the east coast defenses overlooking Harwich

Our First Parade: Mildenhall Town Hall, 1913. Back Row, L. to R.— E. Bates; A. Beckett (killed in Palestine); Bob Jaggard & A. Alecock. Front Row, L. to R.— Jake Mortlock; Vince Rumbelow (died of wounds in Palestine); B. Pooley (killed in France); & S. Smith. (Mortlock family photograph)

harbor.[48] Units which eventually became the 54th (East Anglian) Divisional Artillery were initially deployed at Felixstowe on the opposite bank of the Stour.[49] They practiced on the rifle ranges at Colchester, West Stow, and Thetford, where exceptional prowess gained the reward of the crossed muskets sleeve emblem of "marksman" and carried with it a modest addition in pay. To improve bayonet technique the soldiers thrusted these sword blades attached to their rifle muzzles into suspended stuffed bags in preparation for hand-to-hand combat. During this early period the notorious Black Ace Gang came into being. Founder-member Private Tim Burlham and his cronies became the scourge of small shopkeepers in town and village alike — and their pilfering was not always petty, often more like serious shoplifting, if not outright robbery. (Well within two years they transferred their attentions to the bazaars of Alexandria and Cairo to become a byword among the merchants there.)[50]

Towards the end of 1914 the 1/5th Suffolk became part of the Colchester garrison, and it was probably at this location that Private Jake Mortlock might well have saved the lives of a hut-full of his comrades. On guard patrol during the night he visited his hut to retrieve an item of personal property to discover the room filled with deadly fumes from the stove and all the occupants in a deep coma-like sleep. He thereupon opened all the

2—The Preparations for the Landings

DISS (Norfolk) Camp, 1913. Back Row, L. to R.— G. Ford; Jake Mortlock; George How & S. Smith. Second Row, L. to R.— A. Cobbold & B. [Bill?] Heffer. Front — T. Martin; looking out of tent — Vince Rumbelow. (Martin, a new recruit, has not yet been issued his kit. The rest clearly show the degree to which Territorial Force personnel were fully equipped.) (Mortlock family photograph)

doors and windows, managing to awaken the slumbering soldiers to alert them to the danger of asphyxiation. On Christmas Day, 1914, Private Jake Mortlock and one of his mates wolfed down their Army Christmas dinner and hastened out to borrow two bicycles on which they peddled the thirty-something miles to their homes to enjoy a second one in the evening. On their return both were charged with being absent without leave (AWOL) and upon passing sentence their C.O. said that it was all the more reprehensible that they had eaten their fill at the King's expense prior to absenting themselves (or words to that effect.)[51]

Many of the infantry battalions of the 54th (East Anglian) Division (from 21st May, 1915, when it was constituted) spent spells of duty in the ancient garrison town of Colchester in Essex. While in Colchester some personnel found themselves billeted in the local lunatic asylum where one of the inmates perpetually juggled balls as he perambulated the grounds. One of the town's bakery and confectionery shops purveyed mouth-wateringly delicious gooseberry pies that the troops held in much esteem.[52] Training also entailed a great deal of arduous marching, such as Colchester to Bury St. Edmunds, some thirty miles, in one go![53] Watford, just north of London (where many soldiers were billeted in private homes, where the

Orderly Sergeant's shout was their only reveille) was their final cantonment before they entrained for Liverpool on 29 July. At Watford the 1st/8th (Isle of Wight Rifles) Battalion of the Royal Hampshire Regiment joined the rest of the division — having been quartered at Bury St. Edmunds since April.[54] They, the 1st/5th Suffolk, and the two Norfolk battalions embarked on the recently requisitioned Cunard trans-Atlantic liner the SS *Aquitania*, and at 11:00 P.M. the following night set sail for an eastern destination.[55]

As soldiers, Territorials considered themselves superior to the New Army troops. In the words of Private Jake Mortlock: "We thought we were better than Kitchener's Army."[56] Lance-Corporal Albert Collen with greater bluntness said of the 10th (Irish) New Army Division's soldiers, with whom he later served in Salonika: "All they were good for was for [expletive deleted] fighting among themselves."[57]

So in the early days of August, the 54th (East Anglian) Territorial Division plowed through the Mediterranean aboard various vessels *en route* for its "eastern destination." On the luxury-liner-turned-troopship personnel reported that it sometimes "steering a zig-zag course to confuse submarines" whose periscopes were supposedly vulnerable to the fire from the machine guns the ship possessed.[58] On board was chronically seasick Corporal George How of Freckenham, smitten thus from the very moment his foot touched the deck as he embarked at Liverpool. So bad was his plight that his comrades feared for his life.[59] The soldiers from East Anglia were mostly country lads who, in the main, had never left England's shores. For them this was the beginning of a great adventure, although for most probably not with quite the same kind of classical connotations as their local poet, the recently deceased Sub-Lieutenant Rupert Brooke, envisioned.[60] Lt.-Colonel Thomas Gibbons, in his history of the 1/5th Battalion of the Essex Regiment, recounted that: "At 8 A.M. on the 23rd [July], in dull threatening weather, we steamed slowly out by the winding channel which has been the starting point of so many brave adventures, to the sound of a hearty send-off from all the ships in the harbour."[61]

Things moved towards the fulfillment of the offensive strategy that Hamilton and the ANZAC commander, Birdwood, agreed upon at the end of May. The plan was for an all-out attempt to storm the heights of the Sari Bair Ridge from the northern Anzac sector with surreptitiously strengthened forces. (See Map F.) Starting shortly before, and continuing simultaneously with, Birdwood would launch a strong attack on Lone Pine Ridge at the southern end of the Anzac sector to lead the enemy to conclude that this was where the threat lay. To pin down as many Turkish troops as possible in other areas in order to delay the dispatch of reinforcements to the northern Anzac and Anafarta Plain sectors from elsewhere, Major-General H. de Beauvoir de Lisle (successor to Hunter-Weston as commander of the

29th Division when that officer achieved promotion to 8th Corps commander before being evacuated from the Peninsula with nervous exhaustion) would mount a holding action at Helles. For the same reason a feint at the Isthmus of Bulair and an actual landing on the northern shore of the Gulf of Saros, involving Greek irregulars, were projected, as both locations contained considerable enemy garrisons. Because Marshal Liman von Sanders feared for the Bulair region, he retained a substantial garrison there to combat any potential threat. (See Map C.) In conjunction with the ANZAC breakout, Hamilton planned an entirely new surprise landing of large numbers of troops at Suvla Bay. Once the newly arrived 9th Army Corps successfully landed at Suvla and secured the bay vicinity it would advance to seize the Anafarta Spur, the W Hills, the Kiretch Tepe Ridge, and the Tekke Tepe complex of ridges. (See Map F.)

Good soldier, bad sailor: Corporal George How, D Company, 1/5th Suffolks, suffered from chronic seasickness throughout the voyage out, and, in spite of traveling on the luxury liner-cum-troopship *Aquitania*, arrived at Mudros seriously debilitated. (Mortlock family photograph)

After the accomplishment of those objectives, these units would press in upon the Sari Bair range from the north and west until they linked up with the ANZAC attackers in the Anafarta Hills. Poised in such a position, Hamilton's forces could then turn the Turkish right flank southward towards the Khilid Bahr plateau.[62] (See Map E.)

Once again the Royal Navy and the other Allied warships had crucial roles to play. As in April, the navies would provide firepower in support of the landings for which they acted as major ferrymasters. They must also keep the troops supplied with ammunition, food, and the vital water required for man and beast. The bulk of the water supply from the outset of the campaign was procured and shipped in from Egypt. On arrival it was pumped ashore, transferred to various types of containers which men and mules carried up steep inclines and along traffic-choked ravines to the firing lines.[63] In addition there was the continuance of the responsibility for the transport of the sick and wounded from the peninsula to the hospital ships,

Suvla Plain from Sari Bair. Gives some idea of the rugged nature of the country and the difficulties facing Birdwood's men attacking an enemy entrenched in the higher elevations. (Imperial War Museum, Neg. No. Q13.429)

and thence for further treatment to various destinations such as Britain, Egypt, France, Lemnos, and Malta. This naturally extended to the forthcoming Suvla Bay operations.

At the Anzac Cove and Cape Helles theaters the same old tedium of trench warfare continued. In the former, Sergeant Cyril Lawrence and his fellow Australian engineers burrowed deep into the steep hillsides as they undermined the Turkish frontline trenches. But a different emphasis was now put on this work as, crouched in his dugout (which he now he referred to as "home"), he confided to his diary:

> There's something coming off soon. Our tunnels are being rushed ahead and made wide enough to take a stretcher. We're also filling sandbags ready for tamping charges and making bomb carriers and scaling ladders and all sorts of gear required by us for an advance.[64]

Major John Gillam down in the Cape Helles sector wrote in his diary in the entry of 5 August: "Something big is going to happen soon. I may add that this sentence has been passed from mouth to mouth for the last week, and if that something does not happen soon we shall all be in a devil of a fix on this tiny little tip of the Peninsula."[65]

Meanwhile Padre Dennis Jones, also at Helles, wrote: "There is a great deal of shelling going on by both sides—small attacks by the Turks, constant funerals to attend to, and on the following Sunday I had a busy but gratifying day. The services were well attended and, I think, appreciated by all."[66]

In spite of the Commander-in-Chief's demand for the strictest secrecy with regard to the forthcoming operation[67] his opposite numbers listened to rumors, received intelligence reports and the recounted communications of spies. As a consequence they indulged in much speculation as to where the predicted blow would fall.

> Though the Turks could fairly claim that the first six weeks' fighting on the peninsula had gone in their favour, Enver Pasha and his German advisers were nevertheless persuaded at the beginning of June that their real hour of trial was yet to come.[68]

Marshal Liman von Sanders, commander of the Gallipoli defenders, anticipated that the blow would fall on the Isthmus of Bulair, the waist, or narrowest point, of the peninsula. (See Map C.) It was faintly possible, he conceded, that the enemy might choose the Asiatic shores. In fact Hamilton assembled some of the New Army troops at Mitylene, the Aegean island formerly known as Lesbos, off the coast of Asia Minor opposite Ayvahk, to foster this impression. A plan which entailed exploiting the less rugged country of the Plain of Maidos was also considered a strong possibility and Essad Pasha, the regional army commander, assigned Colonel Hans Kannengiesser the Turkish 9th Division and sent them "to hold and improve the existing trenches on a three-mile front south of Gaba Tepe." Kannengiesser relates in his book, *The Campaign in Gallipoli*, how absolutely impregnable he considered those coastal defenses to be.[69] As to a new landing at Suvla Bay:[70]

> The circumspect and energetic Major Willmer was entrusted with the defence of the Anafarta Plain which surrounded Suvla Bay, and three battalions, one squadron, and three batteries were given him for this purpose. Somewhat little for the far-reaching plain.[71]

It was indeed. Hamilton, in his wildest dreams, could not have hoped for such good fortune, particularly after the horrific carnage of the 25 April landings. So Lady Luck at last condescended to smile upon at least one aspect of his enterprise.

For the second time since March large numbers of troops shipped into the Aegean islands off the Dardanelles and they converged mainly on Lemnos, with its perfect natural harbor of Mudros. But this time there was a distinct difference. For now the vast majority of these troops were straight out from the British Isles, pale-skinned New Army novices with a crash course of military training of less than a year behind them. Equally un-sunburnt were the men of the two Territorial Divisions, who could claim to

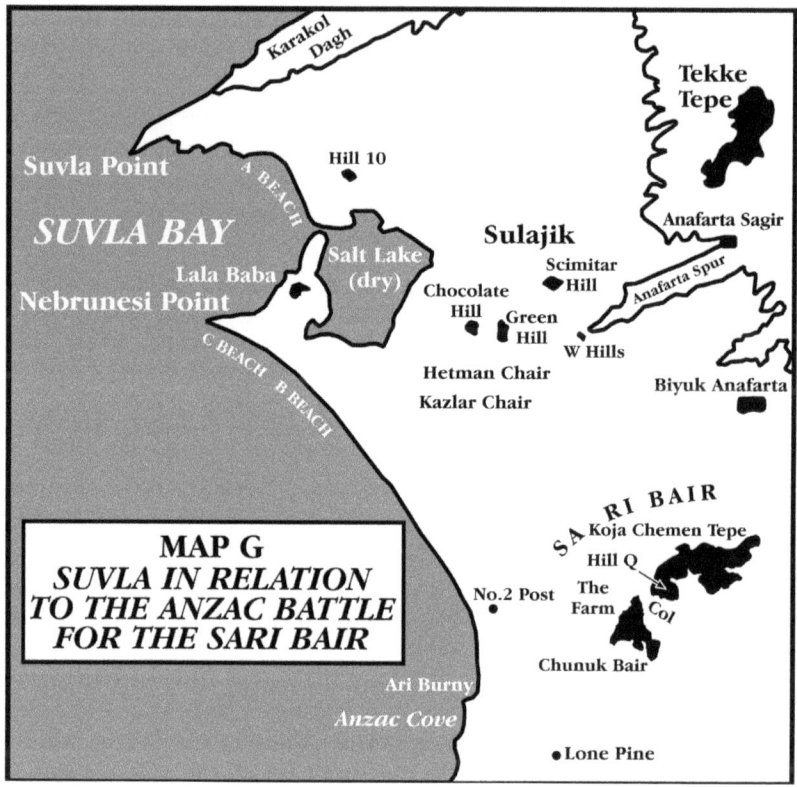

MAP G
SUVLA IN RELATION
TO THE ANZAC BATTLE
FOR THE SARI BAIR

have enjoyed better equipment and endured more lengthy and complete training programs than the aforementioned.[72] In the April assaults nearly all the troops employed were used to, or acclimatized to, hot climates. The exceptions were among the men of the 29th Division, those of whom were sent straight out from Britain. But even here a great many of those were recalled from garrisons in India, and other outposts from Gibraltar to Hong Kong, when the Division was created. The ANZACs left home during the Southern Hemisphere's summer to be stationed in Egypt — not a cool place. The Sikh, Hindu, Punjabi, and Gurkha units of the Indian Army brigades who also served in the Suez Canal Zone prior to joining the MEF were not unaccustomed to hot weather. The French Corps' troops, Senegalese, and Foreign Legionnaires, came mainly from North African garrisons, and were again no strangers to a burning sun. But now the divisions assembled for the forthcoming landings at Suvla Bay consisted entirely of men straight out from the ports of Cardiff, Dublin, Liverpool, Plymouth, and Southampton. Fellows used to the dreary damp of the Welsh mining valleys; the fog-shrouded fells of Lancashire and the industrial north; the moist air of the

Ards of Down, Sandymount Strand, or the blustery cool of Connaught; the invigorating rain-loaded winds which swept the Hampshire Downs; the squall-buffeted uplands of the Isle of Wight; the bracing breezes of the North Sea coast; and the bleak windswept flats of the Fens. They were all accustomed to the dismal chill of a rain-sodden summer, and the raw penetrating cold of a long winter. For all these fresh soldiers 72–80 degrees Fahrenheit was a heat wave, and yet they arrived to do battle on an inhospitable, subtropical, alien shore in high summer, where "the temperature was over 90 degrees F. in the shade by noon!"[73]

At least the men of D ("The Pals") Company, the 7th Battalion of the Royal Dublin Fusiliers, enjoyed a brief spell of acclimatization as they prepared for the coming event while at Mitylene. For it was in and around this town, on the off-the-Asiatic-shore island of the same name, the Lesbos of classical times, that they played out their deceptive role for the benefit of the alleged Greek spies.[74] Sergeant John Hargrave, 32nd Field Ambulance, Royal Army Medical Corps, also with the 10th (Irish) Division, who disembarked on the island of Lemnos, wrote:

> No sooner did we step ashore and sink almost ankle deep in the yellow sand, than the swarms of wicked green and black flies swept upon us. And never again, except at blessed nightfall under the dew-cold stars, were we free from this torment until the campaign ended.[75]

A young anonymous subaltern who served with the same division painted a somewhat rosier picture of that particular locality, and described it as "quite the most beautiful place that possibly could exist ... whitewashed villages half-hidden in vines and figs, pumpkins and pomegranates."[76] Army Chaplain, the Reverend Oswin Creighton, serving the spiritual needs of 86th Brigade of the 29th Division, who spent quite some time thereat, found Lemnos "enchanting."[77] Colonel Gibbons of the Essex Regiment enjoyed his short spell there immensely, especially a bath at some thermal springs. The 13th (Western) New Army Division experienced more exposure to those latitudes than the rest of the 50,000 reinforcements; the advance guard of one of its brigades arrived at Mudros harbor on 6 July. This division, however, was later detached from the 9th Army Corps' command and sent to bolster the intended ANZAC offensive.[78] Royal Army Medical Corps Captain Oskar Teichman, attached to the 1st Worcestershire Yeomanry, 2nd Mounted Division, wrote in his diary:

> *August 17th.* We arrived off Lemnos early in the morning, but as it was not possible to enter Mudros Bay until a fixed hour, our ship kept moving about until we were signaled to come in. We entered the Bay and finally the inner "harbour." Considerable rolling hills flanked the Bay, and it was full of an enormous amount of shipping—British and French battleships, cruisers, torpedo-boat destroyers, mine-layers, mine-sweepers, transports, colliers, provision boats,

captured Turkish steamers, and Greek sailing boats. Naval picket boats and pinnaces were dashing about in all directions. As we entered the Bay we were followed closely by a French troopship, which cheered us and was cheered in return. Then followed the other transport which had conveyed our Division (now fourteen yeomanry regiments strong). In the distance lay the town of Mudros, and numerous white-tented camps were to be seen extending down to the water's edge. The harbour itself was a buzz of activity. It was here that the early landings on the Peninsula were rehearsed before they actually took place. Before reaching our anchorage we passed two French troopships packed with Senegalese soldiers and *tirailleurs Algériens*....[79]

Others were not quite as fortunate to enjoy a short period of acclimatization enabling them to become familiar with the drastic change in temperature and conditions in general.[80] The liners now bearing most of the two British Territorial Divisions, the 53rd (Welsh) and the 54th (East Anglian),[81] would keep some of their human cargoes aboard until the very day of their scheduled landing on the hostile shore. The officer-historians of the 1/5th Suffolk recorded that for over three days they were kept aboard in Mudros harbor, and "life on board the *Aquitania* consisted chiefly of inspections, varied with physical drill, alarms, and numerous guards and picquets. With a complement of 7,000 there was no lack of company."[82]

Earlier, on 11 June, Sir Ian Hamilton confided in his diary his reaction to a personal communication to him from Lord Kitchener, delivered to him by the newly arrived Lieutenant-General the Honourable Sir Frederick William Stopford, who was to command the 9th Army Corps[83] in the projected assault at Suvla. The following portion occasioned food for thought:

> He (Lord Kitchener) is certain that the only way to real success of an attack is by surprise. Also, that when the surprise ceases to be operative, in so far that the advance is checked and the enemy begin to collect from all sides to oppose the attackers, then perseverance becomes merely a useless waste of life. In every attack there seems to be a moment when success is in the assailant's grasp. Both the French and ourselves at Arras and Neuve Chapelle lost the opportunity.[84]

Hamilton told Stopford that what Lord Kitchener stressed only repeated one of the most basic concepts of warfare, and went on to say:

> At our first landing the way was open to us for just so long as the surprise to the Turks lasted. That period here, at the Dardanelles, might be taken as being perhaps twice as long as it would be on the Western front which gave us a great pull. The reason was that land communications were bad and our troops on sea could move thrice as fast the Turks on their one or two bad roads. Yet, even so, there was no margin for dawdling. Hunter-Weston and d'Amade had tried their best to use their brief surprise breathing space in seizing the key to the Narrows—Achi Baba, and had failed through lack of small craft, lack of water, lack of means of bringing up supplies, lack of our 10 per cent reserves to fill the casualties. At that crucial moment when we had beaten the local enemy troops and the enemy reinforcements had not yet come up, we could not get the men

or the stuff quick enough to shore. Still, we had gained three or four miles and there were spots on the peninsula where, today, three or four miles would be enough. Also, supposing he had to run a landing, his (Stopford's) action would take place under much easier conditions than Hunter-Weston's on April 25th.[85]

This extract is of paramount importance — pivotal, possibly, to this entire history, as it illustrates Kitchener and Hamilton's grasp of a fundamental strategy. It is also ironic that Stopford not only carried the miniature lecture on the strategy of surprise to Hamilton from Kitchener, but also received a considerably more detailed one when his Commander-in-Chief expounded its virtues to him!

Sir "Freddy" Stopford, chosen to command the troops to be landed at Suvla Bay, was an amiable, doddering sexagenarian lieutenant-general who had retired seven years earlier to combat chronic ill health. His presence at Gallipoli — indeed, in the army at all — was due to the fact that his country, beginning the war with only a small professional army, had no deep cadre of officers qualified to command an army corps— or even a division. Sir Frederick, called back into service, was given this key assignment by Lord Kitchener even though Sir Ian Hamilton had named at least three other generals he considered better suited for the task.

Lieutenant Compton Mackenzie, a Royal Marine Intelligence officer who happened to lunch at the Officers' Mess at GHQ Imbros the day in June that Stopford arrived, related: "The one next to me was Sir Frederick Stopford, a man of great kindliness and personal charm, whose conversation at lunch left me at the end of the meal completely without hope of victory at Suvla." This was because Stopford allowed one of his divisional generals (not named, but probably Reed) to disparage the whole forthcoming operation, even insisting upon almost mutinous conditions before he would "advance a single yard."[86] Mackenzie recalled that Sir Frederick "was deprecating, courteous, fatherly, anything except the commander of an army corps which had been entrusted with a major operation that might change the whole course of the war in twenty-four hours,"[87] and something that the Commander-in-Chief of the Turkish Army of Gallipoli, Marshal Liman von Sanders, feared the success of "would be a severe blow for us."[88]

Stopford arrived in the middle of June to take up his command, and for a short time succeeded General Hunter-Weston in command of the 8th Army Corps at Helles, so as to gain experience in Peninsula warfare.[89] (It may be of interest to note that in the spring of 1999 an article in the *London Sunday Times* alleged that General Stopford was in possession of some very detailed and up-to-date maps of the Dardanelles and the Gallipoli Peninsula, but that he absent-mindedly left them on the train![90]) As a young man he entered the Grenadier Guards in the early 1870s, seeing the usual service of officers at the end of the nineteenth century, in India, West Africa, and Egypt. During the South African War he acted as military secretary to General Buller, and entered Ladysmith with him at the relief. Since that time he occupied various military positions in Britain, and at the outbreak of war was still on the Active List although just turned sixty — holding the largely nominal post of Lieutenant of the Tower of London.[91] His reputation stood high both as a student and a teacher of military history, and long experience had given him an accurate knowledge of army routine. He, however, had never held high command in the field, and neither history nor routine in itself inspires to action. Rather such a combination tends to suppress the hopeful buoyancy of spirit and rapid fertility of resource essential for good generalship, while it accentuates the hesitating deliberation and caution which too often develop with increasing years. Habits mainly sedentary are also likely to reduce the enthusiasm for physical activity as middle age is passing.[92] While at GHQ Helles, Stopford came under the pessimistic influence of Major-General Hamilton Lyster Reed, a gunner out from the Western Front, who persuaded him that no progress was possible against entrenched positions without a preponderance of howitzer batteries in the artillery.[93] This worthy became Chief of Staff of the 9th Army Corps, which put him in a position to continue his discouragement. As noted earlier, the Territorial divisions *en route* to the field were denuded of their divisional artillery, and thus lacked both howitzer and field gun batteries.

Of the generals selected to command the divisions and some of the brigades which made up the 9th Army Corps, several lacked promising reputations. Major-General Frederick Hammersley, Major-General the Honourable John Edward Lindley, and Brigadier-General William Henry Sitwell did not boast campaign records which inspired confidence, evoked admiration, or suggested brilliant leadership. Among the remainder, Lieutenant-General Sir Bryan Thomas Mahon, Major-General Francis Seymour Inglefield, Major-General Frederick Charles Shaw, and Brigadier-General Felix Frederic Hill demonstrated clear credentials of competence in command. Dug out from semi-retirement, the three had no claim to active service command but seniority. In the case of Hammersley, there was even a touch of mental instability.[94]

Major John Gillam, the supply officer with the Army Service Corps (ASC), whose previously cited eyewitness account of the April landings at Cape Helles depicted those operations so vividly, was also involved with the Suvla Bay landings. He enumerated the complexity of sustaining an army in any location, and that the difficulties are increased when supplies are shipped and unloaded under fire on a hostile shore. The ASC's responsibilities included ensuring that the troops received their daily rations and no lesser an authority than Napoleon declared that: "An army marches upon its stomach."[95] Major Gillam also confirmed what other primary sources contended, that the authorities made every effort to secure and maintain an adequate water ration for the troops. This is further substantiated in the War Office document, *Army: Arrangements made for Water Supply to the Troops during landing at Suvla Bay*, published in October 1915.[96] The Royal Navy bore the burden of transporting and ferrying the Army ashore while at the same time providing a covering bombardment for the landing parties and shipping in supplies to sustain the beachheads. On this occasion, however, the Admiralty would not commit the same vast flotilla of *battleships*. Their Lordships were loath to risk a repetition of the March disasters now that enemy submarines posed a serious threat to all shipping. They recalled the *Queen Elizabeth*, and assigned more naval vessels to combat this underwater menace. It is noteworthy that it was during the Dardanelles Campaign that an "aircraft carrier" was used for the second time in war. (The first was during the disastrous raid on Antwerp in 1914.) HMS *Ark Royal*, which already had float-shod seaplanes that operated from her bows, was adapted so that biplanes could be launched from and landed on her decks. These aircraft carried out invaluable missions of reconnaissance, firedirection and target registration, and aerial photography, as well as harassment of enemy positions and supply routes.[97] As in April, the Navy also had "balloon ships" to which observation balloons were moored.

Midshipman Harry Denham of the *Agamemnon* (so close to Troy and the grave of Achilles), a mere boy of sixteen at the time, furnished some unique insights into the naval preparations for the Suvla attack, as also did fellow officer Lieutenant Eric Bush, serving in the warship HMS *Lord Nelson*. According to their accounts the operation was meticulously planned and executed with every eventuality covered. Commodore Roger Keyes, ever enthusiastic for every aspect of forcing a passage through the Dardanelles, supplied the view of one in the higher echelons of the Silent Service.[98] It is ironic that these two men and a boy of that allegedly mute arm of His Majesty's Forces were eminently better informed about the forthcoming assault by the Army than most of its top brass. This was due to Hamilton's almost paranoiac insistence upon the utmost secrecy. Even Stopford, the Commander of the 9th Army Corps scheduled to make the attack, knew not until 30 July where and when he was to land his forces! In fact this passion for secrecy was carried to such lengths that it kept the detached Company of the 7th Royal Dublin Fusiliers at Mitylene in ignorance of their destination even after they embarked,[99] and the Brigadier (Hill) in command of their Brigade (the 31st) did not know where he was when he landed at Suvla Bay, and was not even in possession of a map of the area![100] When he arrived, Sergeant John Hargrave, with the 32nd Field Ambulance, Royal Army Medical Corps, 10th (Irish) Division, likewise recounted that "we knew not where we were. We had never heard of Suvla Bay."[101]

For all the secrecy involved in the projected landings the Commander-in-Chief of the Turkish Army on the Gallipoli Peninsula, Marshal Liman von Sanders, and his subordinate generals were fully aware of what was going on, and only speculated on the date and place of the impending invasion. Lacking this vital knowledge forced Liman to deploy the troops at his disposal to meet with any eventuality. His inclination favored the blow falling on the Isthmus of Bulair, the waist of, and the narrowest point on the body of, the Gallipoli peninsula. (See Map C.)

To combat this anticipated threat he had ordered the 7th and 12th Divisions to garrison that area "ready to meet the danger in that direction of which he always appears to have been inordinately afraid."[102] He did not rule out the possibility of a thrust on the Asiatic shore, which meant considerable troop dispositions at Bezika Bay and elsewhere. Another spot which appeared to offer Hamilton a good chance of accomplishing his goals was between Anzac Cove and Cape Helles, where a successful invading force could exploit the less rugged country of the Plain of Maidos and thus endanger the lines of communication of the Turkish troops who defended the Helles front. (See Map C.) During the heavy fighting in April and May this neighborhood had been temporarily denuded of its garrison. But early in June, at the first threat of a new landing, urgent steps were taken to reoccupy it, and the Turkish 9th Division, at that time resting and reorganizing in the Krithia sector, was placed under General (then Colonel) Kannengiesser, and sent to hold and improve the existing trenches on a three-mile front from south of Gaba Tepe.[103]

In this area Liman now deployed an additional division, Colonel Mustapha Kemal's 19th, along the coast and inland at that locality. In case of a breakout from the Helles beachhead two more divisions were in readiness. One was on the Asiatic side of the Narrows, the other in the Khilid Bahr region. The Suvla Bay location presented an attacker with advantages, particularly those which relieved and supported the constricted struggle in the Anzac Cove enclave.

> It offered a splendid opportunity for landing, and the towering Kodjadschemendagh [Koja Chemen Tepe, the highest peak of the Sari Bair Ridge] an alluring tactical aim.[104]

Liman did not forget the Gulf of Saros and made a cavalry brigade responsible for meeting any threat to the north of the Isthmus of Bulair.[105] The German Commander-in-Chief of the Turkish 5th Army thus felt that he had strategically spread the forces at his disposal to cover all the likely landing places. He and his divisional commanders now apprehensively awaited the predicted onslaught. On 16 July Liman received definite news of the approach of large numbers of enemy reinforcements. "A report from Salonika then stated that 140 transports and war vessels were assembled in

Mudros harbour, where a force of between 50,000 and 60,000 British troops was waiting ready to embark."[106] Liman knew that, if accurate, these intelligence estimates meant that he could assume that a new landing by a large body of men was imminent. A mighty fleet would support any such landing, giving it mobility far superior to his road-bound forces. Since he could gain no clear indication of the probable point, or points, of the impending assault, "Britain's command of the sea would again offer Sir Ian Hamilton the chance of effecting a tactical surprise."[107]

The recent repeated use of the term "British troops" is no longer a generalization, for, unlike the April landings effected by heterogeneous forces, at Suvla Bay an exclusively British army corps would go ashore. Furthermore, practically all of these soldiers came directly from the British Isles.

The Pre-Landings Offensive

In order to draw the Turks' attention away from the areas on which the plan focused, General Birdwood, the Commander of the forces which occupied the Anzac Cove enclave, launched a savage assault from his southern sector to gain enemy strongpoints which overlooked or enfiladed his tenuous positions. Some of the most horrific hand-to-hand fighting of the entire war ensued thereat. Lone Pine Ridge and Johnston's Jolly became immortalized as blood-tinged chapters of Australia's and New Zealand's annals, steeped with that peculiar mystique associated with the ANZAC epic. In the meantime, to the north, large numbers of reinforcements were landed every night and secreted in the many extra dugouts and trench systems which were excavated to receive them.[108] Colonel Hankey observed "that they [the whole of the 13th (Western) Division and two other brigades] had been introduced as quietly as possible into Anzac on the nights of the 3rd, 4th and 5th August ... and had time to settle down before they were called upon to attack."[109] The same source also related that: "The 11th Division had been out here for some time, part of it had been put in the trenches at Helles, and the whole exercised and hardened since its arrival."[110] Actually it is more likely to have been the 13th Division. The future British Prime Minister, Clement Attlee, who served as B Company Commander with the 6th Battalion, the South Lancashire Regiment, 13th (Western) Division, wrote:

> We stayed our first night [some time in mid or late June, 1915] in the trenches with the Lancashire Fusiliers of the 29th Division. Their battalion strength was about the same as that of my company. Our lads found many old friends and settled in very well. I had three or four weeks at Helles, experiencing the heat and smells and flies. Like many others, I got dysentery, a complaint for which our diet of bully beef, biscuit, and tea without milk was not very suitable. Eventually I fainted and was carried down to the beach and embarked for

Malta. I thus missed the big attack at Anzac, where our division had six or seven thousand casualties, including many of my friends of the South Lancashires.[111]

On the Helles front preparations went ahead for a limited holding action to ensure that no enemy troops from that part of the Peninsula were at liberty to go to the aid of their comrades under attack to the north and west. Major-General Sir Aylmer G. Hunter-Weston, alleged to have remarked, "casualties, what do I care about casualties?"[112] was evacuated, suffering from nervous exhaustion, but his immediate successor, Major-General H. R. Street, was, if anything, even more inclined to persist with broad-daylight frontal attacks after all chances of success had slipped away.

As the great Cunard liner, the SS *Aquitania*, steamed majestically into Mudros harbor on August 5th she was hailed by a boatload of Australians just out of Anzac Cove with: "Are we downhearted!?" The East Anglian troops who crowded the deckrails responded to a man with a hearty "NO!!" Whereupon the reply came back over the water, as quick as a flash: "Well you bloody soon will be!"[113] Later other Australian troops proffered more shouted Antipodean advice: "Sergeants! Tear orf your stroypes! Thair're picking orf N.C.O.s!— Orfficers tew!" It seems that this advice was heeded, as when the units got ashore many officers and N.C.O.s had in fact removed those tell-tale insignias of rank.[114, 115]

The invasion forces started to converge on their objective. From the islands of Imbros, Lemnos, and Mitylene, where the tent cities rapidly emptied, vessels packed with troops weighed down with kit, equipment, arms, ammunition, and iron rations departed. A regular infantryman was burdened with the some seventy (as much as eighty when extra rations were issued) pounds weight he carried. As Major Gillam remarked after he had tried one soldier's pack on before Helles: "How they will fight tomorrow beats me.... I was astonished at its weight."[116] Likewise Captain Aubrey Herbert described a night move up to the line when the infantryman "is only conscious of the dead weight of his load, the braces of his pack biting into his shoulders."[117] Off Cape Helles and Anzac Cove flashes of gunfire illuminated the night sky. Across the water the dull rumble and thud-thud of the artillery bombardment drifted to the ears of the massed ranks of men aboard the invasion fleet. For almost all this was their introduction to war. For those in charge of repulsing the anticipated attack there was no doubt that it was about to take place, but they still could not determine its locality. The vast majority of those about to take part in the attack were in the same state of ignorance.

The first glimpses and sounds of war which greeted the converging convoys of fresh troops resulted from the warships' bombardment and field artillery barrage which supported the commencement of the Helles feint and the heavy fighting which raged at the southernmost end of the Anzac Cove enclave. This latter development was also something of a feint designed to make the Turkish commanders erroneously conclude that this was where the big blow would fall, whereas in actual fact, at the northern end large numbers of reinforcements supplemented Birdwood's ANZACS for the coming offensive. Now those troops stealthily climbed up steep broken ravines in the dark. The August Plan started to erupt and the assault on the Sari Bair Ridges was about to begin.

3

The Landings

The opening phase of the August Plan was markedly similar to that of General James Wolfe's strategy which in 1759 defeated the French in Canada. Prior to the Battle of the Plains of Abraham, British grenadiers scaled the precipitous wooded cliffs known as the Heights of Abraham and struggled up obscure goatpaths in pitch darkness to surprise and overwhelm the French garrison defending Quebec.[1] Over 150 years later, Australian, British, Gurkha, Maori, New Zealander, and Sikh troops clambered upwards along steep scrub- and cacti-choked ravines in the moonless dark to storm the collection of peaks which made up the Sari Bair Ridge. Their objectives included Chunuk Bair, Hill Q, and ultimately the apex of the range, a summit known as Koja Chemen Tepe, slightly less than 1,000 feet above sea level. (See Maps F and G.) These ridges and spurs dominated the Anzac sector and overlooked that of Cape Helles.[2] Possession of these strategic heights would make the Turkish defenses at Helles untenable, and General Sir Ian Hamilton now considered them of equal, if not superior, importance to the Khilid Bahr Plateau. This attempt on the Sari Bair would coincide with the new landing at Suvla Bay. The latter is the prime concern of this work and those of Anzac and Helles only incidental. In the words of *The Official History*: "The stage was set: at Helles and Anzac the actors were already in their places. All that now remained was for the 11th Division to be ferried over to Suvla, and for the two brigades of the 10th to be brought up from Mudros and Mitylene to reinforce at daybreak."[3] Another factor in the equation was that the Turkish observation of Ramadan, the Islamic period of self-denial, had just begun.

As the crescent moon would rise at 2:00 A.M. on the night of 6/7 August it was decided that the August Plan operations would commence on 6 August. The landings at Suvla Bay would begin after dusk on that day.[4] (See Map F.) General Stopford was instructed specifically, in orders issued on 22 July, and signed by General Braithwaite, Hamilton's Chief of the General Staff, to capture Yilghin Burnu (Chocolate Hill) and Ismail Oglu Tepe (W Hills) "*coup de main* before daylight to prevent the guns they contain being used against our troops on Hill 305 [Koja Chemen Tepe, the highest peak of the Sari Bair range, and the prime objective of the August Plan] and to safeguard our hold on Suvla Bay." In the next paragraph it continued: "It is hoped that the remainder of your forces will be available on the morning of the 7th August to advance on Biyuk Anafarta with the object of moving up the eastern spurs of Hill 305 so as to assist General Birdwood's attack."[5] (See Maps E, F, G.)

Hamilton, after inspecting some of his contingents, watched them as they embarked at Mudros. Long rows of pith-helmeted soldiers seemed to stretch interminably across the shimmering wharves.[6] He toyed with the idea of making some impassioned plea "Elandslaagte fashion,"[7] possibly something *à la* Admiral Lord Horatio Nelson on the eve of Trafalgar. But he decided against and lost the opportunity forever. To his diary he expressed disappointment at the absence of Lieutenant-General Sir Frederick Stopford, 9th Army Corps Commander,[8] and Major-General Frederick Hammersley,[9] who commanded 11th (Northern) Division. He reflected thus:

> The morale of the troops about to enter into a battle supplies a splendid field of research for students of the human soul, for then the blind wall set in everyday intercourse between Commander and commanded seems to become brittle as crystal and as transparent. Only for a few moments—last moments for so many? But, during those moments, the gesture of the General means so much—it strikes the attitude of his troops. It is up to Stopford and Hammersley to make those gestures. Stopford was not there, and is not the type; Hammersley is not that type either. How true it is that age, experience, wisdom count for less than youth, magnetism and love of danger when inexperience has to be heartened for the struggle.[10]

At about 8:30, in the gathering dusk, Hamilton saw the whole flotilla glide away and disappear ghostlike northwards. "The empty harbour frightens me," he wrote. "Nothing in legend stranger or more terrible than the silent departure of this silent army."[11] Compton Mackenzie wrote: "The metallic blues and greens and blood-reds in the water had turned to a cold dull grey, eastward the ever increasing surge and thunder of the guns; here an almost horrible quiet."[12]

Sergeant John Hargrave, of the 32nd Field Ambulance, Royal Army Medical Corps, 10th (Irish) Division wrote: "One day came the order to pack up and manhandle all our stuff down to the beach ready for re-embarkation.... August the 6th saw us steaming out at night towards the great unknown climax—the New Landing."[13] Naval Nurse E. Campbell recorded in her diary:

> August 6th. Friday. News arrived for us to go to Cape Helles to sail at 6 P.M. escorted by the *Doris*. They say a big action is going on now. Sailed at 6 for Imbros. Arrived at daylight. Up all night. Many hospital ships passed us during the night. Heard firing & saw flashes from Achi Baba.[14]

The Commander-in-Chief, at Imbros, watched with apprehension "the silent departure of a silent army"[15] when the invasion fleet sailed away to the north, then consoled himself with what aerial reconnaissance reported:

> But it will never do to begin the night's vigil in this low key. Capital news from the aeroplanes. [Commander] Samson has sent in photographs taken yesterday, showing the Suvla Bay area. Not more than 100 to 150 yards of trenches in all; half a dozen gun emplacements and, the attached report adds, no Turks anywhere on the move.[16]

Sergeant John Hargrave spoke with first-hand knowledge of this absence of continuous entrenchments as he "covered the ground many times from August 7th to the 17th." It was true, he conceded, that there were "some short lengths of hastily dug transverse trenches (more in the nature of slit trenches), but very few deeply entrenched positions."[17]

The troops at Mitylene received their orders on the fifth, and embarked on the morning of the sixth. *En route* for their unknown destination "in the dark, early hours of the morning they came in sight of the Peninsula," and Cape Helles, which was a sight wonderful to behold, first appeared with "Achi Baba one mass of bursting shells."[18] These same ferried troops next saw and heard the ANZAC barrage, and moved on to witness the warships' gunfire which supported the landings already in progress at Suvla Bay. "Juvenis" (the *nom de plume* of a subaltern with the 10th (Irish) Division) recorded: "... we glided on among our fellow transports in due order into Suvla Bay, and then, swinging round as we got into line with Lala Baba and Suvla Cape, dropped anchor in the thick of them."[19] "Juvenis" was with the Inniskillings. Henry Hanna recounted the experiences of the 7th Royal Dublin Fusiliers:

> As dawn broke — just before five o'clock — they arrived in Suvla Bay. The morning was beautifully fine and the Bay was full of every kind of shipping, which was partly concealed by a low-lying mist. The naval guns were vigorously shelling the ridges around the Bay. The shells exploded with a bright red flame edged with a fringe of black smoke, just like a tulip with the red leaves [sic "petals"(?)] tipped with black. The noise was terrifying. The Fleet sweepers were ordered to anchor, and did so about a mile from the shore. Day suddenly broke, and the sun as quickly rose, and as the light became stronger nothing was visible to the naked eye save the stretcher-bearers carrying wounded down the slopes of a hill, which the watchers were afterwards to know as Lala Baba. One could see a large number of men digging themselves in just behind a crest about half a mile from the shore. The troops with General Hill immediately got orders to land, that is, the six battalions from Mitylene, including the 7th Dublins, and were to act under the orders of General Hammersley, commanding the 11th Division. About half an hour after they had anchored, shells began to fall round the Fleet sweepers. No ship was struck, but some of the shells burst very close. During the voyage from Mitylene, as indicating the spirit of the men, one could see various groups packed together as tightly as possible,

playing the well-known Dublin game of "House" [Bingo] — which they continued until orders were given to land — even when the shells were bursting round the ship.[20]

Waiting to board at Imbros with his unit, the 6th Battalion of the York and Lancaster Regiment, 11th (Northern) Division, Sheffield scoutmaster 2nd Lieutenant Edmund Priestman observed a camera-armed American gentleman taking motion pictures of the troops.[21] His narrative continued:

> As soon as one of the lighters was packed with khaki from the thick masses of men on the shore, it steamed away and its place was taken by a new one, on to which fresh lines of troops filed, till it too was packed to capacity. Then out it would puff, carrying a dense freight of Tommies, whose legs swung hazardously over the bulwarks and whose heels kicked time to their favourite song: "Are we downhearted? No, not while Britannia rules the waves (not likely!!)"[22] For this new landing "a number of motor-lighters were coming out from home, and with their help a large body of troops could be thrown ashore far more quickly than in the landings on the 25th of April."[23]

The employment of these craft, nicknamed "beetles," greatly supplemented Hamilton's new invasion fleet. These self-propelled flat-bottomed barges conveyed 500 men or 40 horses to the beaches each trip, a distinct improvement on the largely towed invasion craft used in April. Their rate of knots was twice that of the latter, and their construction included bullet- and shrapnel-proof protection, plus a thing to be let down like a drawbridge fixed to their bows "over which men could pour ashore by fours."[24] They were, in fact, the forerunners of the modern landing craft.

The Sheffield scoutmaster, 2nd Lieutenant E.Y. Priestman, whose battalion was part of the 32nd Brigade of the 11th (Northern) Division further related:

> Over the packed decks there hung a tense atmosphere of suppressed excitement, too full for spoken or musical comment, officers and men alike rearranging their respective outlooks upon life to suit the new conditions and the great adventures looming among the shadows ahead. And so the night deepened and our world narrowed down to a vague circle of indigo sea in which we slid quietly forward, alone save for the occasional glimpse of a companion torpedo-boat slipping ghost-like out of the gloom for a moment, to be swallowed again in the darkness. And now came a thrill. The sealed orders containing our programme for the coming landing were to be opened. Crowded round a map, we traced the proposed movements of the various regiments to be engaged, while our Adjutant read from the official memo.... And now on our starboard bow we could see flashes of heavy guns, spurts of yellow light on the flanks of dim hills that came into view, where the shells were bursting, and an occasional glare as a star-shell hung like a lamp over the scene. This was Anzac ... the battleships lying away off the shore, their searchlights throwing vivid beams on to the rugged cliffs, and their guns flinging the crashing shells against these stubborn defenses, while nearer to us a glow of green and red lights showed the outline of a hospital ship against the darkness.[25]

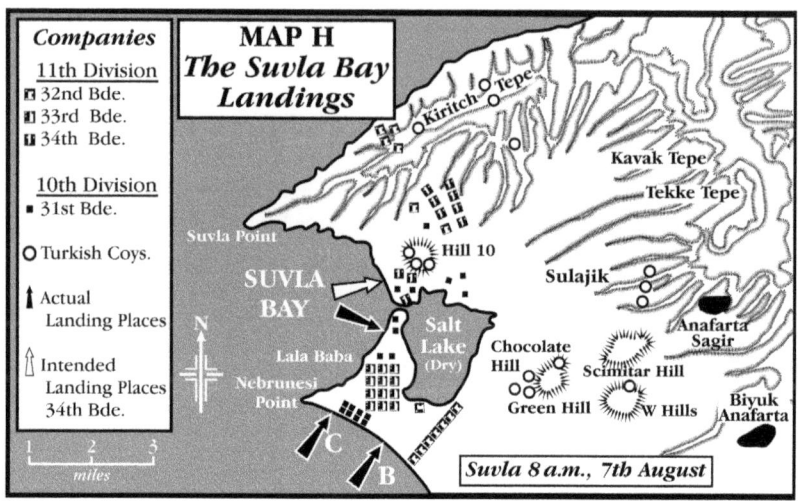

Compton Mackenzie described "the dark night of the Suvla landing,"[26] and possibly he intentionally used that adjective to double in meaning that demonstrated how the Commander-in-Chief was kept "in the dark" as far as reports sent back from the beaches. In fact throughout that murky night General Headquarters (GHQ) Imbros received only one communication.

> At last at 2 A.M. the needle on the dial began to move and a telegraphist spelt out the message: "A little shelling at A has now ceased. All quiet at B." There was no signature — it was simply the signaller on board the *Levant* [off *Levant* Suvla] passing a private message to his mate at the Imbros end — but it did at least serve to reassure the Commander-in-Chief's mind.[27]

"Now, thank God," Hamilton wrote, "the deadliest peril is past. The New Army are fairly ashore."[28]

It was true. That laconic telegraphic contact came after nearly 20,000 troops landed, sustained remarkably light casualties, and caught Marshal Otto Liman von Sanders completely off his guard. (See Map H.) It was also unfortunately true that at the same time:

> All three senior British generals— Hammersley at Suvla, Stopford aboard the *Jonquil* [the flagship of Rear-Admiral Arthur Henry Christian, commander of the naval forces at Suvla Bay] and Hamilton on Imbros— were in almost total ignorance of what was really happening, and the hills which they (or Hamilton, at any rate) had so much hoped to have by dawn, were still several miles away.[29]

For a combatant's experience of the landing 2nd Lieutenant E.Y. Priestman, of the 6th Battalion, the York and Lancaster Regiment, 32nd Brigade, 11th (Northern) Division, continued his narrative:

> And now, away forward, we could see dimly a headland running out into the

sea, silent and deserted, and to the imaginative Bulldog ["Belton Bulldogs"—nickname of his battalion], wrapped in the black mystery; for this was where we were to land. What was waiting for us? What had the first landing party found? You can picture us standing at the rail with our pulses doing tattoos as we strained our eyes into the darkness.

Slowly our boat comes to a stop, and the absence of the rushing water under her bows leaves a silence that can be felt hanging over the waters of the little bay in which we find ourselves. Only away on our right comes the distant rattle of a volley and the dull boom of an occasional gun at Anzac. So the Turkish picquet has been driven in by the-——s and the land is clear. A lighter glides alongside us out of the shadow of the beach, and as it draws near—crack, crack, r-r-r-rattle, rattle, crack!!! From among the black mounds inland a sharp crackling of rifles, and then silence again. As the echo dies away over the still water all our conjectures return. If the Turks have been driven back, whose is this firing? What's happening beyond there, among the shadows? We are still asking these questions as the lighter carries us landward and we step for the first time on to hostile ground. Orders have to be given here quietly, and almost in whispers we get the men into formation on the rough, pebbly beach. We are all ashore now and the boats in the bay are mere brooding shadows on a stretch of dull grey, though the thought of their protecting guns is with us as we lead a way over the gravel into the blackness beyond. To meet—what? As we push on, through sweet, sickly-smelling scrub now, the darkness in front takes the form of a peaked hill [Lala Baba] and we meet the first slopes of its flank.... On the steeper slopes of the peaked hill our formation is altered to four lines, one in front of another, and each man two paces from his neighbor (though they will bunch up for mutual comfort, and one is tempted to shout at times!)

Our front line has met something exciting now, and—"spit, spit, whissss!" a swarm of bullets rushes over our heads into the night.[30]

Many eyes observed the landings, and there is general agreement that the troops met with the minimal opposition described above. Mined approaches in the shallows, foreshore, and beaches inflicted a high proportion of the casualties the landing parties suffered. Sergeant John Hargrave and Lieutenant "Juvenis" both related that they saw the hidden devices blow men up as they went ashore.[31] The former (also a scoutmaster, incidentally) recounted that he and his companion remarked how the landed troops formed up into ranks of four and marched off as if on a parade ground.

> "In fours!" I exclaimed to Hawke, who was peering through my field-glasses. "Sheer murder," said Hawke. No sooner had he spoken than a high explosive shell from the Turkish positions on the Sari Bair range came screaming over the Salt Lake: "Z-z-z-e-e-e-o-o-o-p — Crash!" They lay there like a little group of dead beetles, and the wounded were crawling away like ants into the dead yellow grass and the sage bushes to die. A whole platoon was smashed.[32]

Lieutenant Priestman and Sergeant Hargrave, in addition to a common connection with the Boy Scout movement, sketched graphic scenes and people at Suvla Bay. *With a B.-P. Scout in Gallipoli: A Record of the Belton Bulldogs* by the former, and *Sketches from Suvla*, and *At Suvla Bay* by the latter — their respective books, published in wartime — each contains many illustrations, often humorous, by the authors. One of Sergeant Hargrave's drawings depicted Suvla Bay and indicated what happened at the time, some of which refuted Major Fritz Willmer's assertion that his artillery came through the British warships' gunfire unscathed.[33] At the same time Hargrave witnessed a German aeroplane, a Taube, fly over the bay and drop several bombs, none of which "did much damage."[34] The same account related:

> Mechanical Death went steadily on. Four Turkish batteries[35] on the Kislar Dagh [western end of the Kiretch Tepe Ridge] were blown up one after the other by our battleships. We watched the thick rolling smoke of the explosions, and saw bits of wheels, and the arms and legs of gunners blown up in little black fragments against that pearl-pink sunrise.
>
> The noise of Mechanical Death went surging from one side of the bay to the other — it swept round suddenly with an angry rattle of maxims and the hard echoing crackle of rifle-fire. Now and then our battleships crashed forth, and their shells went hurtling and screaming over the mountains to burst with a muffled roar somewhere out of sight.... The little yellow-skinned observation balloon floated above one of our battleships like a penny toy. The Turks had several shots at it, but missed it every time.[36]

Sergeant J. Watson, of the 8th Battalion the Northumberland Fusiliers, 11th (Northern) Division, in a somewhat confused retrospective account, had a grimmer story to tell. Everything was quite quiet and peaceful, he recalled, until the Captain of their destroyer shouted, "Cast off the lighters!"

> As soon as the Captain had shouted, the Turks opened fire with their machine-guns and rifle fire — also artillery. There were a lot of poor fellows killed and wounded before we left the lighters. The lighters took us as near the shore as they dared, then we had to get into the small rowing boats rowed by the Naval Division. They rowed us until we were about fifteen or twenty yards from the shore, then we had to jump into the sea, up to the waist in water. I always remember the first lighter going out with a load — about five minutes later it returned full of our lads badly wounded. We had to wade for the shore and I remember carrying the Vickers machine-gun on my shoulders when I got near the beach and fell over a tripwire which the Turks had put in the water for that purpose and nearly all the rifles were useless after they had been in the water.[37] The shore was thick with dead and wounded — there were dozens of chaps who never got out of the water. It was bad enough in the dark, but ten times worse when it got daylight. Just at the break of day we got safely landed and the Turks had retreated over the Salt Lake (a name given to a stretch of land which was white as snow with the salt left after the tides from the sea had been up). Our objective was a small hill, which we called Hill Ten; we took it after very heavy losses. I always remember our old Colonel (Lieutenant-Colonel Fishburn) was hit in the shoulder and leg. I was close behind him when he fell to the ground wounded. When he was lying there he took off his cork helmet and waved it to encourage us fellows on, saying, "Go on the same old 'Fifth'!" [The Northumberland Fusiliers were the old 5th Regiment of Foot.][38]

3—The Landings

From the opposite side during the dark watches of that night Colonel (later Major-General) Hans Kannengiesser divulged that:

> As this waiting appeared useless I asked Essad Pasha [General Officer Commanding the Northern Group] to allow me to withdraw to get what sleep I could.... I went to my staff in the officers' mess room where my servant had already placed a thick wolf's skin on the table, my bed. Unfortunately the skin was so full of fleas that I had scarcely any sleep at all.... About 4.30 A.M. I was called to Essad Pasha, who informed me that the enemy had landed troops north of Ariburnu.[39]

Major Fritz Willmer, the German officer commanding the Anafarta detachment, reported the landing to Liman von Sanders as soon as it materialized. He informed the Commander-in-Chief that the obvious first objective of this new development, the line Kiretch Tepe to Chocolate Hill, was firmly in Turkish hands, but urgently requested reinforcements.[40]

Obviously this new development put an end to all the speculation as to the new landing's location, and while Major Willmer's detachment put up a spirited resistance to the incursion, his superiors hurriedly conferred to decide how they best could combat the dangerous turn of events. Already the Anzac breakout was well under way, while very heavy fighting still raged at the southern end of that sector, notably at Lone Pine Ridge. The August Plan was falling into place. Both there and on the Helles front a heavy bombardment from the guns of the Allies' warships and the field artillery batteries still blanketed the Turkish positions, and once the invasion fleet safely anchored in the bay, the Royal Navy's massed ordnance there opened up in support of the Suvla assault.

Liman von Sanders at once realized the significance of the offensives. "The Anafarta landing was an enterprise planned on a grand scale, intended to open the Dardanelles to the Allies by land action while at the same time cutting the Fifth Army from its communications."[41] As John Hargrave wrote: "Turkish and British accounts do not afford him adequate credit for the resolution and skill which he showed as soon as he divined the British plan early on August 7th."[42] But whereas Liman expected the blow to fall on the Isthmus of Bulair, one of his Turkish subordinate commanders, Mustapha Kemal, all along adjudged the British would choose the Suvla area for the fresh landing.[43] His superiors ignored his confident prediction. At the time "he was still only a senior divisional commander, with the rank of colonel, holding the position north of the Anzac front with the 19th Turkish Division. But he was on the spot with his men—alert, watching every move as he looked down from his perch on Battleship Hill."[44]

Colonel Kannengiesser described the scene he surveyed from an adjacent peak, the Djonk Bahir, the top of which was "a long narrow plateau

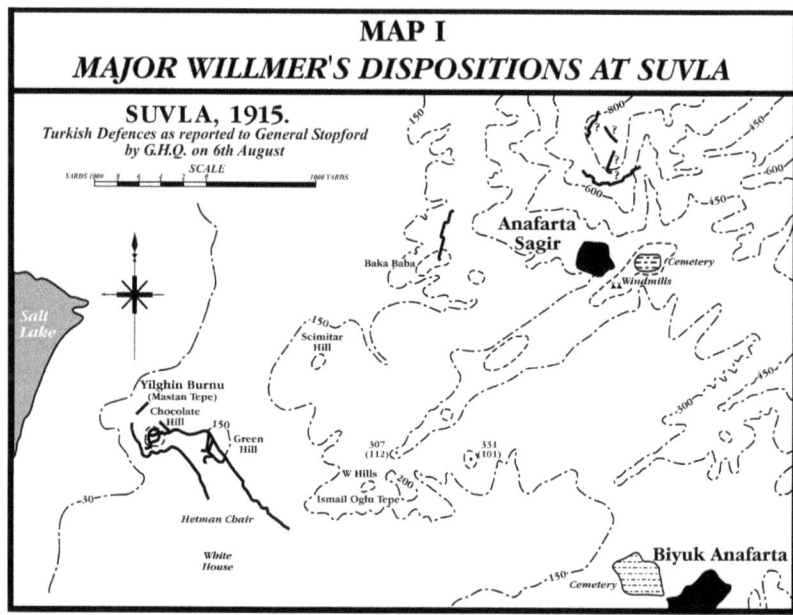

with an astonishingly far-reaching view over rough hilly country to the Aegean Sea."[45] Down below him stretched the placid expanse of Suvla Bay.

> Suvla Bay lay full of ships. We counted ten transports, six warships, and seven hospital ships. On land we saw a confused mass of troops like a disturbed antheap, and across the blinding white surface of the dried salt sea we saw a battery marching in a southerly direction. With our few revolvers we could do nothing about it. All about us was peace and quiet — not a man to be seen and no enemy in front of us in the hills.
> With glasses I was able to pick up bit by bit Willmer's companies north of the Asmak Dere on the east border of the flat country, and I saw English troops on the Lala Baba and, on the flat, in certain places, entrenching. Nowhere was there fighting in progress.[46]

Now all the Turco-German military leaders hastened to re-deploy their forces to check the forward impetus of the invading enemy army. Colonel Feizi Bey was ordered to force-march three battalions from the Bulair garrison to aid Major Willmer's inadequate forces blocking the Suvla threat.[47] (See Map I.)

> At 5.30 A.M. on the 7th — by which hour nine more British battalions had arrived in Suvla Bay to reinforce the thirteen already ashore — these three Turkish battalions were just starting off on their long march from Bulair. [See Map C.]
> The road was a rough track, and there was little chance that they could come into action for another thirty hours.... By 7 A.M. Liman von Sanders had made

3—The Landings

his mind up that Sir Ian Hamilton was throwing his whole weight into the scale at Suvla and Anzac, and that his immediate object was the capture of Hill 971 and Chunuk Bair. Thereupon he ordered Feizi Bey to leave only one division at Bulair and to march south with the 7th and 12th Divisions. He also ordered a second division to be sent north from Helles, and every available man from the Asiatic shore.[48]

So the advance-guard of Feizi Bey's corps could not play an active role in stemming the invasion until around noon of 8 August at the earliest, and the vanguard, at the very least, a couple of hours later. Any additional units brought over from the Asiatic side would take appreciably longer. All of the Helles contingents would go directly to strengthen the defenses opposed to the ANZAC offensive. Not only did the Turco-German military commanders on the spot appreciate the gravity of the threat which now faced them, but in Berlin, leading figures in government, and elsewhere, took a very serious view of the new developments. Grand Admiral Baron Alfred von Tirpitz, Secretary of the Imperial German Navy, wrote on 8 August:

> Heavy fighting has been going on since yesterday in the Dardanelles. The English know, without a doubt, that our submarines there are not available yet for action. In consequence they have brought all their ships there and have opened a frightful bombardment on all the forts and all the positions. The situation obviously is very critical. How earnestly I have urged, alas! in vain, that more of our submarines should be sent thither, and at greater speed. Should the Dardanelles fall, then the world war has been decided against us.[49]

British military intelligence ascertained that a total of only 3,000 men were the entire Turkish troop dispositions within 30 miles of Suvla Bay.[50] Unlike those underestimates made prior to the April landings, these figures were surprisingly accurate, although the actual number concentrated for the defense of the Suvla Plain was roughly half of that total. These assessments did not include forces preoccupied with holding back Lieutenant-General William Birdwood's ANZACs, as these were already under intense pressure from the August Plan attacks in that region. German and Turkish primary sources fully substantiate the foregoing; i.e., Marshal Liman von Sanders, Colonel Hans Kannengieser, Colonel Mustapha Kemal, and Major Erich Prigge, all of whom supplied virtually identical data.[51] This very modest force was all that defended the area which the successful British landing now threatened.

The bay itself and the open plain behind it were dominated on three sides by high ridges—the most distant of which was only four miles from the beach. But once these were occupied, Sir Ian Hamilton would have a sheltered base, secure from enemy shellfire, and would be able to push a force southeastward through the gap between the two Anafarta villages, five miles distant from Suvla, to come in on the flank of any Turkish force still opposing General Birdwood's advance.[52] (See Map E.)

As these three ridges, which combined to encircle Suvla and the Anafarta Plain, will receive frequent mention in the ensuing narrative this is an appropriate juncture at which to elaborate on them, and their strategic importance. The citation which follows is drawn from the definition in *The Official History* whose compiler, Brigadier-General Cecil. F. Aspinall-Oglander, not only participated at Suvla, but was also one of that operation's chief architects. All other works of reputable standing which the author researched agree with those facts, apart from some confusing differences in place names! (See Map G.)

> On the north, from Suvla Point to Ejelmer Bay, was the Kiretch Tepe ridge, running along the northern coast, and attaining at Kiretch Tepe a maximum height of 650 feet. This ridge, low and rocky to start with, is clothed with thick scrub further east, and its northern slopes are abrupt. The Tekke Tepe ridge, running south between Ejelmer Bay and the village of Anafarta Sagir is nearly 900 feet high. Its sides are steep but easily climbable, except for the high prickly scrub which densely clothes its sides. In places this scrub — about six to seven feet high — is only passable by way of narrow goat tracks which zig-zag over the hill. From the top of the ridge the broad plains on either side are spread out at one's feet like a map. On the south the Suvla plain is dominated by the Anafarta spur, a long finger-shaped ridge which runs south-west from near Anafarta Sagir. This ridge, about 350 feet high, ends with a cluster of rugged eminences, in places precipitous, about 300 feet high, known to the British as the W Hills, and to the Turks as Ismail Oglu Tepe. A northern off-shoot from the W Hills is a low, rounded spur, whose summit, known as Scimitar Hill, was later to become the scene of bitter fighting. Rising from the plain, midway between the W Hills and Lala Baba, two small isolated hills also claim attention. These two hills, joined by a low neck, were subsequently called Chocolate Hill and Green Hill from their prevailing colours; but before the Suvla landing they were known as "the Chocolate Hills." On the Turkish map they were collectively called Mastan Tepe (Yilghin Burnu). It will be seen on later pages that this indefinite nomenclature caused serious misunderstandings. It remains to notice here that the Turks had occasionally placed guns on the Chocolate and W Hills to shell the Anzac beaches; that these hills were believed to be defended by trenches and wire against a possible attack from the south and west; and that their northern slopes were said to be undefended. It was reported that there was a small outpost on Kiretch Tepe, and that the Tekke Tepe ridge was unoccupied. The Turks were believed to be keeping three of their five battalions near Anafarta Sagir, and to have distributed the remaining two between the Chocolate and W Hills, the outposts on Kiretch Tepe, and the two horns of the bay.[53]

As to Suvla Bay itself, because of the shifting nature of sea floors, sandbars, and sand dunes, adequate up-to-date information was not available and the naval authorities could supply only old and unreliable charts. In the foreground of the Suvla Plain was the silvery expanse of the Salt Lake with a cut which connected it tenuously to the Bay. This lake was believed completely dry in summer. On 4 August a British warship fired a shell into its surface to ascertain its texture, much to the consternation of secrecy-obsessed Hamilton according to John Hargrave[54] and Alan Moorehead[55]—whereas Hamilton implied that, to the contrary, it was done at his own behest.[56]

Hamilton elected to stay at GHQ Imbros, as it was more or less equidistant from the three theaters of operations (Anzac, Helles, and Suvla), rather than to make his headquarters off Suvla Bay. He now nervously awaited any news, now that his attempt to redeem the Gallipoli *dèbâcle* was underway, but already chaotic situations emerged, unforeseen and unappreciated, embryos which would spawn terrifying monsters. The last-minute renaming of the Suvla landings beaches was but an ill-starred augury of what was to come. These landing sites were originally designated the letters "A," "B," and "C" in logical sequence, to differentiate each beach. But, because of Royal Naval apprehension about putting troops ashore at one landing-point ("B"), in an area reputed to contain treacherous shoals, it was relocated. Regrettably this meant that it placed "A," "B," and "C" Beaches in a nonsequential order. This one seemingly trivial decision unfortunately accounted for a disproportionate degree of chaos during the day ahead.

While the overburdened soldiers[57] of the invasion force endured long, uncomfortable, sleepless hours in the cramped confines of the vessel to which they were assigned,[58] their commanding generals, for the most part aboard ship, hardly deviated from their customary mess routine.[59] The Commander-in-Chief was an exception. Having elected to live under conditions more nearly comparable to those of his combat troops, he thus experienced the pestilential flies and debilitating bouts of dysentery. The others, as usual, had servants constantly in attendance to act as valets, or serve and wait upon them. No "iron rations" for these officers and gentlemen. A typical sample day's provisions, put in menu form, read something like:

Breakfast:[60] wide-ranging menu, from Grapefruit, through Cereal, Bacon, Sausages, and Eggs, to Smoked Herrings; with Fruit Juices, Tea, Coffee, and Milk to drink.
   Tiffin: a Buffet of Cold-Table Meats, Pies, and Savouries; Dessert, Junket, Fresh Fruit.[61]
   Luncheon: Soup; Choice of Entrees; Dessert, Semolina Pudding; Coffee. Up to an hour of sherry, *apéritifs,* mixed drinks, or cocktails preceded
   Dinner at 7.30 P.M.,[62] or 19.30 hours, to put it in military parlance. This was usually the most impressive meal of the day, and consisted of Soup/Hors d'Oeuvres; Fish; Choice of Entrees; Choice of Desserts; Cheeseboard and Fruit; Coffee. A wide selection of Fine Wines, or Ales, complemented this repast, with Port, Brandy, and Liqueurs to round it off. These prime products of vintner, brewer, and distiller were available for the dedicated toper at tiffin and luncheon also on the same monthly mess account. Linen tablecloths, napkins; crystal and silverware. A good cigar, perhaps.... Clearly, this was not soldiering at its most rigorously spartan.

Not nearly as self-accommodating were their Turco-German counterparts. Major-General Hans Kannengiesser (his promotion occurred after this period) recorded, with photographs to substantiate his narrative, in his *The Campaign in Gallipoli*, that his quarters were in a humble clay hutment near Turshun Keui, well within range of the enemy's naval guns. Every day, without fail, this German officer rode around to inspect and encourage the troops under his command. Furthermore, he did all that was in his power to see the summary transportation of the sick and wounded for medical attention. On the morning of 7 August, while he supervised in person the defense of a critical sector of the Sari Bair Ridge, he was hit by a machine-gun bullet "through the breast." He stayed in command till, weakened through loss of blood, he was borne to a hospital ship, and eventually evacuated to Constantinople.[63] (This brave Prussian officer returned to the battle zone in early October 1915 and resumed his account of the campaign.) Liman von Sanders was likewise a man of austere habits in comparison with those of the sybarites on the other side, whose lives seemed to consist of a procession of jolly good meals, and jolly good times with jolly good chaps.

So, whereas all the key figures on the defenders' side were on the spot, peering down from commanding heights, gauging the situation and making the appropriate dispositions with professional efficiency, on the attackers' no such comparable degree of urgency motivated the bemedalled products of the British public schools system. "The Battle of Waterloo" may well have been "won on the playing fields of Eton"[64] but this was a different time and a different place, and the incomparable "Iron Duke" absent. Lieutenant Compton Mackenzie, at GHQ Imbros, recorded his nocturnal reverie of pre-dawn 7 August 1915:

> It was a long time before I fell asleep, for I kept waking to clutch at phantoms. There was no vestige of hope left in my mind that the Suvla landing could now succeed. I felt as if I had watched a system crash to pieces before my eyes, as if I had stood by the deathbed of an old order. The guns I could hear might have been a growling that foretold the murderous folly of the Somme. The war would last now until we had all turned ourselves into Germans to win it. An absurd phrase went singing through my head. "We have lost our amateur status tonight." It was foolish of me who had been old enough to appreciate the muddle of the South African War to go on believing in the practical value of the public school system. I had really for long mistrusted it, but since coming out here I had once more fallen under its spell as I might have fallen under the spell of a story by Rudyard Kipling. Yes, the war would go on now. I must remember to write home tomorrow for more woolen underclothes.[65]

It was this very system, itself the backbone of the British class structure,[66] and its old school tie[67] that bound Sir Ian Hamilton from doing anything that "wasn't quite cricket" in his dealings with fellow members of his caste, which allowed the tragedy of the Suvla Bay failure to occur. "Freddie," "Hunter-Bunter," and "Birdie," all jolly good chaps no doubt, but the two first-named both needed a firmer hand than that of the aesthete Sir Ian Hamilton's.

General Stopford established his 9th Army Corps' Headquarters aboard HMS *Jonquil* anchored at the outer edge of Suvla Bay. Consequently, until the establishment of a naval shore signal-station well into the morning of 7 August, he relied almost exclusively on second-hand reports frequently hours old as the ferried bearer(s) depended on boat-captains preoccupied with other concerns.[68] (What happened to the heliograph of Boer War fame, or the semaphore flags? Sergeant John Hargrave saw, and sketched, the employment of the latter as signallers sent directions to the warships' gun commanders.)[69] Even when Stopford became better informed he did not exactly overburden the telegraphic cable connections with his Commander-in-Chief at GHQ Imbros, or his divisional generals on the beachhead. The commander of the main attacking force, the 11th (Northern) Division, Major-General Frederick Hammersley, elected to set up his headquarters ashore where he got caught up in the confusion which ensued after the landing. He issued orders, countermanded them, and prevaricated to such a degree that he exacerbated and magnified the problems of his subordinate officers and their units. In particular Hammersley failed to ensure that Sitwell's 34th Brigade secured its objectives in accordance with the August Plan's schedule, which, as a direct consequence, meant that the brigade on its right had an unsupported flank which halted its advance.[70] Brigadier-General Felix Frederic Hill was a prime example of one who suffered under the organized chaos which reigned on the beaches of Suvla Bay during the night and day of 6 and 7 August 1915. Landed at a location almost two miles from that originally specified, once ashore his brigade was commandeered by General Hammersley, commanding the 11th (Northern) Division, thus it was detached and separated from Lieutenant-General Sir Bryan Thomas Mahon's 10th (Irish) Division, to which it belonged.

Colonel Maurice Hankey, Secretary of the Dardanelles' Committee, sent out to make a first hand report, witnessed some of notable events of 7 August:

> There was no covering fire from the escorting warships. The 'beetles,' already full laden, were cast off by he towing destroyers, switched on their engines, and ran ashore, lowered he hinged gangways in the bows, and the men ran on to dry land. The 'beetles' then, having thus been lightened, backed out, went back to the parent destroyer and brought ashore the 500 men aboard her in a single trip. Except for those required to land men from the *Theseus* and *Endymion*, the 'beetles' were then free to start landing ammunition, guns, stores, etc.
>
> South of Nibrunesi Point the beach proved very shelving and no physical difficulty was encountered. There was, however, some shelling, and infantry fire from a small Turkish post on the low hill of Lala Baba between Nibrunesi

Point (Kuchuk Kemikli) and the Salt Lake (dry). Before dawn, however, Lala Baba had been captured and a covering position was taken up between the Salt Lake and the shore south of Nibrunesi Point.[71]

In the meanwhile, from their lofty eyries at Anzac, the Australians, New Zealanders, Gurkhas, Indians, and British troops enjoyed a spectacular panoramic view of the new developments. "For looking down from their hillsides they could see Suvla Bay full of ships, the moving marks of boats, dotted specks of men on sandhills, and more ships on the sea marching like chariots to the cannon. In a flash … they realised the truth. A new landing was being made."[72] The Australian engineer, Sergeant Cyril Lawrence, turned his binoculars toward the lightening horizon:

> Away over at Point Anafarta at Suvla Bay I can make out with the aid of my glasses a dull mass on the beach and numbers of tiny craft — some on the beach, some going out and some coming in. I could only surmise that the dull patches were men. If so, then the Tommies had landed at Suvla. I wondered how they were doing.[73]

Like Lawrence many others recorded their observations in diaries, and of those who survived many did likewise in letters, memoirs, reminiscences, or tape-recorded interviews. "Upon this coast and country, roadless, wharfless, beachless and unimproved, nearly 30,000 men landed in the first ten hours of 7 August. At 10 A.M., on that day, when the sun was in his stride, the difficulty of those beaches began to tell upon those upon them."[74] A certain secondary source alleged that much chaos occurred during the hours of darkness when the men landed on that unfamiliar shore. He argued that military discipline is dependent largely upon the spoken command of recognizable officers, and, more particularly, non-commissioned officers; i.e., lance-corporals, corporals, sergeants, and warrant-officers. In the dark on a strange beach in a confused situation, such as pertained at Suvla, units could become mixed up, separated, or fragmented. Men might respond tardily to, or question, the commands of apparent strangers and tend to stick tightly to the familiar members of their section of the platoon. Thus, he contended, just when the situation required vigorous thrusts to secure the crucially important high ground in accordance with the August Plan, inertia paralyzed movement.[75] The eyewitness accounts, however, of two Britons and two Germans refute the foregoing analysis. Second Lieutenant Priestman, whose unit landed under cover of darkness, related how his men fell in and moved off in a thoroughly disciplined manner.[76] Sergeant Hargrave recorded his incredulity when he observed recently landed men falling-in "in fours!"[77] On the opposite side Major Willmer reported that the recently landed British "were walking bolt upright as if on parade,"[78] and Colonel Kannengiesser observed "a battery marching in a southerly direction."[79]

3—The Landings

At this desperately critical juncture the Commander-in-Chief was out of touch and uninformed, and the 9th Army Corps Commander likewise. But whereas the former was impatient and concerned for rapid progress, the latter was complacent and congratulatory.

> 7th August, 1915. Imbros. Sitting in my hut after a night in the G.S. tent. One A.D.C. remains over there. As the cables come in he runs across with them. Freddie Maitland runs fast. I am watching to see his helmet top the ridge of sand that lies between. The 9th Corps has got ashore; some scrapping along the beaches but no wire or hold-up like there was at Sedd-el-Bahr: that in itself is worth fifty million golden sovereigns. The surprise has come off![80]

It had indeed! But the hours passed and no further word came from 9th Army Corps HQ. Unfortunately the old adage "no news is good news" did not hold good in this instance, and Hamilton waited until noon on the seventh for an update on the situation. When at last it came it was:

> ... nearly fourteen hours after the landing began at B Beach on the night of August 6. It was the message that Stopford had sent at or soon after dawn saying that his troops had been able to advance "little beyond the beach." This was bad news. However, the Commander-in-Chief noted that it had been handed in about seven hours ago, and took it for granted that Stopford's troops must have taken their objectives by now.[81]

It is still a mystery why the Commander-in-Chief waited so patiently when others, such as Commodore Roger Keyes, Colonel Cecil Aspinall, and Colonel Maurice Hankey sounded the alarm bells about what they perceived happening (or what they perceived as paralysis) on the Suvla beachhead. At daybreak two whole brigades advanced against the minor elevation of Hill 10, less than half a mile from A Beach. (See Maps G and H.)

> Nor was any forward movement south of the Salt Lake attempted then or at a later hour. During the early hours of the day—from 6 A.M., say, till 10 A.M.— when the heat was not yet trying and when the troops could not have been suffering intensely from thirst, there were thirteen battalions of the 11th Division available to move to the attack. They enjoyed a numerical superiority of at least three to one over the enemy. They were, moreover, sustained by the moral support of part of the 10th Division, already on shore, and the Turks had manifestly already lost the first round in failing to stop the landing and in abandoning Lala Baba.[82]

So while Hamilton fretted for news at GHQ Imbros we have "the picture of Stopford, dawdling on his command ship, distant from the wrought confusion, messaging Major-General Hammersley congratulations for getting his division ashore, seemingly unconcerned about what he does with it after."[83]

At GHQ, the staff, apparently, did not share Sir Ian's concern, as Rear-Admiral Rosslyn Erskine Wemyss, commander of the naval station at

Suvla Bay shortly after the landing, with the Kiretch Fepe Ridge in the background. The dust seen in the middle-distance is from a shell burst. Conveys an air of things being conducted at a leisurely pace. No date given but it may have been taken much later than is implied. (Imperial War Museum, Neg. No. Q13.452)

Mudros, described the complacency at GHQ on 7 August as "something awful."[84] Hammersley, the commander of the 11th (Northern) Division, the main assault force, for his part, also lacked a sense of urgency. One of his contributions to the chaos, as related above, was to "[mis?]appropriate" one of the 10th Division's Mitylene brigades, Hill's 31st. This brigade was "one of Mahon's two brigades" which should have landed at A Beach, but were "most unluckily dumped ashore several miles South at C Beach."[85] (See Map H.) Hill's 31st Brigade was thus a victim of the beach redesignation "which had arrived at Suvla before headquarters and put in on his right, consequently it was separated by the whole 11th Division from the 10th, which was to go into line on the left."[86] Put more simply, according to the Plan the entire 10th (Irish) Division was to have deployed on the Kiretch Tepe Ridge flank parallel with the Gulf of Saros, whereas, because of the mix-up in landing, Hill's Brigade (31st) went into line on the opposite flank and was thus separated from its parent division by the units of Hammersley's 11th (Northern) Division. Such action did not please Lieutenant-General Sir Bryan Mahon, the commander of the 10th (Irish) Division, and Hammersley's senior in rank, who now possessed an emasculated division hardly worthy of a brigadier. Mahon's "division" in all totaled "less than 3,000 men."[87] This was not all. "All [his] Divisional Artillery [various batteries listed] ... had been either left behind in England, or were still in Egypt."[88] It was, however, Mahon's depleted division that penetrated furthest on the first day at Suvla. His Irish infantrymen advanced up and along the Kiretch Tepe Ridge in spite of meeting fierce resistance from the Turkish gendarmerie entrenched thereon.[89] Colonel Maurice Hankey, the visiting Secretary of the Dardanelles Committee and the Imperial General Staff, stated that on 7 August by 5 P.M.:

> when all the troops of both divisions had been put ashore, the amount of ground occupied did not stretch anywhere more than a few hundred yards from the beach, except on the extreme left, where progress had been made to a point about 5,000 yards from Cape Suvla.[90]

D Company of the 7th Battalion of the Royal Dublin Fusiliers ("the Pals," whose ranks included famous rugby football players and other sportsmen) played a notable part in the early hostilities on the left flank high up on the hogsback. Their gallant efforts received neither support, supply, sustenance, nor relief, and it was too late when Hamilton told Stopford "the sooner the Kiretch nettle was grasped the less it would sting."[91] Nor was the chronic inertia prevalent on the beaches at Suvla unobserved from among the heights at Anzac. Major-General Sir Alexander J. Godley, commanding officer of the Australian and New Zealand Division, remarked to Colonel Hankey how "distressful" it was "to see the Suvla troops loafing and bathing [swimming] while my men were fighting like tigers."[92] In the Lone Pine sector alone the fearless Antipodean troops gained seven Victoria Crosses, plus another in the fighting at Rhododendron Spur.[93] Naval Nurse E. Campbell wrote in her diary that:

> 1,380 [wounded arrived in the afternoon and evening of the 7th] mostly stretcher cases & very bad. Had twenty deaths during the voyage.... Heard firing all day. Could see smoke distinctly. We spent all afternoon and night dressing wounds. We left at 8P.M. Men in every corner of the ship. Wards frightfully hot. A good many Australians amongst men. M.O.s [Medical Officers] operated all night.[94]

The desperate struggle and vicious fighting up there was in complete contrast to the atmosphere down below, which, early on 8 August, Colonel Hankey likened to "an August Bank Holiday, with men bathing."[95] The same important primary source shrewdly pronounced:

> By the morning the position was getting really serious. The troops had been ashore thirty-six hours. Instead of being half-way to Maidos, as we had hoped, they were still sitting around the beach. The staff of the Army Corps were still aboard the *Jonquil,* the flagship of Admiral Christian, and, though with admirable promptitude the Navy had run a cable from Kephalos to Suvla and thence to Anzac within a few hours of the first landing, we simply could not get

news at GHQ. We felt great anxiety. All the intelligence reports agreed that in a strategical sense the surprise had been complete. The Turkish reserves were miles and miles away.[96]

Sergeant Hargrave, however, at that same time in the immediate vicinity, "not more than twenty yards from A Beach," felt these observers drew the wrong conclusions with regard to the swimmers in the bay. It was true, he admitted, that close on two hundred men swam off the beaches, but he insisted that they were off-duty cooks, cookhouse orderlies, ASC drivers and farriers, officers' batmen, and so forth; all combat troops not in the firing line, in support, or in reserve, labored in various fatigue parties. "The same bathing carnival was to be seen every day at Anzac," he added.[97] Private Jake Mortlock, who came ashore two days later, gave a completely contrary account when he claimed that he never swam in the sea at all as the Turks "were sniping down to the beach" all the time he was on the Gallipoli Peninsula.[98]

Hamilton's Aide-de-Camp, Captain the Honorable George St. John Brodrick, in a letter written at the time to his father, Lord Midleton, made similar observations regarding the distressing lack of urgency prevalent at Suvla.[99] "Young Brodrick" (he was twenty-seven at the time) did not pull any punches either when it came to summing-up General Sir Frederick Stopford and his staff. "They all seemed a very lifeless crew, with but little knowledge of the general situation and no spirit in them."[100]

Sir Ian Hamilton, writing in retrospect on the 17th, summed up the Suvla landings thus: "The surprise was complete, and the army was thrown ashore in record time practically without loss...." It sounds marvelous—everything went like clockwork! But he was not there, and did not see any of it.[101] "The Staff failed, Stopford mishandled the 9th Corps on shore, the divisional commanders muddled their divisions, and the brigadiers their brigades."[102]

All the while the Suvla commanders dithered and delayed, up among the folds and crags of the Sari Bair Ridge, General Birdwood's gallant troops fought desperate and bloody battles to fulfill their part in realizing the strategy of the August Plan, now beginning to assume a less august aspect. Sergeant Cyril Lawrence expressed profound bitterness at the way "the Tommies are letting our boys down."[103] Condemned by his own words, Hamilton pronounced in retrospect: "*Driving power was required, and even a certain ruthlessness, to brush aside pleas for respite for tired troops. The one fatal error was inertia. And inertia prevailed*" (emphasis added).[104] The youthful Midshipman Harry Denham, however, painted a much more positive picture of events on that day:

> Sunday August 8th. Started at dawn towing boats of wounded from 'A' Beach and then 'C' Beach, the new beaches on the N. side of the Bay; the original 'A' Beach being too exposed, was abandoned. Here I had a bathe, just like being at

3—The Landings

Southsea. *Bacchante* started shelling top of ridge between 'B' and Anzac; big monitors and small ones also occasionally shelling this area. Wounded ceased to come down at 3.30 so we towed all the boats round to old 'A' Beach. One of our aeroplanes dropped a message at 'B' saying that the Turks were bringing up guns to bombard beach, so everyone there was packing up gear in preparation for the shelling. 5 P.M. Monitor *Havelock* went in close to Old 'A' Beach and started shelling possible gun positions on the ridge. It may have done some good, as 'B' did not get shelled that day.[105]

On the opposing side there was widespread wonderment at the absence of attack and lack of purpose. Major Fritz Willmer, the German officer in command of the Anafarta detachment, spent the greater part of 7 August on the Chocolate and W Hills. As the day wore on his anxiety eased to some extent. The invading troops appeared hesitant, the vast majority of them halted on the beaches. He reported to his GHQ that he observed the advance of two or three battalions from the Cut shortly after noon. These headed eastward, and moved "bolt upright, as if on parade." They did not adopt extended order, and "made no use of available cover." He reported that on reaching the northeast corner of the lake these contingents suffered a number of casualties and their advance ended.[106]

Not until 4:20 in the afternoon of the seventh did Hamilton telegraph a message to his Corps Commander:

Have only received one telegram from you. Chief glad to hear enemy opposition weakening, and knows you will take advantage of this to press on rapidly. Prisoners state landing a surprise, so take every advantage before you are forestalled.[107]

Stopford at this time still suffered from a sprained knee and spent much time in a horizontal position. Hamilton was to spend a second night "on tenter hooks." Although he received "a wireless from a warship," and "many messages from Anzac and Helles," it was not until "2.12 A.M.," and "5.10 A.M." of 8 August that Stopford deigned to reply.[108] The second of the two cables from 9th Army Corps HQ to the Commander-in-Chief announced that the minor elevation known alternatively as Yilghin Burnu or Chocolate Hill was "in our hands."[109] (See Map H and I.) This was the least important of the features which the August Plan scheduled for seizure before daylight of 7 August, roughly twenty-four hours previously. In fact, as revealed earlier in this chapter, the wording of Stopford's instructions, communicated to him on 22 July, clearly and categorically stated that: "It is of the first importance that Yilghin Burnu [Chocolate Hill] and Ismail Oglu Tepe [W Hills] should be captured *coup de main* before daylight [of August 7th.]"[110] Only on the heights of the hogsback called the Kiretch Tepe Ridge was anything like a first day's objective achieved, and there General Mahon's depleted division pushed the line further along that rocky eminence.

Hamilton's General Staff Officer for Operations, Lieutenant-Colonel Aspinall, accompanied by Colonel Hankey, was sent to investigate the apparent holdup at Suvla. They arrived at 1:00 P.M. on 8 August, and Aspinall, who with Captain Guy Payan Dawnay "conceived the whole Suvla operation," after "a few minutes walk across the plain was shocked to be told he was in the front line."[111] Thoroughly alarmed, Aspinall boarded the *Jonquil* to alert the 9th Army Corps' commander that his part in the August Plan was very much behind schedule. Stopford, only himself just back from a visit to the Suvla beaches, "seemed well content with the progress made."[112] Aspinall said he was sure General Hamilton would be greatly disappointed that the hills had not been reached, to which Stopford replied that the men needed rest, and that he was going to order an advance for the next day. Aspinall left to send a despairing telegram to Hamilton that read:

> Just been ashore where I found all quiet. No rifle fire, no artillery fire, and apparently no Turks. IX Corps resting. Feel confident that golden opportunities are being lost and look upon situation as serious.[113]

Hamilton, possibly because he was on his way to Suvla Bay, did not receive this communication,[114] and Stopford, perhaps more impressed by Aspinall's urgency than he showed, left the *Jonquil* to order Hammersley to make an immediate advance. Hammersley was not at his headquarters, and when Stopford heard that he was arranging an attack on the W Hills for the following morning, abandoned his proposal.[115]

Hamilton's extraordinary patience became exhausted as alarming evaluations reached him from go-getters such as Commodore Roger Keyes and Colonel Maurice Hankey, and he at last decided to visit the scene to see for himself what caused the lack of progress. To his chagrin the vessel which was to take him over to Suvla from Imbros developed boiler trouble and could therefore not sail as planned. It was not until 4:15 P.M. that he obtained passage aboard Admiral de Robeck's yacht, *Triad*. "Hamilton arrived in a fever of anxiety, and was met by Keyes, and Aspinall, who were distraught at the deplorable turn of events."[116] These stalwarts realized the real urgency of the hour and nicely gauged the remedial action needed. With the certain dispatch of strong enemy reinforcements to the Suvla sector the British forces must occupy the heights before these arrived for the planned strategy to stand a chance of success. As Colonel Maurice Hankey, who was also present, wrote: "If the Turks reached the Anafarta Sagir ridge first and entrenched there, our plan had failed, and we were again up against trench warfare."[117] Hamilton immediately re-embarked and hastened out to the *Jonquil*. There he confronted General Stopford who lay on a valise spread on deck. "A short and strained conference took place."[118] The 9th Army Corps Commander stressed all kinds of reasons for not pressing home attacks, one of which was totally absurd. He had "decided to postpone the occupation of the ridge (which might lead to a regular battle) until next morning."[119] Stopford insisted that his divisional generals wanted more time "to rest, reorganize, and water their troops" before they could undertake any offensive operations, and added that "nothing would please him more than if I could succeed where he had failed."[120] Hamilton took him at his word without extending an invitation for Stopford to accompany him. Thus the two knights parted, and Hamilton "tumbled into Roger Keyes' racing motor boat and with him and Aspinall we simply shot across the water to Lala Baba. Every moment was priceless. I had not been five minutes on the *Jonquil* and in another two I was with Hammersley."[121]

Hamilton found Hammersley rather shaken as the result of a recent uncomfortably close shell-burst and more intent upon ensuring his personal safety than directing aggressive maneuvers against the enemy. Hamilton demanded the mounting of an immediate attack to capture the heights which, according to the August Plan, one recalls, should have been occupied within a matter of hours following the landing. Colonel Hankey related that Hamilton managed to prevail over Hammersley's reluctance and "organized a night advance, as a result of which a part of a battalion actually set foot on the vitally important ridge just north of Anafarta Sagir, but, not being well supported, fell back ... and the net result was a trifling advance to a line roughly north and south through Kuchuk Anafarta Ova."[122] Aircraft reconnaissance now reported large bodies of enemy troops converging on the Suvla Bay and northern Anzac sectors. The sands of time were running out, and the whole August Plan was now in serious jeopardy.

At 7.00 P.M. on 7 August Major Willmer again reported to Fifth Army Headquarters:

> The landing of hostile forces has continued all day. Estimate their present strength as at least one and a half divisions. No energetic attacks on the enemy's part have taken place. On the contrary, the enemy is advancing timidly. His skirmishers were fired on by our artillery to good effect. Hill 10 had to be evacuated in the face of superior forces. Kiretch Tepe and Mestan Tepe [Chocolate Hill] still in our hands. Am expecting a powerful attack against the latter tonight. Hostile artillery fire till now only from men-of-war. Our artillery has suffered no damage.... Will hold Ismail Tepe [W Hills] position under all circumstances. Beg you to hasten arrival of XVI Corps.[123]

While Hamilton at the eleventh hour wrestled with recalcitrant generals under the in-name-only leadership of an aged and unsuitable corps commander, a far greater sense of purpose prevailed among the German and Turkish military hierarchy. Liman von Sanders consulted with his subordinate commanders on how most effectively to deploy the reinforcements which converged on the Suvla-Anzac battlefields. Their first priority was to secure all the high ground. In particular they needed to expel the small units now lodged on Chunuk Bair and Hill Q, high up on the Sari Bair Ridge just below the commanding height of the Koja Cheme Tepe, hold the enemy from further advancement along the Kiretch Tepe Ridge, and secure the Tekke Tepe Ridge, the Anafarta Spur, and the Ismail Oglu Tepe before the invaders could reach those heights. (See Map F.) The Turkish divisional commander, Colonel Mustapha Kemal, had already performed sterling work in rallying a dispirited defense to repulse a dangerous advance among the peaks of Sari Bair.[124] All the while, the footsore soldiers under Feizi Bey's command drew ever closer to the critical Tekke Tepe heights, which they needed to occupy before the enemy could.

Held up by a mere three battalions of troops and a handful of guns that composed Major Willmer's Anafarta detachment, the numerically vastly superior forces of the British 9th Army Corps now faced a desperate water shortage. On the evening of 8 August Midshipman Harry Denham wrote in his diary that: "Fresh water at Suvla Bay is running very short and all H M [His Majesty's] ships are distilling hard while the merchantmen are having their tanks emptied. Wounded at 'A' are not getting sufficient water and other troops are doing without it."[125] General Mahon's infantrymen up on the Kiretch Tepe Ridge suffered from raging thirst as much as any as they strove to hold the positions they gained, as, exposed to the full force of the fierce sun they endeavored to entrench at places where the surface was solid rock. In such cases they constructed sangars (structures made with rock boulders where the soil depth is insufficient for entrenchments) for protection. Mahon's gallant men faced continuous Turkish counterattacks as they desperately fought to retain the tenuous positions they occupied. Sergeant John Hargrave and his fellow Royal Army Medical Corps Field Ambulancemen, as they worked desperately around the clock to locate and bear away the wounded on stretchers, received the same request wherever they went: "Any water?"[126] Just behind the Turkish lines up on that hogsback was a deep and most elaborate well, which a British advance would have secured, as it would elsewhere according to the following testimonies. Colonel Aspinall claimed he saw water trickling down from the side of a rock up on the Kiretch Tepe ridge location which engineers could have tapped to supplement the meager supply in the area. The last paragraph in GHQ's 22 July instructions to the 9th Army Corps commander stated that: "Water is plentiful throughout the Anafarta Valley...."[127] General de Lisle, giving evidence before the Dardanelles Commission the following year, stated that:

> There were wells within a quarter of a mile of the shore which I had opened out. On the Kiretch Tepe ridge there were two wells 400 feet above the sea. Between Kiretch Tepe and the Salt Lake were as many wells as you liked to dig.

You had not to go more than 15 feet before you got as much water as you wanted.[128]

As 7 August 1915 passed into history, the British 9th Army Corps' only additional gain was the modest elevation known as Chocolate Hill.

> Throughout the 7th August General Headquarters exercised no influence over the course of the Suvla operations, and their inactivity on this day, which in the light of after events, may be regarded as one of the crises of the World War, can only be explained as the result of over-confidence.[129]

Sunday, 8 August followed it, a day that John Hargrave aptly designated: "Sunday — the day of rest." He remarked at sunrise that dew-spangled cobwebs festooned the coarse grass and scrub to observe that: "Only the Suvla spiders — and Feizi Bey's troops coming down from Bulair — had toiled through the night."[130] It was on this same day that Colonel Maurice Hankey, the Secretary of the Dardanelles Committee, accompanied by the man who later compiled *The Official History of the Gallipoli Campaign*, Colonel Cecil Aspinall, went ashore at Suvla Bay to behold what he evocatively described as "an August Bank Holiday scene" of relaxation "with men bathing in the sea."[131] What distressed him even more was the attitude of the Staff of Corps and Divisions:

> [They] were settling themselves in dug-outs. The pioneers, who should have been making rough roads for the advance of the artillery and supply waggons soon to be landed, [or digging wells] were engaged on a great entrenchment from the head of the bay over the hills to the sea 'to protect headquarters'..." You seem to be making yourself snug," I said to a staff officer. "Are you not going to get a move on?" "We expect to be here a long time," was his reply.[132]

Colonel Hankey also commented on the absence of enemy shellfire and any bellicose action on the part of the British army.[133] Also interesting reading is what Lieutenant-Colonel W.J.K. Rettie, who commanded the 49th Brigade, Royal Field Artillery, experienced. He and his unit arrived in Suvla Bay at break of day on the 7th of August, but remained aboard the *Minneapolis* until the afternoon of the next day. The following are some impressions he set down in a diary:

> I was struck by the restfulness of all around. There appeared to be little going on, a good many infantry sitting about, or having a bathe. The impression conveyed to my mind was that of a 'stand fast' at some field day. Having located the C.R.A. [Commander Royal Artillery] on the beach near Lala Baba, I was told to bring the batteries into action under cover of that hillock. This was rather a shock, as we had at least expected to go forward to Chocolate Hill. On expressing surprise, and asking what we were waiting for, I was met with the grim reply: "For the Turks to reinforce;" and so it proved.[134]

General C.E. Callwell, at that time Director of Operations at the War

Office, wrote: "The second day of the IXth Corps' stay at Suvla was, from the fighting point of view, practically a day of rest."[135]

Hamilton's cardinal virtue, patience, was by now utterly exhausted, and it was Hammersley who received the full force of the Commander-in-Chief's demand for immediate action. Instead of postponing an attack until the dawn of the ninth, as Hammersley proposed, Hamilton insisted that the one brigade ready to advance, the 32nd, should do so forthwith, and he ordered that it ascend, seize, and consolidate on the Tekke Tepe Ridge. But it was late in the day and the orders given had to be transmitted to the units involved, instructing them of the change in plans before they could respond to the new strategical situation. This was completed only shortly before the time Hammersley's attack was scheduled to begin. "Throughout the second day at Suvla, therefore, with 22 battalions ashore and only 1500 Turks opposed to them, the IXth Corps had accomplished nothing."[136]

It is the opinion of some experts that Hamilton's last-minute intervention contributed to the failure. Military historian Robert Rhodes James called it "disastrous."[137] There is little doubt that the Commander-in-Chief introduced an element of confusion into what seemed at least to have some semblance of sound strategy. After all, even reluctant warriors such as Hammersley had at last consented to a general offensive of some considerable force aimed at the Tekke Tepe Ridge. Whereas, because of Hamilton's intrusion, only one brigade would assault a feature already receiving the weary Turkish reinforcements who had slogged their way along the long rough roads from Bulair.

Unfortunately, confused orders and uncertainty as to the whereabouts of various units caused the tragic abandonment of other lodgments on the adjacent Scimitar and W Hills. The fact was that a unit of the 32nd Brigade, the 6th battalion of the East Yorkshire Regiment, had already entrenched on Scimitar Hill (unbeknownst to Hamilton for several years) and these soldiers were recalled to take part in the planned attack. Tragically, this key position was thus abandoned without a shot fired. As Churchill wrote: "It is extraordinary that on such a quiet day this should not have been known at Divisional Headquarters less than two miles away."[138] Also, at the same time, an officer and a signaler of the same 6th East Yorkshires practically reached the summit of the Tekke Tepe to find it still unoccupied. "Their report, like so many others went astray, and Hamilton himself did not learn of it until 1923."[139]

> An attempt was made on the same day [9 August] to seize Ismail Oglu Tepe by 33rd Brigade, which included the 6th Battalion, the Lincolnshire Regiment. "It was a recipe for disaster soon to be fully realised. Hardly had the Lincolns begun their advance on Ismail Oglu Tepe, when heavy rifle fire broke out from the north-east. At the same time Turkish artillery began shelling Chocolate Hill. Far from finding their left flank protected, the 6th Lincolns, commanded

3—The Landings

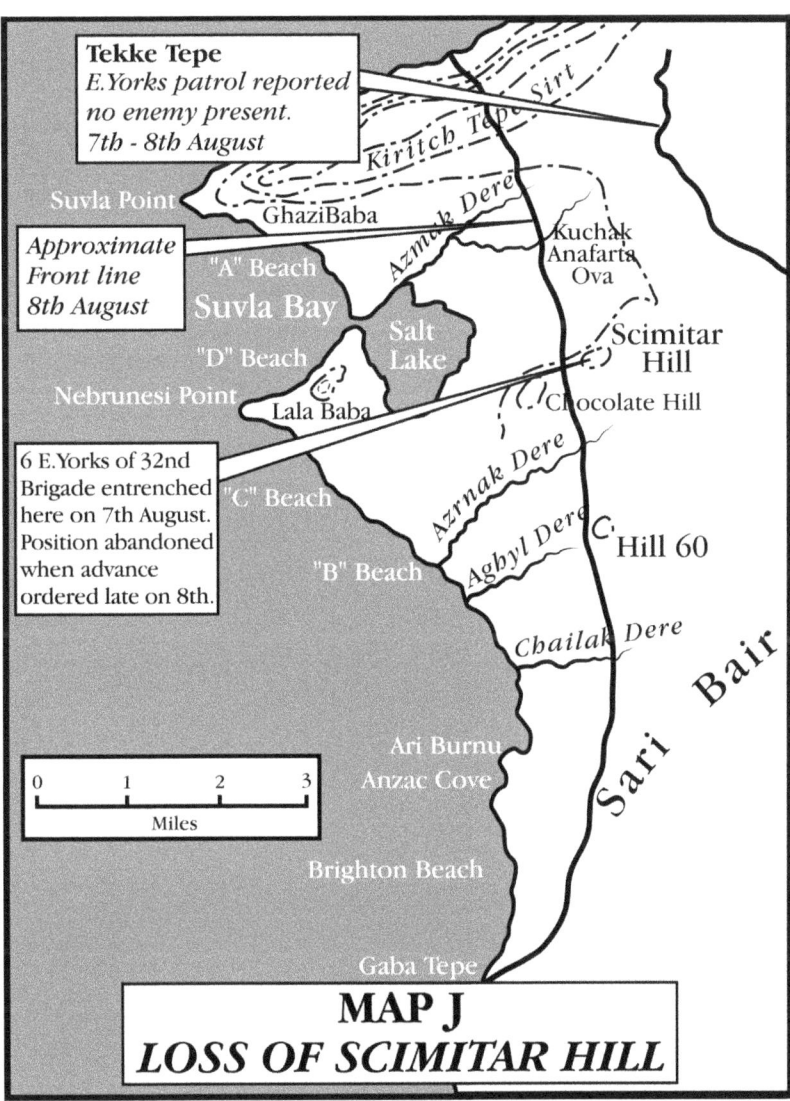

MAP J
LOSS OF SCIMITAR HILL

by Lt.-Col. M. P. Phelps, came under heavy fire from Turks dug in on the crest of Scimitar Hill."[140] An inferno broke out in the dense scrub and a retirement ordered, leaving many wounded at the mercy of the flames. Captain Percy Hansen [6th Battalion, the Lincolnshire Regiment, 33rd Brigade, 11th (Northern) Division] led a volunteer party of three men back up the slopes and into a pall of smoke. According to Col. Phelps, they advanced 400 yards through the burning scrub and succeeded in rescuing six wounded men in despite "exploding ammunition and crossfire from the Turks." For his action Capt. Hansen was awarded the Victoria Cross "for conspicuous bravery."[141]

As for the half-hearted attempt to redeem the well-nigh unbelievable inactivity since the landing, it was almost dawn before the 32nd launched its attack on the heights, and it was too late. The troops encountered withering fire, rifle, machine-gun, and shell, and the units which reached the summit met vastly superior Turkish forces which overwhelmed and completely repulsed them. Their comrades-in-arms on the lower slopes became subjected to intense shellfire, and as they moved higher the slowly traversing machine guns cut them down in swathes. Those who survived moved upwards into an inferno of fierce flame as the brittle dry scrub, ignited by shell bursts, erupted into wind-driven fiery furnaces which cremated dead, wounded, and living alike. From one of the eyrie heights at Anzac, Private Leonard, a New Zealander with the 1st Otago Infantry Battalion recalled the scene.

> We could plainly see the Tommies charging across the flat under a perfect mass of bursting shells and shrapnel. The scrub with which the flat was covered had caught fire and I afterwards heard that many of the wounded, unable to escape, were burnt to death in it. At one point I saw the Tommies charge right through the burning scrub with shrapnel bursting over them in clouds. The chaps who fell at this point would not have had to wait for the fire to creep up on them as some of the other poor beggars had to do.[142]

The race for the Tekke Tepe was over; in effect the Turks had the trophy handed to them "by British irresolution."[143]

On 9 August, military intelligence officer, Lieutenant Compton Mackenzie wrote bitterly in his diary:

> The enemy was absolutely surprised: they thought we were attacking in the same old place: their best troops were in the Southern Zone. It is believed that my own little stunt at Mytilene really did draw the submarines south to wait for phantom transports that never came. And the Ninth Army Corps bitches [botches?] the whole thing. There were forty ships with their guns pointing at the Anafarta ridge, and the general wouldn't advance because there had been no artillery preparation. He had been reading about artillery preparation in France, and his men were digging themselves in three hundred yards from the shore. There was a chance of open fighting: there was no need of artillery preparation: there were no Turks to fire at, and the aeroplanes said only three guns, which would have been captured. It's a tragedy.[144]

Driven practically to distraction, Hamilton once again did the rounds; i.e., Stopford, Hammersley, Mahon, with only the last-named responding with anything which approached enthusiasm for positive military action. Sir Ian, however, still had some cards unplayed. Two reserve divisions waited in the wings: the 53rd (Welsh) Territorial Division, and the 54th (East Anglian) Territorial Division. He ordered the 53rd to land at Suvla Bay. Its commander, Major-General the Honourable John Edward Lindley, did not possess an impressive record of battlefield command; in fact he had spent most of his military life holding positions of an administrative capacity: i.e., Commandant of the School of Instruction, the Imperial Yeomanry, 1901–1903, and ditto of the Cavalry School, 1905–1907. His appointment to the divisional command of the Welsh Division dated from the peaceful days of 1913. The troops under General Lindley's command stayed cooped up on the SS *Mauretania,* the second of the Cunard liners pressed in for service as troopships. They experienced no acclimatization whatsoever, yet their Commander-in-Chief, Sir Ian Hamilton, intended for them to straightaway storm the Tekke Tepe Ridge, now stoutly defended by seasoned Turkish troops from positions which dominated the whole Anafarta Plain. The sad fact was that all of Liman von Sanders' reinforcements had now arrived, and these included many more machine-guns sections, field-gun and howitzer batteries. Now these units were in place, and digging in for all they were worth, it seemed, strangely enough, that the Suvla generals bordered upon eagerness for the fray. Once ashore, however, the Suvla bug smote General Lindley's Welshmen as it had their predecessors. Their numbers merely added to the over-crowded conditions on the beaches, spawning incohesion and disorganization. Chaos reigned to such a degree that Lindley more or less threw in the towel, and Stopford, ever the pessimist, started making uncharitable allusions to "sucked oranges."[145]

Determined that the procrastination must cease, Hamilton ordered his last reserves, the 54th (East Anglian) Territorial Division to land in Suvla Bay with a definite objective in view. At one point Hamilton intended to fling this division in to supplement Birdwood's Corps in its attempt to take the Sari Bair heights, but the latter advised him that supplying such additional numbers would present great difficulties at that moment. Once more space was gained and "communication trenches … dug," giving greater access to the firing lines, then they could accommodate, and would welcome, such reinforcements. In the meantime the ANZAC commander and his generals "agreed they would rather the extra pressure was applied from Suvla."[146] In the light of his discussions at Anzac, Hamilton now planned for the 54th Division to support the 53rd in its seizure of the Tekke Tepe Ridge, and if necessary storm the feature unaided.[147] (See Map F.)

Hamilton visited Suvla at 8:30 A.M. on 9 August, and experienced almost exactly the same thing as Colonel Hankey had the previous day. He arrived and:

> found Stopford, about four or five hundred yards East of Ghazi Baba, busy with part of a Field Company of Engineers supervising the building of some splinter-proof huts for himself and Staff. He was absorbed in the work, and he said that it would be well to make a thorough job of the dug-outs as we should probably be here for a very long time. I retorted, "Devil a bit; within a day or two you will be picking the best of the Anafarta[148] houses for your billet."[149]

The Official Historian related that Hamilton discovered General Stopford, Officer-Commanding His Majesty's 9th Army Corps, ashore at last, preoccupied with the construction of "a shrapnel-proof shelter close to the shore."[150] Still as adamant that no move to seize the vital heights was feasible at present, Stopford repeated his previously stated reasons, and declined to order an immediate attack on the Tekke Tepe Ridge or the Anafarta Heights.

The East Anglian troops that Sir Ian intended to attack the Tekke Tepe Ridge stayed aboard the *Aquitania* in Mudros harbor for three days, in the case of the 1/5th Suffolks; and from the 7th to the 9th August aboard the *Grampian* for the 1/5th Essex.[151] As for the 1/8th Battalion, the Royal Hampshire Regiment, its personnel "did not land but were transferred almost at once to smaller vessels for transport to Suvla Bay, where they disembarked on August 9th."[152] The Suffolk Regiment's officer-historians related that the men were:

> ... chafing at being idle, while [they] knew the big push was being made. However, on August 9th [their] turn came, and at 3.40 P.M. [they] were transferred to a smaller vessel, the *Fauvette*, and proceeded to Imbros harbour, where the night was spent. The afternoon of August the 10th saw [them] sail into Suvla Bay.[153]

Lt.-Col. Gibbons recorded that when his battalion dropped anchor, some considerable distance offshore, at 5:00 A.M. on the 10th August:

> Heavy firing was distinctly heard, and puffs of smoke could be clearly seen as the shells burst on the distant shores of the Peninsula. Though we did not know it at the time, a keen struggle was taking place, the 53rd Division, supported by the 11th, making a final attempt to capture Ismail Oglu Tepe (afterwards known as "W Hill," from its peculiar formation) and the ridge known as Anafarta Sagir.[154]

Captains A. Fair and E.D. Wolton, the officer-historians of the 1/5th Battalion of the Suffolk Regiment, continued their narrative thus:

> We landed in lighters at "A" Beach and marched to a point about two miles inland. All was new, country, climate, conditions, and work. The country where we landed might be described as mildly rugged, scrub covered and rock strewn, apparently devoid of fresh water, and altogether most inhospitable. The weather was scorchingly hot, and the sun's rays beating down from almost overhead were reflected from the sparsely covered rocks. We felt this fierce heat doubly as we had not had time to get acclimatized and, coming as we did straight from the ship where there was little room to exercise, were not in the best of condition.... What little vegetation there was varied in species, but always had one point (or points) in common, for every plant possessed sharp prickles.... Although within artillery range the Turks did not cause us much harm.... [155]

1/5th Suffolk infantryman Private Jake Mortlock's account of the landing at A Beach differed somewhat from that of his battalion's historians. Upon coming ashore one of his first exclamations was: "Those silly buggers are shooting at us!!"[156] "Those silly buggers" were not fellow British soldiers, as Mortlock assumed, but Turkish infiltrators, who for the remainder of the campaign would be "sniping down to the beach."[157] The same source recalled that someone in authority pointed out heights in the distance (most probably the Tekke Tepe Ridge) and said "we had to be up there within three days."[158] As the August Plan entailed the occupation of all the high ground which encompassed Suvla Bay and the Anafarta Plain well before this date it meant that, if the above statement carried the stamp of authenticity, those in command now thought in terms of 13 August to achieve those objectives, almost a week after the initial landing! In other words, features scheduled for capture "by dawn on 7 August," when the element of surprise was complete, had been rescheduled for occupation by 13 or 14 August. The big difference was that now a resolute enemy stoutly defended them.

Someone at Battalion Headquarters, the 1/5th Suffolks' *History* goes on to relate, possessed the foresight to ensure that the fifty camp kettles belonging to the battalion "were carried full of water from the ship."[159] Very soon a water ration of one pint per day made the sweating tired soldiers crave to slake their thirsts in the rain puddles of England, and even their households' soapy washing-water.[160]

> The Essex, once the move was made, "lost no time in landing." Transferring to flat-bottomed steam lighters they "were soon at quite a respectable pier, with our feet at last on enemy soil. A few shells were bursting on the beach, and the occasional spurt of a Mauser bullet, but as far as the Battalion was concerned we got ashore without a casualty."[161]

The same primary source goes on to relate:

> The enemy was indeed too much taken up with events on his immediate front to have much time for us. We were in fact effecting a landing under cover of an infantry attack. We landed at "A" beach, Suvla Bay, and rendezvoused a short distance inland. Concealment was almost out of the question. The heights of Sari Bair overlooked the whole beach, though from a considerable distance making observation difficult, and we were not subjected to any aimed fire. *No orders were received for an advance, and we settled down into our bivouac* [emphasis added].[162]

On the evening of 10 August the 1/5th Suffolks received orders to move into the firing line close to the southern face of the Karakol Dagh (a feature at the Suvla Point end of the Kiretch Tepe Ridge), to prolong the right flank of the 9th Battalion of the Lancashire Fusiliers who occupied the trenches there, thus filling a gap which existed between that unit and the northeastern edge of the Salt Lake. According to the August Plan schedule, this area was to the rear of ground to be captured within the first few hours, i.e., the dawn of 7 August; it was now the evening of 10 August. Once in this position orders were given for the posting of outposts while the rest of the battalion dug themselves in.¹⁶³ One of D Company's platoon commanders, Lieutenant H. Cœur de Wolton, detailed Corporal Reginald E.S. Lane to take a detachment forward into what in actuality was no man's land. Lane recalled that Lieutenant Wolton's specific instructions were "that if we saw or encountered any enemy we were to open fire, thereupon alerting those in the main party who would respond accordingly." Lane asked, "Yes, sir. But what will happen to us?" To which Lieutenant Cœur de Wolton rather regally replied something along the lines of that it would be a case of "a few being sacrificed for the good of many." Corporal Lane stated that the first order he gave his detachment as they moved off was: "Put those

Portrait of a pragmatist: Reg Lane. Enlisted with a hangover on 5th August, 1914. Was one of a very few who put on weight while on the Gallipoli Peninsula. Served in Egypt and Palestine. Commissioned into Egyptian Labour Corps in 1917, ending the war in France with the rank of Captain. (Mortlock family photograph)

safety-catches on, and don't take 'em off until I tell you to!"¹⁶⁴ As it happened, during that night Lane's detail encountered nothing which forced him to rescind his safety-catch directive. The 1/5th Suffolk's *History* continued: "Early next morning we took up a more forward position, which we occupied until the afternoon of August 12th."¹⁶⁵

As previously stated, Hamilton decided to call upon his second reserve division to storm the Tekke Tepe Ridge, either with or without the collaboration of his first, the 53rd (Welsh) Division. This, its general, Lindley, now pathetically claimed he could not control, although he did not go into specifics, and General Stopford, with Kaiser-like derision, denigrated as "sucked oranges," a term he now (11 August) applied to both his Territorial Force divisions.[166]

It is interesting to note that at least one brigade of the 54th (East Anglian) Division was immediately dispatched to the left flank in support of units holding ground in the Kiretch Tepe sector, whereas one would have supposed that logic pointed to the center. Instead of digging in on the left during their first evening and night ashore, surely their orders ought to have had them toiling up the foothills of the central mass in preparation for the assault on the objective specified in the first instance. The very weak chain of command at Suvla is clearly demonstrated as *The Official History* relates that *"it was decided that this gap must be filled by units of the 54th Division without reference to G.H.Q."* (emphasis added).[167] Or, as *The Regimental History of the Royal Hampshire Regiment, Vol. II* puts it: "Accordingly, despite G.H.Q.'s intentions, several units of the Fifty-Fourth Division were hurried forward into this gap and among them the 8th Hampshire, who found themselves on outpost with the very vaguest idea of the ground, of the situation and what was expected of them."[168] On the same day (10 August) Hamilton received a bluntly worded cable from Lord Kitchener which read:

> I am sorry about the Xth and XIth Divisions in which I had great confidence [Kitchener's New Army Divisions.] Could you not ginger them up? The utmost energy and dash are required for these operations or they will again revert to trench warfare.[169]

Unfortunately, the qualities "energy and dash" were both aliens to Generals Stopford, Hammersley, Lindley, and Sitwell. "Hardly had my cable [reply] to K. been despatched when Stopford gives us a specimen of 'dash' by his answer to my reminder."[170] This was that he "foresaw very great difficulty" in carrying out Hamilton's wishes. Likewise General Lindley, commander of the 53rd (Welsh) Division, displayed very little of either animation when he responded negatively to his orders, saying he "could not undertake to clear the Anafarta Ova of snipers and to hold it as a cover to the advance of the LIVth."[171] At least Generals Inglefield, General Officer Commanding the 54th (East Anglian) Division, and Mahon seemed motivated with the offensive spirit. The former, when "told off for the attack," was "keen." Mahon was keen too, and:

> After sitting for three days where I left him on the morning of the 9th, has got tired of looking at the gendarmes and has carried their trenches by the forbidden frontal bayonet charge without much trouble or loss although, naturally, these trenches have been strengthened during the interval.[172]

Lt.-Col. Thomas Gibbons relates in his history *With the 1/5th Essex in the East:*

> There was heavy fighting all day on the left, some Battalions of the 10th Division making an advance and capturing the crest of the Kiretch Tepe Sirt, known to us afterwards as the "Razor-back." The sound of heavy rifle fire at a distance is difficult to describe, it wasn't a "roar," and it wasn't exactly a "crackle." It gave the impression of a high wind blowing, through which could be heard the incessant and monotonously distinct pup-up-up-up of the machine guns. The enemy were evidently being rapidly reinforced and made a spirited counter attack on the salient we were holding. The men showed their first signs of excitement as at last they saw live moving "running man" targets to fire at. At one time we were outflanked on the left, and there was talk of retirement. But no such thought entered the heads of the 5th or the 6th Essex on our left, and the attack was successfully driven back by steady and well-controlled fire. One enemy aeroplane dropped bombs on the 6th [Essex]. The peculiar sound of bombs dropping through the air was a novel one to most of us. We saw the Irishmen of the 10th Division cheering and waving their helmets on the crest of the Razorback, which they had won, though at a heavy cost. They were obliged, however, to withdraw during the night to their old line a short distance behind the culminating point, at a place called "Jephson's Post," after the gallant Major Jephson of the 6th Munsters, who was killed at the very post which had been named after him when he had captured it with his men the week before.[173]

Later this same day (12 August) Colonel Hankey showed Sir Ian a cable from Maurice Bonham-Carter, the Prime Minister's Private Secretary, saying that "the Prime Minister (Asquith) wishes him to stay on longer and that Lord K. would like to know if he can do anything to give impetus to the operations."[174] But still the Commander-in-Chief did not take the hint and personally project and inject "energy and dash" into the deteriorating Suvla situation.

> Early on the 11th, an order reached General Stopford from G.H.Q. that the 54th Division was to seize the Tekke Tepe ridge at dawn next morning, following a night advance to the foothills.[175]

The actual text of the cable went into specifics and alerted its recipient to expect the imminent arrival of a General Staff Officer armed "with detailed instructions."[176] Owing to the fact that "between the landing place and the Kuchuk Ana Ova [Ova = plain] lay a very difficult and intricate country in which it would be almost impossible to avoid intermixture of units and confusion before the final attack on the morning of the 13th it was decided to send the 163rd Brigade forward on the afternoon of the 12th to clear this area of any enemy detachments in it, and establish itself about the Kuchuk Ana Ova, thus enabling the main attacking force next morning to get so far on its way to the ridge without the confusion which must result from having to fight its way through a country of small fields surrounded by deep ditches and high hedges, with forest in the background. To add to the difficulties of the 163rd Brigade, its orders were generally to clear the country, and no definite objective was assigned to each unit."[177] Colonel Sir H. Beauchamp, commanding 1/5th Norfolk, was placed in local command of the Brigade. The orders the 163rd Brigade HQ received duly filtered down to its Battalions' HQs, and reached that of the 1/5th Suffolk in mid-afternoon of that same day:

> We received verbal orders to advance 1,200 yards due east at 4 P.M. The 1/5th Norfolks were to be on the right, the 1/8th Hants [Hampshires] in the centre, the 1/5th Suffolks on the left which directed the attack. The 1/4th Norfolks were in support on the left. The direction was pointed out, and the optimistic, if erroneous, information added that it was "just a sniper drive to push back stray Turks." We had just half an hour in which to plan and issue orders for an advance against an enemy whose position was not known. An issue of water and rum which was being made when the advance was ordered had to be abandoned, and the attack commenced forthwith. The 54th Divisional Artillery having been left behind in England, there was no Field Artillery support, but the naval guns supported the advance with high explosive. This sounded comforting, even if it was unable to do much harm. High explosive is useful for pounding trenches and other known positions, but its effect is very local, and for open warfare with an enemy in unknown positions it is of little use. However, the mere fact of having some sort of artillery support gave us additional confidence.[178]

In reference to this action *The Official History* recorded that:

> Orders were vague, and, as commanding officers had never seen the ground, there was great doubt as to the exact whereabouts of their objective. Subordinate leaders for the most part had only a hazy idea of what was required of them; and, although a number of maps were hurriedly issued at the last minute, most of them depicted another part of the peninsula.[179]

The Royal Hampshire Regimental History states the Brigade's objective as: "... some huts about a mile ahead of its outpost line.... Immediately ahead lay open grazing ground with a few scattered trees and patches of cultivation, with some ditches and hedges. Beyond this scrub extended to the foothills, which it covered."[180] So the 54th (East Anglian) Division went into battle in place of the 53rd (Welsh) Division with the distinction of having been extended the same Kaiser-like contempt of Lieutenant-General the Honourable Sir Frederick Stopford, K.C.V.O., Commanding Officer of His Royal Highness King George the V's 9th Army Corps, by his also likening them unto "sucked oranges,"[181] implying that the best troops found their way to the Western Front. This was certainly not the case as every single battalion of the 54th (East Anglian) Division bore a 1/ prefix, indicating that they contained all "those who volunteered for foreign service, while those who elected to remain for home service" became designated 2/— and eventually went to France nonetheless.[182]

The Royal Hampshire historian recorded that: "An 18 pounder battery, two mountain batteries and some naval guns were to provide artillery support, but, like the infantry, the gunners had little idea of the enemy's dispositions and without more definite targets could give little help."[183]

An eyewitness observed that the Suffolk soldiers advanced on the left of the 163rd Brigade through a withering fire, with no artillery support of their own. They gained about 1,300 yards (slightly more than their orders specified) and occupied a position which was to remain the front line until evacuation. Another spectator, the C.O. of 1/5th Essex, 161st Brigade, recounted: "As far as we could see the 163rd Brigade had driven back the enemy."[184] Lack of water and swarms of flies added their peculiar discomforts to those of enemy action. After three days the Suffolks were relieved, and their casualties found to have been 186 killed and wounded, and three missing. In addition nearly 160 men and officers were sick — mostly ill with dysentery.[185]

Its historians recorded that the 1/5th Battalion of the Suffolk Regiment, "in spite of the heavy fire encountered, went forward as steadily and coolly as if they were still in training at Watford, and reached a position about 1,500 yards in advance of their jumping-off line."[186] The enfilade fire from the high ground of the Kiretch Tepe Ridge on the left and the Anafarta Spur to the right intensified, the ground to be negotiated was clothed with thick prickly scrub, casualties mounted, and at some points units began to lose cohesion.

Isolated parties of the 163rd Brigade [163rd] pushed on, in particular a company of the 1/5th Norfolks on the right, led by its C.O., Lieutenant-Colonel Sir Horace Beauchamp, "a bold and self-confident officer who had seen service in Egypt, the Sudan, and South Africa," waving a cane as if directing beaters on one of his estate's pheasant shoots. "This party, consisting of 15 officers and 250 men, was not supported, and was never seen again."[187] Lt.-Col. Gibbons, in his history, however, has it that "two companies of the 1/5th Norfolks pushed too far and were swallowed up in the scrubby slopes of Tekke Tepe never to be seen again ...," citing the "Commander-in-Chief's historic dispatch."[188] Members of a British Graves Registration Unit discovered the remains of these soldiers in September 1919.[189] They were "scattered over an area of one square mile, at a distance of at least 800 yards behind the Turkish front line."[190] Allegations that many of these soldiers met their deaths after being captured were made, together with supporting evidence, in an article in the *Sunday Times* (London).[191] The Reverend C. Pierrepont Edwards, M.C., C.F., Brigade Chaplain during this incident, was directed by Queen Alexandra following the war to investigate the fate of the missing men. His conclusion was that they were forced to surrender and were then shot by their captors.

3—The Landings

The plain stretching inland from Suvla Bay is covered with long grass and trees, and the hills with tough prickly bushes, breaking up an attack and forcing troops to wind in and out in single file. The fighting at Suvla was not static warfare, but hill warfare, requiring long practice and a high standard of training to prevent loss of cohesion, co-operation, and direction, and to avoid confusion. Some of the troops engaged had not had sufficient training to carry out in its entirety so ambitious a programme.[192]

For the 1/8th Hampshire soldiers: "It had been a hard trial for inexperienced troops, especially when so little artillery support was available. Casualties now proved to have amounted to nearly half those in action."[193]

Following this action after barely two days ashore their military historian recorded that: for the next three days the battalion (1/5th Suffolk) was subjected to persistent sniping and desultory artillery fire. But that was not all, for the great shortage of water and the lack of shelter from the powerful rays of the sun caused further trouble. Sleep by day was rendered almost impossible by the swarms of flies, while at night little could be obtained, every available man being employed. On 15 August the battalion, having been relieved, returned to the reserve trenches where its casualties were ascertained to have been 186 killed and wounded and three missing. In addition, 6 officers and about 150 other ranks were sick, mostly suffering from dysentery. The casualties among the officers were as follows:

Killed: Lieut.-Colonel W. M. Armes, T.D.[194] [Commanding Officer]; Major R. H. Kendle, T.D.; Captain G. W. Ledward; 2nd Lieuts. C. W. Cory, T. S. Hinnell, G. K. Alston, and O. B. Wolton.

Wounded: Lieuts. N. Rooke, G. G. Warnes, E. M. Ashton, A. S. Parker and H. F. Everett (R.A.M.C.).

The great majority of these casualties occurred on August 12, after which action the Rev. C. Pierrepont Edwards, Brigade Chaplain, greatly distinguished himself while in charge of a volunteer stretcher-party, being shortly afterwards awarded a Military Cross. Colonel Armes, an energetic and popular officer with many years of volunteer and territorial service to his credit, had been in command of the 1/5th Suffolk Regiment since June 1911, and his death was deeply deplored. Captain Lacy Scott assumed temporary command of the battalion.[195]

Lt.-Col. Thomas Gibbons, speaking for his Battalion, 1/5th Essex, 161st Brigade, wrote: On the 14th we were ordered to advance to the relief of the 163rd Brigade, who were holding on to the ground they had won but were having rather a bad time. Colvin, with a small patrol, made an excellent reconnaissance of the ground to be covered, whilst Mackenzie Taylor, with his platoon, made good a small hillock to our left front, which was occupied by enemy snipers. Colvin's party in particular were sniped nearly all the way out and back, but brought some good information as to the ground. At 4 P.M. the advance commenced. The distance to be covered was little over a mile, for the

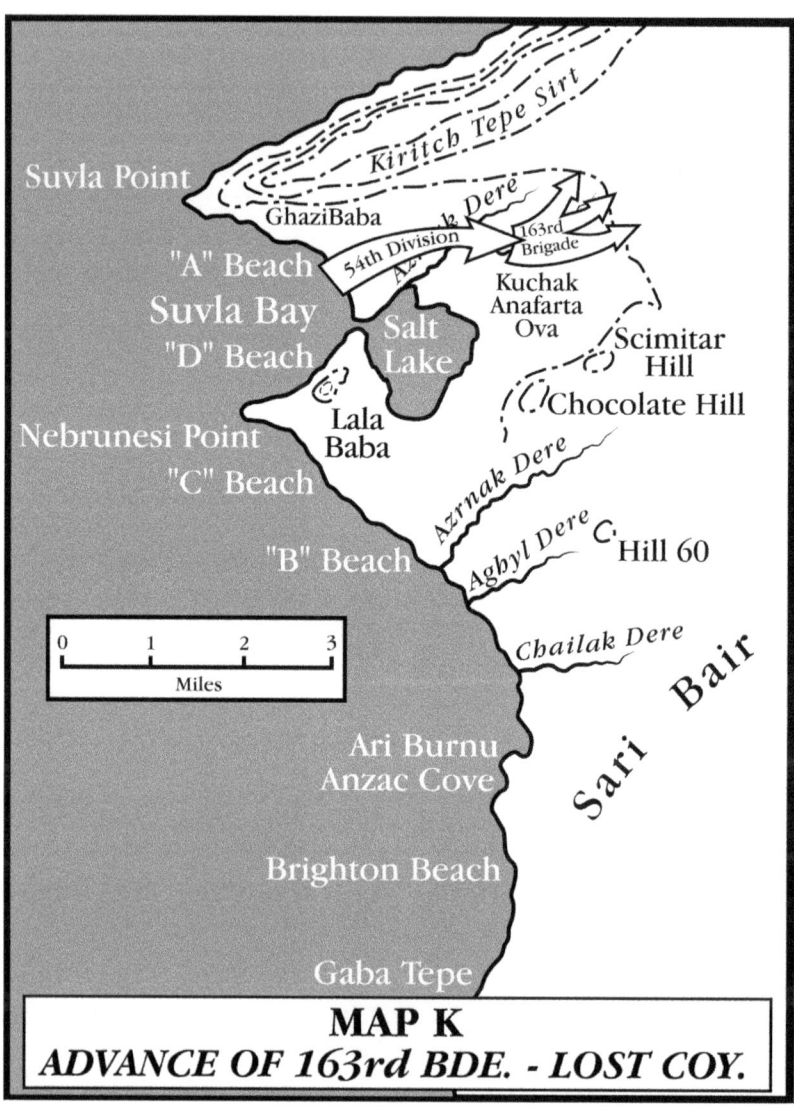

MAP K
ADVANCE OF 163rd BDE. - LOST COY.

most part on the level plain which was thickly covered with prickly scrub. The formation was lines of platoons in single file. The moment the leading platoons came into the open heavy shrapnel fire commenced. Rifle fire was also opened from the heights in front, also from the plain on our left. The latter could have only been from snipers who were behind the forward line held by our own troops, but the volume was considerable. It sounds hardly credible that many of these troublesome individuals could continue behind our line but it must be remembered that this line was by no means continuous for the first few days after the landing; this constant sniping was a regular thing, and it was some time before the pests were all disposed of. Australian sharpshooters would set forth in pairs, as if they were going to shoot rabbits, with haversacks, waterbottles, and ammunition, and would be out the whole day, taking on the Turk at his own game, and beating him at it. But it was slow work. The cover was thick, and the quarry knew just how to use it, and they got busy on that afternoon of our advance over the plain. We could not, of course, return the fire for fear of hitting the troops in front, and there was nothing to do but walk past it, though it was anything but pleasant when it began to come from the left rear. Everyone was carrying something, water-cans, camp-kettles, tools, machine guns, etc., and it was hot work, with the sun still blazing. The men were absolutely steady.

It must be recalled that these soldiers were straight out from England where a summer temperature of 80º F. is regarded a heat wave, and here it must have been close to 100º! Colonel Gibbons goes on:

> Direction was not perfectly kept, but this was not surprising, considering the nature of the country and the fact that we had to change direction twice to avoid going over the crest of a hill. However, the majority of the Battalion reached the line occupied by the 5th Norfolks and the 8th Hants. Some platoons on the right of the Battalion struck the line held by a Brigade of the 53rd Division, between whom and the 163rd there was a considerable gap. The detached platoons found the Battalion about dusk, after a somewhat trying movement across the enemy's front, feeling for the open flank, and the gap was eventually filled by the 7th Essex, making a thin but continuous line. 14 N.C.O.'s and men of the Battalion [1/5th Essex] were killed and about 30 wounded in the advance. It was our baptism of fire.[196]

Lt.-Col. Gibbons continued his account of subsequent action:

> At dark there was considerable uncertainty as to the situation on our right and the patrol work was particularly difficult. One patrol was unfortunately ambushed, and 2/Lieut. Turner, the leader, and Sergt. Rice were killed, but two men made their way back under a heavy fire. Turner was an old "Artists" Rifleman. He had served in France and had not been with us long, but had made himself deservedly popular. Rice was an old comrade and the steadiest of N.C.O.'s. During the night the relief took place and the battle-worn 163rd got out of the line without incident.
> There was little in the way of sleep for anybody that night. Our predecessors had been unable to do much in the way of digging in, owing to the exhaustion of the men and the shortage of tools, and the night was spent in strengthening the position, a work which continued all the next day in the face of continual fire from the unseen enemy in front. Whilst superintending the work of his Company Captain Denton was shot through the head and killed instantly. Poor "Pat" Denton. He was the keenest of us all, and none was loved better by his men or by his brother officers.[197]

It proved much the same sad story — or even worse — for each of the combatant units. Added to which they suffered utter fatigue, raging thirst, pestilential plagues of flies, the awful stench of putrefying corpses, the constant sniping and the systematic shellfire. It had been, as Lt.-Col. Gibbons summarized:

> A trying ordeal for men who had no previous experience of war; the want of sleep and fresh food, the constant strain, the blazing heat, the black plague of flies, the dirt and squalor of it all, and perhaps more than anything the all pervading smell of death, had proved too much for others more hardened than they, and it was no disgrace that the ordeal had proved too severe for a time for some sorely tried natures to bear.[198]

A private in the London Regiment closely echoed Private Jake Mortlock's opinion of the conditions:

> One of the biggest curses was flies. The whole side of the trench used to be one black swarming mass of flies. Anything you opened, like a tin of bully [corned beef], would be swarming with flies. If you were lucky enough to have a tin of jam and opened that, swarms of flies went straight into it. They were all around your mouth and on any cuts or sores that you'd got, which then turned septic. Immediately you bared any part of your body you were smothered. It was a curse, it really was.[199]

The August Plan was a failure. Even as early as the 11th of August it was clear that the new venture, the August offensive, had completely faltered. Major Jack Churchill wrote to his brother Winston that day: "The golden opportunity has gone, and positions that might have been won with a little perspiration would only be gained now by blood."[200]

The Turks under Mustapha Kemal had cleared Chunuk Bair with bloody attacks flung at the enemy with an unprecedented fury. Yet, on the evening of 10 August, the Commander-in-Chief of the Mediterranean Expeditionary Force wrote in his diary:

> We had Chunuk Bair in our hands for the best part of two days and two nights.... The Turks are well commanded: that I must admit. Their generals knew they were done unless they could quickly knock us off.... So they have done it. Never mind: never say die.[201]

This statement is typical of the man. At the moment it was recorded the whole structure of his August Plan lay in ruins. The Helles garrison had failed to prevent the Southern Group from sending reinforcements to Sari Bair; the Anzac Corps had fought itself to a standstill; and a large part of the 9th Army Corps was exhausted. None of the original objectives had been gained. But the Commander-in-Chief refused to accept defeat.[202]

Hamilton knew that Birdwood's troops could not attack again for several days, and that when they could they stood no chance of success without the aid of a flank-turning movement from Suvla. In spite of everything he remained supremely confident that not only was such a maneuver possible, but it would prove successful. But first a general overturn (no pun intended) needed to occur. This happened at "an interview aboard HMS

3—*The Landings* 97

Private Mortlock (with cap) is seated center front, 4th from left. Capless to his right, same row, is Bob Jaggard; Maurice Williams is third from right, same row. Inscribed on reverse of the original: *"Some of the Boys of the Old Brigade— Suvla/Anzac 8th & 12th August, 1915, A.D."* (Mortlock family photograph)

Triad between 6 and 7 P.M. on the 13th August, 1915, between the General Commanding and Sir Frederick Stopford, commanding 9th Corps."[202] When "Sir Frederick represented that the 9th Corps were not fit to undertake an advance at the present moment," Sir Ian's patience could stand no more.[203] Thus he cabled Lord Kitchener on 13 August in which he hinted at the relief of Stopford and Company, and the dispatch of replacement generals. On 17 August Hamilton sent the Secretary of War "a complete *résumé*" of the operations, an outline of his future intentions, and a list of his requirements. The latter consisted of "45,000" replacement drafts, plus "new formations totaling 50,000 rifles" deemed essential to give him "the necessary superiority ... to bring the operations to a happy conclusion."[204] The powers in London responded, as was their custom, with "too little too late." They did, however, replace the timid, tired old men in charge of, and responsible for, the Suvla *fiasco* with Western Front generals who met with Hamilton's delighted approval. Why it was not possible to assign this caliber of commander to the Gallipoli theater in the first instance is difficult to comprehend. In Winston Churchill's wise words: "These new Generals could be spared on the morrow of disaster, but not while their presence might have commanded success."[205] As for reinforcements they ordered the 2nd

Mounted (Yeomanry) Division, minus horses, to sail from Egypt. "The Incomparable 29th Division" would come round from Helles to augment and stiffen the 53rd (Welsh) Division, and some troops from Anzac moved across, mostly Australian counter sniping marksmen. Although this total did not begin to approach what Hamilton asked for, he and his colleagues planned to launch another offensive in an attempt to retrieve the rapidly deteriorating Suvla situation.

With the new developments planned, the accounts of those who took part in the Suvla Bay landing and the subsequent operations thereat proliferate because of the extra troops assigned to that theater. Thus, there is a wealth of additional primary source material available. Particularly this is true where it comes to the personal accounts of the author's kith and kin, friends of his family, and local veterans. Sometimes one is faced with difficult choices when it comes to actual selection. It is the author's aim to let as many as possible of those seldom-heard voices speak, whenever appropriate, and accord their narratives the credence which he is certain they fully deserve.

4

Failure

It was indeed ironic that the powers in London granted General Sir Ian Hamilton's original wish for vibrant Western Front generals only after they dismissed the hopeless failures they appointed in the first instance.[1] On 14 August 1915 Lord Kitchener's reaction to Hamilton's cable explaining the Suvla setback was that "if you should deem it necessary to replace Stopford, Mahon and Hammersley, have you any competent Generals to take their place? From your report I think Stopford should come home."[2] Even then Hamilton's gentility remained intact as the following day he wrote: "I had meant to make time to run across to Suvla today but Stopford may wish to see me on his way to Mudros so I shall sit tight in case he does."[3] The 18 August, following the meeting of the Dardanelles Committee, saw "on Hammersley's report, Sitwell, Brigadier of the 34th Brigade, 11th Division ... relieved of his command,"[4] and the resignation of Lindley, general officer commanding the 53rd (Welsh) Territorial Division. This occurred after the latter confessed to his Commander-in-Chief that "his Division had gone to pieces and that he did not feel it in himself to pull it together again."[5] His reward was a base command at Mudros. The following week Hammersley[6] himself "was taken off the peninsula in a state of collapse."[7] Hamilton, ever the perfect gentleman, had in fact done nothing positive about his incompetent and dilatory generals, in particular Sir Frederick Stopford, the 9th Army Corps commander, "and it was Kitchener who extricated him from the skein of chivalry in which he was enmeshed."[8] "Asquith voiced his own annoyance, indicating that it was difficult to understand, after Suvla Bay, how Hamilton could remain confident of victory; and he wrote to Kitchener that Stopford and his staff ought to be court-martialled and dismissed from the Army."[9] Radical changes in the 9th Corps' hierarchy indeed:

> Day by day, the Suvla command disappeared.... Hill, suffering from acute dysentery, had to go on August 22.... Never before in military history had there been such a clear-out of brass-hats during a campaign. Six commanding generals in nine days, and none below the rank of brigadier-general.[10]

As Captain Eric Bush, who served as a midshipman on HMS *Baccha-*

nte throughout the entire Dardanelles/Gallipoli Campaign, observed: "Six commanding officers, none of them below the rank of brigadier-general, packed off must surely constitute a record in British military history. And the tragedy is that the changes came too late. By August 16th the battle was already lost."[11]

Hamilton telegraphed Kitchener on 14 August to the effect that the one man on the spot who could pull the 9th Corps together again was Major-General H. de Beauvoir de Lisle, presently commanding the 29th Division at Helles—an officer whom John Hargave maintained advocated evacuation as the only solution to the Gallipoli dilemma.[12] A snag existed, though: Lieutenant-General Sir Bryan Mahon was his senior in rank and needed to agree to waive his seniority in order for de Lisle to take command. On 15 August Hamilton telegraphed Mahon to that effect.[13]

Prior to the receipt of Sir Ian's telegraphed request "General Mahon was still holding his original line astride the ridge at Jephson's Post. The 30th Brigade (Br.-General L. L. Nicol) was on the northern slopes of the ridge, and the 31st Brigade (Br.-General F. F. Hill) on its southern slopes. To support the advance the 162nd Brigade [54th (East Anglian) Division] (Br.-General C. de Winton), then in bivouac near A Beach, was also placed at Mahon's disposal."[14]

One of Lieutenant-General Sir Frederick Stopford's last actions was to order Mahon to advance along the Kiretch Tepe Ridge. "Orders to this effect were issued at 8.40 A.M. on the 15th—without further reference or report to G.H.Q."[15] Thus, around midday on 15 August—at the behest of reluctant warrior Sir Frederick Stopford—Irish troops, supported on their right flank by units of the 54th (East Anglian) Division, thrust forward to seize a feature known as "the Pimple."

The 162nd Brigade of the 54th (East Anglian) Division operating on the right flank of the 10th (Irish) Division prepared to advance at 1 o'clock with the 1/5th Bedfordshire leading. Its brigadier, Brig.-General C. de Winton, had only three battalions at his disposal, as the fourth—the 1/4th Northamptonshire—did not land until noon of that day. "It was understood that that the brigade was to act as flank guard to the 10th, and little fighting was anticipated. There had been no time to reconnoiter the very difficult ground over which the battalions were to move, and General de Winton had no information about the probable whereabouts of the enemy."[16]

> After advancing some 400 yards the Bedfordshire came under increasing rifle and machine-gun fire. It was not easy for inexperienced troops to wheel left-handed and continue their advance astride the numerous gullies which run down from the ridge. The very enthusiasm of the battalion—for all ranks were eager to get on—led to loss of cohesion. Progress became very slow, and parties

SHRAPNEL ELUCIDATED

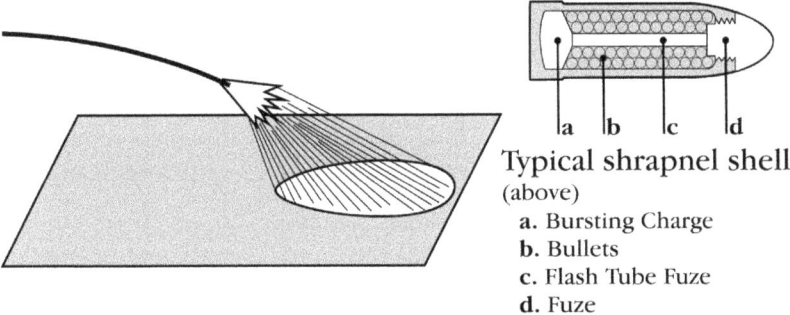

Typical shrapnel shell
(above)
a. Bursting Charge
b. Bullets
c. Flash Tube Fuze
d. Fuze

Shrapnel elucidated. Adapted from an overhead lecture slide projection, courtesy of Major Nicholas C. Jenkinson, T.D., the Commanding Officer, 202 (Suffolk & Norfolk Yeomanry) Battery, 100 Medium Regiment, Royal Artillery, T.A., King's Road Cavalry Barracks, Bury St. Edmunds, Suffolk, England. (*Action Graphics of Virginia*)

of the 1/10th and 1/11th London were dribbled forward to reinforce the line. Br.-General Hill, hearing that the advance of the Inniskillings was not being supported, was soon sending out messages to urge the attack forward, and late in the afternoon Br.-General de Winton went up with his brigade-major (Major Stuart Hay) to lead the troops in person. He was gravely wounded while doing so, but his example was not without effect. Though the Territorials had already suffered crippling losses, a last effort by small parties of all three battalions advanced the left of the line to the south-western shoulder of Kidney Hill. Here the troops held on for many hours, entirely unsupported, but during the night the whole brigade fell back to a line prolonging the original front line of the 31st Brigade. Major G. F. M. Davis, 1/11th London, was killed while covering the retreat of the rear party. In the three battalions of the 162nd Brigade engaged the total casualties in this attack amounted to 37 officers and 900 men.[17]

Unbeknownst to all on the British side connected with the assault "the main enemy ammunition dump happened to be established" further along that ridge.[18] General Liman von Sanders regarded this attack as extremely threatening and wrote: "If on August 15 and 16 the British had taken the Kiretch Tepe they would have outflanked the entire Fifth Army and final success might have fallen to them."[19] But the British had no such great objectives in view. The attack was no more than an afterthought on Stopford's part,[20] and the men were so ill-provided with ammunition that they were reduced at one stage to throwing rocks and stones at the Turks; and so in a day or two it petered out.[21] It was up on that same hogsback ridge that Private Jake Mortlock recalled:

> We were supporting the South Wales Borderers, and the Turks were bursting shrapnel[22] over us. It was sweeping right down to the sea [Gulf of Saros.] Then there was the case — if *that* hit you you'd know all about it. [He seemed to attribute the accuracy of the fuse-settings on the shells to the fact that] ... they [the Turks] had German officers.[23]

Sergeant John Hargrave waxed lyrical in his description of this facet of warfare: "All along the ridge shrapnel flashed and blossomed like magical death-flowers, budding and overblown on the instant, shedding their death-seed in a whanging clangour that rang on the hard sandstone like a thousand hammers on a giant anvil."[24]

In his first book, *At Suvla Bay*, published in 1916, Hargrave graphically described "a great gaping wound" in the abdomen which a shrapnel ball inflicted on a little Welsh private who implored "the Medical Officer in the Gaelic tongue to 'put him out' and terminate his agony. After a morphia tablet was administered the patient began singing "at the top of his high-pitched voice":

> When the midnight chu-chu leaves for Alabam!
> I'll be right there!
> I've got my fare ...
> All aboard!
> All aboard!
> All aboard for Alla-Bam!....
> Midnight ... chu-chu ... chu-chu ...

"And so, slowly his soul steamed out of the wrecked station of his body and left for 'Alabam!'"[25]

The troops who assaulted along the Kiretch Tepe, for the first time at Suvla, attacked with an unusual amount of artillery in support. The 15th Heavy Battery arrived a few days before, and the 58th Brigade Royal Field Artillery (10th Division) came safely up the coast from Anzac. All these guns were engaged, besides a mountain battery, some machine guns, and the guns of the destroyers *Grampus* and *Foxhound*, firing from the Gulf of Saros.[26] In all probability the Royal Naval warships mentioned above were those Private Mortlock looked down on amidst the carnage, squalor, flies, heat and raging thirst to behold the sailors in their immaculate white drilling on deck. "It was a picnic," he observed acidly.[27] Lieutenant "Juvenis," in a similar location, "knew that on most of them a bottle of beer would be obtainable for sixpence."[28]

A prisoner revealed to interrogators from the 7th Royal Dublin Fusiliers that "the Turks had six fresh battalions in line or in strongly fortified redoubts, each battalion provided with twelve machine-guns."[29] If the prisoner's revelations warranted credence, and subsequent developments suggest that they did, then Stopford's last act, therefore, was to order Mahon to send his reduced numbers of men forward to storm a key position now approximately seven times as strongly held as a week previously (7/8 August) when he dithered and dallied to avoid getting involved in "a regular battle."[30] Mahon's gallant Irishmen rose to the occasion and advanced to capture "the Pimple" redoubt at bayonet-point. Unreinforced and virtually forgotten, they withstood fierce counterattacks and continuous bombing from the enemy entrenched in higher ground on the south face of the ridge. Many of the very best officers fell, including Lieutenant "Juvenis" with a bullet-smashed arm, and the 5th and 6th Battalions of the Royal Irish Fusiliers were almost exterminated. "Lieutenant Hamilton [was] the only officer left in D ['The Pals'] Company [of the 7th Royal Dublin Fusiliers, and] though wounded in the foot, was in command."[31] Mahon's men faced an enemy who possessed ample ammunition and a seemingly endless supply of bombs whereas the Irish troops now lacked both, as unsupplied they repulsed attacks with bayonet, rifle-butt, fist, and even rocks. Private Wilkin, of D ("The Pals") Company, the 7th Royal Dublin Fusiliers, threw back five Turkish grenades before a sixth blew up in his hand, killing him instantly.[32] The shattered brigades were withdrawn before the dawn of the seventeenth from the untenable positions, which were never recaptured.[33]

> At 7 P.M. what remained of the three Irish battalions on the Kiretch Tepe were ordered to withdraw to their old front line: the position they had gained on August 7, about 700 yards west of Jephson's Post. "Not a man moved until he received the order, and then slowly, deliberately, almost reluctantly, they retired." So at nightfall on the August 17, the Kiretch battle—that might have been the turning-point in the campaign—came to an end, and the Turks regained the hogsback.[34]

This incidentally was Mahon's last action for a time, as he declined to waive his seniority and serve under de Lisle, whom Hamilton appointed to replace Stopford as 9th Army Corps commander. The former packed up his things and departed to Mudros to cool off. For a general to desert his division in the midst of a battle was something virtually unheard-of; for the common soldier it would have resulted in a court martial and the firing squad. Hamilton nominated Brigadier-General Frederick Hill to succeed him as Officer Commanding the 10th (Irish) Division. John Hargrave, in his book *The Suvla Bay Landing*, devoted a whole chapter, entitled "Chaos in Command," to this and several similar episodes to demonstrate why he bitterly named it thus.[35] "Mahon had gone—and neither Hill nor anyone else knew what to do. Stopford was busy packing up. De Lisle was busy taking over.... There was, literally, *no one in command*."[36]

At Imbros on August 17th Hamilton inscribed in his diary his notion of the Suvla Landing: "The surprise was complete, and the army was thrown ashore in record time practically without loss...." As John Hargrave adjudged: "It sounded marvelous—everything went like clockwork! But he was not there, and did not see any of it. Six days later, on the 23rd, when explaining the Suvla landing in his 'weekly budget,' he writes:

> ... Not that I have yet got any very clear conception of the details myself. It seems clear that this great mass of young and inexperienced troops failed simply because their leaders failed to grasp the urgency of the time problem when they got upon the ground, although, as far as orders and pen and ink could go, it had been made perfectly clear.

The truth is that the "time problem" in his written battle orders had not been made "perfectly clear." Instead, as already stated, the fatal words *"if possible"* had taken all the "urgency" out of them, and reduced them to little more than polite requests.

The nearest Hamilton came to any self-criticism, or any inkling that his G.H.Q. staff might be too light-heartedly confident—counting their lighter-loads before they had landed—was a diary jotting dated August 26th: "... Anyway, whether by my own fault or those of others, one thing is certain, namely, that up to date there has been misunderstanding."

Hargrave goes on to observe:

> We may wonder whether, in fact, we are dealing with a pack of incompetent Old Army Generals who misunderstood their "perfectly clear" orders—or with various forms of dry-rot at the top of the Victorian/Edwardian social structure? Perhaps of our phase of civilization?[37]

The Commander-in-Chief advised Lord Kitchener in a lengthy *résumé* that his "British Divisions are at present 45,000 under establishment, exclusive of about 9,000 promised or on the way. If this deficit were made up, and new formations totaling 50,000 rifles sent out as well ... [these] should give me the necessary superiority."[38] Presumably this meant the ability to forcibly occupy the Anafarta Heights, thrust further along the Kiretch Tepe Ridge, and make sizeable gains in the Sari Bair sector. Members of the Dardanelles Committee greeted this shopping-list with incredulity. As one, Andrew Bonar Law, put it: "General Hamilton is always *nearly* winning."[39] It is well to bear in mind that the Committee now possessed a most detailed first-hand account of the Suvla fiasco from its Secretary, Colonel Maurice Hankey, dispatched to Prime Minister Asquith on 12 August.[40]

Front and inside page reports which appeared at this time in the daily newspapers, however, painted a much rosier picture of events in the Gallipoli theater. An "AUSTRALIAN POSITION TREBLED" headline emblazoned *The Times*,[41] and although this was true from the purely geographical aspect its substance was misleading. While in much smaller print: "To the north no further progress has been made" by the newly landed forces, was more exact and nicely exemplified the British capacity for understatement.[42]

Following the departure of the unfortunately appropriately named Stopford and Sitwell, together with their kindred-spirited colleagues, Hamilton now hoped to inject some vigor into the 9th Army Corps and its attached divisions. As a start he assembled a strong force to storm Scimitar Hill and the Ismail Oglu Tepe (W Hills). These were somewhat modest objectives compared to the grandiose ones of the original scheme which envisioned the capture of those and many other features "by dawn" of 7 August.[43] As previously stated at the end of Chapter Three, Hamilton ordered the infantry brigades of the 29th Regular Army Division ("The Incomparable 29th"— now, alas, but a shadow of the fine, highly trained contingent that landed on 25 April) round from Helles to stiffen his attack, and brought the 2nd Mounted (Yeomanry) Division up from Egypt, minus their horses, to augment his reserve. From the ANZACs he borrowed the services of sharpshooters trained to combat the Turkish sniping menace, these latter, all told, amounted to a little over 100 personnel. To coordinate the new effort required time, especially in view of the recent upheaval among the top echelons of the 9th Army Corps, therefore Hamilton planned the assault for 21 August.

In an 18 August meeting of commanders and General Staff Officers, which Sir Ian described as "a Council of War," final arrangements were made for the new attack.[44]

> Even now, on August 18, he was prepared to fight on with nothing but sick men and the shadow-shapes of field artillery and howitzers that had never been landed — or had only just been landed —(at Anzac!) and were "at the disposal of" General de Lisle "as soon as horses could be provided to mobilise them." At this moment there were three more field artillery brigades and two batteries of 4–5inch howitzers waiting at Lemnos, "ready to be brought up as soon as they could be landed, but they would have to be landed without horses and taken into position by horses of other units." (See *Dardanelles Report,* Part II, Section 102, page 46.)[45]

The frontage of the intended offensive was narrow, and confined to the Anafarta Spur area. As the Turkish positions overlooked the entire Suvla Plain, and no communication trenches to the firing line existed, units would assemble during the night of 20/21 August. The schedule allowed for short preparatory bombardment to begin at 2.30 P.M. prior to the launching of the attack at 3.00 P.M., at a time when the glare of the sun would dazzle the Turkish gunners and their observation-post officers. Remembering the frustrated hours spent while he waited for word of the earlier *contretemps,* Hamilton planned to witness these operations firsthand on shore at Suvla Bay.

The following evening (19 August) after dinner, Colonel Maurice Hankey took his leave and departed for London in the company of "the King's Messenger." Hamilton hoped that Hankey's report to Prime Minister Asquith and the Dardanelles Committee would do much to combat the "flood of false gossip" that these received.[46] Presumably he referred to the critical cables war correspondents, Ellis Ashmead-Bartlett and Keith Murdoch, telegraphed from the Gallipoli theatre. What he did not know was that on the very same day the Dardanelles Committee met to discuss the failure at Suvla. Subsequently Lord Kitchener told the members that: "If it was the fault of the Generals, the Generals must be relieved," and later expanded:

> I would be glad if we were rid of the Dardanelles problem, but in my opinion, after consultation with Sir John French and his staff, there were two main points to be borne in mind in considering what action should be adopted. One was that it would be impossible to embark all the troops in the case of a withdrawal, and that a certain portion must surrender.[47] Such a course seemed impossible of adoption to me. It would have the worst effects in Egypt and India. The other was that we could not desert the British forces now in the field, and leave them there unsupported.[48]

The next day's entry in the Commander-in-Chief's *Gallipoli Diary* succinctly unfolded the train of events:

> *21st August, 1915.* Sailed for Suvla about 1 o'clock with Braithwaite, Aspinall, Dawnay, Deedes, Ellison, Pollen and Maitland. The first time I have set forth with such a Staff. *Not wishing to worry de Lisle*[49] [emphasis added] I climbed up to the Karakol Dagh, whence I got something like a bird's eye view of the arena which was wrapt from head to foot in a mantle of pearly mist. Absurdly the Ancients would have ascribed this phenomenon to the intervention of an Immortal. Nothing like it had ever been seen by us until that day and the cloud — mist — call it what you will — must have had an unfortunate bearing on the battle. On any other afternoon the enemy's trenches would have been sharply and clearly lit up, whilst the enemy's gunners would have been dazzled by the setting sun. But under this strange shadow the tables were completely turned; the outline of the Turkish trenches were blurred and indistinct, whereas troops advancing from the Aegean against the Anafartas stood out in relief against a pale, luminous background. As a result of our instructions; of conferences and of the war council we had got our plan perfectly clear and ship-shape. Everyone understood it. The 10th Division was Corps reserve and was lying down in mass about the old Hill 10 in the scrub. We had to trust to luck here as they were under enemy's fire if they were spotted. But very strict orders as to keeping low and motionless had been issued and we just had to hope for the best. The Yeomanry were also Corps reserve at Lala Baba where they were safe. But when they advanced, supposing they had to, they would have to cross a perfectly open plain under shell fire. This was the special blot on the scheme but there was no getting away from it. There was no room for them in the front line trenches and the communication trenches to the front had not yet been dug. As to the attack: on the extreme right the Anzacs and Indian Brigade were to push out from Damakjelik Bair towards Hill 60. Next to

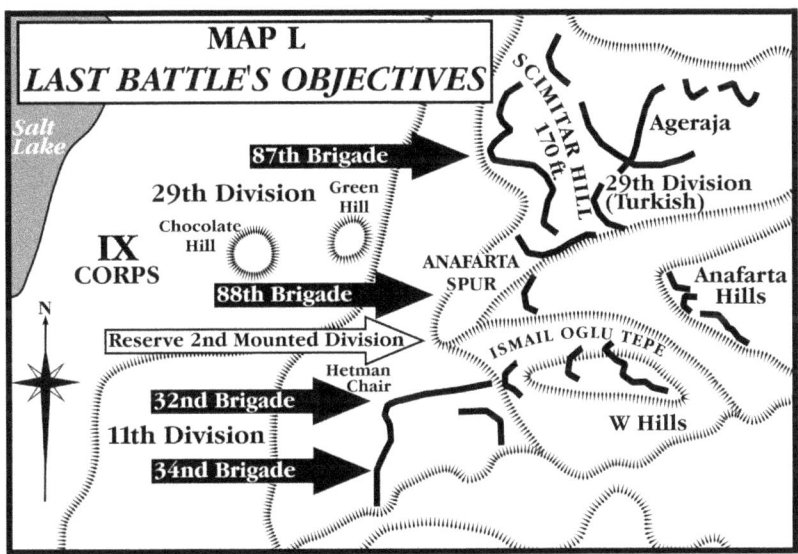

them in the right centre the 11th Division was to push for the trenches at Hetman Chair. On the left centre the 29th Division were to storm the now heavily entrenched Hill 70 [Scimitar Hill]. Holding that and Ismail Oglu Tepe we should command the plateau between the two Anafartas; knock out the enemy's guns and observation posts commanding Suvla Bay, and should easily be able to work ourselves into a position whence we will enfilade the rear of the Sari Bair Ridge and begin to get a strangle grip over the Turkish communications to the Southwards. To the extreme left on the Kiretch Tepe Sirt by the sea, to Sulajik where they joined the 29th Division the 53rd and 54th Divisions were simply holding the line.[50]

Since the whole plan revolved on the assumption of the existence of conditions "A," when Sir Ian arrived at "about 1 o'clock"[51] to find that conditions "B" pertained, one would have expected he would reappraise the situation in the light of this untoward development. Why had no one reported this freak occurrence of nature to GHQ? At all events, with almost two hours before he launched his attack one could conclude that, as a strategist, he had the option of postponing his offensive. "Same time tomorrow, chaps," when the chances of a return to conditions "A" were overwhelming. Hamilton revealed that he "wished to postpone the attack, but for various reasons this was not possible,"[52] so the battle commenced according to plan. Undoubtedly the erstwhile commander of the 9th Army Corps, General Stopford, would not have felt thus constrained.

Major John Gillam watched the battle as it unfolded, and wrote a moving account of what he witnessed:

> 2.30. The four battleships and all our guns on shore open a heavy bombardment on the Turkish positions on the hills in front, and especially Burnt Hill [Scimitar Hill], and an hour later the gorse on that hill and on the low ground to the right of Chocolate Hill catches alight, and is soon burning like a roaring furnace, spreading like the fire on a prairie. At 3.30 I hear rifle fire and learn that our attack on Burnt Hill has started. The artillery simultaneously increases its range.[53]

Padre Dennis Jones, recently arrived from Helles with the 29th Division, also observed the action from the 53rd (Welsh) Division's Casualty Clearing Station on the beach in the middle of Suvla Bay. "The artillery and ships' fire was very rapid and fierce. An attack was made at 3 P.M. by my Brigade [the 87th] led by the Inniskillings, who suffered severely. They gained the ridge but were constantly compelled to retire."[54] Young Midshipman Harry Denham observed from aboard HMS *Euryalus* that "our shooting was pretty bad; I know for a fact that one casement had 7 on their fuse instead of 27 and hence wasted shrapnel on our own troops."[55]

This, then, was not the same walk-over situation that existed on 7 August. The assaulting contingents faced a determined enemy, fully prepared, deeply entrenched, well armed, well led, and who occupied all the dominating geographical features of the surrounding landscape. In short, theirs was a formidable task, which only an incorrigible optimist such as Hamilton expected them to perform successfully.

Henry Nevinson, the War Office–accredited veteran war correspondent of *The Guardian* for the Dardanelles Campaign, from a site on Chocolate Hill, recorded a very heavy Turkish bombardment of that position before and after the infantry started their advance. (He himself sustained a wound in the head from shrapnel.) His account continued:

> On the right the 34th Brigade advanced successfully across the narrow front of plain between the small farms of Hetman Chair and Air Kavak (a quarter-mile south of Hetman). They took the trenches on the plain without great loss. But the 32nd Brigade which was to have kept in touch with them at Hetman Chair, and to have seized the long trench running thence towards W Hill, lost direction and kept edging off to their left or north-east, instead of due east. The plain is open but for a sprinkling of small trees, and the mist was not thick enough to confuse. They may have been attracted by the chance of cover among the slopes leading up to the hills on their left, and the fire from the long communication trench was certainly very severe. It was still more unfortunate that when the 33rd Brigade was sent up to capture the trench at all costs, they "fell into precisely the same error," as we are told.[56]

Sergeant Hargrave stated that the battalion on the 32nd Brigade's left "had been told to march by a compass bearing" owing to the poor visibility, and during the first few hundred yards of the advance lost all its officers.

"As no one else knew the compass bearing it soon lost direction."⁵⁷ (See Map J.)

"The Incomparable 29th" meanwhile stormed Scimitar Hill, the W Hills (Ismail Oglu Tepe), and also attempted to advance up the Anafarta Spur. As the Reverend Dennis Jones commented, his Brigade (the 87th) successfully gained its objective "but were constantly compelled to retire,"⁵⁸ because of what John Hargrave called "a tornado of shrapnel and machine-gun fire from the Anafarta Spur."⁵⁹ Hamilton from the western end of the Kiretch Tepe Ridge watched anxiously, and "by 3.30 P.M. it seemed as if distinct progress was being made."⁶⁰ His narrative continued:

> About that time (3.30 P.M.) it was I saw the Yeomen marching in extended order over the open ground to the South of the Salt Lake in the direction of Hetman Chair. The enemy turned a baddish shrapnel fire on to them, and although they bore it most unflinchingly, old experience told me that their nervous fighting energy was being used up all the time. If only these men could have been brought within charging distance, fresh and unbroken by any ordeal! But here was just one of the drawbacks of the battlefield and no getting over it.⁶¹

Padre Jones viewed the same spectacle from the A beach area:

> It was during the afternoon that I witnessed the splendid advance over the Salt Lake made under a curtain of shrapnel by the Yeomanry Brigade. The whole countryside seemed to be one continuous blaze of fire and smoke. The bushes had caught fire and many of our men were burnt on the blazing hillsides.⁶²

From practically the same location Major John Gillam saw:

> The Yeomanry now marching steadily in open order across the Salt Lake. It is the first time they have been in action. Several years ago I was a trooper in the Warwickshire Yeomanry, who are now with the rest marching into battle. The Worcesters, Gloucesters, Middlesex, Sharp-shooters, Sherwood Foresters, Notts and Derby are there, and I think several other regiments, all troopers and troop leaders on foot, their horses left in Egypt. Little did they think, when they trained on Salisbury Plain for cavalry work, that when the hour came for them to go into battle they would go in on foot as infantry.... Ah! The real thing has come for them at last, though many of them only landed this morning, for I see a white puff of shrapnel burst over their heads. It is quickly followed by another and another, developing to a rapid concentrated fire. They run the gauntlet without losing their Salisbury Plain steadiness, except for occasional bunching together here and there. Soon casualties occur and prostrate khaki figures can be seen lying on the sandy salt of the lake for the stretcher-bearers and ambulance-wagons to pick up — the harvest of war. At last they are at Chocolate Hill, where they nestle under its slopes for protection till further orders.⁶³

"That day I saw an unforgettable sight," wrote Major Aubrey Herbert, who was watching the battle from No. 2 Outpost, West Anzac.

The dismounted Yeomanry attacked the Turks across the Salt Lake of Suvla.

Shrapnel burst over them continuously; above their heads there was a sea of smoke. Away to the north by Chocolate Hill fires broke out on the plain. The Yeomanry never faltered. On they came through the haze of smoke in two formations, columns and extended. Sometimes they broke into a run, but they always came on. It is difficult to describe the feelings of pride and sorrow with which we watched this advance, in which so many of our friends and relations were playing their part.[64]

The artist Norman Wilkinson immortalized the scene on canvas from a picture he drew at the time.[65] This not only faithfully depicts the advance, but also its futility, given the awesome fortress heights featured in the background.

By far the best primary source is the account of Captain Oskar Teichman, R.A.M.C., attached 1st Worcestershire Yeomanry, who moved up within the advancing columns. His vivid description is incomparable:

At 3.10 P.M. our Division and part of the Tenth formed up behind Lala Baba, and then, crossing the ridge, commenced to descend to the Salt Lake plain. We were in the following order: Second Brigade (Berks, Bucks and Dorset Yeomanry), Fourth Brigade (three London Yeomanry Regiments), First Brigade (Worcester, Warwick and Gloucester Yeomanry), Third Brigade (Derbyshire and two Notts Yeomanry Regiments), Fifth Brigade (Hertfordshire and Westminster Yeomanry). Each Medical Officer and bearer party followed his own Brigade. Not a shot was fired until we had gone a quarter of a mile and were well into the plain, when suddenly we seemed to walk into an inferno of shrapnel and H.E. [High Explosive]. Our first casualty was a Worcester Yeoman with a spent bullet in his thigh. After that men seemed to be dropping like flies. Finding an old Turkish trench, we made it our first Aid Post; this was soon full of wounded, dressed and labeled and fairly safe, as it was deep. Then I looked for a Field Ambulance, but ours was at that moment only just starting down the hill behind the last Brigade, and the only Red Cross flag to be seen was 2 miles away across the Salt Lake. So, noting the position of our trench, we move on. Selecting another Aid Post in a slight depression behind a stunted oak-tree, we were soon busy again bringing in the wounded. It was heart-rending work, as so many were past hope of recovery; the proportion of killed was very great and many were quite unrecognizable. Three slightly wounded men were killed in our Aid Post as a shell burst over us. The H.E. caused ghastly effects, as men were literally blown to pieces.

Such graphic descriptions are indeed uncommon, and the fact that Captain Teichman and his staff moved forward in the thick of things make his account all the more dramatic. He continues:

My bearers worked splendidly, and brought the wounded in a perfect inferno of bursting shells. We found that we were now picking up chiefly Notts, Derbys, Inniskillings, Irish Fusiliers, Sherwood Foresters and Hertfordshire Yeomanry, as our Brigade had turned slightly northwards and we, being busy, had not noticed this, and had kept straight on. Our Aid Post now contained about fifty wounded and dying, and I was very relieved to suddenly see a Red Cross flag about 200 yards behind our position. This turned out to be our Second

Mounted Brigade Field Ambulance, so, after detaching an orderly to inform them of the position of our first Aid Post and the one we were just vacating, we pushed on to form our third. We now entered a piece of land covered with tall rushes, which made the search for wounded difficult. Here I was working with several M.O.'s, but we each had our own zone to draw. On one occasion practically nothing was left of what had been two stretcher-bearers carrying a man. I came upon a group of five yeomen, quite dead in realistic attitudes, without a scratch on them, probably the concussion effect of H.E. Several men unwounded had completely lost their reason and some were blind. Huge holes seemed to be torn in the squadrons as they advanced, but, to quote Ashmead-Bartlett's report, "they moved as if on parade, and losing many, they never wavered but pressed steadily on." The Indian Mule Corps advancing with us showed the greatest contempt for the enemy's fire. Our men bore their wounds with the greatest of courage, and our stretcher-bearers worked in the calm routine fashion, as if they were working at a Field Day on the Berkshire Downs or on the marshes of the East Coast. One recognized now how important discipline and routine are on these occasions, when one saw each squad of three or four men performing their duties methodically. As we advanced men of the Signal Companies, R.E., kept laying their field telephone, and if one man, rolling his wheel over the ground, fell, there was always another behind to take it on. Here and there one came upon large holes made by the H.E. shells; they were useful to put men into, as they were safe from rifle fire. We had to work as fast as possible in order to keep ahead of our Third and Fifth Brigades, which were following us, as we knew that if they passed us they would draw more fire on our wounded. My next Aid Post was just in front of a little wood of scrub; there were now more bullet wounds as we were nearer to the trenches.

Captain Teichman now vividly recounts how:

The fleet in the Bay now opened fire again, and we could hear the big shells roaring overhead. To quote Ashmead-Bartlett: "The rifle fire was deafening, and I do not think that I have ever heard such a din as that produced by the ships' guns, field pieces, bursting shells and thousands of rifles, on any battlefield before." Snipers in the low scrub in front of the hill now became very troublesome, remaining behind and firing on our men after they had passed. My Aid Post was now full, so, sending back another messenger, we pushed on again. We came to a point where a little path forked in the wood, and there we found quite a pile of men, all evidently shot by the same sniper as they passed that spot. As we were removing one of them another man was shot by the sniper. About this time the scrub on our right caught fire and burnt furiously. This made the immediate search for wounded very urgent. We could hear those who could not move crying for help as the flames crept in. Some men of another Division advanced along little footpaths amongst the flames, and when they were wounded badly, it was very difficult to remove them. I now moved on to form my next Aid Post at the base of the hill, but to get there we had to leave the scrub and double across two fields, which were continually being searched by snipers; some of these were left exposed by the fire and were shot by our men on sight.... On forming my Aid Post under the hill, I saw a Field Ambulance in a small wood just beyond the reach of the flames. This turned out to be our Fourth (London) Brigade Field Ambulance, and we then commenced to evacuate our wounded to it. From this spot stretchers were carried to the dugouts of the advanced dressing station of the 32nd Field Ambulance [Sergeant John Hargrave's unit] on the Salt Lake. At this point mule transport took them across the bed of the lake to the Welsh Casualty Clearing Station on the beach.[66]

War Correspondent Ellis Ashmead-Bartlett wrote:

On Chocolate Hill I met General Peyton, who commands the 2nd Mounted Division of Yeomanry. He gave me some details of the unfortunate experience of his division during the attack on the 21st. All are now agreed that it was one of the worst managed affairs yet seen on the Peninsula, which is saying a great deal. It seems that many generals resented having de Lisle, a cavalryman, placed over their head. No one knew their orders on the 21st, and some of the Yeomanry regiments had no idea of their objectives. Why on earth they were brought across the Salt Lake in broad daylight under a heavy shrapnel fire, instead of being massed behind Chocolate Hill under cover of night, remains a mystery to this day. But this is only on a par with everything else.[67]

Had history repeated itself? Shades of the Crimea arose spectre-like. In attendance were three of the Four Horsemen of the Apocalypse: War, Death, and Pestilence. Siege warfare. On 21 August 1915, over sixty years after the Charge of the Light Brigade at Balaclava and the exploits of the "noble six hundred," immortalized by Tennyson, a much greater number, nearly 5,000, without the mobility of mounts, marched through a "Valley of Death" with "cannon to right of them, cannon to left of them, cannon in front of them, [which] volleyed and thundered."[68] My Lords Raglan ..., Lucan ..., Cardigan ..., the order.... Lord George Paget ... his cigar lasted until he reached the Russian guns.[69] The North Valley, the Fedioukine Hills, and the Causeway Heights.[70] The Commander-in-Chief, Field-Marshal Fitzroy James Henry Somerset, Baron Raglan, made Gallipoli his headquarters. Brigadier-General James Thomas Brudenell, Earl of Cardigan. Lieutenant-General George Charles Bingham, Earl of Lucan. Every bit as well-bred and just as amateurish as were their subsequent Suvla counterparts. As to the cavalry troopers under their command, those "noble six hundred" were sent (because "someone had blundered") in pursuit of an unclear objective into an almost identically homicidal salient in which their dismounted British Army cavalry brethren of later years now found themselves advancing.

Of the 673 soldiers who, on October 25, 1854, charged into the North Valley above Balaclava in the Crimea, 113 were killed, 134 were wounded, and 251 were missing and presumed captured. The order, scribbled in pencil by General Richard Airey, was perhaps unclear: "Lord Raglan the Commander-in-Chief wishes the cavalry to advance rapidly to the front, and try to prevent the enemy carrying away the guns...."[71]

Captain Nolan[72] galloped with the order and died a hideous death moments after he delivered it, which sealed his lips forever.

4 — Failure

The Mounted Division numbered 5,000 (a cavalry division differed in composition from that of an infantry division), but went into battle without their mounts. Not for them "the wild charge" into "the valley of Death," they marched "into the jaws of Death, into the mouth of Hell."[73] Nevertheless, these, "upholding the traditions of their forefathers at Poitiers, Crecy, Agincourt, kept their formation."[74] Sergeant John Hargrave looked down, and:

> From Two Tree Hill we had a magnificent view of the dismounted, or rather unmounted, Yeomanry as they moved out from Lala Baba and began their march across the Salt Lake in open formation. This was sometime between 3.30 and 4 P.M. On the Karakol Dagh, Hamilton and his staff were also watching. It was a sight to behold. There were five brigades, each nearly 1,000 strong, marching in extended order (column of squadron) — wave after wave — with about seven paces between each man. [Less than a year later, 1 July 1916, the British Army would advance thus on the opening day of the Battle of the Somme to suffer unprecedented decimation, 55,000–60,000 casualties in just a few hours.] They stretched from just below the Cut to the scrubby ground south of the Salt Lake, a distance of 2,000 yards. And they presented such a target as artillerymen dream of. They marched steadily, like an army of soldier ants that cannot be deflected, and almost as soon as they came into the open from their bivouacs behind Lala Baba, shrapnel began to thin them out.[75]

But bravery was not enough. As Norman Wilkinson's depiction graphically illustrated, the Turks held all of the daunting heights in the background. Chocolate Hill, the only British lodgment, was an insignificant semi-foothill at their base. The Yeomanry advanced splendidly "under a curtain of shrapnel."[76] They were "stormed at with shot and shell,"[77] and, as evening rapidly approached, deployed to storm the Ismail Oglu Tepe and reinforce the abortive assaults on Scimitar Hill, now a burning and smoldering corpse-strewn ruin. (The 2nd Battalion of the Hampshire Regiment, up from Helles, also "advanced in open order across the Salt Lake, now virtually dry, to reserve trenches behind Chocolate Hill. Though shelled during this advance they suffered only one casualty, Lieutenant-Colonel Harland being hit in the leg, but while digging in they caught more shell-fire and had over 20 more casualties.")[78]

> The advance of these English Yeomen was a sight calculated to send a thrill through anyone with a drop of English blood running in their veins. Such superb martial spectacles are rare in modern war.... Despite the critical events in other parts of the field, I could hardly take my glasses from the Yeomen; they moved like men marching on parade.[79]

Compared with:

> And now the watchers on the heights saw the lines of horsemen, like toys down on the plain, were expanding and contracting with strange mechanical precision. Death was coming fast, and the Light Brigade was meeting death in per-

fect order; as a man or horse dropped, the riders on each side opened out; as soon as they had ridden clear, the ranks closed again. Orderly, as if on the parade ground, the Light Brigade rode on, but its numbers grew every moment smaller and smaller as they moved down the valley. Those on the heights who could understand what that mechanical movement meant in terms of discipline and courage were intolerably moved, and one old soldier burst into tears. It was at this moment that Bosquet, the French general, observed, "*C'est magnifique mais ce n'est pas la guerre.*"[80]

Major John Gillam wrote the epitaph for the last battle of the Gallipoli Campaign. It is quite brief and astonishingly accurate.

August 22nd. We did not attack at dawn, and so the 88th have not been in action. We are as we were — yesterday's battle is not to be recorded as a victory for us. Machine guns again from right, left, and centre fired from behind great boulders of stone and hidden hillocks covered with gorse, and wave after wave of our men were mown down as if with a scythe. Twice we captured the Burnt Hill[81] [Scimitar Hill], but twice were driven off, and Burnt Hill remains Turkish. The Yeomanry were unable to get to grips with the enemy; but for gallantry in that march from Chocolate Hill to our front line, four hundred yards in front across the open in daylight, under a hail of shrapnel and machine gun bullets, their behavior could not have been excelled.[82]

The Commander-in-Chief sadly recalled "there was nothing for it but to fall back under cover of darkness to our original line. The losses in this attack fell most heavily on the 29th Division. They were just under 5,000."[83] The Reverend Dennis Jones found: "The Inniskillings ... had been severely cut up, for only 250 men and two officers left."[84]

The best-laid plans of General de Lisle and his staff had gone hopelessly awry. By nightfall it was over. The greatest battle fought on the peninsula in terms of numbers had become the most costly and the least successful. Intended as an attempt to capture the W Hills, Scimitar Hill and 112 Metre Hill, objectives which should have been attainable within the first twenty-four hours of the Suvla Bay operations.[85]

On the smoldering battlefield there was, however, still time for acts of great gallantry. Two troopers of the 1/1st Berkshire Yeomanry, Andrews and Potts, lay badly wounded to the rear of a section of Turkish frontline trench which they overran in their storming assault on the summit of Scimitar Hill. The Berkshires had been on the peninsula only three days, and the attack was their first operation. A more testing baptism of fire seems hard to imagine. Led by Major E. S. Gooch, the unit had gone into action with 9 officers and 314 men. By nightfall, only 4 officers and 150 men remained. Potts, a member of B Squadron, came through the march across the Salt Lake unscathed to reach the foot of Scimitar Hill, officially styled Hill 70 but more familiarly known to the troops as Burnt Hill. Advancing in short spurts, their presence partially masked by the tall scrub, the Berkshires made good progress at first. Pausing beneath the summit, Potts and his companions were ordered to "fix bayonets," and then an officer led them in the final rush, shouting: "Come on, lads! Give 'em beans!"[86]

4—Failure

Captain Teichman wrote:

It was now 11.30 P.M., and we began to descend the eastern exposed slopes of Chocolate Hill in very open order. There was little moon, and we could see, as we approached Hill 112, the fires which had broken out all over that hill, and also on Hill 60 to the south and Hill 70 to the north. As these fires increased the surroundings were brilliantly illuminated. We did not know at the time that there was a large communication trench leading from the top of the hill to our advance trenches. We were told that if we went on about half a mile we should come to a lane which passed behind the trenches held by our First Brigade. We missed the lane, but stumbled into a trench held by the Sherwoods. We were glad to get into it, as the rifle fire was getting hot and bullets meant for this trench were breaking the ground at our feet. Here we attended to some wounded, and then proceeded along the trench in a north-easterly direction to where we heard cries for help. Doubling across the open, we found ourselves in a hot position, so dropped into the nearest trench, which turned out to be a Turkish one recently evacuated. I proceeded carefully, thinking that we might meet the Turk any moment; however, we did not meet any live ones. The fires on Hill 112 were now burning low, but one could see the neutral ground between our lines, with heaps of Turkish dead. Our Brigades had advanced up this hill, but had had to retire. I got out of our trench and found one of our machine guns at work, and waited for a time in a well-built Turkish shelter. Thus ended August 21st.[87]

In a letter written to his sister from a hospital ship shortly after the battle, Trooper Frederick Potts of the Berkshire Yeomanry recounted his severe ordeal:

We had already captured a Turkish trench, and when the order was given to charge over we went. About 20 yards from the other side I received a wound in the thigh. It completely knocked me off my feet and I had to lie there. Presently, another of our chaps crawled to where I was. He was shot in the groin. There we lay all that night suffering from thirst, but it was much worse the next day. It seemed though we should go mad for want of a drink. When the second night came we decided to move if possible. This was no light job, as firing had been going on all around us—one bullet actually grazed my ear. However, we managed it somehow. Then we were able to get some water from the water bottles of the men who had been killed. Rather a painful job taking it, but one of necessity.

Soon after we moved away the Turks visited the place, and by the terrible screams and groans we judged that they were killing off the poor chaps who still had a spark of life in them. We found a hiding place for the remainder of the night and next day. We dared not show ourselves for fear of snipers, and oh, the thirst! I crawled from one body to another getting water. It was like wine, although it was nearly boiling. At nightfall we decided that anything was better than to die of thirst, so we endeavoured to crawl to where we could find the British lines. The other chap could hardly move and after a few yards had to give up, so I laid him on a shovel and dragged him down the hill bit by bit for about three-quarters of a mile. Before we started I prayed as I have never prayed before for strength, help and guidance. I felt confident that we should win through. On reaching the bottom of the hill we came to a wood. Here I left the other chap to find a way through. I had not gone more than 20 yards when I received the command to halt. By good luck I had struck a British trench. I soon told my tale, and it was not long before they found stretchers for both of us and took us into their trenches, where we were treated with every kindness.

From here we were conveyed to a Field Ambulance dressing station and had some hot tea. Oh it was grand! We were then put on an ambulance and sent to a Welsh casualty clearing station and thence on board this boat.[88]

In the above account Trooper Frederick Potts very much played down what actually happened. How eventually he had to stand up to pull the shovel-sledge under enemy fire. On October 1, 1915, the *London Gazette* announced the award of the Victoria Cross to N0.1300 Tpr. Frederick Potts: "For most conspicuous bravery and devotion to a wounded comrade...."[89]

The unsuccessful attack of August 21st was the last offensive effort of the Gallipoli venture, after that only local attacks were made for the improvement of the line. Before another advance could be attempted substantial reinforcements must be provided, over and above the drafts needed to bring the existing forces up to establishment and relieve the many men who were carrying on though debilitated and really unfit for hard work.[90]

Captain Teichman's entry for the following day makes for somber reading:

August 22nd. The fires on the hills had now burnt out: it was 2 A.M., and not knowing the general scheme of the trenches, I thought it best to wait until daylight before making a move. At 3 A.M. two infantry subalterns, evidently having lost their units, tumbled in on top of us and immediately fell asleep. At 4 A.M. we got the order to retire, and fell in with the Worcester Yeomanry, who skirted the hill and formed up with the remains of the Division on the west of Chocolate Hill. The greater part of the Division then retired over the same ground which we had crossed on the previous day and returned to the ridge behind Lala Baba. Fortunately, in the dim dawn the enemy did not see our move, or we should have been shelled again. By 7 A.M. the regiments were formed up again and were going through the sad ordeal of the roll call. We then learnt that the Second and Fourth Mounted Brigades had made an heroic attack on Hill 70, had reached the top, and had then been thrown back by sheer force of numbers. Their losses were very great, including two Brigadiers. It transpired that during the advance from Lala Baba to Chocolate Hill alone there had been five hundred casualties in our Division before it came within rifle range, and that our total casualties had been 30 per cent. A message now came up that sixty wounded were still lying on the edge of the Salt Lake, at the original first position of the Second Mounted Brigade Field Ambulance. They had been left there, under cover of a slight ridge, the afternoon before, but owing to the extreme pressure of work it had not been found possible to evacuate them to the southern beach. The Field Ambulance bearers were quite worn out with twelve hours' continuous carrying; volunteers were therefore called for to carry them to the beach, as it was now light and shells were beginning to fall in the plain again. My own bearers were not fit to go, but we managed to get ten men per regiment in the Brigade, and I accompanied them, as, not having done any

4—Failure

manual work, I was fairly fresh in spite of the last sixteen hours. We ran down and got to work at once, and acting as a bearer, I realized what hard work it was as I helped to carry a fat Major over very rough ground to the Casualty Clearing Station on the beach. Here we were rewarded with enormous bowls of tea and bread, which was very much appreciated, as we had eaten nothing since the previous afternoon. At this Casualty Clearing Station every wounded man was redressed if necessary, received hot food, his anti-tetanic injection, and was shipped off to the hospital ships in the Bay.

Captain Teichman and his companions returned to their position behind Lala Baba to find most of their men asleep from exhaustion — in spite of a battery of 60-pounders which were firing only a hundred yards away. He resumes his account:

Meanwhile, the sections of our Field Ambulances which had remained under Chocolate Hill, I could see with my glasses, were having a rough time. After a bathe we lunched again in the little ravines by the sea; it was quite peaceful when the guns ceased to fire for a while, but we were not the merry party we had been twenty-four hours before — some were missing, some killed and some wounded. At 7 P.M. we again left Lala Baba and crossed the Salt Lake to Chocolate Hill. Not a shell was dropped on us, only an occasional rifle shot. What a scene of desolation — dead men, mules, rifles, ammunition, helmets and emergency rations lay everywhere. As we marched slowly along, we came across some of our dead and hastily buried them while it was possible. Most of these had not fired off any ammunition, as they had been killed by shell fire long before they were within rifle range of the enemy. It was sad work, burying these men, mostly yeomen farmers in the prime of life and of splendid physique — this senseless slaughter of war seemed appalling, when viewed calmly after the excitement of battle was over. Eventually we caught up our Brigade, who were lying on the ground at the foot of the hill. While sitting on the ground, one man gave a little cough and rolled over against his neighbor quite dead. We could not find the cause of death at first, but it turned out that a dropping spent bullet had entered the left lung just behind the clavicle, leaving hardly any wound. The Division now ascended the hill; each Brigade had a small area allotted to it, and we all began to dig in for the night. It was very hard work in the stiff clay, but a certain amount of corrugated iron and balks of timber were obtainable. Extra sandbags were issued to the men, as they had used up those which they carried on the previous day.[91]

Two days later, on the 24th, Captain Teichman confided in his diary:
"During the morning one of our wells ran dry and we were limited to one water-bottle a day each and a little extra water per ten men for making tea. One was afraid of eating one's fill of bully beef, as it caused such a thirst...."[92]

On the next day Captain Teichman wrote:

August 25th. We stood to at daylight, but bar the usual rifle fire nothing was doing. After breakfast I attended some Irish wounded, brought into the reserve trenches at the top of the hill. During the morning we were heavily shelled, and had several men killed and wounded in their primitive dugouts. Fifty men per

Sixty-pounders in action. Presents an accurate action still of a gun crew on a fire mission — as well as showing a lack of uniformity of dress. The gun is at full recoil, the No. 2 having just pulled the lanyard. The gunners in the foreground are fitting the fuses to the shells. (Imperial War Museum, Neg. No. Q13.340)

> regiment were sent into the advance trenches to strengthen the Eleventh Division and learn their duties in stationary trench warfare. Burial parties were again sent out into the plain to search for missing and collect equipment. After supper our Divisional General [Peyton] joined us; he told us that one of his R.E. officers had discovered a new Turkish well, and that probably our supply of water would be increased.[93]

The day after he continued:

> *August 26th.* In the afternoon two of us walked to the Welsh Casualty Clearing Station [53rd (Welsh)] on the beach; taking a different route across the lake, we came upon several unexploded shells embedded in the clay, and examined the large craters formed by the enemy's H.E. Here were situated some of the hastily made Turkish trenches of the original landing. They contained Turkish equipment, broken rifles and dead Turks. On arrival at our hill we found that an Intelligence report had just come in (aeroplane) announcing the appearance of six large red cylinders behind the village of Kutchuk Anafarta; these were supposed to contain gas. Respirators (of the most primitive type!) were served out to all, and Brigade M.O.'s instructed the men how to use them.
> In the evening a large packet of maps was delivered to Brigade H.Q.; we were all very pleased, as the maps which had been served out were scarce and lacking largely in detail. When the packet was opened it was found to contain maps of the Cromer, Sheringham and King's Lynn [Norfolk, England] districts where we had been stationed in 1914!

August 27th. While having tea with the officers of the Second Mounted Brigade Field Ambulance in a tunnel in which they were living (they could no longer exist above ground in their exposed position at the bottom of the hill), we heard a tremendous bombardment going on about two miles to the right of our position. Seizing our glasses, two of us ran up the hill and lay down in the scrub on its righthand shoulder. Here we had a wonderful view of an Australian and a Ghurka Brigade advancing south of the Kasa Dere valley on Hill 60. We saw these troops, aided by the Connaughts and the South Wales Borderers, drive the enemy out of three rows of trenches amidst clouds of H.E. smoke and ultimately take the hill. It was a brilliant piece of work.[94]

Several reports appeared in the *New York Times* between 24 and 30 August, these ranged from the euphoric "Four-Day Suvla Battle Threatens Disaster to Whole Moslem Campaign," which headed a totally erroneous report which stated that the Allies now commanded the Narrows, to an official Turkish government announcement that their army had inflicted a severe defeat on the enemy forces. Furthermore, the Turco-German Commander, Marshal Liman von Sanders, in a *communiqué* published in the *New York Times* on 27 August, expressed complete confidence in his ability to repulse any future attacks, and of achieving eventual victory.[95] He also found it necessary to rebut "such incorrect statements published on August 23 in several well known British papers about great British progress on the Gallipoli peninsula and false statements about the relations between the German and Turkish officers, that four weeks later when I learned of it, I sent the following telegram to the German headquarters to contradict the press, the contents of the telegram giving the view prevailing at our headquarters":

> Camp at Boghali, 23 Sept. 1915
> The Anafarta operations undertaken by the British may be considered a total failure. As at Ari Burnu, so in the Anafarta section and in Suvla Bay the British hold but a narrow strip directly on the coast where they are entrenched and have been able to maintain themselves under the protection of the fleet. Everywhere the British camps are directly on the coast. All elevations commanding this narrow strip of land in front are in possession of the Turkish Army. The communications on the peninsula are completely open and nowhere interrupted. All British attacks have been repulsed with enormous losses. The news of discord between Turkish and German officers are pure inventions. The dirty source, which is spreading such news from Constantinople, would like to spread discord and is unable to do so. Present relations between Turkish and German officers are the best imaginable. Both are proud of the continued success of the brave Osman Army.
> Sgd. Liman v. Sanders.[96]

Needless to say news of the disaster appalled Cabinet and Dardanelles Committee members alike, and aroused much fury amongst Members of Parliament. At the meeting held at 10 Downing Street on Monday, 19 August

1915, Major-General C.E. Callwell, Director of Military Operations, War Office, reported that the Suvla forces sustained 23,000 casualties, plus many more evacuated sick. Andrew Bonar Law, Secretary of State for the Colonies, said, "General Hamilton was always *nearly* winning." Prime Minister Herbert Asquith thought that Sir Ian's fresh demands "should be examined to see if they were reasonable. While Sir Ian Hamilton had lost 23,000 men, he was still confident. The reason was not easy to see." Bonar Law "considered that a further attack would be a useless sacrifice of life." Sir Edward Carson, Attorney-General, agreed. Bonar Law advocated denying Hamilton reinforcements as a way of compelling him to cease launching further futile attacks.[97] Almost certainly this posed a defeat for the pro–Gallipoli faction and marked a distinct turning-point towards the acceptance of eventual evacuation as a means to extricate the Allied troops from an *impasse*. Once Colonel Hankey returned to resume his post and delivered his *Memorandum on the Situation, August 30, 1915*, this apparently spawned a very secret document which dispassionately considered the implications of "alternative (b) To find a pretext for withdrawal from the campaign," which the Committee members debated.[98] The following month at the 31st Meeting the Committee's agenda included Lloyd George's pet scheme for going to the assistance of Serbia. Soon this upstaged Gallipoli with the planned dispatch of French and British forces to Salonika, for already they talked of taking British divisions out of the line at Gallipoli for that purpose.

The month of August petered out with a vicious engagement in the Hill 60[99]-Kaiajik Dere salient. At a cost of 1,000 ANZAC, Indian, and British casualties this offensive gained a position which was enfiladed to the point of untenability.[100] The sum total of all the August action secured, at a cost of "some 45,000 Allied soldiers," was an area which Major-General Sir Alexander John Godley, Australian and New Zealand Division commander, described as "five hundred acres of bad grazing ground."[101] The same general stated that because of the development of a bridgehead at Suvla the Allied armies now faced "three sieges instead of two."[102]

"At the height of the August campaign casualties had been so great that the medical services for a few days were almost as bad as anything which Florence Nightingale had found at Crimea."[103] On the positive side, however, the Indian troops captured a well at Kabak Kuyu which yielded a plentiful supply of water which, although of dubious quality, greatly supplemented the meagre daily ration, and enabled much-needed ablutions to be performed.[104] The advance also effected the important Suvla Bay–Anzac Cove juncture. The Turks, however, still occupied the crest-line of Hill 60 and for the rest of the campaign this eminence was the scene of ceaseless bombing, undermining, and sniping which typified the Gallipoli stalemate.

Earlier, on 20 August, Private Mortlock "celebrated" his 20th birthday

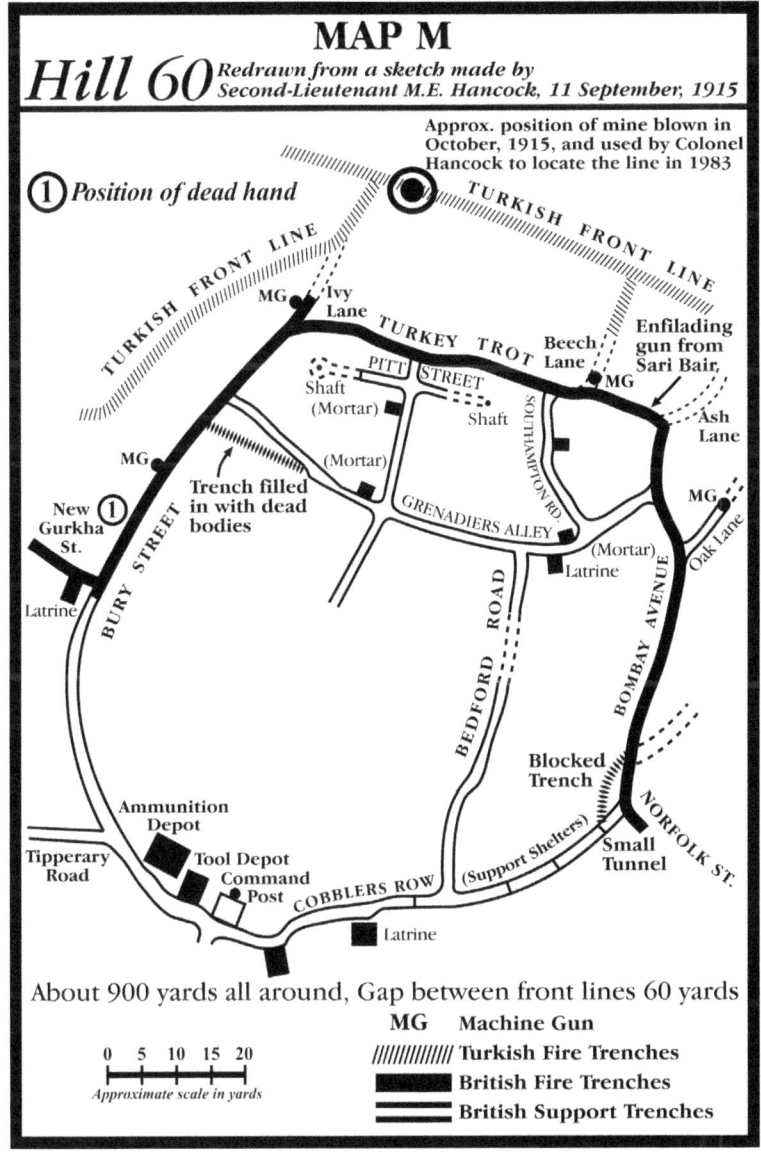

Map by Action Graphics of Virginia.

on the Kiretch Tepe Ridge. While in reserve for over a week he and his comrades excavated trenches and dugouts, furnished water-carrying parties, constructed roads, and otherwise improved communications. In temperatures which Sergeant Hargrave maintained "reached over 110 degrees [Fahrenheit]"[105] they worked hard night and day, with only the pitifully inadequate daily ration of a pint of water, "and were continually under shrapnel and sniper fire."[106] A month later Mortlock wrote to his cousin Jack Parker after a tour of duty on Hill 60:

> We get on a bit better for water now [the well at Kabak Kuyu?].... The worst thing we have to put up with is the flies, they are a plauge [sic] if you like swarm over everything and in everything. Oh for a row on the river.... I would sooner be shooting rabbits [on the farm] than Turks.[107]

On September 3, Ellis Ashmead-Bartlett wrote: "I then had a talk with General Mahon [10th (Irish)]. He complained bitterly of the manner in which his division had been split up at the landing; and even now one of his brigades is at Anzac, and he has never seen it since the operations began. He declared that both Hamilton and Braithwaite ought to go, and only this could restore the confidence of the troops."[108]

Another chapter of the Gallipoli saga drew to its close. The War Office and Dardanelles Committee refused to send more troops to General Sir Ian Hamilton's Mediterranean Expeditionary Force, mainly to prevent him expending them in further abortive and bloody assaults. The members greeted his irrepressible optimism with nothing but skepticism and cynicism. They used the word "evacuation" unequivocally, and planned that the Secretary of State for War, Lord Kitchener, should go out to make a firsthand assessment of the situation. The commitment at Salonika not only strengthened the opposition to the dispatching of further troops, whether reinforcements or replacements, to the Gallipoli Peninsula, it actually took the 10th (Irish) Division out of the line there in late September destined for that new theater of operations.

On 3 September 1915, wartime nurse and Oxford undergraduate Vera Brittain wrote her friend, 2nd Lieutenant Roland Aubrey Leighton, a seemingly appropriate obituary—albeit premature—for the Dardanelles venture:

> It was such a surprise to me this morning to see in *The Times* the death of a cousin of mine from wounds received in the Dardanelles. I didn't even know he was out. These casualties in Gallipoli are really terrible. So little seems to be accomplished for the loss of so much. At the present rate of advance—about half a mile in six months—it will take 28 years to get through, by which time all the men of this generation & the next will have been annihilated. Shall *we* see 'the morning break'?[109]

5

The End

The chorus of criticism of the conduct of the Gallipoli campaign swelled ever louder as more and more voices joined in. On the War Council and Dardanelles Committee the advent in mid-August 1915 of an extremely anti-Gallipoli member, Sir Edward Carson,[1] weakened the already-evaporating support General Sir Ian Hamilton enjoyed. Impending offensives on the Western Front, plus the Salonika commitment, would, in any event, have ruled out much in the way of additional men and *materiél* for the Mediterranean Expeditionary Force. But with dogged determination the Commander-in-Chief still refused to accept defeat, a forlorn figure in the midst of a welter of condemnation and recrimination, continuing his pleas for the wherewithal to achieve success. Lieutenant-Colonel Basil Liddell Hart in his "Gallipoli Judgement" chapter of the serialized *Purnell's History of the First World War* offered his retrospective analysis: "Hamilton erred in pursuing aims, which his plans had made possible, after they had become impossible, whereas his Western Front counterparts had persisted, at far greater cost, in pursuing aims that had never been possible."[2] While former British Prime Minister Clement Attlee (who served as a company commander at Suvla) adjudged in his autobiography:

> The Gallipoli campaign will always remain a very vivid memory. I have always held that the strategic conception was sound. The trouble was that it was never adequately supported. Often I have thought how near we came to victory, and I have tried to work out what the consequences would have been in that event. Unfortunately the military authorities were Western-Front-minded. Reinforcements were always sent too late. For an enterprise such as this the right leaders were not chosen. Elderly and hidebound generals were not the men to push through an adventure of this kind. Had we had at Suvla generals like Maude, who came out later, we should, I think, have pushed through to victory. Even as it was we came near to success. But for General Baldwin's column losing its way, it would have joined the Gurkhas and the South Lancashires on Sari Bair. But for Mustapha Kemal Pasha being in command of a Turkish division at the crucial point, we might have held that height. It was a tragic failure. I always feel a sympathy with all old Gallipolitans; as James Thomson the poet says, I "feel the stir of fellowship in all disastrous fight."[3]

As the summer of 1915 ebbed away, and the Allied troops now confined to an exclusively defensive role, many gave thought to what would be the next step in the series of blunders that epitomized the campaign. Not many of these thoughts were likely to be anything but gloomy.

> Regimental officers and men serving on the Gallipoli peninsula in the autumn of 1915 were naturally not aware of the course of the discussions about the future of the expedition which followed the check of August 21st. Still they could hardly fail to realize that sooner or later something must be done to break down the existing stalemate, and they could form their own opinions as to the prospects, about which few can have been very optimistic.[4]

The British Secretary of State for War, Earl Kitchener, addressing the House of Lords on the 15th of September, 1915, somberly summed up the depressing situation:

> On the Gallipoli Peninsula operations were carried on during June against the Turkish positions. Several Turkish trenches were captured and our own lines were appreciably advanced and our positions consolidated. Considerable reinforcements having arrived, a surprise landing on a large scale at Suvla Bay was successfully accomplished on August 6 without any serious opposition. At the same time an attack was launched by the Australian and New Zealand Army Corps from the Anzac position and a strong offensive was delivered from Cape Helles in the direction of Krithia. In this latter action the French troops played a prominent part and showed to high advantage their usual gallantry and fine fighting qualities. The attack from Anzac, after a series of hotly contested actions, was carried to the summit of Sari Bair and Chunuk Bair, which are the dominating positions in this area.
> The arrival of the transports and the disembarkation of the troops in Suvla Bay were designed to enable the troops to support this attack. Unfortunately, however, the advance from Suvla was not developed quickly enough, and the movement forward was brought to a standstill after an advance of about two and a-half miles. The result was that the troops from Anzac were unable to retain their position on the crest of the hills, and, after being repeatedly counter-attacked, they were ordered to withdraw to positions lower down. These positions, however, have been effectively consolidated, and now, joining with the line occupied by the Suvla Bay force, form a connected front of more than twelve miles. From the latter position a further attack on the Turkish entrenchments was delivered on the 21st, but after several hours of sharp fighting it was not found possible to gain the summit of the hills occupied by the enemy, and, the intervening space being unsuitable for defence, the troops were withdrawn to their original position. Since then comparative quiet has prevailed and a much-needed rest has been given to our troops.[5]

On the peninsula the days became less hot and the nights distinctly cooler as September wore away. It was still far from a holiday camp, though. The awful stench of decomposed corpses, and the activities of flies, lice, and what the 1/5th Suffolk's Battalion historians refer to as "vermin"[6] made everyday life uncomfortable. Death, mutilation, disease, and disillusionment are factors which try the most buoyant of spirits. Private Mortlock stated that the Gurkhas[7] "were the only ones who were cheerful on Gallipoli."[8] He also related how these resilient little warriors would only unsheathe their *kukris* to draw blood, and to fulfill this condition would make a tiny nick on a person's hand, say, so a drop of blood showed. He said they used to disappear into the night in search of unwary enemies, and had their haversacks partially filled with Turks' ears, grisly trophies of their nocturnal exploits.[9] (The *kukri* is an unusual weapon, something of a cross between a knife and a machete, shaped like a boomerang.) Later during his war service Captain Reginald Lane somehow acquired a pair of *kukris* which he brought home after the war; he was also, incidentally, according to Private Mortlock "the only one [of us] who got fat on Gallipoli."[10] Indeed, many became walking skeletons as the result of the ravages of dysentery. For some the contagion proved fatal. Lady Diana Cooper, in her autobiographical *The Rainbow Comes and Goes*, recorded that: "George Vernon, that dependent boy we had so cherished and petted as one does the youngest and weakest of the family, got dysentery at Suvla in Gallipoli and died, too slowly, in a hospital in Malta."[11] John Masefield observed in 1916:

> The dysentery, which had been present ever since the heats began, increased beyond all measure; very few men in that army were not attacked and weakened by it. Many thousands went down with it; Mudros, Alexandria and Malta were filled with cases; many died. Those who remained, besides carrying on the war by daily and nightly fire, worked continually with pick and shovel to improve the lines. Long after the war, the goatherd on Gallipoli will lose his way in the miles of trenches which zigzag from Cape Helles to Achi Baba and from Gaba Tepe to Ejelmer Bay.[12]

The troops belonging to the opposed armies on the Gallipoli peninsula now did, indeed, "live like moles."[13] Every day and every night each side improved their positions, repaired any which suffered detrimental effects from shellfire or mine detonation, and worked on additional communication thoroughfares, without which the soldiers in the firing lines would have been virtually isolated. Captain Aubrey Herbert painted a depressing picture of an infantry unit moving up at night to relieve another.

> When at last we came into a deep communication trench we felt that the end of [our] weariness must surely be near. But the worst exasperations of relieving an unknown line were still before us. It was a two-mile trudge in the narrow ditches to the front line. No war correspondent has ever described such a march; it is not included in the official 'horrors of war'; but this is the kind of thing, more than battle or blood which harasses the spirit of the infantryman and composes his life.... Each man [becomes] a mere lifeless automaton ... Mechanically each man grapples with obstacles, mechanically repeats the ceaseless messages that are passed up and down ... to those behind, and stumbles on. He is only conscious of the dead weight of his load, and the braces of his

SOME REGIMENTAL BADGES—KUKRIS DEPICTED

Some regimental badges. All these units participated in the Suvla/Anzac fighting. The 6th contained the Gurkha riflemen Jake Mortlock so admired. Note the depiction of their kukais. (*Action Graphics of Virginia*)

> pack biting into his shoulders, of his thirst and the sweat of his body, and the longing to lie down and sleep. When we halt men fall into a doze as they stand and curse pitifully when they are urged on from behind.[14]

On the same day that Private Mortlock penned the letter to his cousin Jack Parker, Major John Gillam wrote in his diary:

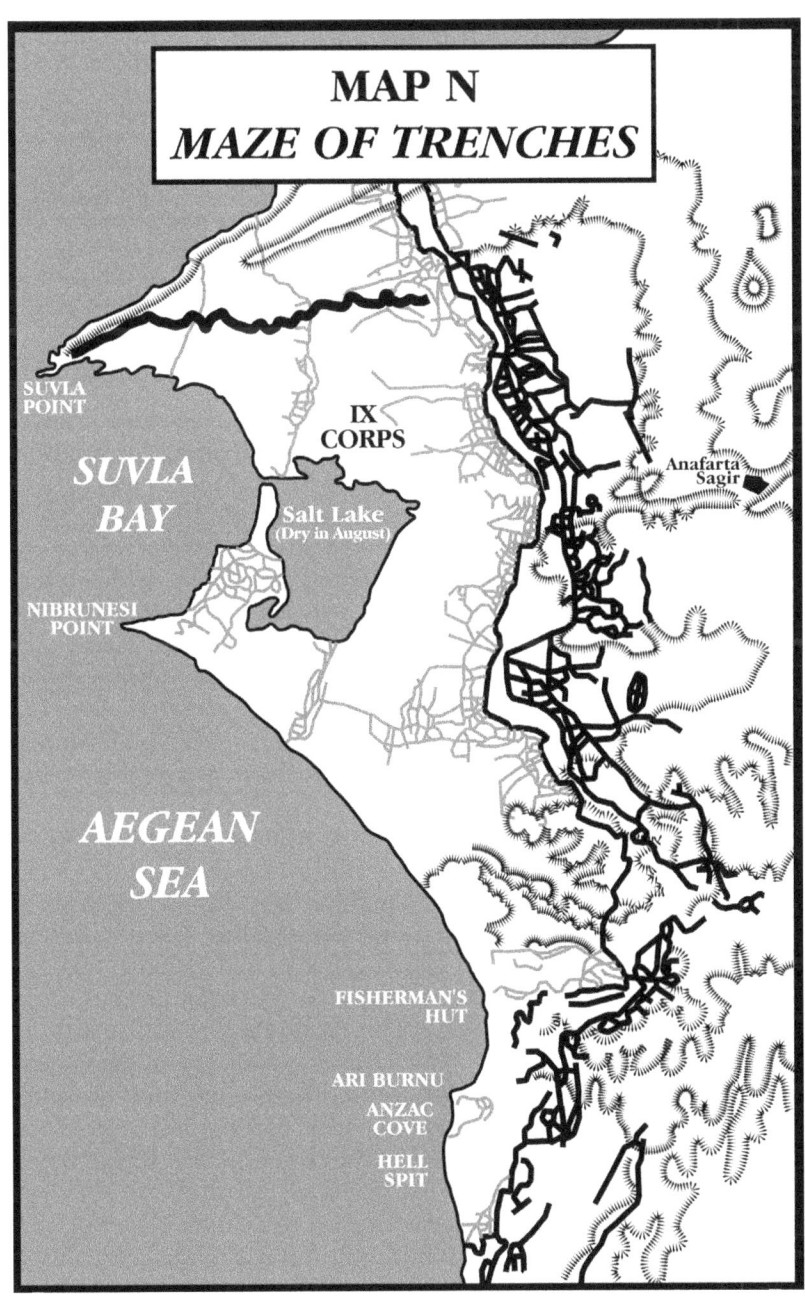

September 25th. A quiet day; just the usual artillery duels, no shells coming our way. Walked up to Brigade H.Q. in the evening. Battalion of the London Regiment joins Brigade. Lovely moonlit night. Rather a lot of firing on our front, and bullets a bit free. Meet Stewart and Lachard at Brigade, Stewart having come to relieve Lachard, who is going back to Helles. Walked back together. A bright flash. *Swiftsure* in the bay denotes that she has fired one of her big guns, and a few seconds after a loud report is heard, and the rumble of the shell as it passed over Sari Bair on to "somewhere" goes on for a long time before one hears the distant report of its burst. I hear the sound of propellers overhead, and think I can see the airship from Imbros sailing over towards Anarfarta. The *Swiftsure* fires once more, and then all is quiet for an hour. Then a Turkish battery puts a shell over us, and follows this up with one every ten minutes, continuing for an hour![15]

The Commander-in-Chief's diary entry for 25 September actually mentioned that he visited the 54th (East Anglian) Division: "lunched with General Inglefield[16]; then plodded through the trenches held by his Division (the 54th; nice looking boys) and by the Indian Brigade."[17]

Also on that date, after remaining anchored in the Mersey for a whole day on the White Star liner *Olympic,* the Suffolk Yeomanry—without their horses—sailed for Gallipoli. The voyage was not entirely free from dangers. In the Mediterranean, after picking up thirty-five sailors from a French ship sunk by a torpedo, the *Olympic*—now no longer escorted—opened fire on an enemy submarine, causing it to dive to safety.[18]

Private Mortlock maintained that Suvla Bay was never accorded the same share of publicity in the newspapers as the other two sectors. "It was always Helles and Anzac," he said.[19]

The tedium of trench warfare went on. At night the garish glare of Verey-lights[20] and star-shells fitfully illuminated the landscape as they hung in the sky above no man's land and the firing lines. At listening posts in frontline trenches and forward saps former Welsh miners laid their ears to the ground in order to detect the sounds of enemy undermining.[21] Shortly after the link-up between Suvla and Anzac on 28 August the 54th (East Anglian) Division took over the line from Aghyl Dere to Hill 60, and the 1/5th Battalion of the Suffolks, now reduced to a quarter of its original strength, garrisoned Hill 60 (see Map M) for the first time from 5th to the 13th of September. "During these nine days on Hill 60 we lost three killed, 8 wounded, and 32 to hospital. 9,000 rounds of S.A.A.[22] [Small Arms Ammunition] were expended. These figures never include machine-gun ammunition."[23] On 15 September the battalion relieved the 1/4th Norfolks in what was known as Norfolk Trench, which was a continuation of the front line from Hill 60. There "a well[24] was found a few yards from the front line and was of priceless value, for, although the water was not supposed to be fit for drinking purposes, this order was not rigidly enforced. So while here we did not suffer from water shortage and took the opportunity of having a good wash."[25] This mention of water shortages and ablutions brings to mind the amusing anecdote from Anzac. The story goes that General Birdwood was making his customary rounds one day when he happened upon an Australian soldier busy shaving with the aid of a small quantity of water in a mess tin.

"Having a good clean-up?" said the General.

"Yes, sir. Pity I ain't a bloody canary!"

It was at the end of this spell on Hill 60 that Private Mortlock wrote his only letter from Gallipoli to survive the passage of time (most probably written in the harbor area of Australia Gully West.) His battalion's historians vividly described that awful place in the pages of their work:

> Hill 60 formed a salient in both the British and Turkish lines, and was badly enfiladed from Chunak Bair and other hills on our right flank in possession of the Turks. [See Map M.] They were quick to turn this to advantage, and practically all their artillery fire was enfilade. One battery of 75's was particularly enterprising and unpleasant. With most guns we could hear the report and then the approach of the shell, and were able to take cover, but with these guns the velocity of the shell was so great that it exploded almost as soon as the sound was heard, hardly giving time even to duck our heads[26].... The parapets were in many places made up of dead bodies.[27] [As in Captain Aubrey Herbert's verse: "... The corpses on the parapet, the maggots in the floor."][28]

The men eagerly awaited parcels from home, especially those which contained food to vary their depressingly predictable diet of bully beef,[29] very brittle weevil-infested biscuits, and apricot jam. The preserve last-named was an exceedingly magnetic attractor of flies.[30] 2nd Lieutenant Edmund Priestman, of the 6th Battalion, the York and Lancaster Regiment, drew a humorous sketch which depicted himself with his head enveloped in a swarm, and Private Mortlock of the 1/5th Battalion, the Suffolk Regiment related how one's mouth would be disgustingly encrusted with flies whilst trying to eat in daylight.[31] Lieutenant "Juvenis" recorded his excitement at the arrival of "a Harrods' hamper," and the subsequent feast he and his fellow officers enjoyed that evening in the Company mess.[32] For less exalted beings the delivery of a humble airtight tin of homemade fruitcake was a godsend. Private Jake Mortlock received a parcel from his Aunt Kate, who obviously rated his spiritual well-being much above that of his physical. To his and his comrades' great disappointment the opened package contained not food, or even cigarettes, but a substantial pile of issues of a periodical publication called *Little Gleaner*, which was entirely devoted to the dispensing of intensely innocent Christian literature aimed at children and juveniles. In spite of their initial reaction Mortlock recalled that he

General William Birdwood outside his dugout. The largely popular Commander of the ANZAC forces (which eventually included the 54th [East Anglian] Division) was once described as "the soul of Anzac." (Imperial War Museum, Neg. No. Q13.796)

handed the magazines out one apiece to his fellow soldiers who accepted them, as "they were glad of something to read."[33]

Although determined offensive warfare virtually ceased on the Gallipoli Peninsula and what Alan Moorehead described as "a dull implacable *ennui* began to settle on the Allied Army,"[34] politicians and generals fought verbal battles across tables in Whitehall to decide what to do with the problems that the theater posed. At a meeting of the Dardanelles Committee on 6 October the initiator of the strategy and the most pro-Gallipoli member, Winston Churchill, stated:

> The only question is whether there is still time to save the situation at Gallipoli. There appears to me to be two alternatives: (1) To cut our losses at Gallipoli, retire from the campaign, and abandon Turkey to Germany; (2) To try and save the situation at Gallipoli, and force the Straits.... In fact, the whole question resolves itself into this: have we time to force the Dardanelles before the Germans can get through to Constantinople?[35]

Lord Selborne, an ardent supporter of the enterprise and author of the recently circulated "Selborne Memorandum" which strenuously advocated a more aggressive stance in Gallipoli, agreed with this general presentation of the question.[36] Lords Curzon and Crewe opposed the idea of evacuation because of its likely detrimental Imperial repercussions. All the while they

5—The End

deliberated, to their consternation, that sublime optimist Hamilton continued to pester them for replacement drafts, reinforcements, and artillery ammunition.

But on the peninsula severe critics of the conduct of the operations conferred, and became, as it were, blood brothers, after which their arguments coagulated. They made plans to take their case to the drawing-rooms of members of the Cabinet.

At the forefront of this anti-Hamilton, anti-General Staff group of critics were two especially vociferous—an English War Office–accredited correspondent, Ellis Ashmead-Bartlett, and an Australian journalist, Keith Murdoch, who had been granted conditional permission to visit the battlefields. Both perceived what they considered the utter incompetence of the Gallipoli generals, and their almost criminal disregard for the men under their command. The former wrote a letter to the Prime Minister, dated 8th September, 1915:

> Dear Mr. Asquith,
> I hope you will excuse the liberty I am taking in writing to you but I have the chance of sending this letter through by hand, and I consider you should know the true state of affairs out here. Our last great effort to achieve some definite success against the Turks was the most ghastly and costly fiasco since the battle of Bannockburn.
> Personally, I never thought the schemes decided on by Headquarters ever had the slightest chance of succeeding and all efforts now to make out that it only just failed, owing to the failure of the 9th Corps to seize the Anafarta Hills, bears no relation to the real truth. The operations did, for a time, make headway, owing to the superlative gallantry of the Colonial troops, and the self-sacrificing manner in which they threw away their lives against positions which should never have been attacked.
> The main idea was to cut off the southern portion of the Turkish Army by getting astride of the Peninsula from Suvla Bay. Therefore, the whole weight of the attack should have been concentrated on this objective; instead of which the main attack, with the best troops, was delivered against the side of the Turkish positions which are a series of impossible mountains and valleys covered with dense scrub. The Staff seemed to have carefully searched for the most difficult points, and then threw away thousands of lives in trying to take them by frontal attacks. A few Gurkhas obtained a lodgment on Chunuk Bair, but were immediately driven off by the Turkish counter-attacks, and the main objective, Koja Chemen Tepe, was never approached.
> The 9th Corps, miserably mishandled, having failed to take the Anafarta Hills, is now accused of being alone responsible for the ultimate failure of the operations. The failure of the 9th Corps was not due so much to the employment of new and untried troops, as to bad Staff work. The generals had but a vague idea of the nature of the ground in their front, and no adequate steps were taken to keep the troops supplied with water. In consequence many of these unfortunate volunteers went three days in very hot weather on one bottle of water, and were yet expected to advance, carrying heavy loads, to storm strong positions. The Turks, having been given ample time to bring up strong

reinforcements to Anafarta, where they entrenched themselves up to their necks, were again assaulted in a direct frontal attack on August 21st. The movement never had the slightest chance of succeeding and led to another bloody fiasco in which the unfortunate 29th Division, who were brought up especially from Helles, and the 2nd Mounted Division (Yeomanry), were the chief sufferers....[37]

Ashmead-Bartlett also stated that Hamilton and his staff were openly referred to by the troops at Gallipoli with derision.[38] While Murdoch stated in his celebrated letter to Andrew Fisher, the Australian Prime Minister that "Braithwaite [Chief of the General Staff] is more cordially detested in our forces than Enver Pasha [Turkish Minister of War]."[39] Even Private Mortlock's expressed wartime opinion was: "All the generals ought to be shot!"[40] Although such a drastic formula was not contained in Messrs. Ashmead-Bartlett and Murdoch's actual messages their esteem was roughly on the same par. Besides these somewhat sensational gentlemen of the press, a much more conservative and expert opinion ranged itself against the tired men who botched the golden Suvla opportunity and then launched their attacks when no hope remained. This voice was very influential indeed, for it came from none other than Major Guy Dawnay, one of the architects of the Suvla Bay strategy. Paradoxically, Lieutenant-General the Honourable Sir Frederick Stopford, now back in London, seeking to exonerate himself, added his voice too and accused GHQ Imbros of "interference."[41] The sands of time trickled out for Hamilton; his enemies and detractors agreed upon his fate; the only thing not settled was the type of scaffold.

The first of many blows struck the Commander-in-Chief of the Mediterranean Expeditionary Force on:

26th September, 1915. Imbros. Last night after dinner, Braithwaite came across with a black piece of news in his pocket: —
(No. 8229, cipher). From Earl Kitchener to General Sir Ian Hamilton. On account of the mobilization of the Bulgarian Army Greece has asked the Allies to send a force to Salonika in order to enable her to support Serbia should the latter be attacked by Bulgaria, as well as by German forces from the North.... It is evident that under these circumstances some troops will have to be taken from the Dardanelles to go to Salonika ... required for Salonika would be two divisions, preferably the Xth and the XIth.... The Dardanelles Committee consider a withdrawal from Suvla to be advisable under the circumstances.[42]

Lieutenant-General Sir Bryan Mahon and his 10th (Irish) Division sailed from Suvla Bay on the last day of September. They disembarked at Salonika on 9 October 1915. General Mahon was destined to command the British contingent thereat — and initially the Anglo-French Army of Salonika, prior to the appointment of French General Maurice Sarail as Commander-in-Chief. Sergeant Hargrave was with them. Lance-Corporal Collen would join them later. Lieutenant "Juvenis" could not go.

5—The End

Wounded on the Kiretch Tepe Ridge he was bound for old Blighty on a hospital ship.

> The 54th (East Anglian) Division which had replaced the 10th (Irish) astride Kiretch Tepe Ridge when that division took part in the abortive August 21st attack, moved to General Birdwood's command early in September to allow of the 13th (Western) Division joining the Ninth Corps, to which it properly belonged. This brought the 8th Hampshire to the Rhododendron Spur-Damakjelik sector, where the 10th [Hampshire] had undergone its strenuous initiation to active service. Thus the paths of the three battalions did not cross.[43]

The writing was on the wall for the Gallipoli venture, and no one was more appalled than its instigator, Winston Churchill, who wrote: "The conduct of the 9th Corps at Suvla would be incredible if it were not true."[44] The deliberations in Whitehall and elsewhere on the future of the Gallipoli war zone had, however, almost no immediate effect on the everyday lives of troops involved. The exception was that, as Lord Kitchener communicated to Hamilton on 5 October, the Dardanelles Committee expected him to adopt "only a purely defensive attitude,"[45] he could plan no more offensives and the campaign degenerated into a defensive stalemate. Hamilton observed: "The Dardanelles is not a sanatorium; Suvla is not Southend. With the men we have lost from sickness in the past six weeks we could have beaten the Turks twice over."[46] Although the last part was typical Hamilton wishful thinking, the rest of the statement was only too true. Moorehead maintained that "800 sick men were being evacuated from the peninsula every day."[47] It was sometime in early October that Private Jake Mortlock reported sick, suffering from a terribly sore throat. It will be remembered that his division sailed without, among other ancillary units, its Field Ambulance detachment. Marched to an Advanced Dressing Station, he was given a cursory examination, and then had two teeth extracted without the pain-dulling benefit of novocaine, laughing gas, or the like. A suspected malingerer, he was sent on his way with the callous pronouncement: "That'll make you feel better."[48] A few days later he returned on a stretcher to renew his acquaintanceship with those gentle Royal Army Medical Corps philanthropists. Diagnosed with a severe case of diphtheria,[49,50] Mortlock was evacuated from that awful peninsula and in a matter of weeks found himself aboard a hospital ship[51] bound for Malta. He thus sailed away from the hell-hole of Gallipoli, but most of his mates remained, including at least one boy.[52]

Shortly thereafter the fellow-Suffolk lads of the Suffolk Yeomanry, following hours out on a gale-tossed sea, landed at Walker's Pier, Anzac Cove, during the night of the 10th–11th October. It and the other regiments composing the Eastern Mounted Brigade were attached to the 54th (East

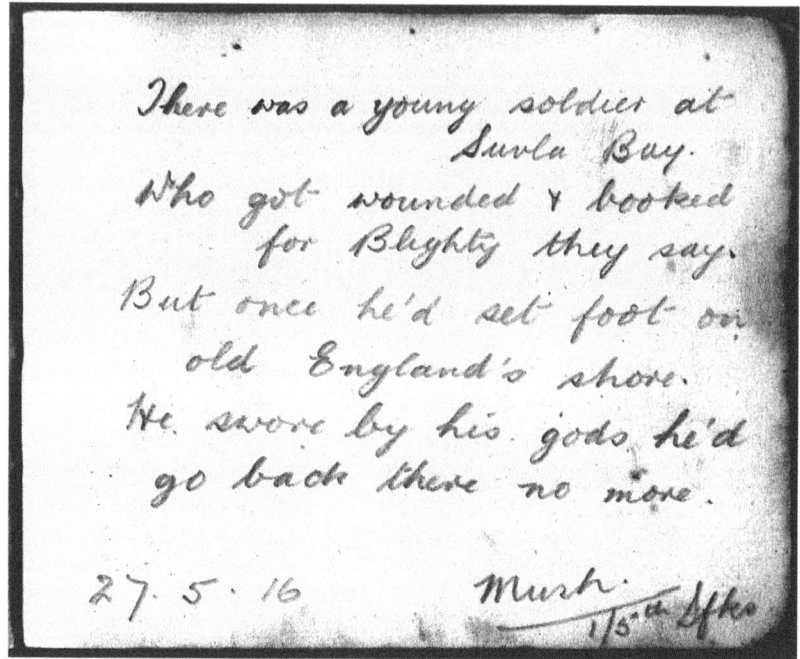

This unique contribution is an entry in Private Jake Mortlock's autograph album, which spans the years 1913–1918. (Mortlock family papers)

Anglian) Division. All units, short of both officers and men, eagerly welcomed the newly arrived regiments, and soon the Suffolk Yeomanry were allotted a considerable sector of the line. There the newly-arrived soldiers found that during the daytime things were generally quiet except for sniping and shelling, the latter occurring with almost timetable predictability, so the regiment soon came to know when to expect such displays of activity. During the night hours rifle fire was incessant.[53]

Throughout October controversy raged in Britain. The opinion of the public had been aroused and there was a great deal of criticism of the Gallipoli campaign. As these arguments amassed the fate and the very future of the Gallipoli operations swung in the balance. When the Dardanelles Committee convened on the 11th of October two papers lay before them and "each was a bombshell." The first was the report of Lt.-General the Honourable Sir Frederick Stopford, ignominiously relieved of his command of the Ninth Corps, and now back home in Britain, who hastened to defend his inaction and disclaim responsibility for the Suvla Bay *fiasco*.[54]

> It was a farrago of half-truths and downright lies and it implied harsh criticism of Sir Ian Hamilton's conduct of operations, not only at Suvla but on the penin-

sula as a whole. It was viciously unfair, but it went unchallenged. Sir Ian Hamilton, who had not even seen it, was given no opportunity to reply, but Lord Kitchener had already made up his mind.... The second document was the virulent Murdoch letter.[55]

The golden opportunity that Suvla Bay offered in early August would never return. The Dardanelles Committee sought a face-saving pretext for extricating their Mediterranean Expeditionary Force from the Gallipoli Peninsula, and as a first step on 14 October "they did reach one unanimous decision. Sir Ian Hamilton was to be sacked."[56] Hamilton's *Gallipoli Diary* relates how the deciphered message was worded:

> The War Council held last night decided that though the Government fully appreciate your work and the gallant manner in which you personally have struggled to make the enterprise a success in face of terrible difficulties you have had to contend against, they, all the same, wish to make a change of command which will give them an opportunity of seeing you.[57]

Sadly Hamilton opined that the choice of his successor, Lieutenant-General Charles Carmichael Monro, was intended "to force K. to pull down the blinds."[58] In Winston Churchill's bitter paraphrase: "He came, he saw, he capitulated."[59] As previously related, "K." (Kitchener) already accepted a withdrawal from Suvla,[60] and it would take only a personal visit to convince him that evacuation was the only feasible course of action. Interestingly enough at about the same time Kaiser Wilhelm II went out "to view the battlefields of the Dardanelles Campaign...."

> His Majesty the Emperor [Kaiser Wilhelm II] visited the battlefields of the Dardanelles on the 17th of October. I delivered a brief discourse on Suvla Bay in the presence of a great suite, in which there were several high naval officers, explaining the limited activity of the U-boat war in the Dardanelles and the reasons for it, without His Majesty appearing in the least displeased.[61]

Lord Kitchener would also come out in person to appraise the situation on the Gallipoli Peninsula. Before he did so, in a long, and often bluntly worded speech to the House of Commons on November 2, Sir Henry James Dalziel, Liberal Member of Parliament for the Scottish constituency of Kirkcaldy Burghs, made some very profound observations. Some of the most far-sighted points made by the Honourable Member are contained in the following extracts of his peroration:

> Of the initial delays and procrastinations:
> There are in this country photographs of Blue Jackets having tea on the top of Achi Baba, which shows how simple it would have been, and that if we had only the military to lend aid at the same moment it would have been a walkover with no trouble at all. Those are serious matters since you gave two months' notice to your enemy as to what you were going to do. I think some explanation is required when the Colonies send their best blood to be destroyed

by machine guns which were there awaiting them. That is not all. What about the men we sent to the Dardanelles—new, unseasoned men who had never seen fire, and, after being stowed up on a troopship, were walked ashore into fire without a moment's rest—I mean at Suvla Bay, which is only an instance and an indication of what has been going on all over the place? I say it was not fair to send men under those conditions to attack, especially where they were landed. Who was responsible for the men who were placed in charge? Who decided the staff that was going to be in charge and have influence over thousands of men? It was not, as I understand, General Sir Ian Hamilton; he was not responsible for the men; he did not get his own staff. Some of the men who were responsible for that disaster were men who were sent from home by the authorities, and who were not suggested by the Commander-in-Chief himself. We had this statement at the Table the other day from the Under-Secretary of State for War, that the General concerned has been retired. Why did he not tell us the truth? Probably he was not answering that question, and I know he is the last man to keep anything back, and I wish he had his way with regard to these matters, and I am sure he would give us information. The answer to which I refer was that a general had been retired, but is it not a fact that not one, but two, three and four generals have been retired? Why keep these facts from the public? The man in the street practically knows them, but they are not stated publicly. What is the result? The men themselves lose confidence when they know of those who have made mistakes costing the loss of thousands of men.[62]

A couple of days later, on November 4th, Lloyd George received the following letter from Prime Minister Herbert Asquith:

Secret.

10, Downing Street,
Whitehall, S.W.
3rd November, 1915.

My Dear Lloyd George,
What I wanted you to know before tomorrow's Cabinet was that, in view of the conflicting opinions now to hand of Monro and the other generals in regard to the future of the Dardanelles, I arranged to-day that K. should proceed without delay (tomorrow, Thursday night) to Alexandria, and after visiting Gallipoli and Salonika, and conferring with all our military and diplomatic experts in that quarter of the world, advise us as to our strategy in the eastern theatre.

In the meantime I propose to take over the War Office, and I am confident that in the course of the next month I can put things there on a better footing, and in particular come to a complete understanding with you on all the important problems which are connected with the design, fabrication and supply of munitions.

We avoid by this method the immediate supersession of K. as War Minister, while attaining the same result. And I suppose even B.L. [Bonar Law] would hardly object to such a plan.

Yours very sincerely,
H. H. A.

P.S.—This is for yourself alone; I have not said anything to any of our colleagues. But I regard it as of the first moment that in this matter you and I should act together.[63]

5—The End

Unaware of these political machinations designed to severely curtail his authority, Lord Kitchener duly sailed from Marseilles, where "he was diverted from Alexandria and asked to go direct to Mudros, where MacMahon, Maxwell, Monro, and Birdwood had been ordered to meet him."[64] "Kitchener anchored at Mudros on November 10, and spent the next few days and nights in close inspections of the positions and long conferences on board the *Lord Nelson,* to which he was trans-shipped for a few days.... Helles drew from him expressions of genuine surprise that its seizure could have been effected in the teeth of strong opposition.... On November 13 the Anzac position was thoroughly overhauled, and Kitchener was rapturously received by the Australians and New Zealanders, to whom he gave messages of congratulations from King and nation."[65] The difficulties of the terrain and the precarious footholds to which the troops clung depressed him. He appraised the situation, and, on 15 November, cabled the government that evacuation might not prove as costly as had been previously calculated. On 22 November Kitchener advised the War Committee[66] in London by telegram to recommend that Suvla and Anzac should be evacuated, while the Cape Helles garrison should continue to hold out.[67]

David Lloyd George commented acidly on these developments:

> One culminating illustration at this period of our military leaders' capacity for blundering remains to be recorded. Upon the return of Lord Kitchener, at the end of November, 1915, from his expedition to the Balkans, the antipathy of the British General Staff to any operations in that theatre crystallized into a definite recommendation that the Salonika expedition should be recalled. Rumour had it that Kitchener had somehow been talked over by the plausible and adroit King Constantine of Greece into favouring this step. The General Staff advised that we should withdraw from both the Dardanelles and Salonika and concentrate our forces on the defence of Egypt.[68]

Early in November the 1/5th Suffolks "moved to Dixon's Gully, where 2nd Lieutenant G.G. Oliver had a lucky escape, his nose being grazed and several teeth knocked out by a bullet which had killed Private W. Hume. Orders were now received that no unnecessary risks were to be incurred, the reason for this precaution — though not given out the time — being that the evacuation of the peninsula was already under very secret consideration."[69] Colonel Gibbons also narrowly escaped death while in a forward sap the 8th Hampshires christened "Carisbrook Castle."

> I was shooting from here on November 5th when I saw the enemy bring his machine gun into action in the new emplacement. We started with our usual deliberate methods — and the Turk fired first. Something struck me on the side of my neck with a blow like a sledge hammer and knocked me off the parapet. Hugging the place, which was very painful, I went back to my dugout and discovered that the bullet had not penetrated far, but had burned a large hole in the surface of my neck. It had glanced off a sandbag and hit me sideways. I had

to go to the ambulance and get it seen to, but it did not necessitate my leaving the Battalion. It stopped my sniping for a time though, and it was two months before the wound healed up."

Still on Laindon Hill, Anzac, Colonel Gibbons described the magnificent view it afforded of the spectacular sunsets and the rugged height of Samothrace. He goes on:

> Time had wrought great changes in our organization, and we were now getting fairly regular supplies of fresh meat and bread once or twice a week. Water had still to be strictly husbanded as it all had to be brought up on mules. Rum was almost a daily issue and the men appreciated it highly, for the nights were getting very cold and this increased the strain of night duty. Talking of mules, it must be stated that these much maligned animals served us well, as they have all through the war. No draft or pack animal will do its work so well under all conditions of terrain, weather, and subsistence, as the mule. The breed used on the Peninsula were small, wiry, and extraordinarily handy when properly handled. The drivers and leaders were almost exclusively Indians, who seemed to possess the "mule sense" to a remarkable degree.[70]

As autumn ebbed away and the Northern Hemisphere winter approached, Nature followed her time-honored routine. On 20 November Captains Fair and Wolton of the 1/5th Suffolks narrated that:

> For some time big flocks of migrating geese had been pressing south over Gallipoli, and some men in the trenches, to relieve their boredom, started to blaze away at them. But this proved infectious and, day by day, the firing continued, and even machine-guns took part in the fun. The Turks soon joined in the game, and their rifles could be seen pointing straight up into the air above their parapets. A rattle of musketry proceeding from the British or Turkish trenches on the flank did not mean that an attack was taking place, but merely that the geese were coming, and finally strict orders were issued that firing at geese must cease. Only one goose was known to have been brought down as a result of all our efforts, and as that observed strict neutrality by falling in "No-Man's-Land" no one benefited.[71]

The history of the 1/5th Battalion of the Essex Regiment gives a slightly different version of this phenomenon—although, admittedly, this was observed roughly a month earlier (late October):

> Great flocks of geese and storks flew over every day going west. Both sides fired at them with rifles, without effect, except to increase the "overs." We could have done with a goose. The Turks even tried their "Archies" (anti-aircraft guns) at them, but still no result.[72]

Fair and Wolton divulged that owing to the opening of a front at Salonika, artillery ammunition in the Suvla/Anzac sector was limited to three rounds per gun a day. This ration was insufficient for the purpose of demolishing barbed wire. When the Turks pushed out barbed-wire "knife rests"[72] in front of a mine crater the Suffolks resorted to a catapult-launched bomb with a thin rope attached. This projectile, however, fell into the enemy's trench and a strenuous tug-of-war ensued which ended abruptly when the Turks cut the rope![73] So the soldiers of both sides enjoyed their lighter moments.

Corporal Reg Lane recalled that a bugle was sounded when "Asiatic Annie," the big gun opposite Helles which fired shells across the Hellespont, opened up.[74] Presumably flash-spotters detected this and activated the order to the warning bugler.

The geese which hastened southward did so instinctively to escape the onset of winter. The Allied troops on the Gallipoli peninsula had no immediate plans to migrate, although the people in high places started to make provision for the projected abandonment of the Suvla/Anzac sector.

Captains Fair and Wolton recounted, "the weather became extremely cold culminating in a three-day blizzard from November 27th to 29th inclusive."[75] The battalion suffered severely as at 3.00 P.M. on 26 November they received orders that "the 54th (East Anglian) Division is to proceed to Mudros on night 27th/28th November to rest," and preparations for the move entailed the dismantling of "carefully constructed bivouacs" and "the handing in of baggage ... including Officers' kits, valises, and mess boxes."[76] The Division was totally unprepared for the weather which now struck the peninsula. The trenches were already "rivers and the gullies raging torrents" because of torrential rains.

A senior officer, Lt.-Colonel Frederic W.D. Bendall, commanding a battalion of the London Regiment, described at length the awfulness of it all. The author makes no apology for quoting it almost in its entirety.

> If you broke a wash basin in half, the line of the break would give you a good idea of the trench lines at Suvla. High, almost mountain high, to the north, they ran down the stony slopes, where nothing grew but prickly Turkish holm-oak in dense, scrubby patches, down to the cultivated flat land at the bottom of the basin. Over grassy hillocks they ran, and away southward to the Anzac position, which we saw dimly, but did not know, and up the distant cliffs to the precarious foothold we had on the summit there. From 70 to 400 yards apart they ran, our trench and the Turkish line.
>
> Standing in the middle of the basin, we saw a curved line of hills some miles away. To the left these hills went on behind us to the northern end of the blue bay, where battleships rode snugly at anchor inside protecting nets. The ground here was like a rough farm at home. There were hedges and ditches, trees, some poor olive-groves, and here and there a vineyard.
>
> All the ravines and water-courses on the distant hills led the winter rainfall into the middle of the basin, and in August we found in the clayey soil hoof-marks and foot-marks inches deep, made in the previous winter, when the farms were a puddle, and the farmers were at peace, and now baked and set till the rains should come again.
>
> Our division held the middle of the basin. My battalion was on the left flank of the divisional sector, and my left-hand company was on rising ground,

where the slope of the northern hills began. The battalion trenches were shaped like a bent bow with an arrow on it. The front trench was the string, about three-quarters of a mile long. From each end a communication trench led back. These curved towards each other and met some 300 yards behind the firing-line. They formed the bow. The arrow was a third trench, which was really a field ditch dug out and widened, which ran from the middle of the front line to the junction of the two communication trenches. Battalion headquarters were just off this straight trench on the south side. A trench with a fire-step led to them, and from this ran several narrow slits in the ground 2 feet wide and 6 feet deep. Each of these opened out into a small room, about 6 feet by 7, in which an officer, or some men lived. One room was a good deal larger than the others. This was the mess-room. These rooms were covered with corrugated iron and a few inches of earth, and in them lived four or five officers and about twenty men, runners, signallers, and the like.

Not exactly the Ritz — but British soldiers are very adaptable creatures and tend to make the best of a bad job. Colonel Bendall continued his narrative thus:

It was a Friday in the last week of November 1915. I had been out some hours with the Brigadier and the other C.O.'s, walking over the line of the trench which was being dug close to the beach to cover the evacuation, which we knew was coming. Heavy rain had fallen all day, and I was very wet. When I got back to my little room in the earth I changed, putting on dry "slacks" and shoes, a British warm overcoat, and a Balaclava helmet, for it was quite cold. The time was about six o'clock, and it was quite dark.

So I walked down my private slit and turned into the mess-room, where we had a lamp. There the second-in-command, the M.O., and the adjutant were sitting on seats made of filled sand-bags, at a rough table made of rum cases. The Adjutant told me nothing had happened, and we all cursed the weather, for the floor was muddy and the roof was dripping. There was an hour before dinner, and we began to discuss the evacuation, some details of which I had learnt during the afternoon.

As we sat talking there were noises of splashing in the slit outside, and a figure of an orderly was dimly seen, saluting with difficulty in the restricted space.

"Front line all correct, sir," he said.

"Very good," said the adjutant, and looked at me.

"All right, Jones, no messages," I said, and the splashing sound faded away up the slit. This was the usual procedure during the hours of darkness. Each company reported to battalion headquarters every hour, and we reported to the brigade.

The rain sounded more heavily than ever, and there were by now some 3 inches on the floor. To keep our feet dry we took the top row of sand-bags from the seats, and used them as footstools. Hopes of a meal seemed rather dim. The cook-house was not likely to be drier than the mess-room, and it would be no joke carrying things along the slit. Even as the M.O. gave voice to this thought there was more splashing, and the adjutant's servant appeared, a waterproof sheet over his head.

"Sorry dinner will be a bit late, sir," he said. "Cook's doing 'is best, but it's raining something awful, and keeps puttin' the primus out."

5—The End

"All right, Smith," said the M.O., who was Mess President on the grounds that he had less to do than anyone else. "Tell him not to worry. We'd sooner have it late and dry," and Smith paddled away.

Colonel Bendall related that while they waited for dinner to arrive:

Another unpleasant quarter of an hour went by, and the water on the floor rose slowly but steadily. Then, almost suddenly, the heavy drumming noise became less heavy, died down to a mere patter and ceased. The M.O., who had on gum-boots, splashed outside and sniffed.

"It's stopped, sir," he said: "I can see a star or two."

"Thank Heaven!" I replied. "If that's so I'll just wade around to my dug-out and see how much of my kit is dry. I'm afraid I didn't cover up my valise."

It was very unpleasant in the slit. The water was over my shoes, and it was pitch dark. Gradually I began to see a little, and by the time I reached my dug-out had picked out several stars to the north.

My dug-out was furnished simply. There was a stretcher resting on filled sand-bags, and a packing-case in the corner. My valise went on the stretcher, and my kit on or under this. I lit a candle and began to pile things on the valise. The cover was turned over, after all, so my flea bag was dry. As I fished about underneath for gum-boots I heard a strange sound. I could have sworn it was the sea, washing on the beach! But the sea and the beach were four miles away. I stood in the doorway and listened. And as I listened in the flickering light there was a curious slapping noise in the slit outside, and a great snake of water came round the curve — breast high — and washed me backwards into the dugout. I was off my feet for a moment, and then, sodden and gasping, I was in the doorway again. Another moment and I was in the open air, and the horror of drowning under the dug-out roof was gone. What was left was bad enough! The water was at my throat, waves of it licked my face. I reached both hands to the top of the walls, but I could get no hold there.

A desperate plight indeed! But Colonel Bendall managed to hold on and gradually extricate himself.

My fingers tore through the mud. Slowly I forced my way along the slit. If I could get to the main headquarters trench I should be better off, for this, like all trenches that faced east, had a fire-step, a broad ledge, some 2 feet from the trench bottom. I do not know how long it was before I turned the last corner. But suddenly I felt that the slit was wider. I turned round and with great difficulty got one foot up. Thank God! There was the ledge. A great heave and I was on it — another heave and scramble and I was on the top — panting and dripping — but out of the water, out of the greasy prison walls of that horrible slit.

I stood there in the dark for a minute to get my breath. Then I called out: "Hullo, headquarters party, is anyone here?"

Answering voices came from a few yards away, and, moving towards them, I found the M.O. and five or six men standing by the hedge which ran along the centre communication trench. They were all sodden and shivering, and the M.O. and one of the men were clearly in a bad way — the others were supporting them. The ground was covered by the water — my feet told me that — and I realized that there was a flood from the hills, and that the water must have come through the Turkish lines. They were worse off than we were! But our lot was bad enough.

I could see the hedge clearly now, and the break in it where the trench I had just left opened into the centre trench. Taking two men with me, I walked carefully to the break, and turned along the headquarters trench, which, of course, I could not see for flood water, calling out as I went. Answers came from more than one point, and I heard the adjutant and the second-in-command. Moving on, I found they were on the top, each with two or three men, but separated from me and each other by the small trenches that led to the dugouts. Gradually, going carefully hand in hand, and feeling with one foot ahead so that we might not step into a hidden trench, we came opposite them, and, as one man had a stick which could reach across the slit, we were able to help them over in turn, and in the end we collected most of the party, though some were missing. We moved cautiously back to the hedge, and in it or near it we spent the night. Most of us stood on the lower branches to keep out of the water. It was bitterly cold. [The poor Medical Officer later died of hypothermia.][77]

"The rain was followed by a piercing north wind and a black frost. With the north wind came snow, and the tempest grew into a veritable blizzard."[78] As *The Times History of the War* stated: "Since the days of the Crimea no British Army had been exposed to more suffering from the elements." The troops were:

frozen, buffeted by wind and sleet with hardly the possibility of motion to keep the circulation alive, the men endured agonies. Sentries watching through the loopholes in the parapet were found dead at their posts when their turn came to be relieved, frozen rigid, their stiff fingers still clutching the rifle with an ironfast grip, the blackened face still leaning, under its sackcloth curtain, against the loopholes.[79]

As Captain Clement Attlee, of the South Lancashire Regiment, 11th (Northern) Division, recalled: "During that time the most notable incident was the blizzard; heavy rain turned our trenches into moats, and frost and snow followed. Numbers of men had to be evacuated with frozen feet, and a good many died."[80]

"There was an unofficial armistice in places where the soldiers of both sides had been forced out of the flooded trenches and huddled in groups in the open with no attempt at concealment and no stomach for a fight. But the guns were still firing from batteries miles behind."[81]

Australian Intelligence Officer, Captain R. Hugh Knyvett, wrote:

Without warning, winter came down upon us. No one guessed he was so near. We were still in our summer clothing, and were not prepared for cold weather, when like a wolf on the fold the blizzard came down upon us. This was the worst enemy those battered troops had yet encountered. Hardly any of the boys had ever seen snow and now they were naked in the bitterest cold. There were more cases of frostbite than there were of wounds in the whole campaign. More had their toes and fingers eaten off by Jack Frost than shells had amputated. In those open, unprotected trenches, in misery such as they had never dreamed could be, the lads from sunny Australia stood to their posts. When the snow melted the trenches fell in and Turk and Anzac stood exposed to each other's fire, but both were fighting a common enemy and so hard went this battle with them as to compel a truce in the fight of man against man.[82]

A fellow Australian, Official Correspondent Captain C.E.W. Bean, in his *Official History of Australia in the War: The Story of Anzac: From the 4th of May Until the Evacuation of the Gallipoli Peninsula* recorded that:

> A destroyer was driven ashore in Suvla Bay. At Anzac the trenches were filled with water, and streams roared down the gullies. The fate of Suvla was more terrible. Across a long and deep ravine leading obliquely down from the "whale-back" ridge of the Kiretch Tepe Sirt, high parapets had been constructed by Turks and British alike. Against these parapets the water was dammed up, as in a reservoir. They gave way, as when a reservoir's embankment bursts, and the weight of accumulated water swept down the ravine into the valley, and from the valley into the Salt Lake and the shore, bearing with it stores and equipment, and mule-carts and mules, and the drowning bodies of Turks and Britons, united in vain struggles against the overwhelming power of nature. Along other sections of the lines, the men stood miserably in the trenches, soaked to the skin, and in places up to the waists in water.
>
> Then, of a sudden, the wind swung round to the north and fell upon the wrecked and inundated scene with icy blast. For nearly two days and nights snow descended in whirling blizzards, and two days and nights of bitter frost succeeded the snow. The surface of the pools and trenches froze thick. The men's greatcoats, being soaked through with the rain, froze stiff upon them. Men staggered down from the lines numbed and bemused with the intensity of the cold. They could neither hear nor speak, but stared about them like bemused bullocks. The sentries and outposts in the advanced trenches could not pull the triggers of their rifles for the cold.... Few can realize the suffering of those four days.[83]

Owing to the gale-force winds and the abysmal conditions no troop transports could leave the harbor, so the 54th's move was canceled. They had no bivouacs, their clothes and equipment were sodden, and the officers had no greatcoats or blankets, the only shelter available were water-filled dugouts, and because of the difficulties of supply "all ranks were on half-rations."[84] One can imagine the absolute misery of such a situation, and of the three sectors, the troops on the Suvla Plain were the most vulnerable as the flood waters rushed down the gullies from the heights to literally sweep men and matter away.[85] Some even drowned; others abandoned the dubious safety of the trenches to climb onto the parapets and paradoses (earthworks or sandbagged protective shields at the rear of a trench) to risk drawing fire from the enemy. Either the enemy were too preoccupied with their own plight, or inclined to compassion when they witnessed that of the other, but there is no instance of the Turks taking advantage of a helpless enemy. This is very much in keeping with the popular concept of "Johnny

Turk," among ANZAC and British alike. He won esteem as a warrior and for his gentlemanly attitude to war, such as not using poison gas.

The severe wintry weather, which followed hard on the heels of the torrential rains, exacted an awful toll. "... many froze to death. Fifty Gurkhas lost one or both feet from frostbite."[86] Capt. W. Smith, B Company Commander, 1/6th Gurkhas, feelingly described the horrors of this terrible period:

> The 29th was the first time since the 26th evening that I was able to get off the men's boots, and the state of their feet appalled me. In nearly every case they had lumps of ice between their toes; their feet were white as far as the ankle and insensible to touch. Throughout all this time I never heard a single complaint. The men were cheerful and ready to laugh at a joke. No praise could be too high for them.[87]

Another primary source witnessed the very same highly commendable trait. Private Jake Mortlock described how his Gurkha ward-companions aboard the hospital ship *en route* to Malta would push their feet out of the beds to relieve the pain in their frostbitten toes.[88]

The Regimental History of the Royal Hampshire Regiment states "the great November blizzard was perhaps less felt at Anzac than at Suvla. Being high up in the hills the 163rd Brigade [54th Division] escaped the flooding from which the troops in the lower ground suffered so severely."[89]

Finally the weather improved enough so that the 54th (East Anglian) Division came out of the line. Once this happened the Suffolk Yeomanry and the other regiments of the Eastern Mounted Brigade found themselves allotted to Major-General Godley's Australian and New Zealand Army Corps. They were the only English troops in the corps. The last personnel left the peninsula on December 21st, eventually bound for Egypt. Total casualties suffered by the Suffolk Yeomanry in ten weeks were 11 officers and 282 other ranks—the majority caused by sickness.[90] The 1/8th Battalion the Hampshire Regiment left the peninsula for Mudros on the 3rd December, and after ten days in camp thereat sailed for Alexandria aboard HMS *Victorious* on the 15th.[91] As for the 1/5th Suffolk: "Eventually, after many warnings and cancellations, the battalion, consisting of 19 Officers and 249 other ranks, embarked on HMT *Osmanieh* during the night of December 6th/7th.... On December 19th we disembarked at Alexandria.... We had reached a land of peace and plenty at last!"[92] Likewise other units of the Division sailed for Egypt where the prospect of rest, rejuvenation, and a return to good health were almost immediately invigorating.[93] Speaking in the House of Commons the following day (20th December, 1915) Lloyd George used the following words: "Having in mind the fatal tardiness which had brought so much disaster to the Allied cause in the Dardanelles, the Balkans, Russia and Mesopotamia:

... Too late in moving here, too late in arriving there, too late in coming to this decision, too late in starting with enterprises, too late in preparing! In this war the footsteps of the Allies have been dogged by the mocking spectre of 'too late,' and unless we quicken our movements damnation will fall on the sacred cause for which so much gallant blood has flowed....

"That summed up my considered opinion at the time on the muddled campaign of 1915. That is my judgment today [1933] after a careful perusal of all the documents and histories written on the subject from every point of view."[94]

Thus the unhappy saga of the Dardanelles venture drew steadily to its conclusion, and although some on the other side expected that the British would turn Cape Helles into another Gibraltar, no one with any influence in Whitehall ever advocated an indefinite stay of that nature. As before at the landings in April and August, the Royal Navy bore the brunt of the burden of arranging, supplying, and carrying out transportation. Only this time it evacuated the Mediterranean Expeditionary Force, which in palmier days Lord Kitchener designated "the Constantinople Expeditionary Force," and only (of ill omen?) its newly appointed Commander-in-Chief persuaded him to change it for something less presumptuous.[95] Of all the operations conducted in the Dardanelles theater this, the evacuation, was by far the most brilliantly executed. An unqualified success, with only two casualties. The German Commander-in-Chief General Liman von Sanders confessed that he did not at all suspect what was about to happen.[96] However, at least one voice of cynicism echoes through the Halls of Time, it is that of Private Jake Mortlock when he commented on this much-vaunted operation, the evacuation of the peninsula: "They *knew* we were going; they *let* us go."[97]

Successful it was, although the Allied armies left behind a prodigious quantity of undestroyed *materiél*. Marshal Otto Liman von Sanders stated that it took two years to remove the vast amounts of stores and equipment. He specified at length what some of it consisted of:

Between Suvla Bay and Ari Burnu five small steamers and more than sixty boats were abandoned on the beach. We found large quantities of material for dummy rail lines, telephones and obstacles, piles of tools of all kinds, medicine chests, medical supplies, and water filters.

A great mass of artillery and infantry ammunition had been abandoned and whole lines of carriages and caissons, hand guns of all kinds, boxes of hand grenades and machine gun barrels. Many stacks of conserves, flour, food and mountains of wood were found. The tent camps had been left standing and sacrificed. This probably served better than anything else to mask the withdrawal.[98]

The haul at Helles was even greater, Marshal Liman von Sanders recounted:

The booty at the south group was extraordinary. Wagon parks, automobile parks, mountains of arms, ammunition and entrenching tools were collected. Here too most of the tent camps and barracks had been left standing, in part with all their equipment.... The immense booty of war material was used for other Turkish armies. Many ship loads of conserves, flour and wood were removed to Constantinople. What the ragged and insufficiently nourished Turkish soldiers took away, cannot be estimated. I tried to stop plundering by a dense line of sentinels but the endeavour was in vain. During the ensuing time we saw the Turkish soldiers on the peninsula in the most incredible garments which they had made up from every kind of uniform. They even carried British gas masks for fun. There were also hundreds of dead mules and horses which were shot to deny their usefulness to the enemy, although quite a few of each were captured and turned over to the Turkish artillery. And in the end the line had not advanced further than at 30 August.[99] [See Maps J and N.]

Among all the accolades and exuberant praise for the Allied accomplishment Henry Nevinson soberly observed:

No doubt they [the enemy] were glad at our going; naturally they were glad. And so, by the evacuation, our authorities, whether political or military, were acting contrary to Napoleon's maxim of war: "Never do what you know your enemy wants you to do."[100]

Where did they go after evacuation? Those who survived saw action at Salonika, Mesopotamia, or the Western Front — Bullecourt, Festubert, the Somme, Arras, Vimy Ridge, Ypres, Passchendaele, Cambrai, Albert and Amiens. The 54th (East Anglian) Division and its infantry battalions, including the 1/5th Suffolks, remained in Egypt to press into the Sinai desert, up to Gaza, Palestine, Syria, and ending up in Beirut. They earned the nickname of "Allenby's pets," as most British troops in Palestine were hastily recalled to help stem the alarmingly successful German offensive breakthroughs on the Western Front in the spring and summer of 1918. Private Mortlock recalled they had actually entrained for that theater when the order was canceled.[101] Those who did not live to fight another day lay, in the prophetic words of one of them, "in some corner of a foreign field...."[102] Sadly, poor 2nd Lieutenant Priestman, the sketching scoutmaster of the 6th York and Lancaster Regiment, 11th Division, was one.

The Suvla *fiasco*, which aroused bitter controversy in Britain, effectively negated the entire Gallipoli Campaign. In some ways it also sounded the death-knell of the British Empire, whose mighty Royal Navy, and companion Mediterranean Expeditionary Force, in not achieving their objectives, in reality sustained a humiliating defeat. All the more significant, in the eyes of world opinion, it was sustained at the hands of the Ottoman Empire, derisively known as "the Sick Man of Europe," and thus was a major contributory factor to the hesitancy of Greece and the decision of Bulgaria to join the Central Powers.

The story of the Gallipoli campaign from the side of the Allies is at once heroic and pitiful, a story of courage and incompetence, and of life, material, and prestige wasted, culminating in a withdrawal in January, 1916.[103]

The blame for the failure to grasp the golden opportunity that presented itself in the early days of August 1915 must rest with the hopelessly incompetent General Stopford and his like-minded subordinate generals. Stopford's vacillating disposition failed to press an advance against the minimal initial resistance doomed the enterprise from the start.[104] The human cost, which victory could seek to justify, would in defeat intone an awful tally of "blood, toil, tears and sweat."[105]

Henry Nevinson and Captain C.E.W. Bean, in their separate works computed identical figures—suggesting they drew from the same source—in their lists of casualties of the British, Dominion and Imperial land forces, including the Royal Naval Division but excluding Navy and French figures. The former's, tabulated in 1917, amounted to:

	Killed	*Wounded*	*Missing*	*Total*
Officers	1,745	3,143	353	5,241
Other ranks	26,455	74,952	10,901	112,308
Totals	28,200	78,095	11,254	117,549

> A large proportion of the missing must be counted as killed. The number of sick admitted to hospital between April 25 and December 11, 1915, was 96,683, of whom also a considerable proportion died. If we may take about one-quarter of the missing as killed, and about one-twentieth of the sick as having died, the total lives lost amounts to about 36,000.
>
> The total losses of the Turks have been variously estimated ... [some inflated as high as half a million] but those estimates are conjectural.[106]

Those of the Official Historian's, compiled after the war, break down to figures which suggest an almost equal human cost if the French casualties are included; i.e., Allied and Turco-German each at around a quarter of a million.[107] *The Official History* states that a total 410,000 British, ANZAC and Imperial, and 79,000 French and French Colonial, troops took part in the Gallipoli Campaign.

> Of this total 43,000 British officers and men had been killed, taken prisoner, or posted as missing, or had died of wounds or disease. The total British casualties, including those evacuated sick, had amounted to 205,000; those of the French to 47,000. By a curious coincidence, the Turkish casualties are placed by the Turkish official account at the almost identical figure of 251,000; but Turkish records were very loosely kept, and other Turkish authorities place the total losses as high as 350,000.[108]

Marshal Liman von Sanders, the Commander-in-Chief of the other side, in his *Five Years in Turkey*, gives figures which certainly warrant as much credence as the foregoing:

The total loss of the Fifth Army in the Dardanelles Campaign is very high and corresponds to the duration and severity of the fighting. It amounted to about 218,000 men, of whom 66,000 were killed and of the wounded 42,000 were returned to duty. There were Turkish infantry regiments which in this campaign needed and received 5,000 replacements.[109]

One of those evacuated sick was Private Jake Mortlock. He was eventually transported to Malta in a hospital ship along with Gurkhas suffering from frost bitten toes.[110] At No. 1674 in the Isolation Block of Imtarfa Hospital[111] in the Maltese interior he lay in a ward where night and day he listened to the sounds of church and convent bells continually tolling and chiming. There, in the watches of the night, he claimed his fevered brain heard the duty nurse say to the doctor making his rounds, "I don't think he'll be with us in the morning." He resolved he would, and was. Early in the New Year (1916) he was transported to Blighty and St. Bartholomew's Hospital in London. Paralyzed from the waist down and fed by tubes through the nostrils, he wasted down to six stones (84 pounds). Electrical-shock treatment, administered *via* feet immersed in water, gradually restored the use of his lower limbs, and Time, the great healer, took care of the rest. The love of an Australian nurse may also have helped. Within a year of leaving Gallipoli, Private Mortlock rejoined his remaining comrades of D Company, 1/5th Battalion, the Suffolk Regiment in Egypt to serve on active duty in Sinai, Palestine and Syria. He went "over the top" in practically all the battles. Certainly he was actively engaged in the three attempts to take Gaza—in particular the fighting for the El Arish Redoubt in the third and successful Battle of Gaza, where he mortally wounded a Turkish sniper. He celebrated the Armistice in Beirut.[112] After demobilization early in 1919 he resumed working on the family farm in Worlington. He served throughout the Second World War in the Special Constabulary. He died in a hospital at Bury St. Edmunds on December 23, 1971, aged 76.

Regarding some of the other primary sources: Sergeant John Hargrave went to Salonika whence he was evacuated sick in 1916 and declared unfit for further military service. After his discharge, as its chief, "White Fox," he founded a boys' organization to rival the Boy Scouts. This, however, perished due to adverse reaction to the Fascist paramilitary movements. He also became an inventor of considerable talent, an advanced navigational instrument being the one for which he is best known. In addition he established a semi-political social-credit group which gained a greater following in Canada than in the U.K. Major John Gillam served in France where he was awarded the Distinguished Service Order (D.S.O.). Returning to the City as a businessman he fell in love with a spunky salesgirl at Harrods whom he introduced to the London stage. She later became the celebrated Sheila Graham, authoress of *Beloved Infidel*—her account of her liaison with

F. Scott Fitzgerald.¹¹³ Padre Dennis Jones was appointed precentor of Manchester Cathedral, a post he held for many years. Sergeant Cyril Lawrence of the Australian Engineers went to the Western Front, where he received decorations for bravery and a commission. There he admitted that he radically changed his opinions of the British "Tommies" for the better.¹¹⁴ In peacetime he rose to become one of Australia's leading civil engineers. The violin-playing New Zealand infantryman, Alexander Aitken, entered academia, rising to become a university professor of mathematics, a Fellow of the Royal Society, and a scholar of some considerable renown. His account of his wartime experiences, *Gallipoli to the Somme: Recollections of a New Zealand Infantryman*, won the 1963 Hawthornden prize. Lance-Corporal Albert Collen served in France, Flanders and Salonika; he also fought with the British contingents sent to support the White Russians in their struggle with the Bolsheviks. After all this excitement he returned to work on his family's farm in Worlington.¹¹⁵ Reginald Lane followed the fortunes of the 1/5th Suffolks until late 1917 when he was commissioned into the Egyptian Labour Corps and later posted to France. After the war he married and settled in Queen Adelaide, Ely, Cambridgeshire. There he secured a job at the first sugar beet processing factory in Britain (Ely), eventually rising to an executive position. Captain E.D. Wolton, one of the 1/5th Suffolks' historians, ended up as an auctioneer and valuer with the family firm. Sergeant George How — after having been detailed to stay behind in Egypt to help deal with the riots and tumults that followed the end of the war — eventually resumed his civilian occupation as a miller, and later became the licensee of the Golden Boar public house in Freckenham.

Poor 2nd Lieutenant Edmund Priestman was killed in an engagement in which he displayed the utmost gallantry; his remains are interred in a cemetery near where he fell on the Kiretch Tepe Ridge. In the words of the idolized Georgian poet, Sub-Lieutenant Rupert Brooke, yet another name on the horrendous list of a massacred generation:

> These laid the world away; poured out the red
> Sweet wine of youth; gave up the years to be
> Of work and joy, and that unhoped serene,
> That men call age; and those who would have been,
> Their sons, they gave, their immortality.¹¹⁶

Of some of the other actors in the tragedy of Suvla Bay who survived the War: Lt.-Col. Frederic W. D. Bendall, who not only survived the floods and blizzard but wrote such a graphic account of those horrors, went on to be wounded in France and mentioned twice in dispatches. Promoted to full Colonel and created a C.M.G., he later became Director of Army Education at the War Office, 1940–42. Retiring to live in a small village in Hampshire, he died at an uncertain date. General Sir Ian Hamilton received no further commands during the war. He published his account of the operation in 1920, and died in London on October 12, 1947, aged 94. General the Hon. Sir Frederick Stopford resumed his post as Lord Lieutenant of the Tower of London. He never commanded troops in the field again. He retired in 1920 and died in 1929, aged 75. Stopford's Chief of Staff—the man who sowed the seed of uncertainty in the Corps Commander's mind—Major-General Hamilton Lyster Reed, V.C., went on to command the 15th (Scottish) Division, 1917–1918. He was General Officer Commanding the 52nd (Lowland) Division, Territorial Army, from 1923 to 1927. He retired on pay in 1928, and died on March 7, 1931, aged 61 or 62. Major-General Frederick Hammersley—whose Great War service is overlooked by all volumes of both *Who's Who* and *Who Was Who*—died on March 28, 1924, at the age of 65. Lieutenant-General Sir Bryan Mahon, one of the few Suvla generals to show any enterprise, went on to command the British Salonika Expeditionary Force, 1915–1918, and initially the Allied Army of Salonika, 1915–1916—until the appointment of the French General Maurice Sarrail as Commander-in-Chief. He emerged with an agreeable amount of credit, and the Grand Cross White Eagle of Serbia (1917) to boot. He retired on pay with the rank of general in 1921, and died at his country residence in County Kildare on September 24, 1930, aged 68. Like Mahon, General Sir William Birdwood was one of the few senior officers to emerge from the Gallipoli Campaign with an undamaged reputation. Promoted Lieutenant-General in August 1915, and knighted later the same year, Birdwood continued to lead the Australian and New Zealand Army Corps (ANZAC)—now on the Western Front—until the end of May 1918, when he took over command of the reconstituted British Fifth Army. Promoted to full general in 1917 he guided the Fifth Army through the climactic Courtrai Offensive in the autumn of 1918. He died in 1951, aged 85. The Chief of the General Staff of the Mediterranean Expeditionary Force throughout Sir Ian Hamilton's tour of duty, Major-General Walter Pipon Braithwaite, served throughout the war and was awarded many foreign decorations. He was knighted in 1918, and retired on pay in 1931 with the rank of general. He died September 8, 1945, at the age of 79. The Commanding Officer of the 54th (East Anglian) Division, Major-General Francis Seymour Inglefield, went with his division to Egypt, and remained in command for a time, 1915–1916, until forced to leave because of health reasons. He retired from the Army and died on July 23, 1930, at the age of 74. One of the most enthusiastic and confident advocates of the Dardanelles strategy, Admiral of the Fleet Sir Roger Keyes continued his naval service well into World War II, when he was appointed Director of Combined Operations 1940–1941. He was created Baron Keyes

5—The End

of Zeebrugge and Dover in 1943. He died on December 26, 1945, at the age of 72. Brevet Colonel Thomas Gibbons commanded the 1/5th Battalion of the Essex Regiment for the remainder of the war in Egypt, Palestine, and Syria. Thrice wounded, he was awarded the D.S.O. and the Order of the Nile, 3rd Class. He, in fact, stayed in Egypt until the early summer of 1919, playing an active role in controlling the riots and unrest that occurred in the spring. Returning to Dunmow, he resumed his position as a partner in the Dunmow Brewery firm of Randall, Gibbons, Ingold & Company, and, also, of course, published a truly splendid account of the fortunes of his command in *With the 1/5th Essex in the East* in 1921. The exact date of his death is somewhat uncertain, sometime in 1943 or 1944, which would make him around seventy. The valiant and much-decorated Captain Oskar Teichman went on to serve in Egypt and Palestine, and ended the War on the Italian front. He continued his fascinating diary entries throughout the entire war.

On the other side, Field Marshal Otto Liman von Sanders retained high command of forces of the Ottoman Empire until after the war. On February 27, 1918, he was given the thankless and impossible task of shoring up the Turkish front in Palestine as commander of Army Group F in Syria, and twice repelled British attacks in the Jordan Valley. But denied supplies and reinforcements by Enver Pasha, the War Minister, and the new German Chief of the General Staff, General Hans von Seeckt, he was unable to check the eventual breakthrough. After the Armistice he returned to Constantinople until January 1919 to oversee the repatriation of German troops in Asia Minor. On his way home in February, the British held "Pasha Liman" at Malta for six months as a suspected war criminal. Finally released in August, he was permitted to return home. Field Marshal Liman von Sanders retired from the army in October 1919 at the age of 64 to write his memoirs, and he died in Munich on August 22, 1929, aged 74. German historian Ulrich Trumpener described him as "one of the most capable field commanders the Turks had during the war." Also it should not be overlooked that in November he energetically — albeit, unsuccessfully — attempted to halt the Armenian deportations to Smyrna. General Mustapha Kemal, whose rugged determination was largely responsible for the thwarting of the Allied aims at Gallipoli, rose rapidly from divisional commander, to corps and army commander opposing the Russians on the Caucasian front during 1916–17. He alone emerged with any credit. His reward was an army command in Syria for the 1917 Yilderim offensive to recapture Baghdad, but his army was diverted to meet the menacing British advance out of Egypt. But disagreeing strongly with his government's policy, he resigned his command. In the closing months of the war, the young general gave a final display of his skills. In August 1918, he took charge of the skeletal remains of the Seventh Army in Palestine. Harried by British cavalry and Arab insurgents,

Kemal conducted a fighting retreat from Palestine to Damascus, and finally to Aleppo. By the close of the war, Kemal, by then an army group commander, held the southern gateway to Anatolia. One historian's assessment has him "the greatest Ottoman military hero to emerge from the war." It was after the war, however, that he truly rose to the occasion by defending the Turkish nation, opposing its partition, and expelling the Greeks. Afterwards he was instrumental in the modernizing, westernizing and secularizing of the Republic of Turkey.[117] Known as "Ataturk," he died in Istanbul (Constantinople) of cirrhosis of the liver on November 10, 1938, aged 58. Enver Pasha, of whom it has been said that his strategic ambitions outran his talents, left his country with German assistance in November 1918. After a shadowy career in exile he finally took up the cause of the Turkic peoples of Central Asia, joining them in combat against Soviet rule. He was killed in a clash with the Red Army on August 4, 1922; he was only 40 years old.[118]

Practically everyone connected with the Dardanelles exploits, who survived, has passed on. Those few who still remain are most certainly centenarians at this time (2007).

6

The Conclusion

The strategically sound conception of the August Plan that could, and indeed should, have been the masterstroke of the Gallipoli Campaign was bungled at Suvla,[1] not amongst the high peaks of the Sari Bair range at Anzac. At Suvla the golden opportunity to redeem past blunders on this peninsula slipped away. The August landings at Suvla Bay successfully achieved complete surprise, and because of this, unlike those in April, suffered remarkably few casualties. But these failed because of lamentable faults which followed in the train of their execution. "At Suvla the root of the failure to develop a splendid opening and exploit surprise must lie at the door of Corps and Divisional headquarters, where energy, initiative and promptitude in appreciating the situation and the urgent value of time were conspicuously lacking."[2] One of the — if not *the* — leading scholars in the field of Official War Histories, Professor Andrew Green, maintains that Brig.-Gen. Cecil Aspinall-Oglander, author of *Official History of the War: Military Operations; Gallipoli*, "... succeeded in publishing an Official History not just of great academic integrity but of great literary interest."[3]

Until August, the Allied local commanders apparently lacked any strategical conceptions other than those of forlorn hope. Indeed, it is debatable whether they possessed the requisite troops and munitions to permit any other. Certainly General Sir Ian Hamilton, the Commander-in-Chief of the Mediterranean Expeditionary Force, continually stressed these two chronic shortages in his frequent telegraphic correspondence with the British Secretary of State for War, Lord Kitchener. The combined Suvla-Anzac maneuver of the August Plan, which followed, was of a different order. It was a sound plan; there were sufficient forces enough to carry it out. Thrusting between the two Anafarta villages and penetrating along the Kiretch Tepe Ridge would have cut off both the Anzac and Cape Helles Turkish garrisons, and such a success would have given the Allies the whole western shore of the Dardanelles — allowing the naval task force to force through to the Marmora. On the opposing side, the Commander-in-Chief of the Turkish Fifth Army entrusted with the defense of the Gallipoli Peninsula, Marshal Otto Liman von Sanders, and his subordinates, Colonels Mustapha Kemal

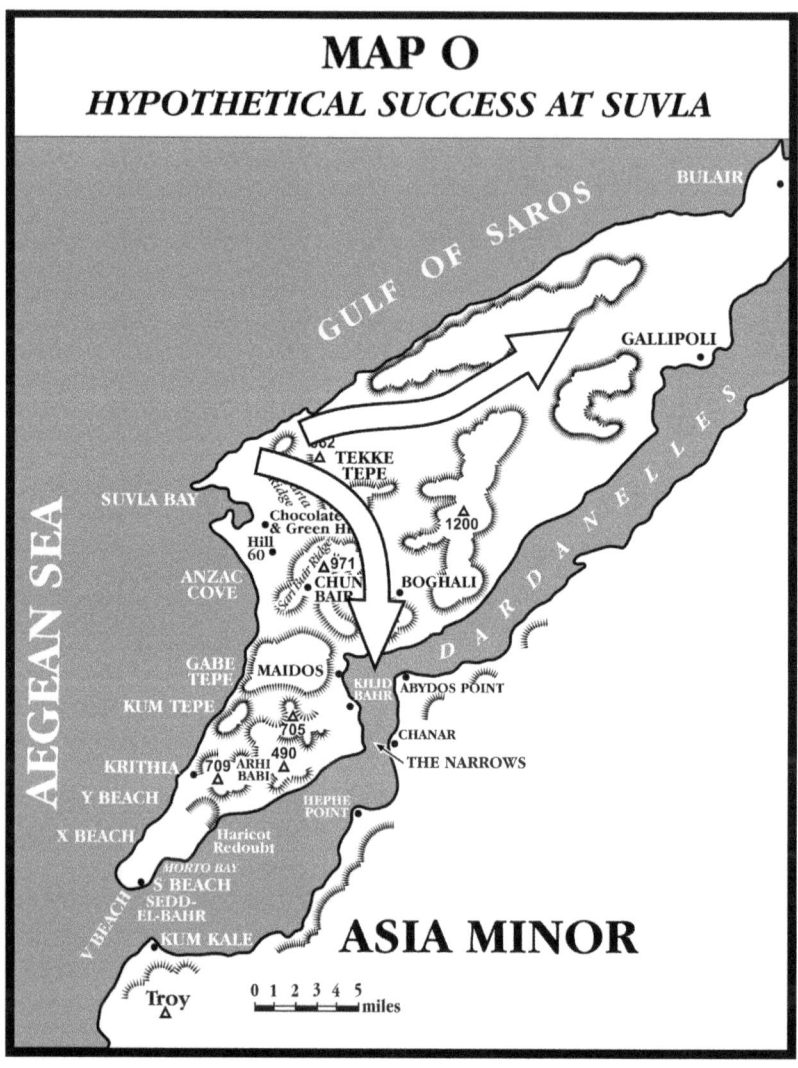

and Hans Kannengiesser, adjudged that there was a very great danger of that likelihood. Clement Attlee, later in life, spoke with conviction of potential success. However, David Lloyd George aptly summarized the dual handicaps of amateur attitude and bumbling incompetence which unfortunately characterized the British approach:

> A small force of a few thousands landed in time would easily have overwhelmed the wretched garrison to whom the defence of Gallipoli had been entrusted by the careless Turks. When we sent an army numbering tens of

thousands to attack in April, Turkish reinforcements had arrived which were strong enough to prevent us capturing one of our objectives. We were always too late. We ran race after race with the sluggish Turks and each time he invariably won, and arrived first at the winning post. He delayed and procrastinated according to his wont, but we beat him in the dawdling game. He gave us many chances and we never took one.... As soon as they [the Germans] saw how feckless our efforts were in the Dardanelles they ceased to worry about that operation and postponed dealing with it until the autumn. They were right. Scores of thousands of Allied troops fell in belated and therefore fruitless assaults on Achi Baba and the heights above Suvla and in clinging to the rocky slopes of Anzac.[4]

The principal fault which lost this priceless chance of open warfare across the Suvla Plain and up the Anafarta Heights was the shameful indecision of the 9th Army Corps Commander, Lieutenant-General the Honourable Sir Frederick Stopford, and certain other equally dilatory and incompetent officers, in particular Hammersley, Sitwell, and Lindley. As one historian summed it up:

On August 6 a new landing was made at Suvla Bay which found the Turks wholly unprepared. Then a swift and vigorous advance might have given Stopford's troops the Anafarta Ridge, which was the key to the whole position. But the opportunity was missed. While forty-eight precious hours were lost by his assailants, Mustapha Kemal Bey, a young Turkish officer, collected a sufficiency of troops and, rushing to the vital point, saved the situation.[5]

General Stopford's altogether preposterous excuse for not ordering an advance along the strategically crucial Kiretch Tepe Ridge, that it would lead to "a regular battle," is unbelievable coming from the mouth of a wartime army commander. (Forty-two years later Private Jake Mortlock reacted with incredulity upon reading about the incident in Alan Moorehead's *Gallipoli*— "That's what we were there for!"[6]) Equally incredible, the Commander-in-Chief, to whom the plea was directed, kept the obvious *riposte* to himself, contenting himself to merely inscribing it later in his diary. At this point he should have spoken bluntly and insisted on an immediate move to seize the objectives of the August Plan. He, himself, in a retrospective judgment contained in his *Final Despatch*, admitted that inertia was allowed to prevail on the beaches of Suvla Bay. *The Times* (London) pronounced that it "was not the inexperience of the troops, nor the lack of water, but the incompetence of some of the Corps and Divisional commanders" that ultimately doomed the operation.[7] Gallipoli war correspondent, Ellis Ashmead-Bartlett, wrote: "The Staff failed, Stopford mishandled the 9th Corps, the divisional commanders muddled their divisions, and the brigadiers their brigades."[8] *The Times* also believed that "Sir Ian Hamilton cannot escape some share of the criticism he quite rightly applies to others."[9] Able Seaman Joseph

Murray of Hood Battalion, the Royal Naval Division, nicely summarized the failure at Suvla in a fitting epitaph written in his diary in early 1916:

> Perhaps as the years roll by we will be remembered as the expedition that was betrayed by jealousy, spite, indecision and treachery. The Turks did not beat us—we were beaten by our own High Command.[10]

The failure of the 9th Army Corps to advance in accordance with the August Plan timetable meant that they did not occupy the features vital to success, which of itself would have secured wells yielding an abundance of water. (See Maps E and F.) In addition, it allowed vast numbers of troops to congest the restricted beachheads, which magnified the confusion, and exacerbated the problem of water supply to the firing lines, as Midshipman Denham, Colonel Aspinall, Henry Nevinson, Henry Hanna and others related.

Nor can the Commander-in-Chief of the Mediterranean Expeditionary Force escape responsibility. He let the element of surprise, which Lord Kitchener, in a pre-Suvla message, so clearly emphasized was an absolute essential ingredient of successful warfare, slip away completely. Neither did Hamilton project or inject much of the "energy and dash" he himself said was needed into the Suvla situation until it was too late. Everything, even his dismissal, he took with the graciousness of a truly refined gentleman, when occasion demanded a bit of the bully-boy approach of a Hunter-Weston. He needed to recapture the spirit with which he inspired his men before the Battle of Elandslaagte on 21 October 1899, when he told them that the next morning newsboys in the streets of London would be calling out the news of their victory. The same spirit that, with conspicuous bravery, he later rallied them at a critical moment during an enemy counter-attack.

After the failure at Suvla Bay the whole Gallipoli enterprise was doomed, unless another large reinforcement of men and *materiél* had enabled the prompt delivery of yet a further stroke. But the skeptical and unhelpful attitudes of many of the members of the Dardanelles Committee, plus the projected battle of Loos and the commitment to the Salonika venture, resulted in Gallipoli being put on hold. When Bulgaria came into the war on the side of the Central Powers it opened up a vital supply route which linked Germany's industrial might to Turkey's war efforts and the chance was lost forever.

At the very core of the Suvla *débâcle* was the British class system. In a society still in some respects largely feudal and which retained much of its structural origins there was, and is, a definite and clearly delineated system of class strata. The retention of the monarchy and the continued existence of vast land-owning lesser lords are obvious illustrations of this. Other aspects are not so apparent. There was, however, a great difference between the aristocracy, the upper, upper-middle, and middle classes on the one hand, and the working class on the other. This disparity was even more accentuated by the education the children of the different classes received.[11] The British public school system[12] (which means exactly the opposite of the American model) is primarily a preserve of the middle and upper classes and the aristocracy. All of the leading public schools could be categorized on a par with Eton.

> Eton College in the eighteen-seventies and eighteen-eighties was a vast incubator dedicatedly engaged in the task of hatching out the future rulers of the greatest Empire the world has ever known. From the headmaster down to the youngest fag in the school, everyone was serenely aware that the cachet of an Eton education would, in future life, put every scholar two jumps ahead of the rest in the race for the choicest positions in politics, the Church, diplomacy and the more rewarding branches of the Civil Service. It was the most exclusive, and the most influential club in the world; and any boy who did well could be sure that, at the head of practically every department of the State, there was an Old Member waiting with a helping hand and promise of preferment.[13]

"A public school and then club life in Oxford or Cambridge, and then another club in town; London in June, when London is pleasant, the moors in August, and pheasants in October, Cannes in December, and hunting in February and March."[14] It lays firm foundations, from preparatory-school days onwards, for the turning out of a breed of human beings superior in intellect, accent, culture and manners. What Matthew Arnold described as "the religion of inequality," and what Disraeli wrote of as the formation of "two nations"—Marx's "*bourgeoisie* and proletariat."[15] In other words, a breed that thinks, speaks, and acts differently. Patrician, as opposed to plebeian. Journalist Jack Pitman, in his delightfully malicious book, *England Ebbing*, wrote:

> But most of all, class is linguistic. One false step, one slip of the tongue, and the game's up. How one speaks, the inflection, locutions, accent, and the like, can literally mean the difference between life and limbo. Language is simply the great stigmata.[16]

The products of the public school system automatically gravitated to Oxford, Cambridge, the Royal Military Academy at Sandhurst, the Royal Naval College at Dartmouth, and Cranwell, the home of the Royal Air Force Academy. They dominated Parliament, the judiciary, academia, the City, the Civil Service, the *Corps Diplomatique*, the armed services, most of the other professions, and the Church of England—the established church. Since Eton, Harrow, Rugby, Marlborough, Charterhouse, and the rest were exclusively boys' schools the above-mentioned occupations were consequently preponderantly peopled by males. After leaving public school, a common bond, "the Old School Tie," still unites the "Old Boys," as they are called.[17] This brotherhood is steeped in courtesy, chivalry, and gentility, with an innate abhorrence of anything that is "not cricket." Compton Mackenzie confessed he distrusted it.[18] The system spawned two distinct types of fellow, one the soft aesthete, the other the manly athlete. Robert Graves in his largely autobiographical *Goodbye to All That* nicely differentiated these divergent species, as, to a lesser extent, did R.C. Sheriff in his play *Journey's End*. Much of Hamilton's makeup smacked of the former, with his slightly effeminate posture and his penchant for poetry. Furthermore it also spawned — as another commentator put it — "… a slack, uncompetitive crowd of 'leaders' brought up on a games ethic where the point was not to win but to 'play the game'; where team spirit was more important than team victory."[19]

The same "Old School Tie" mentality impeded Sir Ian Hamilton's ability to exert effective leadership in his role as Commander-in-Chief of the Mediterranean Expeditionary Force. He did not like to interfere, intervene, countermand, or reprimand. Largely due to this attitude, the unopposed "Y" Beach landing of 25 April went unexploited, as he did not wish to question Hunter-Weston's judgment. He allowed Stopford to waste the precious days at Suvla, and at the crucial battle for Scimitar Hill and the Ismail Oglu Tepe he took a back seat rather than "bother de Lisle." Stopford to a lesser extent suffered from the same constraints. When he did condescend to go ashore after Aspinall's agitated visit he returned to the *Jonquil* without so much as speaking to the officer and gentleman he specifically went to see. This was because one of Hammersley's staff-officers told him that General Hammersley planned an offensive for the following day (9 August), and one does not question the word of a gentleman. As John Hargrave observed:

> We may wonder whether, in fact, we are dealing with a pack of incompetent Old Army Generals who misunderstood their "perfectly clear" orders— or with various forms of dry-rot at the top of the Victorian/Edwardian social structure? Perhaps of our phase of civilization?[20]

There was also the easy informality of the Mess and the Club. "Freddie" Stopford, "Hunter-Bunter," "Young Brodrick," "Birdie," "Bobs," and "K." They still called on one another, lunched or dined together, were waited upon by servants, and enjoyed the nicer things of life, such as ice, table-linen and silverware, only a few hundred yards from the absolute squalor and degradation of the trenches the men they commanded inhabited.

It was not until the First World War, with the partial exception of the South African campaign, that the rigid polarization of the classes in the armed services was broken down. Prior to 1914, a great social gulf existed between the common soldiers immortalized by Kipling, and disparaged by the Duke of Wellington as "the scum of the earth who enlisted for drink," and the commissioned officers who commanded them. Again, this was something similar to the patrician and plebeian concept. Although the "other ranks" might grouse and curse, most subconsciously acknowledged their officers' unquestioned right to, and capability of, leadership. Few had the same respect for those oddities who rose from the ranks on the strength of merit and diligence.

Warfare on the Western Front followed a rigid and predictable timeframe, and had developed its firmly established procedures, of: 1. Heavy artillery bombardment of enemy positions. 2. Massed frontal assault by infantry to penetrate the enemy's defenses. 3. (In theory only.) After the (anticipated) breakthrough of the enemy's lines the cavalry would exploit the breach. 4. Almost automatic counterattacks by the enemy to retake any ground lost in 2. Whereas, in comparison the Suvla Bay landings differed considerably. Firstly, *the element of surprise was absolute.* Secondly, *the successfully accomplished landings met little opposition and suffered few casualties.* Thirdly, *the invading forces enjoyed overwhelming numerical superiority, a ratio of at least seven or eight to one.* Fourthly, *the assaulting troops were supported by the heavy caliber gunfire of the Allied navies' warships, and these vessels possessed ample stocks of ammunition.* Fifthly, and finally, *all of the most important geographical features scheduled for seizure were all well within five miles of the beaches, lightly defended, with minimal entrenchments protected by little or no barbed-wire, and without the possibility of rapid reinforcement.* In plain language *it was the perfect situation for a vigorous thrust.* As Ellis Ashmead-Bartlett wrote at the time: "It was at Suvla where the full main thrust should have been delivered instead of launching forlorn assaults against impregnable semi-mountain positions from Anzac."[21]

Practically all of the troops who landed on the night of 6/7 August and from dawn onwards of 7 August were Kitchener's New Army volunteers. What they lacked in experience and training they more than made up for in patriotism and enthusiasm. Attlee, Cooper, Gillam, Graves, Hall, Hanna, Hargrave, Jones, "Juvenis," Masefield, Priestman, and Raymond all verify this. All they required was efficient, positive, directive leadership from Corps, Divisional and Brigade HQs. The eyewitness accounts of Aspinall, Bush, Cooper, Denham, Hankey, Hanna, Hargrave, "Juvenis," Kannengiesser, Nevinson, Priestman and Willmer do not speak of the landings as a shambles. Just the opposite, both British and German accounts refer to good order and discipline, albeit inappropriate, on the beaches. 2nd Lieutenant Priestman, a scoutmaster, of the 32nd Brigade, 11th (Northern) Division, did not seem at all in the dark as to what his objectives were as he and his men moved forward on schedule to secure them. Likewise Lieutenant "Juvenis" of the Royal Iniskilling Fusiliers, 10th (Irish) Division, gave a similar account. Even when the beaches became thoroughly congested, good order and military discipline were certainly maintained in at least some units. Captain Fair, Captain Wolton, and Corporal Lane of the 1/5th Suffolks all testified to this on the 10 August, and the orderly advance of the Yeomanry under fire on the 21 August surely demonstrated it beyond question. The impetus was there, it only required competent generalship to sustain its forward momentum. This was when the generals squandered the golden opportunity presented to them at Suvla Bay. To borrow Winston Churchill's words: "History will vindicate the conception, and the errors in execution will on the whole leave me clear."[22]

The never-to-be-repeated chance had already slipped away when the Welsh and East Anglian Territorial Divisions landed. The former possessed a general who immediately abdicated his responsibility. Major-General the Honourable John Edward Lindley commanded the 53rd (Welsh) Division for two years prior to Suvla yet as soon as it was ashore confessed he could not control it. The 54th (East Anglian) Division possessed a distinguished veteran commander in Major-General Francis Seymour Inglefield, who, like the men under him, "was keen" for the fray. It will be remembered that the 54th Division arrived on Gallipoli without transport mules, so the soldiers had to manhandle everything, frequently in full battle order. To do so in high summer on one pint of water a day was extremely taxing — if not debilitating. Notwithstanding they performed their allotted tasks in an exemplary manner. The gross mismanagement of the Suvla invasion forces meant it was too late for them or anyone else to turn the tide of battle on the Gallipoli Peninsula. For the 9th Army Corps Commander, with Kaiser-like contempt, to dismiss these Territorial Divisions as "sucked oranges" was to add insult to injury and confirm the truth of the old adage "a bad workman always blames his tools." The Official Historian, Brig.-General Cecil Aspinall-Oglander — who, as a General Staff Officer, was not only one of the chief architects of the Gallipoli Campaign strategy, but was an eyewitness throughout — was not afraid to single out incompetence and failure. While he "avoided attempting to identify a single scapegoat for the misfortune and error of Gallipoli, nevertheless, Hamilton and Stopford, along with their subordinates, suffered explicit criticism which was considerably damaging to their public and military reputations. In addition Kitchener and the government as a whole were openly rebuked for what Aspinall considered their part in the failure."[23]

From 10 August onwards, every death which occurred, or would occur, on the Gallipoli Peninsula was a wasted life, and the bitter rivulets of bereaved mothers' tears would never wash away the purple stain of culpability from the inept hands of Lieutenant-General the Honourable Sir Frederick William Stopford, 9th Army Corps Commander, his staff, and his equally blameworthy subordinate generals. To a lesser extent, because he permitted what he himself called "the fatal inertia on the Suvla beaches" to develop, the Commander-in-Chief of the Mediterranean Expeditionary Force, General Sir Ian Monteith Hamilton, must also bear a burden of responsibility. This is the author's judgment on the failure at Suvla Bay.

Appendix A

"Dead Men's Diaries Laud Turkish Foes"

PATHETIC ENTRIES IN NOTEBOOKS OF BRITISH SOLDIERS WHO FELL AND WERE BURIED BY THE MOSLEMS TELL OF STIFF FIGHTING

One writer thought he bore a charmed life, but finally was slain — showed mental strain.

Source: The New York Times, *Section II, Sunday, August 8, 1915, p. 2, columns 6 & 7.*

GALLIPOLI PENINSULA, June 19 [1915] (Correspondence of The Associated Press.)

Many dead British soldiers have been buried by the Turks—usually after a trench has been taken. Before the body is disposed of it is searched for letters or some other means of identification. In the course of this many interesting documents, among them diaries of fallen officers and men, have been found. A number of these were placed at the disposal of The Associated Press correspondent with permission to copy such parts he might care to make use of.

A dozen of the diaries were read. Parts of them are given here. Life in the trenches is pictured as one long round of "fatigue and squadding" and keeping back the Turks, whom nearly all had come to respect and fear.

The diary of Private R. Charlesworth, Eighth Manchester Regiment, 32 years old, is somewhat typical of those kept by men of his station. There is a quaint charm in his simple description of the trip to Egypt and the installing of the regiment in Mustapha Pasha camp, Alexandria. The insects there were a plague, his diary says, and the men were glad when they were transferred to Polymedia camp, in the island of Cyprus.

Then came references to long route marches and much drill. Later the regiment was sent to Cairo. More marches followed. Many men fell out and often officers with humane inclinations would help some poor enlisted youngster by carrying his rifle for him. The regiment was picked for service in the Dardanelles. It was embarked on the steamer *Ionian* of Glasgow.

For about a month Private Charlesworth fought at Sedd-el-Bahr, life being a series of alternate shifts of "work and rests." Then comes the last entry: "On the 26th (May) we finished the trench. On the 27th we moved to the second line of trenches."

"A march past for Sir Ian Hamilton" in Egypt appears to have been the most important event to another, whose other entries, made in a calendar, consist entirely of "on" and "off" duty and similar routine remarks.

The diary of another contains the owner's will on the inside page of the cover. It reads:

My will: Everything I possess goes to my father.

[Signed] WILFRED HAYES, 6th Batt., Manchester Regiment. The entries are extremely matter-of-fact.

May 15th. Turks advance.

May 16th. One of our officers shot dead.

May 21st. Nothing doing all day.

May 27th. Not a minute's sleep for three days and nights.

May 28th. We were obliged to remove our reserve trench.

May 29th. During the afternoon the 8th B., M. R. (8th Battalion, Manchester Regiment,) were digging in a trench, which they had advanced to during the night, when they were surprised by the Turks. They retired, leaving rifles and equipment behind. The artillery and infantry peppered them. The Eighth Essex were to take back the trench, and the Sixth, who were in the reserve trenches, resting after two nights of advancing and trench digging, had to go and support them. The 8th lost heavily, although the 6th had few casualties. The 8th got the order to advance with fixed bayonets, but funked it, so we 6th would not let them stay in the trench and pushed them over the parapet. Same day a wounded man crawled into our trench and said that a Sergeant and four men were the only survivors in a trench. Reinforcements were sent.

May 30th. We are still in the trenches and are getting very worn and tired.

May 31st. Turks attacking. Eighth unable to hold their own; one of our platoons to aid. The 8th begin to retire, but the Sergeant in charge of the 6th will not allow them to retire.

Then comes the penultimate entry. It reads:

June 3rd. Cousin Richard killed — only me left out of the three of us.

And then the last:

June 4th. [Battle of the Fourth of June/Third Battle of Krithia?] Preparing to take Hill 700 at the point of the bayonet. Twelve o'clock we charge the Turks at the point of the bayonet. Private William Sykes of the Eighth Battalion, Manchester Regiment, who enlisted as No. 2029, at the age of 17 years and 5 months, had nothing but his letters on his person when found. Most of them were written by his mother, a gentle middle-aged woman, according to her photograph, which the boy carried with him. The letters are addressed to: "Our dear son Will." There is a photograph that shows Will among his five sisters and there is another taken when he enlisted showing Will as a chubby youngster with a wondering, innocent stare in his large eyes. He is clothed in a very smart uniform that is a trifle too large. One can almost sense his endeavor to fill it.

The most remarkable document in the lot is that of a Captain F. I. Lynch, regiment unknown. There is some doubt as to the second initial, which may be intended for an "I" or a "J." His diary is well kept, and gives the most minute details, and mirrors a mind constantly under great strain. There are in it many allusions to himself as a "lucky man" or a man with a "charmed life."

The Captain left Rugby on March 17th for Alexandria. The French he met en route he refers to as "those funny little Frenchmen." His stay in Egypt is given in the diary in bleak notes devoid of interest. On April 21st his ship arrived in Saros Bay. On the same day the Turks fired on the British transport *Manita*, with the result that about seventy soldiers jumped overboard, of which number sixty were drowned, according to the entries in Captain Lynch's diary.

Of the many entries a few will be given here in the exact words of Captain Lynch:

> *Sunday, April 25th.*— I was the sole survivor out of a company of eighty-five rank and file, the majority of whom were killed outright. In the morning, just before we retired, I bandaged a Sergeant of the R. M. L. I. [Royal Marines Light Infantry, Royal Naval Division], whose brains were hanging out of the back of his head. A sniper suddenly fired a couple of shots, wounding again some of the wounded. I took a little time to locate the devil, and fired a shot bringing him down a hill 200 feet above. I took the belt from his rifle and put it in my pocket for a keepsake. I was very much surprised to find him to be a German. I gave him a fine death, about six or seven bayonet thrusts just to finish him off. I didn't try to kill him [sic].

On May 15th Captain Lynch speaks of a deserter who had been caught and, as he thinks, will be sentenced to death. Four others, he says, have already been sentenced to death, but sentence had been commuted to ten years penal servitude. Of the four, one was a sergeant-corporal and three were privates, belonging to the Munster Fusiliers and the Worcester Regiment.

There is little sleep to be had, and the Turks give no quarter, says the entry, nor do they permit the care of the wounded and killed, because the German officers are against this. Captain Lynch writes of his own trench as being filled with dead men and accoutrements.

> *May 19th.*— Turks show great pluck. We like the way the Turks come up to us in great bundles as the Germans. You can't help hitting the brutes; they simply walk into our bullets.
>
> *Saturday, May 22nd.*— Had a very narrow escape. Was unbuttoning my greatcoat. I bent my head to see what had happened, when a bullet hit me bang

on the topknot. Had I not bent my head I would have been buried by now. My luck must have been in. The bullet was like a ton of bricks falling on top of me. Fighting at its worst at present. The firing is awful.

Tuesday, May 24th. — The Manchester Brigade has been split up and sent to different units for discipline, some of them giving us great laughs. Of course they are only Terriers [Territorials.]

Saturday, May 29th. — Turkish shells are dropping terribly near. Four fragments of German, French, English, and Turkish made shells. They are splendidly equipped as regards firearms and ammunition.

Tuesday, June 2nd. — Digging communication trenches all day long, wishing we were in the firing line. Getting messed around something awful. Some strong chemicals have been put in the water to discourage men in drinking it. Wrote Addie [wife or *fiancée*?] another letter.

The last entry reads:

Wednesday, 3rd June. — Called out last night to go to base, but the order was very soon cancelled. We are not sorry to go to our beds. Captain Lynch must have mistaken some of the blond Turks, with Georgian and Circassian ancestry, for Germans. An inspection by The Associated Press correspondent of the Sedd-el-Bahr Turkish trenches and camps has established that today [June 19th, 1915] there are not more than a score of Germans at the front and that up to May 4th none at all were active there.

Appendix B

"Why French Left Kum Kale"

COULDN'T HOLD THE ASIATIC SHORE AGAINST THE TURKISH GUNS

Source: The New York Times, Part II, Sunday, August 8, 1915, p. 2, column 7.

The correspondent of The Associated Press recently visited Weber Pasha, the German General commanding the Turkish troops operating against the Allies near Sedd-el-Bahr. The General said the situation was most favorable to the Ottoman forces. Had it not been that the Allied ships literally overwhelmed the peninsula with artillery fire during the landing operations, he said, not a single British or French soldier would have set foot ashore. But for days and days the allied ships had bombarded every square yard on the southern point of the peninsula, making it impossible to move the Ottoman troops without exposing them to almost instant annihilation. But day after day the Turks dug more trenches and improved them. Then it was the allied land forces that ran into a wall of Turkish pluck and endurance.

In those days Weber Pasha was in command of the Ottoman forces behind Kum Kale. Here the French tried their luck. General Weber forced them back. The operations against the Asiatic side at Kum Kale were no feint. Weber Pasha has in his possession the general order of the French landing troops. Kum Kale and its neighborhood were to be taken and held at all cost in order that the Turkish batteries in that locality might be captured. It was feared that these batteries would prove a thorn in the side of the allied troops at Sedd-el-Bahr, because they could sweep, and at present do sweep, every day, the positions on the allied right wing. The French failed to hold Kum Kale because the Turkish batteries mowed down everything on the ground held by the French troops, and the Ottoman infantry waded in with the bayonet in a manner which not even the French, no mean performers with the bayonet themselves, could stand. So they re-embarked and went to Sedd-el-Bahr, where today they form the allied right wing and are almost daily subjected to a galling fire by the Turkish batteries that they were to silence.

Appendix C

Contemporary Views Expressed by Ministers and Members of Parliament

November 2, 1915. Debate on the Naval and Military Situation in the House of Commons. Speech by Sir Henry Dalziel, Member of Parliament for the Scottish constituency of Kirkcaldy Burghs

Sir H. Dalziel: If I supported the Noble Lord's suggestion my speech would be in jeopardy, and however much I may appreciate the Noble Lord's intention his suggestion would not serve the purpose he has in view. The country should take note of the contempt, the supreme contempt, which the Government still shows for the House of Commons after the Dardanelles operations have been going on for about eight months when they will not even come and listen to the criticisms we have to offer. [There was not a single Minister on the Front Bench from the Departments concerned] That is a sign of the sort of way in which they are conducting this War. I come back to an important point. I do not want to make capital of any kind, but I want to say that the Government began this Dardanelles business without making the slightest inquiry, or without taking the highest advice to which they ought to have referred it.

[Of the initial delays and procrastinations:] There are in this country photographs of Blue Jackets having tea on the top of Achi Baba, which shows how simple it would have been, and that if we had only the military to lend aid at the same moment it would have been a walk-over with no trouble at all. Those are serious matters since you gave two months' notice to your enemy as to what you were going to do. I think some explanation is required when the Colonies send their best blood to be destroyed by machine guns which were there awaiting them. That is not all. What about the men we sent to the Dardanelles—new, unseasoned men who had never seen fire, and, after being stowed up in a troopship, were walked ashore into fire without a moment's rest—I mean at Suvla Bay, which is only an instance and an indication of what has been going on all over the place? I say it was not fair to send men under those conditions to attack, especially where they were landed. Who was responsible for the men who were placed in charge? Who decided the staff that was going to be in charge and have influence over thousands of men? It was not, as I understand, General Sir Ian Hamilton; he was not responsible for the men; he did not get his own staff. Some of the men who were responsible for that disaster were men who were sent from home by the authorities, and who were not suggested by the Commander-in-Chief himself. We had this statement at the Table the other day from the Under-Secretary of State for War, that the General concerned had been retired. Why did he not tell us the truth? Probably he was not answering that question, and I know he is the last man to keep anything back, and I wish he had his way with regard to these matters, and I am sure he would give us information. The answer to which I refer was that a general had been retired, but is it not a fact that not one, but two, three and four generals have been retired? Why keep these facts from the public? The man in the street practically know them, but they are not stated publicly. What is the result? The men themselves lose confidence when they know of those who have made mistakes costing the lives of thousands of men.

6 December, 1915. Questions and Answers by M.P.s and Ministers in the House of Commons, Mediterranean Expeditionary Force

Mr. King asked the Prime Minister whether he is in a position to give any information as to the results of Lord Kitchener's visit to the Eastern Mediterranean?

The Prime Minister: No, Sir.

Mr. S. Benn asked the Under-Secretary of State for War if the percentage of sickness amongst our troops on the Gallipoli Peninsula is greater than the percentage of sickness amongst the French troops; and if he can state if the French medical authorities consider that the ration of claret served out to the French troops has caused a good deal of immunity from a prevalent disease?

Mr. Tennant: The Army Council have no information as to the comparative immunity from sickness of the British and French troops on the Gallipoli Peninsula, nor whether the ration of claret stated to be served out to the French troops has proved salutary as a prevention of disease. Even if this were so, it does not, I think, follow that like results would follow if claret were served out to British troops, nor am I perfectly certain that such a step if adopted would commend itself to all Members of this House.

Mr. Leif Jones: Apart from Members of this House, is there any member of the medical profession who recommends it?

Mr. King: Is the right hon. Gentleman aware that the late M. Pasteur made inquiries and investigations into the value of claret, and found it an exceedingly good thing for killing germs of all kinds?

Mr. Tennant: I quite sympathize with that statement.

Mr. Lynch: Is the right hon. Gentleman aware that a Commission of eminent medical men have been considering this very subject, and that it was on their recommendations that the French light wines were supplied?

Mr. Pringle: Is the right hon. Gentleman aware that some of our soldiers have exchanged their jam for French claret?

Appendix D

Private Mortlock's Letter from Hill 60

Mediterranean Expeditionary Force
25/9/15
Dear Jack,

    Just a line to let you know that I am still quite all right (thank God) and to thank you for your letter which I just received. I was jolly glad to hear from you and to know that you are all quite well, also glad to hear that you have had nice weather for the harvest. Thanks very much for saying you are sending a parcel. It will be a treat I am sure. Parcels from England are one of the greatest luxuries you can possibly get out here.

    We get on a bit better for water now as the weather is not so hot. The worst thing we have to put up with is the flies. They are a plague if you like, swarm over everything so that you have quite a job to eat anything during the day. Talk about another row on the river, don't I wish we could, and I know there is one thing if I get home again safe (which I hope please God I shall) I shall surprise some of you at the amount of good things I shall eat.

    But there we are getting a bit used to it now, we live more like moles than anything else, and I think I would rather be shooting rabbits [on the farm] than Turks, you have to keep your head down so out here unless you want a hole through it.

    And now I must close.
With love to all of you.
Hoping to hear from you as soon as you get a chance to write.
With love
From your cousin Jake
P.S. Bob Jaggard is alright, wishes to be remembered to you.

Appendix E
August 1915 Order of Battle

Source: Based upon Aspinall-Oglander's The Official History of the War: Military Operations; Gallipoli, Vol. II, Appendices.

Mediterranean Expeditionary Force

Commander-in-Chief — General Sir Ian M. Hamilton, G.C.B.
Chief of the General Staff — Major-Gen. Walter P. Braithwaite, C.B.
Deputy Adjutant-General — Brig.-Gen. E. M. Woodward
Deputy Quartermaster-General — Major-Gen. G. F. Ellison[1]

VII Corps [Cape Helles]

G.O.C. — Lt.-Gen. Sir F. J. Davies, K.C.B.[2]
Brig.-Gen. General Staff — Brig.-Gen. H. E. Street

29th Division
Major-Gen. H. de B. de Lisle, C.B.

86TH BRIGADE:
2/Royal Fusiliers
1/Lancashire Fusiliers
1/Royal Munster Fusiliers
1/Royal Dublin Fusiliers

87TH BRIGADE:
2/South Wales Borderers
1/King's Own Scottish Borderers
1/Royal Inniskilling Fusiliers
1/The Border Regiment

88TH BRIGADE:
4/Worcestershire Regiment
2/Hampshire Regiment
1/Essex Regiment
1/5th Royal Scots (T.F.).

XV Bde. Royal Horse Artillery (B, L, & Y Btys.).
XVII Bde. Royal Field Artillery (13th, 26th & 92nd Btys.).
CXLVII Bde. Royal Field Artillery (10th, 97th & 368th Btys.).
460th (Howitzer) Bty. Royal Field Artillery

August 1915 Order of Battle 173

90th Heavy Bty. Royal Garrison Artillery
14th Siege Bty. Royal Garrison Artillery
1/2nd London, 1/2nd Lowland & 1/1st
 W. Riding
Field Coys. R.E. (T.F.) Divisional
 Cyclist Coy.

42nd (East Lancs.) Division (T.F.)
Major-Gen. W. Douglas, C.B.[3]

125TH BRIGADE:
1/5th Lancashire Fus.   1/7th Lancashire Fus.
1/6th Lancashire Fus.   1/8th Lancashire Fus.

126TH BRIGADE:
1/4th East Lancs. Regt.   1/9th Manchesters
1/5th East Lancs. Regt.   1/10 Manchesters

127TH BRIGADE:
1/5th Manchester Regt.   1/7th Manchesters
1/6th Manchester Regt.   1/8th Manchesters
1/1st E. Lancs. Bde. R.F.A.
 (4th, 5th & 6th Btys.).[4]
1/2nd E. Lancs. Bde., R.F.A.
 (15th, 16th & 17th Btys.)[5]
1/3rd E. Lancs. Bde., R.F.A.
 (18th, 19th & 20th Btys.)[6]
1/4th E. Lancs. (How.) Bde., R.F.A.
 (1st & 2nd Cumberland Btys.)
1/1st E. Lancs., 1/2nd E. Lancs., &
1/2nd W. Lancs.[7] Field Coys.,
 Royal Engineers.

52nd (Lowland) Division (T.F.)
Major-Gen. G.G.A. Egerton, C.B.

155TH BRIGADE:
1/4th R. Scots Fus.   1/4th K.O.S.B.
1/5th R. Scots Fus.   1/5th K.O.S.B.

156TH BRIGADE:
1/4th R. Scots.   1/7th Scottish R.
1/7th R. Scots.   1/8th Scottish R.

157TH BRIGADE:
1/5th H.L.I.   1/7th Highland L.I.
1/th H.L.I.   1/5th Argyle & S.H.
1/2nd Lowland Bde. R.F.A.
1/4th Lowland (Howitzer) Bde. R.F.A.
 (1/4th & 1/5th City of Glasgow Btys.)
 2/1st and 2/2nd Lowland Field Coys.,
 R.E. Divisional Cyclist Coy.

13th (Western Division)[8]
Major-Gen. F.C. Shaw, C.B.

38TH BRIGADE:
6/King's Own
6/E. Lancs. Regt.

6/S. Lancs. Regt.
6/Loyal N. Lancs. Reg.

39TH BRIGADE:
9/R. Warwich Regt.
7/Gloucestershire R.

9/Worcestershire Regt.
7/N. Staffordshire Regt.

40TH BRIGADE
4/S. Wales Borderers
8/R. Welch Fus.
8/Welch Regt. (Pioneers)
LXVI Bde. R.F.A. (A, B, C, & D Btys.)[9]
LXVII Bde. R.F.A. (A, B, C & D Btys.)[10]
LXVIII Bde. R.F.A. (A, B, C & D Btys.)[11]
LXIX (How.) Bde. R.F.A.
 (A, B, C & D Btys.)[12]
71st, 72nd and 88th Field Coys. R.E.
Divisional Cyclist Coy.

8/Cheshire Regt.
5/Wiltshire Regt.

Royal Naval Division
Major-Gen. A. Paris, C.B.

1ST BRIGADE:
Drake Bn.
Nelson Bn.

Hawke Bn.
Hood Bn.

2ND BRIGADE:
No. 1 Bn. R.M.L.I.
No. 2 Bn. R.M.L.I.
1st, 2nd & 3rd Field Coys,
 R.E., Divisional Cyclist Coy.

Howe Bn.
Anson Bn.[13]

IX Corps G.O.C.
Lt.-Gen. Sir F. Stopford, K.C.M.G.

BRIG.-GEN., GENERAL STAFF: Brig.-Gen. H.L. Reed, V.C.

10th (Irish) Division
Lt.-Gen. Sir B. Mahon, K.C.V.O.

29TH BRIGADE[14]:
10/Hants.
6/R. Irish Rifles

5/Connaught Rgs.
6/Leinster Regt.

30TH BRIGADE:
6/R. Munster Fus.
7/R. Munster Fus.

6/R. Dublin Fus.
7/R. Dublin Fus.

31st Brigade:
5/R. Inniskill. Fus.
6/R. Inniskill. Fus.
5/R. Irish Regiment (Pioneers)
LIV Bde. R.F.A. (A, B, C & D Btys.)[15]
LV Bde. R.F.A. (A, B, C & D Btys.)[16]
LVI Bde. R.F.A. (A, B, C & D Btys.)[17]
LVII (Howitzer) Bde. (H, Q, with
  A & D Btys. only)
65th, 66th & 85th Field Coys., R.E.
Divisional Cyclist Coy.

5/R. Irish Fus.
6/R. Irish Fus.

Corps Troops

4th (Highland) Mountain Artillery Bde.
(T.F.): Argyllshire Bty. and Ross & Cromarty Bty.

11th (Northern) Division

Major-Gen. F. Hammersley, C.B.

32nd Brigade:
9/West Yorks. Regt.
6/Yorkshire Regt.

8/W. Riding Regt.
6/York & Lancs.

33rd Brigade:
6/Lincolnhire Regt.
6/The Border Regt.

7/S. Staffordshires
9/Sherwood For's.

34th Brigade:
8/Northumberland F.
9/Lancashire Fus.
6/East Yorkshire Regt. (Pioneers)
LVIII Bde. R.F.A. (A, B, C & D Btys.)
LIX Bde. R.F.A. (A, B, C & D Btys.)
LX Bde. R.F.A. (A, B, C & D Btys.)[18]
67th, 68th and 86th Field Coys, R.E.
Divisional Cyclist Coy

5/Dorsets
11/Manchesters

Attached IX Corps

53rd (Welsh) Division (T.F.)

Major-Gen. the Hon. J. E. Lindley.[19]

158th Brigade:
1/5th Royal Welch Fusiliers
1/6th Royal Welch Fusiliers

1/7th Royal Welch Fusiliers
1/1st Herefordshire Regt.

159th Brigade:
1/4th Cheshire Regt.
1/7th Cheshire Regt.

1/4th Welch Regt.
1/5th Welch Regt.

160th Brigade:
2/4th Queen's (Royal West Surrey Regt.) 2/4th Royal West Kent Regt.

1/4th Royal Sussex Regt.
1/1st Welsh & 2/1st Cheshire Coys. R.E.

2/10th Middlesex Regt.
Divisional Cyclist Coy.

54th (East Anglian) Division (T.F.)

Major-Gen. F. S. Inglefield, C.B.

161ST BRIGADE:
1/4th Essex Regt.
1/5th Essex Regt.

1/6th Essex Regt.
1/7th Essex Regt.

162ND BRIGADE:
1/5th Bedfordshire Regt.
1/4th Northamptonshire Regt.

1/10th London Regt.
1/11th London Regt.

163RD BRIGADE:
1/4th Norfolk Regt.
1/5th Norfolk Regt.
1/2nd & 2/1st East Anglian
   Field Coys. R.E.

1/5th Suffolk Regt.
1/8th Hampshire Regt.

Divisional Cyclist Coy.

2nd Mounted Division[20]

Major-Gen. W. E. Peyton, C.B.

1ST (SOUTH MIDLAND) BRIGADE:
1/1st Warwickshire Yeomanry
1/1st Royal Gloucestershire Hussars.

1/1st Worcestershire Yeomanry

2ND (SOUTH MIDLAND) BRIGADE:
1/1st Royal Buckinghamshire Hussars
1/1st Dorset Yeomanry.

1/1st Berkshire Yeomanry

3RD (NOTTS. & DERBY) BRIGADE:
1/1st Sherwood Rangers
1/1st South Nottinghamshire Hussars.

1/1st Derbyshire Yeomanry

4TH (LONDON) BRIGADE:
1/1st County of London Yeomanry
1/1st City of London Yeomanry.

1/3rd County of London Yeomanry

5TH BRIGADE:[21]
1/1st Hertfordshire Yeomanry

1/2nd County of London Yeomanry
(Westminster Dragoons.).

1st Australian Division

Major-Gen. H. B. Walker, D.S.O.

1ST AUSTRALIAN BRIGADE:
1st (New South Wales) Battalion
2nd (New South Wales) Battalion

3rd (New South Wales) Battalion.
4th (New South Wales) Battalion.

August 1915 Order of Battle

2ND AUSTRALIAN BRIGADE:
5th (Victoria) Battalion
6th (Victoria) Battalion
7th (Victoria) Battalion
8th (Victoria) Battalion.

3RD AUSTRALIAN BRIGADE:
9th (Queensland) Battalion
10th (South Australia) Battalion
11th (Western Australia) Bn.
12th (S. & W. Aus. & Tas.) Bn.
I.(N.S.W.) Field Artillery Bde.
  (1st, 2nd & 3rd Btys.). II. (Victoria)
  F.A. Bde. (4th, 5th & 6th Btys.).
  III. Field Artillery Bde. 7th
  (Queensland), 8th (W. Austr.) &
  9th (Tasmania) Btys.
1st, 2nd & 3rd Field Coys. Australian
  Engineers.
4th (Victoria) Light Horse Regt.[22]

New Zealand & Australian Division

Major-Gen. Sir A. J. Godley, K.C.M.G.

NEW ZEALAND BRIGADE:
Auckland Battalion
Canterbury Battalion
Otago Battalion
Wellington Battalion

4TH AUSTRALIAN BRIGADE:
13th (New South Wales) Battalion
14th (Victoria) Battalion
15th (Queensland & Tasmania) Bn.
16th (S. & W. Australia) Battalion.

NEW ZEALAND MOUNTED RIFLES BRIGADE:[23]
Auckland Mounted Rifles
Canterbury Mounted Rifles.
Wellington Mounted Rifles

1ST AUSTRALIAN LIGHT HORSE BRIGADE:
1st (New South Wales) Regiment
2nd (Queensland) Regiment.
Maori Detachment
I. N.Z. Field Artillery Bde. (1st & 3rd
  Btys. & 6th Howitzer Bty.).[24]
II. N.Z.F.A. Bde. (2nd & 5th Btys.
  & 4th How. Bty.).[25] 1st & 2nd Field
  Coys. New Zealand Engineers. N.Z.
  Field Troop, Engineers.
Otago Mounted Rifles.[26]
3rd (S. Austr. & Tasmania) Regt.

2nd Australian Division[27]

Major-Gen. J. G. Legge.

5TH AUSTRALIAN BRIGADE:
17th (New South Wales) Battalion
18th (New South Wales) Battalion
19th (New South Wales) Battalion
19th (New South Wales) Battalion

6TH AUSTRALIAN BRIGADE:
21st (Victoria) Battalion
22nd (Victoria) Battalion
23rd (Victoria) Battalion
24th (Victoria) Battalion.

7TH AUSTRALIAN BRIGADE:
25th (Queensland) Battalion
26th (Queensland & Tasmania) Bn.
4th & 5th Field Coys. Australian
  Engineers.
13th (Victoria) Light Horse Regiment.[28]

27th (South Australia) Bn.
28th (Western Australia) Bn.

Australian & N.Z. Army Corps Troops

2ND AUSTRALIAN LIGHT HORSE BRIGADE:
5th (Queensland) Regiment
6th (New South Wales) Regiment.

7th (New South Wales) Regiment

3RD AUSTRALIAN LIGHT HORSE BRIGADE:
8th (Victoria) Regiment
9th (Victoria & South Australia) Regt.
7th Indian Mountain Artillery Bde.[29]
Consisting of: one 4.7-inch gun;
  three 6-inch Howitzers.

10th (W. Australia) Regiment

Attached New Zealand & Australian Division
Major-Gen. H. V. Cox.

29TH INDIAN INFANTRY BRIGADE:
14th Sikhs
1/5th Gurkha Rifles

1/6th Gurkha Rifles
2/10th Gurkha Rifles

G.H.Q. Troops

20TH BRIGADE ROYAL GARRISON ARTILLERY:
10th, 15th & 91st Heavy Batteries R.G.A.

24TH BRIGADE ROYAL GARRISON ARTILLERY:[30]
17th, 42nd & 43rd Siege Batteries R.G.A.

ARMOURED CAR DIVISION (R.N.A.S.):
Nos. 3, 4, 9, 10, 11 & 12 Squadrons—(3, 4, & 12 Squadrons in Egypt.).

Corps Expeditionnaire D'Orient
Commander:- General Bailloud.

1st Division: Gen. Brulard.

1ST METROPOLITAN BRIGADE:
175th Regiment
1st Regiment de marche d'Afrique
  (2 Bns. Zouaves, 1 Bn. Foreign Legion).
Foreign Legion Battalion (2 Coys.).

2ND COLONIAL BRIGADE:
4th Colonial Regiment.

6th Colonial Regiment.
6 Batteries of Artillery (75-mm.).
2 Batteries of Artillery (65-mm.).

2nd Division

3RD METROPOLITAN BRIGADE:
176th Regiment.
2nd Regiment de marche d'Afrique (3 Bns. Zouaves).

4TH COLONIAL BRIGADE:
7th Colonial Regiment.
8th Colonial Regiment.
9 Batteries of Artillery (75-mm.).

Corps Artillery

One Heavy Battery, 120-mm., long (4.7-inch).
One Heavy Battery, 155-mm., long (6-inch).
Two Heavy Batteries, 155-mm., short (6-inch).
Two Siege Guns, 240-mm. (9.4-inch).
Battery of Naval Guns.

Notes

Preface

1. Sir Edward Grey, British Foreign Secretary. Remark made on standing by the window of the Foreign Secretary's room in the Foreign Office at dusk on 3 August 1914. From Sir Edward Grey (Edward, Viscount Grey of Fallodon), *Twenty-Five Years, 1892–1916*, vol. 2 (New York: Frederick A. Stokes Company, 1925), 20.

2. Brian Bond, "The First World War," in *The Shifting Balance of World Forces, 1898–1945*, vol. 12 in *The New Cambridge Modern History*, ed. C. L. Mowat, 2nd ed. (Cambridge: Cambridge University Press, 1968), 171.

3. Ibid., 173–74.

4. H.H. (Herbert Henry) Asquith, *Memories and Reflections, 1852–1928, by the Earl of Oxford and Asquith, K. B.*, vol. 2 (Boston: Little, Brown, and Company, 1928), 68.

5. An empire created by Turkish tribes in Anatolia that lasted from the decline of the Byzantine Empire in the 14th century until the establishment of Turkey as a republic in 1922. (See Map A for area of influence in 1914.) The seat of government was the Sublime Porte in Constantinople. Russia was the traditional enemy of the Ottoman Turks, but pre-1914 relations with Britain and France were tolerably good, their investments considerable, and trade substantial. The Ottoman entry into World War I resulted from an overly hasty calculation of likely advantage. German influence was strong, but not decisive. Condensed from M.E. Yapp, "Turkey and Ancient Anatolia," in *The New Encyclopedia Britannica*, 15th ed., vol. 9, 6.

6. David Lloyd George, *War Memories of David Lloyd George, 1914–1915*, vol. 1 (Boston: Little, Brown, and Company, 1933), 338–39.

7. Asquith, *Memories and Reflections*, vol. 2, 66–67.

Introduction

1. Brigadier-General Vincent J. Esposito, ed., *A Concise History of World War I* (New York: Frederick A. Praeger, Publishers, 1964), 11.

2. Ibid., 7.

3. Ibid., 8.

4. Grey, *Twenty-Five Years, 1892–1916*, Vol. II, 20.

5. Ibid.

6. Private S. Jacob P. Mortlock, D Company, 5th Battalion, the Suffolk Regiment, Territorial Force. Interview, 5 August 1965.

7. F. Loraine Petrie, O.B.E., *The History of the Norfolk Regiment, 1685–1918*, vol. 2, 4th August 1914, to 31st December 1918 (Norwich: Jarrold & Sons, Ltd., The Empire Press, 1924–1926), 120.

8. B.H. Liddell Hart, *Strategy* (New York: Frederick A. Praeger, 1954), 14.

9. Justin Wintle, ed., *The Dictionary of War Quotations* (New York: The Free Press, 1989), 296.

10. Henry Morgenthau, *The Secrets of the Bosphorus* (London: Hutchinson & Company, 1918), 14. Also *Ambassador Morgenthau's Story* (New York: Doubleday & Page, 1920), 20. David Childs, *Germany in the Twentieth Century* (London: B.T. Batsford, 1991), 12–13.

11. General Otto Liman von Sanders, *Five Years in Turkey* (Annapolis: U.S. Naval Institute Press, 1927), 21.

12. Esposito, *A Concise History of World War I*, 13. Barbara W. Tuchman, *The Guns of August* (New York: Macmillan Publishing Company), 137–62.

13. Richard Hough, *The Great War at Sea, 1914–1918* (Oxford: Oxford University Press, 1983), 150–151.

14. Edwin P. Hoyt, *Disaster at the Dardanelles, 1915* (London: Arthur Barker, 1976), 30–32.

Notes — Chapter 1

15. Minutes of the two Meetings of the War Council at 10 Downing Street, London, 28 November 1914; and 13 January 1915 (London: H.M.S.O., 1916), 3, and 2–3 respectively.
16. R. Ernest Dupuy and Trevor S. Dupuy, *The Encyclopedia of Military History*, rev. ed. (New York: Harper & Row, 1977), 766.
17. Bernard and Fawn Brodie, *From Crossbow to H-Bomb: The Evolution of the Weapons and Tactics of Warfare*, rev. and enlarged ed. (Bloomington: Indiana University Press, 1973), 46–47.
18. Minutes of the Meeting of the War Council at 10 Downing Street, London, 13 January 1915, 3.
19. Anthony Bruce and William Cogar, *An Encyclopedia of Naval History* (New York: Facts on File, Inc., 1998), 69.
20. Minutes of the 12th Meeting of the War Council at 10 Downing Street, London, 16 February 1915, 1.

Chapter 1

1. Minutes of the 12th Meeting of the War Council at 10 Downing Street, London, 16 February, 1915, 1.
2. Alan Moorehead, *Gallipoli* (New York: Harper & Brothers, 1956), 80.
3. General Sir Ian Hamilton, *Gallipoli Diary*, vol. 1 (New York: George H. Doran Company, 1920).
4. *Ibid.*, 3–4.
5. Lord Hankey, *The Supreme Command 1914–1918*, vol. 1 (London: George Allen & Unwin, 1961), 290. Lyn Macdonald, *1915: The Death of Innocence* (New York: Henry Holt & Company, 1995), 142–3.
6. H. Gordon Phillips. Unfulfilled prophecy made to Private S. Jacob P. Mortlock, while transporting him to the station upon mobilization, 5 August 1914. Later this worthy served as a Royal Engineers' sapper in the waterlogged trenches of Flanders during the Passchendaele offensive of 1917. Recounted by Private Mortlock. Interview, 5 August 1964.
7. Serge Sazonov, *Fateful Years, 1909–1916: The Reminiscences of Serge Sazonov, G.C.B., G.C.V.O.* (New York: Frederick A. Stokes Company, 1928), 239–50.
8. "Dreadnought" was the name of the first modern armor-plated, steel-hulled warship (launched February 1906) of a powerful type superior in armament to all its predecessors, whose introduction set the trend for the navies of the world and made the previous vessel designs obsolete. Peter Kemp, ed., *Oxford Companion to Ships and the Sea* (Oxford: Oxford University Press, 1976), 334, and *Oxford English Dictionary*, 2nd ed., vol. 4, (Oxford: Clarendon Press, 1989).
9. E.B. Potter, *Sea Power: A Naval History*, 2nd. ed. (Annapolis: Naval Institute Press, 1981), 216.
10. Hoyt, *Disaster at the Dardanelles*, 29.
11. Captain Eric Wheler Bush, *Gallipoli* (New York: St. Martin's Press, Inc., 1975), 39.
12. The author's uncle, Ord. Tel. Albert Joseph Brown, served aboard the ill-fated HMS *Irresistible*. He received a "Mentioned in Dispatches" while in that theater of war.
13. "It will be seen that the mine, like the submarine, was used both offensively and defensively. It helped bar the Allies from the Dardanelles and the Germans from Riga." Bernard and Fawn Brodie, *From Crossbow to H-Bomb: The Evolution of the Weapons and Tactics of Warfare*, 187.
14. Admiral Sir Roger Keyes, *The Naval Memoirs of Admiral of the Fleet Sir Roger Keyes*. vol. 2: *The Narrow Seas to the Dardanelles, 1910–1915* (New York: E. P. Dutton & Company, 1934), 297.
15. Morgenthau, *The Secrets of the Bosphorus*, 42.
16. *New York Times*, 26 March 1915, 2.
17. Morgenthau, *Ambassador Morgenthau's Story*, 186–188.
18. Dr. Harry Stuermer, *Two Years at Constantinople* (New York: Doubleday, Doran, & Company, 1918), 93–94.
19. Hoyt, *Disaster at the Dardanelles*, 163.
20. Sanders, *Five Years in Turkey*, 53.
21. *Ibid.*, 53–4.
22. Joseph Pomiankowski, *Der Zusammenbruch des Ottomanischen Reiches: Erinnerungen an die Turkei aus der Zeit des Weltkrieges* (Zurich: Amalthea-Verlag, 1928), appendix 2.
23. Hoyt, *Disaster at the Dardanelles*, 164.
24. H.G. Wells, *The Outline of History* (Garden City, N.J.: Doubleday, 1931), 1,090.
25. Sanders, *Five Years in Turkey*, 56.
26. *Ibid.*, 17.
27. J. Williams, *The Geography of Gallipoli* (Perth, Australia: Kookaburra Press, 1932), 2–3.
28. Tuesday, April 13. "I saw the Commander-in-Chief tearing along through the village [Mudros]. They say he always walks very fast, and is of a quick, nervous disposition." The Reverend Oswin Creighton, C.F., *With the Twenty-Ninth Division in Gallipoli:*

A Chaplain's Experiences (London: Longman, Green and Company, Limited, 1916), 37.

29. *Ibid.*, 12–13. Also Frederick R. Dickinson, *War and National Reinvention: Japan in the Great War, 1914–1919* (Cambridge, MA: Harvard University Asia Center, 1999), 45–46. Britain committed 2,800 troops; Japan 29,000.

30. Christopher Hassall, *Rupert Brooke* (New York: Harcourt, Brace & World, 1964), 461.

31. It seems that the intelligence estimates of Turkish troop strengths on the Gallipoli peninsula were conservative in the extreme. Hamilton estimated, "34,000 and about a 100 guns." Hamilton, *Gallipoli Diary*, vol. 1, 98, 251.

32. Liddell Hart, *Strategy*, 194.

33. Hamilton, *Gallipoli Diary*, vol. 1, 89.

34. *Ibid.*, 89–90.

35. The Members of the Dardanelles Committee were also on the War Council and their deliberations took place whenever the latter was in session. C. F. Aspinall-Oglander, *The Official History of the War: Military Operations: Gallipoli*, vol. 1 (London: Heinemann, 1929), 111.

36. Liddell Hart, *Strategy*, 194.

37. Sanders, *Five Years in Turkey*, 101–102.

38. The Greek government allowed the Allies to use several of its islands in the area, notably Lemnos, Imbros, and Mitylene (Lesbos) as bases for operations.

39. Bush, *Gallipoli*, 73.

40. Christopher Marlowe, *Dr. Faustus*, Act V, Scene 1. From *The Oxford Dictionary of Quotations*, 4th. ed.

41. Private Mortlock. Interview, 10 August 1965. Also Major John Gillam's account in his *Gallipoli Diary*, page 22.

42. Liddle, *Men of Gallipoli*, 46.

43. Weber Pasha, the German general commanding the Turkish forces at Cape Helles, in an interview granted the Associated Press correspondent, maintained, "The operations against the Asiatic side at Kum Kale were no feint." He stated further that he had in his possession the general order of the French landing troops which entirely substantiated this. *The New York Times*, Sunday, August 8, 1915, Part II, p. 2, column 7. See also Appendix B.

44. Sir Ian Hamilton, *Gallipoli Diary*, vol. 1, 80–81.

45. Williams, *The Geography of Gallipoli*, 11.

46. Hamilton, *Gallipoli Diary*, vol. 1, 80–81.

47. *Ibid.*, 66–67.

48. Colonel Maurice Hankey, Secretary of the War Council, on 28 February 1915 put the expected Russian contribution as "... their fleet and an army corps of 47,600 men and 120 guns to operate from the Black Sea against Constantinople...."

Lord Maurice Hankey, *The Supreme Command, 1914–1918*, vol. 1 (London: George Allen & Unwin, 1961), 284.

General Sir Ian Hamilton wrote in his diary on 14 April: "Now that the [extra] French Division has been snuffed out, how about Grand Duke Nicholas, General Istomine and their Russian Divisions? Are they also to prove phantoms?"

Later, on 30 May, he lamented: "A message from Hanbury Williams, who is with the Grand Duke Nicholas [Chief of the Russian Imperial General Staff], to say that, because of a terrific Austro-German attack near Gorlice, all idea of sending me a Russian Army Corps to land at the Bosphorus has been abandoned!!!" Hamilton, *Gallipoli Diary*, vol. 1, 108 and 255, respectively.

49. Hans Delbrück, *Delbrück's Modern Military History*, ed. & trans. by Arden Bucholz (Lincoln: University of Nebraska Press, 1997), 132.

50. Rear Admiral (Retired) Prof. N. B. Pavlovich, ed., *The Fleet in the First World War. Vol. I: The Operations of the Russian Fleet.* Translated from Russian (New Delhi: Amerind Publishing Company, Pvt., Ltd., 1979), 330.

51. Sir George Arthur, *Life of Lord Kitchener*, vol. 3 (New York: The Macmillan Company, 1920), 120–121.

52. *Ibid.*

53. *Ibid.*, 123.

54. *Ibid.*, 124.

55. G.P. Gooch, *The History of Modern Europe, 1878–1919* (New York: Henry Holt & Company, 1922), 572.

56. Creighton, *With the Twenty-Ninth Division in Gallipoli*, 47.

57. Quoted in Sanders, *Five Years in Turkey*, 70.

58. A member of this unit was an uncle of one of the author's colleagues: Private David Anderson Mackenzie, of the 1/5th Battalion (the Edinburgh Rifles) of the Royal Scots. An old boy of Stewart's College, where he played cricket and rugby for the 1st teams and enrolled at Edinburgh University as a medical student at the outbreak of war. He chose to volunteer and was killed at Cape Helles on May 3, 1915.

59. Geoffrey Moorhouse, *Hell's Foundations: A Town, Its Myths, and Gallipoli* (Man-

chester: Manchester University Press, 1991), 40.

60. The defenders "had their target on the front and both flanks at ranges between 100 and 300 yards in clear daylight, 30 boats bunched together and crammed with men and a good big ship. The first outbreak of fire made the bay as white as a rapid, for the Turks fired not less than 10,000 shots a minute for the first few minutes of that attack. Those not killed in the boats at the first discharge jumped overboard to wade or swim ashore. Many were killed in the water, many, who were wounded were swept away and drowned; others, trying to swim in the fierce current, were drowned by the weight of their equipment." John Masefield's "The Landing at V Beach, near Sedd-el-Bahr," in *Pen Pictures of British Battles: Painted by Author and Artist* (London: Eyre & Spottiswoode, Limited, 1917), 44–45.

61. Private David Anderson Mackenzie, 1/5th Battalion, (the Edinburgh Rifles) the Royal Scots (see endnote 56), was one of those soldiers.

62. Major John Gillam, D.S.O., *Gallipoli Diary* (Stevenage: The Strong Oak Press/ Tom Donovan Publishing, 1989), 28–31.

63. Hamilton, *Gallipoli Diary*, vol. 1, 210.

64. John F. Williams, *Anzacs, the Media and the Great War* (Sydney: University of New South Wales Press, Ltd., 1999), 83.

65. Keyes, *The Naval Memoirs of Admiral of the Fleet Sir Roger Keyes*, vol. 1: *The Narrow Seas to the Dardanelles, 1910–1915*, 332–33.

66. Major-General J. F. C. Fuller, *A Military History of the Western World*, vol. 3 (New York: Funk & Wagnalls, 1954), 263.

67. Charles Fair, *From the Jaws of Victory* (New York: Simon & Schuster, 1971), 329–30.

68. Liddell Hart, *Strategy*, 194.

69. Nigel Steel and Peter Hart, *Defeat at Gallipoli* (London: Macmillan, 1994), 334.

70. David R. Woodward, *Field Marshal Sir William Robertson, Chief of the Imperial General Staff in the Great War* (Westport, Connecticut: Praeger, 1998), 11.

71. H.G. Wells, *The Outline of History* (New York: Garden City Books, 1931), 1,091.

Chapter 2

1. Allegation made by Mr. F.W. Roch, Liberal Member of Parliament for Newcastle-upon-Tyne, during a debate on the floor of the House of Commons, 10 November 1915. *Parliamentary Debates (Hansard)*, vol. George V, 75–76, 1914/15 (London: H.M.S.O., 1915–16), 1280. The contention is supported by combatants, notably Sergeant John Hargrave, Captain A. Fair, M.C., and Captain E.D. Wolton. The *Official History* also goes into specifics. More recently evidence has come to light of even bigger blunders. Research carried out for, and to be published by, the Royal Geographic Society, will expand these considerably. Source: article in *The Sunday Times* of 21 March 1999.

2. Ellis Ashmead-Bartlett, C.B.E., *The Uncensored Dardanelles* (London: Hutchinson & Company, 1928), 14–15.

3. Michael Asher, *Lawrence: The Uncrowned King of Arabia* (Woodstock, New York: The Overlook Press, 1999), 138.

4. On 24 March 1915, Enver Pasha, the Turkish Minister of War, appointed the German Marshal Otto Liman von Sanders to command the Turkish Fifth Army at the Dardanelles, with his headquarters at the town of Gallipoli. Martin Gilbert, *Winston S. Churchill*, vol. 3: *1914–16, The Challenge of War* (Boston: Houghton Mifflin Company, 1971), 400.

5. Ashmead-Bartlett, *The Uncensored Dardanelles*, 14.

6. Captain the Hon. Aubrey Herbert, *The Secret Battle* (London: Methuen & Company, 1919), 79.

7. Private Mortlock. Interview, 10 August 1965.

8. Captain Aubrey Herbert, "Half Hours at Helles." Composed in commemoration of the Battle of the Fourth of June (Third Krithia) in that theater on its first anniversary in 1916. Quoted in Robert Rhodes James, *Gallipoli* (London: B.T. Batsford, 1965), 209.

9. Alexander Aitken, *Gallipoli to the Somme: Recollections of a New Zealand Infantryman* (London: Oxford University Press, 1963), 24.

10. C.E.W. Bean, *Official History of Australia in the War: The Story of Anzac: From 4 May, 1915 to the Evacuation of the Gallipoli Peninsula* (Canberra: Angus & Robertson, 1941), 200. Hamilton, *Gallipoli Diary*, vol. 1, 248, 357.

11. *British Documents on Foreign Affairs: Reports and Papers from the Foreign Office Confidential Print. Part II: From the First to the Second World War. Series H: The First World War, 1914–1918*, vol. 1: *The Allied and Neutral Powers: Diplomacy and War Aims, I: August 1914–July 1915*, ed. David Stevenson (New York: University Publications of America, 1989), 368.

12. Private Mortlock on snipers: "You have to keep your head down so out here, unless you want a hole through it." Excerpt from page 3 of "Letter from Hill 60, Suvla/Anzac," written on 25 September 1915. Later in the war he turned the tables on the enemy and accounted for a Turkish sniper during the fighting for the El Arish Redoubt in the Third Battle of Gaza.

13. Actually only a Lance-Corporal at the time, the inventor's name was Beech, formerly a Sydney builders' foreman.

Richard Wright, "Gallipoli: The Second Stage," in Brigadier Peter Young, ed., *The Illustrated Encyclopedia of World War I* (New York: Marshall Cavendish, 1984), 905.

14. Hankey, *The Supreme Command, 1914–1918, vol. 1*, 379–80.

15. Sir Ronald East, ed., *The Gallipoli Diary of Sergeant Lawrence of the Australian Engineers — 1st A.I.F., 1915* (Melbourne: Melbourne University Press, 1981), 111–13.

16. Australian slang for "mate," "chum," "pal," "buddy."

17. Alistair Thomson, *Anzac Memories: Living with the Legend* (Melbourne: Oxford University Press, 1994), 37.

18. Prime Minister Herbert Henry Asquith and his Cabinet established the War Council, originally composed only of Asquith, Lloyd George, Grey, Churchill, Fisher, Kitchener, and Wolfe immediately after war was declared; this body first met on 5 and 6 August 1914. It was expanded to include Murray and Balfour, with Hankey as Secretary.

In December Crewe was added; Haldane and Wilson in January 1915, and in March McKenna and Harcourt became members. Hankey, *The Supreme Command, 1914–1918, vol 1*, 233, 237.

19. 27 May 1915: The Cabinet of the new Coalition Government created the Dardanelles Committee. It contained the Prime Minister Asquith, Lansdowne, Curzon, Kitchener, Balfour, Bonar Law, Grey, Crewe, Lloyd George, Churchill, and Selborne. In mid-August an additional member, Carson, an outspoken critic of the Dardanelles Campaign, joined its ranks. The original conception of the Committee was a Cabinet Committee of the pre-war type, i.e., a committee composed of members of the Cabinet created to deal with a specific area. For the first two and a half months of its existence there were no Service members, and the Chiefs of Staff or other technical officers attended only rarely, to give information on some particular subject. Its first meeting was held on the afternoon of 7 June. The Committee would soon encounter great difficulties in trying to confine its activities to the Dardanelles, as events there instantaneously affected other theaters of war. In these circumstances the Dardanelles Committee would inevitably become a War Committee with the virtual dictatorial powers associated with it, in fact, if not in name. *Ibid.*, 336–7.

20. Churchill, *The World Crisis, 1915*, vol. 2, 411.

21. They maintained that the successful prosecution of the war entailed defeating the German armies on the Western Front. Their ranks included the British High Command Generals: French, Haig, Rawlinson, and Robertson, together with the majority of their French counterparts, Joffre in particular. The Chairman of the War Council and Dardanelles Committee, British Prime Minister Herbert Asquith was a convinced disciple of this philosophy, and, on the Opposition benches, Andrew Bonar Law, while not exactly a "Westerner," opposed the Gallipoli involvement. Lord Kitchener changed his stance over the course of the development from a proponent of the "Westerner" concept, to a reluctant subscriber to the Dardanelles strategy, and thence to becoming a lukewarm advocate of it.

22. Woodward, *Field Marshal Sir William Robertson, Chief of the Imperial General Staff in the Great War*, 17.

23. Captain A. Fair, M.C., and Captain E.D. Wolton, *The History of the 1st/5th Battalion of "The Suffolk Regiment"* (London: Eyre & Spottiswoode, 1923), 15.

24. Private Jake Mortlock. Interview, 20 August 1965.

25. The Commander of the 29th Division, Major-General Sir Aylmer Hunter-Weston, on one occasion sat out in the open, entirely exposed to shellfire, working on some papers. As to the incompetence, more on that anon.

26. Hamilton, *Gallipoli Diary*, vol. 1, 268–9.

27. *Ibid.*, 269.

28. Aspinall-Oglander, *The Official History of the War: Military Operations; Gallipoli*, vol. 2, 63.

29. War Council/Dardanelles Committee, Minutes, 7 June 1915, 1. Aspinall-Oglander, *The Official History of the War: Military Operations; Gallipoli*, vol. 2, 60.

30. War Council/ Dardanelles Committee, Minutes, 10 June 1915, 2.

31. Aspinall-Oglander, *The Official History of the War: Military Operations; Gallipoli*, vol. 2, 127.

Notes — Chapter 2

32. *Ibid.*, 61–62.
33. *Ibid.*, 127.
34. Sir Ian Hamilton, *Sir Ian Hamilton's Final Dispatch: The Tragic Story of the Dardanelles* (London: George Newnes, 1916), 14.
35. *Ibid.*
36. Edwin Blackwell & Edwin C. Axe, *Romford To Beirut, via France, Egypt and Jericho: An Outline of the War Record of "B" Battery, 271st Brigade, R.F.A.* [Royal Field Artillery], *(1/2nd Essex Battery, R.F.A.), With Many Digressions* (Clacton-on-Sea, Essex, England: R.W. Humphries, 1926), 7: "About the middle of July the Infantry Brigades found themselves under orders for Gallipoli, but contrary to general expectation the Divisional Artillery was not detailed to accompany them."
37. Private Mortlock. Interview, 10 August 1965.
38. Aspinall-Oglander, *The Official History of the War: Military Operations; Gallipoli*, vol. 2, 491.
39. James Norman Hall, *Kitchener's Mob: The Adventures of an American in the British Army* (New York: Grosset & Dunlap, 1916), 2, 21, 23, and 25.
40. Richard Burdon Haldane, *Richard Burdon Haldane (Viscount Haldane): An Autobiography* (New York: Doubleday, Doran & Company, 1929), 206.
41. Lieutenant-Colonel Howard Green, *The British Army in the First World War: The Regulars; the Territorials; and Kitchener's Army* (London: William Clowes, 1968), 38.
42. *Ibid.*
43. Edgar Wallace, *Kitchener's Army and the Territorial Forces: The Full Story of a Great Achievement* (London: George Newnes, 1916), 161–2.
44. *Ibid.*
45. It is interesting to note that 2nd Lieutenant Ian Hamilton, following a year at the Royal Military College, Sandhurst, was gazetted to the Suffolk Regiment in April 1874—although he transferred to the Gordon Highlanders in 1875. Of equal interest is the revelation that prior to Sandhurst he also spent six months studying at a German Military Academy in Dresden! Source: Lieutenant-General Alan Sheppard's "Gallipoli: The Generals," in Edward Young, ed., *The Illustrated Encyclopedia of World War I*, vol. 3 (New York: Marshall Cavendish, 1984), 912.
46. Fair and Wolton, *The History of the 1st/5th Battalion "The Suffolk Regiment,"* 9–10.
47. Wallace, *Kitchener's Army and the Territorial Forces: The Full Story of a Great Achievement*, 162.
48. Fair and Wolton, *The History of the 1st/5th Battalion "The Suffolk Regiment,"* 8.
49. Blackwell & Axe, *Romford To Beirut, via France, Egypt and Jericho: An Outline of the War Record of "B" Battery, 271st Brigade, R.F.A. (1/2nd Essex Battery, R.F.A.) With Many Digressions*, 7.
50. Private Mortlock, and Captain Reginald Lane. The gang members often held up an ace of spades—their badge of membership. Interviews, Christmas 1964. After the war, Tim Burlham became an Eastern Counties' bus driver and sometimes stopped in the village to have a word with his former comrade-in-arms.
51. Private Mortlock. Interview, Christmas 1964. The two soldiers undoubtedly received seven days C.B. (confined to barracks—"jankers" in Army parlance), which also entailed—among other things—nightly mounting with the guard in full battle order. Apparently this punishment did not have the desired deterrent effect as within three months Mortlock went AWOL again to attend a family party. Postcard dated 21st March 1915. Source, Mortlock Family Papers.
52. *Ibid.* Much to his amazement Mortlock discovered these delicacies were still obtainable, and of unchanged quality, over fifty years later! Interview, 10 August 1965.
53. Some of these unfortunate soldiers had to march a further three miles to private-house billets in the village of Risby—where Private Mortlock had his first encounter with a bed bug. Interview, 18 September 1965.
54. C.T. Atkinson, *The Regimental History of the Royal Hampshire Regiment*: vol. 2, *1914–1918* (Glasgow: Robert Maclehose & Company, Limited), 1952.
55. Fair and Wolton, *The History of the 1st/5th Battalion "The Suffolk Regiment,"* 11, 13–14. Also, Petrie, *The History of the Norfolk Regiment, 1685–1918*, vol. 2, 4th August 1914 to 31 December 1918, 121.
56. Private Mortlock. Interview, 10 August 1965.
57. Lance-Corporal Albert E. Collen, C Company, the 2nd Battalion, the Royal Fusiliers. Interview, 6 July 1963. The Royal Fusiliers is the only regiment in the British Army whose officers do not make the loyal toast. Their loyalty is considered beyond question.
58. Fair and Wolton, *The History of the 1st/5th Battalion "The Suffolk Regiment,"* 14–15.

Notes—Chapter 2

59. Private Mortlock. Interview, 10 August 1965.
60. Henry W. Nevinson, *The Dardanelles Campaign* (New York: Henry Holt Company, 1919), 86–7. Brooke, a former classical scholar at King's College, Cambridge, enthused about his destination in a letter to Violet Asquith. In it he alluded to the Plains of Troy, Lesbos, and Hero's Tower, and wondered whether the sea really would "be polyphloisbic and winedark and unvintageable...." Hassall, *Rupert Brooke*, 488.
61. Gibbons, *With the 1/5th Essex in the East*, 3.
62. John Hargrave, *The Suvla Bay Landing* (London: Constable & Company, 1964), 62–5.
63. Great Britain: War Office. *Army: Arrangements made for Water Supply to the Troops during the Landing at Suvla Bay* (London: H.M.S.O.; Harrison & Sons, 1915), 2.
64. East, ed. *The Gallipoli Diary of Sergeant Lawrence*, 44.
65. Gillam, *Gallipoli Diary*, 184.
66. The Reverend Dennis Jones, C.F., *The Diary of a Padre at Suvla Bay* (Manchester: The Faith Press, 1916), 60.
67. Hargrave, *The Suvla Bay Landing*, 71.
68. Aspinall-Oglander, *The Official History of the War: Military Operations; Gallipoli*, vol. 2, 159.
69. Major-General Hans Kannengiesser, *The Campaign in Gallipoli*, trans. Major C. J. P. Ball (London: Hutchinson & Company, 1927), 199.
70. Mustapha Kemal, who played a key role in containing the April Anzac Cove landing, predicted that the blow would fall at Suvla Bay. His warning went unheeded.
71. Kannengiesser, *The Campaign in Gallipoli*, 200–01.
72. Private Mortlock and many of his chums had enlisted in the Territorial Force as early as 1912–13. In the fateful summer of 1914 the 5th Suffolks struck their Annual Training Camp on the 26 July—four weeks after Princip's fatal shots at Sarajevo on 28 June, and a mere ten days before being mobilized!
73. Hargrave, *The Suvla Bay Landing*, 110.
74. Henry Hanna, *The Pals at Suvla Bay: Being the Record of "D" Company of the 7th Royal Dublin Fusiliers* (Dublin: E. Ponsonby, 1916), 53.
75. Hargrave, *The Suvla Bay Landing*, 65.
76. "Juvenis," *Suvla Bay and After* (London: Hodder & Stoughton, 1916), 1.
77. The Reverend Oswin Creighton, *With the Twenty-Ninth Division at Gallipoli: A Chaplain's Experiences* (London: Longmans, Green & Company, 1916), 19, 20, 22, 21, and so on. The author, following his bout of diphtheria, was stationed on Lemnos.
78. Nevinson, *The Dardanelles Campaign*, 293.
79. Captain Oskat Teichman, D.S.O., M.C., R.A.M.C. *The Diary of a Yeomanry M. O.: Egypt, Gallipoli, Palestine and Italy* (London: T. Fisher Unwin, Ltd., 1921), 16–17.
80. Gillam, *Gallipoli Diary*, 162–3.
81. Units from both Divisions were carried aboard vessels which put into Alexandria. In the case of the 1st/5th Essex some personnel were allowed ashore. Gibbons, *With the 1st/5th Essex in the East*, 6–7.
82. Fair and Wolton, *History of the 1st/5th Battalion "The Suffolk Regiment,"* 14–15.
83. For the Regimental Badges of some of the units which comprised this Army Corps, and the 54th (East Anglian) Division, see the accompanying illustrations.
84. General Sir Ian Hamilton, *Gallipoli Diary*, vol. 2 (New York: George H. Doran Company, 1920), 1–2.
85. Ibid., 2–3.
86. Compton Mackenzie, *Gallipoli Memories* (New York: Doubleday, Doran, & Company, 1930), 340–41.
87. Ibid.
88. Sanders, *Five Years in Turkey*, 22.
89. According to a study published by the Royal Geographic Society in 1999, Stopford obtained some accurate maps of the Dardanelles prior to taking up his command, but "left them on a train." Source: an article by the paper's Defence Correspondent, Hugh McManners, entitled "Bad Maps led to carnage of Gallipoli," in *The Sunday Times*, (London), 21 March 1999, 11.
90. Ibid.
91. *Dictionary of National Biography: The Concise Dictionary; Part II, 1901–1970* (Oxford: Oxford University Press, 1982), 1023.
92. Nevinson, *The Dardanelles Campaign*, 292–3.
93. (a) The basic differences between a "gun" and a "howitzer" or "mortar" are the angles of elevation and muzzle velocities. The former can achieve a maximum elevation of 45 degrees and possesses a high muzzle velocity. The latter two categories can fire comparatively larger and heavier projectiles at steeper angles—as much as 75 degrees in the case of the "mortar"—with very much lower muzzle velocities than those of the "gun" (sometimes enabling the shell or bomb to be detected in flight). Because of the high

angle of elevation and the steep "splash-down" resultant, these artillery pieces can be ranged to drop their shells or bombs into deeply entrenched fortifications, and thus are much more effective at their destruction than the gun. It was in the First World War that the monster siege cannon, such as the Krupps 410 centimeter mortar, came into their own. One of the several drawbacks to naval bombardment was the flatter trajectories of their high-explosive shells, which meant that upon impact the explosive energy fanned forwards rather than blasting downwards. This was an inherent weakness of the naval gunfire employed at Gallipoli. Source: Former 22626479 Gunner Mortlock, M.J., 22 Gibraltar and 46 Niagara Batteries, the Royal Regiment of Artillery (founded by King Henry VIII), and Q Battery, 358 Medium (the Suffolk Yeomanry) Regiment, R.A., Territorial Army.

(b) The Turkish artillery possessed batteries of German *Minenwerfers* (minethrowers), nicknamed by the soldiers on the receiving end as "Moaning Minnies," an onomatopoeic nomenclature. Private Jake Mortlock. Interview, 10 August 1965.

94. Hargave, *The Suvla Bay Landing*, 75–6; and Alan Moorehead, *Gallipoli*, 243. Both accounts related that "Major-General Hammersley ... had suffered a breakdown a year or two before [Suvla]."

95. Angela Partington, ed., *The Oxford Dictionary of Quotations*, 4th ed. (Oxford: Oxford University Press, 1992), 490.

96. Gillam, *Gallipoli Diary*, xviii, xix, 224–5. Also, Great Britain: War Office, Army: *Arrangements Made for Water Supply to the Troops During Landing at Suvla Bay* (H.M.S.O., Harrison & Sons, 1915), 1–2.

97. Liddell Hart, *Strategy*, 100.

98. Keyes, *The Naval Memoirs of Admiral of the Fleet Sir Roger Keyes: The Narrow Seas to the Dardanelles; 1910–1915*, 399–400.

99. Hanna, *The Pals at Suvla Bay*, 53–54.

100. Hargrave, *The Suvla Bay Landing*, 99.

101. John Hargrave, *At Suvla Bay* (London: Constable & Company, 1916), 58.

102. Major-General Sir C.E. Callwell, K.C.B., *The Dardanelles* (Boston: Houghton Mifflin Company, 1919), 228.

103. *Ibid.*

104. Aspinall-Oglander, *The Official History of the War: Military Operations; Gallipoli*, vol. 2, 160.

105. Kannengiesser, *The Campaign in Gallipoli*, 201.

106. *Ibid.*, and Aspinall-Oglander, *The Official History of the War: Military Operations; Gallipoli*, vol. 2, 160–61.

107. *Ibid.*

108. East, ed., *The Gallipoli Diary of Sergeant Lawrence of the Australian Engineers*, 77–78.

109. Hankey, *The Supreme Command, 1914–1918*, vol. 1, 392, 395.

110. *Ibid.*, 395. One feels that Colonel Hankey may well have confused the 13th Division with the 11th, as the former did go into the line at Helles, whereas the latter was the last of the three Kitchener's Army divisions to arrive (28th July.)

111. The Right Hon. Clement R Attlee, *As It Happened* (New York: The Viking Press, 1954), 58–59.

112. Wintle, ed., *The Dictionary of War Quotations*, 322.

113. Fair and Wolton, *The History of the 1st/5th Battalion "The Suffolk Regiment,"* 15. Date of arrival given in Petrie's *The History of the Norfolk Regiment, 1685–1918*, vol. 2, 4 August 1914 to 31 December 1918, 122.

114. Private Mortlock. Interview, 10 August 1965.

115. Donna Condell, Curator, Department of Exhibits and Firearms, the Imperial War Museum, Lambeth Road, London, SE1 WC4, and her colleagues. Letter dated 4 October 1993, and enclosure in reply to my query. One section of the enclosed material was a transcript of an archival sound recording of a veteran of the Gallipoli Campaign reminiscing about how officers and N.C.O.s used indelible pencil mark to inscribe their stars ("pips"), crowns, and chevrons on sleeve or shoulder so that they would be apparent only at close proximity.

116. Gillam, *Gallipoli Diary*, 29.

117. John Ellis, *Eye-Deep in Hell: Trench Warfare in World War I* (New York: Pantheon Books, 1976), 33.

Chapter 3

1. Harry Judge, ed., *Oxford Illustrated Encyclopedia*: vol. 3: *World History from Earliest Times to 1800* (Oxford: Oxford University Press, 1988), 284, 385.

2. The Hampshire Regiment had a battalion at Anzac (2nd) and another at Helles (10th) both involved in the pre- Suvla assaults, while a third (8th) went to Suvla Bay with the rest of the 54th (East Anglian) Division. C.T. Atkinson, *The History of the Royal Hampshire Regiment*, vol. 2: *1914–1918*

(Glasgow: Robert Maclehose & Company, Limited, 1952), 92–100.
  3. Aspinall-Oglander, *The Official History of the War: Military Operations: Gallipoli*, vol. 2, 158.
  4. *The Times History of the War*, vol. 7 (London: The Times, 1916), 169.
  5. Hamilton, *Gallipoli Diary*, vol. 2, Appendix III, 309. However, because of Stopford and Reed's remonstration an amended version was issued into which what John Hargrave called "the fatal phrase '... if possible ...'" was inserted. *Ibid.*, 311.
  6. Hargrave, *The Suvla Bay Landing*, 257.
  7. As an army commander prior to the Battle of Elaandslaagte in October 1899, Colonel Hamilton, in a speech to his troops, told them that "tomorrow the newsboys on the streets of London will be calling out the news of your victory." Later, at a critical juncture of the battle, Hamilton, with conspicuous bravery, rallied his men to repulse an enemy counterattack. Thomas Pakenham, *The Boer War* (New York: Random House, 1979), 139–44.
  8. Stopford had slipped and sprained his knee that morning. Colonel Aspinall found him lying on his valise spread out on the floor of his tent, as he recounts in *The Official History*, 159. Moorehead, *Gallipoli*, 256.
  9. Whereabouts uncertain. Probably organizing his Divisional Headquarters.
  10. Hamilton, *Gallipoli Diary*, vol. 2, 53–54.
  11. *Ibid.*, 54.
  12. Mackenzie, *Gallipoli Memories*, 351.
  13. John Hargrave, *At Suvla Bay* (London: Constable and Company, 1916), 55, 57.
  14. *The Virago Book of Women and the Great War, 1914–1918* (London: Virago Press, 1998), 133.
  15. 2nd Lieutenant Priestman of the 6th York & Lancasters at the same location recorded a completely contrary observation. (See page 72 below.) E.Y. Priestman, *With a B.-P. Scout in Gallipoli: A Record of the Belton Bulldogs* (London: George Routledge & Sons, 1917), 161–62. B.-P. = Baden-Powell, the founder of the Boy Scout movement.
  16. Hamilton, *Gallipoli Diary*, vol. 2, 54–55.
  17. Hargrave, *The Suvla Bay Landing*, 129.
  18. Hanna, *The Pals at Suvla Bay*, 59.
  19. "Juvenis," *Suvla Bay and After*, 15.
  20. Hanna, *The Pals at Suvla Bay*, 60–61.
  21. A movie camera was not a commonplace in 1915 and one wonders whether any of those unique reels survived.
  22. Priestman, *With a B.-P. Scout in Gallipoli*, 161–62.
  23. Aspinall-Oglander, *The Official History of the War: Military Operations: Gallipoli*, vol. 2, 131.
  24. Hamilton, *Gallipoli Diary*, vol. 2, 3.
  25. Priestman, *With a B.-P. Scout in Gallipoli*, 162–63.
  26. Mackenzie, *Gallipoli Memories*, 349.
  27. Moorehead, *Gallipoli*, 264.
  28. Hamilton, *Gallipoli Diary*, vol. 2, 55.
  29. Moorehead, *Gallipoli*, 264.
  30. Priestman, *With a B.-P. Scout in Gallipoli*, 164–67.
  31. Hargrave, *At Suvla Bay*, 59. "Juvenis," *Suvla Bay and After*, 23–24.
  32. Hargrave, *At Suvla Bay*, 59.
  33. Aspinall-Oglander, *The Official History of the War: Military Operations: Gallipoli*, vol. 2, 266.
  34. Hargrave, *At Suvla Bay*, 62.
  35. It is well to bear in mind that Hargrave was a medic. It seems more than likely that his reference to "four batteries" must have meant "guns," as is later indicated. The whole Anafarta Detachment possessed only three batteries at that time and Major Willmer would not have concentrated them all on the Kiretch Tepe Ridge. A battery is a subdivision of an artillery regiment containing four to eight guns.
  36. Hargrave, *At Suvla Bay*, 60–62.
  37. This is extremely debatable, as a well-oiled weapon would be unlikely to suffer this kind of ill-effect from momentary submersion in seawater.
  38. Lyn Macdonald, *1914–1918: Voices and Images of the Great War* (London: Michael Joseph, 1988), 96.
  39. Kannengiesser, *The Campaign in Gallipoli*, 204.
  40. Lieutenant George O. Van Orden, U.S. Marine Corps. "The Gallipoli Landings: Suvla Bay, 6 August–20 December, 1915," from *The Gallipoli Campaign Studies*, at the U.S. Marine Corps School. Thesis, U.S. Naval College, 1935.
  41. Sanders, *Five Years in Turkey*, 88.
  42. Hargrave, *The Suvla Bay Landing*, 283.
  43. Holger H. Herwig and Neil M. Heyman, eds. *Biographical Dictionary of World War I* (Westport, CT: Greenwood Press, 1982), 203.
  44. *Ibid.*, 112.
  45. Kannengiesser, *The Campaign in Gallipoli*, 205.
  46. *Ibid.*
  47. Sanders, *Five Years in Turkey*, 81–82, and Callwell, *The Dardanelles*, 228.
  48. Aspinall-Oglander, *The Official History of the War: Military Operations: Gallipoli*, vol. 2, 265.

49. Grand Admiral Baron Alfred von Tirpitz, *My Memoirs*, vol. 2, trans. Georg Hans Krefeld (New York: Dodd, Mead & Company, 1919), 369.
50. Hamilton, *Gallipoli Diary*, vol. 2, 50–51.
51. Sanders, *Five Years in Turkey*, 81. Kannengiesser, *The Campaign in Gallipoli*, 198–99. Major E.R. Prigge, *Der Kampf um die Dardanellen* (Berlin: Kiepenhaver, 1916), 72–73.
52. Aspinall-Oglander, *The Official History of the War: Military Operations: Gallipoli*, vol. 2, 128.
53. Ibid., 128–29.
54. Hargrave, *The Suvla Bay Landing*, 100.
55. Alan Moorehead, *Gallipoli*, 255.
56. Hamilton, *The Tragic Story of the Dardanelles: Ian Hamilton's Final Despatch*, 89. Also Hamilton, *Gallipoli Diary*, vol. 1, 329.
57. Gillam, *Gallipoli Diary*, 30. When witnessing the April landings put their burden at 70 lbs., Gillam observed, "how they will be able to fight tomorrow beats me" with that kind of encumbrance.
58. "Some of the men had been on their feet for seventeen hours." Aspinall-Oglander, *The Official History of the War: Military Operations: Gallipoli*, vol. 2, 236.
59. Creighton, *With the Twenty-Ninth Division in Gallipoli: A Chaplain's Experiences*, 38, 41–2, 50.
60. Gillam, *Gallipoli Diary*, 29.
61. Lieutenant-Colonel Peter Champness, T.D. Interview, 10 June 1955.
62. "Juvenis," *Suvla Bay and After*, 2.
63. Kannengiesser, *The Campaign in Gallipoli*, 210.
64. Angela Partington, ed., *The Oxford Dictionary of Quotations*, 727.
65. Mackenzie, *Gallipoli Memories*, 360–61.
66. Vivian Ogilvie, *The English Public School* (New York: The Macmillan Company, 1957), 196–98.
67. Jack Pitman, *England Ebbing* (New York: Stein & Day, Inc., 1987), 53–54, 59, *et al.*
68. Keyes, *The Naval Memoirs of Admiral of the Fleet Sir Roger Keyes*: vol. 1: *The Narrow Seas to the Dardanelles, 1910–1915*, 333.
69. Hargrave, *At Suvla Bay*, 70.
70. Hargrave, *The Suvla Bay Landing*, 102–05. Aspinall-Oglander, *The Official History of the War: Military Operations: Gallipoli*, vol. 2, 165–66. James, *Gallipoli*, 290.
71. Hankey, *The Supreme Command, 1914–1918*, vol. 1, 395–396.
72. John Masefield, *Gallipoli* (New York: The Macmillan Company, 1916), 175.
73. East, ed. *The Gallipoli Diary of Sergeant Lawrence*, 62–63.
74. Masefield, *Gallipoli*, 183.
75. Brigadier-General S. L. A. Marshall, United States Army Reserve, Retired, "Suvla Bay," in *The Military Review*, 43, 11 (November, 1963): 65–66.
76. Priestman, *With a B.-P. Scout in Gallipoli*, 165.
77. Hargrave, *At Suvla Bay*, 59.
78. Aspinall-Oglander, *The Official History of the War: Military Operations: Gallipoli*, vol. 2, 165.
79. Kannengiesser, *The Campaign in Gallipoli*, 205.
80. Hamilton, *Gallipoli Diary*, vol. 2, 55.
81. Hargrave, *The Suvla Bay Landing*, 111.
82. Callwell, *The Dardanelles*, 225.
83. Marshall, "Suvla Bay," *The Military Review*, 66.
84. James, *Gallipoli*, 283.
85. Hamilton, *Gallipoli Diary*, vol. 2, 75.
86. Hankey, *The Supreme Command, 1914–1918*, vol. 1, 396.
87. Hargrave, *The Suvla Bay Landing*, 128.
88. Ibid.
89. Major Bryan Cooper, *The 10th (Irish) Division in Gallipoli* (London: Herbert Jenkins, 1918), 145, 148, 157–8.
90. Hankey, *The Supreme Command, 1914–1918*, vol. 1, 396–97.
91. Hamilton, *Gallipoli Diary*, vol. 2, 77.
92. Hankey, *The Supreme Command, 1914–1918*, vol. 1, 401.
93. Snelling, *VCs of the First World War: Gallipoli*, 147–187.
94. *The Virago Book of Women and the Great War, 1914–1918*, 133.
95. Hankey, *The Supreme Command, 1914–1918*, vol. 1, 397.
96. Ibid.
97. Hargrave, *The Suvla Bay Landing*, 145.
98. Private Mortlock. Interview, 10 August 1965.
99. Hamilton, *Gallipoli Diary*, vol. 2, quoted by permission.
100. Ibid.
101. Hargrave, *The Suvla Bay Landing*, 236.
102. Ashmead-Bartlett, *The Uncensored Dardanelles*, 230.
103. East, ed., *The Gallipoli Diary of Sergeant Lawrence*, 69.

Notes—Chapter 3

104. Hamilton, *The Tragic Story of the Dardanelles: Ian Hamilton's Final Despatch*, 94–95.
105. H.M. Denham, *Dardanelles: A Midshipman's Diary, 1915–1916* (London: John Murray, 1919), 146.
106. Aspinall-Oglander, *The Official History of the War: Military Operations: Gallipoli*, vol. 2, 265–66.
107. Hamilton, *Gallipoli Diary*, vol. 2, 56.
108. Ibid., 56–57.
109. Ibid., 57.
110. Bean, *Official History of Australia in the War: The Story of Anzac: From 4 May, 1915, to the Evacuation of the Gallipoli Peninsula*, 467.
111. Aspinall-Oglander, *The Official History of the War: Military Operations: Gallipoli*, vol. 2, 272.
112. James, *Gallipoli*, 294.
113. Churchill, *The World Crisis*, vol. 2, 1915, 470.
114. James, *Gallipoli*, 294. Colonel Hankey stated that this cable reached GHQ, Imbros just after Sir Ian arrived at Suvla. Hankey, *The Supreme Command, 1914–1918*, vol. 1, 398.
115. James, *Gallipoli*, 294.
116. Ibid.
117. Hankey, *The Supreme Command, 1914–1918*, vol. 1, 397.
118. James, *Gallipoli*, 294.
119. Hamilton, *Gallipoli Diary*, vol. 2, 62.
120. Ibid., 64. Also Keyes, *The Naval Memoirs of Admiral of the Fleet Sir Roger Keyes*: vol. 1: *The Narrow Seas to the Dardanelles, 1910–1915*, 337.
121. Hamilton, *Gallipoli Diary*, vol. 2, 64.
122. Hankey, *The Supreme Command, 1914–1918*, vol. 1, 398.
123. Aspinall-Oglander, *The Official History of the War: Military Operations: Gallipoli*, vol. 2, 266.
124. Kannengiesser, *The Campaign in Gallipoli*, 211–12.
125. Denham, *Dardanelles: A Midshipman's Diary, 1915–1916*, 146.
126. Hargrave, *The Suvla Bay Landing*, 115.
127. Hamilton, *Gallipoli Diary*, vol. 2, Appendix III, 310.
128. Aspinall-Oglander, *The Official History of the War: Military Operations; Gallipoli*, vol. 2, 318.
129. Ibid.
130. Hargrave, *The Suvla Bay Landing*, 133.
131. Hankey, *The Supreme Command*, vol. 1, 398.
132. Ibid., 399–400.
133. Ibid., 398.
134. Aspinall-Oglander, *The Official History of the War: Military Operations: Gallipoli*, vol. 2, 275.
135. Callwell, *The Dardanelles*, 229.
136. Ibid., 275.
137. James, *Gallipoli*, 295.
138. Churchill, *The World Crisis*, vol. 2, 472.
139. Ibid.
140. Snelling, *VCs of the First World War: Gallipoli*, 189–190.
141. Ibid., 191, 193.
142. Lyn Macdonald, *1914–1918: Voices and Images of the Great War* (London: Michael Joseph, 1988), 100.
143. Lord Kinross, *Ataturk: A Biography of Mustapha Kemal, Father of Modern Turkey* (New York: William Morrow, 1965), 102.
144. Mackenzie, *Gallipoli Memories*, 374.
145. Aspinall-Oglander, *The Official History of the War: Military Operations: Gallipoli*, vol. 2, 314.
146. Hamilton, *Gallipoli Diary*, vol. 2, 81.
147. Ibid.
148. Private Mortlock said wistfully of the village of Anafarta: "We could see it. But we never got there...." Interview, 10 August 1965.
149. Hamilton, *Gallipoli Diary*, vol. 2, 72–73.
150. Aspinall-Oglander, *The Official History of the War: Military Operations: Gallipoli*, vol. 2, 277–78.
151. Gibbons, *With the 1/5th Essex in the East*, 6.
152. Atkinson, *The Regimental History of the Royal Hampshire Regiment*, vol. 2, *1914–1918*, 101.
153. Fair and Wolton, *The History of the 1st/5th Battalion "The Suffolk Regiment,"* 15.
154. Gibbons, *With the 1/5th Essex in the East*, 6–7.
155. Ibid., 15–16.
156. Private Mortlock. Interview, 10 August 1965.
157. Ibid.
158. Ibid. According to *The Official History*, Sir Ian Hamilton insisted that "... the 54th Division must assault the crest of the ridge at dawn on the 13th, and the 10th and 11th Divisions must render as much as assistance as possible." Aspinall-Oglander, *The Official History of the War: Military Operations: Gallipoli*, vol. 2, 314. Also Hamilton, *Gallipoli Diary*, Appendix IV, 311.
159. Fair and Wolton, *The History of the 1st/5th Battalion "The Suffolk Regiment,"* 16.
160. Private Mortlock. Interview, 10

August 1965. Mortlock vowed at the time never again to waste water and is known to have adhered to this undertaking until his death in late December 1971.
161. Gibbons, *With the 1/5th Essex in the East*, 7.
162. *Ibid.*
163. Fair and Wolton, *The History of the 1st/5th Battalion "The Suffolk Regiment,"* 16.
164. Corporal (at that time) Reginald E.S. Lane, D Company, the 1/5th Battalion, the Suffolk Regiment. Interview, 5 November 1965. Incidentally, it is of interest to reveal that the very same officer, Lt. H. Coeur de Wolton was later to be instrumental in obtaining Lane a commission in the Egyptian Labour Corps.
165. Fair and Wolton, *The History of the 1st/5th Battalion "The Suffolk Regiment,"* 16.
166. Aspinall-Oglander, *The Official History of the War: Military Operations: Gallipoli*, vol. 2, 314.
167. *Ibid.*, 313.
168. C.T. Atkinson, *The Regimental History of the Royal Hampshire Regiment*: vol. 2, *1914–1918*, 101.
169. Hamilton, *Gallipoli Diary*, vol. 2, 94–95.
170. *Ibid.*, 95.
171. *Ibid.*, 95, 97.
172. *Ibid.*, 97–98.
173. Gibbons, *With the 1/5th Essex in the East*, 12.
174. Hamilton, *Gallipoli Diary*, vol. 2, 98.
175. Aspinall-Oglander, *The Official History of the War: Military Operations: Gallipoli*, vol. 2, 314.
176. Hamilton, *Gallipoli Diary*, vol. 2, 90.
177. Petrie, *The History of the Norfolk Regiment, 1685–1918*, vol. 2, 4 August 1914 to 31 December 1918, 124.
178. Fair and Wolton, *The History of 1st/5th Battalion "The Suffolk Regiment,"* 16–17.
179. Aspinall-Oglander, *The Official History of the War: Military Operations: Gallipoli*, vol. 2, 317.
180. Atkinson, *Regimental History of the Royal Hampshire Regiment*: vol. 2, *1914–1918*, 102.
181. Aspinall-Oglander, *The Official History of the War: Military Operation; Gallipoli*, vol. 2, 314.
182. Fair and Wolton, *The History of the 1st/5th Battalion, "The Suffolk Regiment,"* 9–10. Gibbons, *With the 1/5th Essex in the East*, 1–2.
183. Atkinson, *The Regimental History of the Royal Hampshire Regiment*: vol. 2, *1914–1918*, 102.
184. Gibbons, *With the 1/5th Essex in the East*, 9.
185. Guthrie Moir, *The Suffolk Regiment*. Famous Regiments Series, ed. Lieutenant-General Sir Brian Horrocks (London: Leo Cooper, 1969), 91–92.
186. Fair and Wolton, *The History of the 1st/5th Battalion "The Suffolk Regiment,"* 17.
187. Bush, *Gallipoli*, 273. Aspinall-Oglander, *The Official History of the War: Military Operations: Gallipoli*, vol. 2, 317–18.
188. Gibbons, *With the 1/5th Essex in the East*, 9.
189. "Some Hampshires were among them." Atkinson, *The Regimental History of the Royal Hampshire Regiment*, vol. 2, *1914–1918*, 102.
190. Bush, *Gallipoli*, 273.
191. *The Sunday Times* (London), 3 May 1998 Article on "The lost Company of the 1/5th Norfolks," 12. Also *All the King's Men*, a television dramatization of Nigel McCrery's novel based on the incident on Masterpiece Theatre, February 20, 2000. Repeated on PBS, March 18, 2002. Also F. Loraine Petre, *The History of the Norfolk Regiment, 1685–1918*: vol. 2, 4 August 1914 to 31 December 1918 (Norwich: The Empire Press/Jarrold & Sons, Ltd., 1953), 125–126.
192. Murphy, *The History of the Suffolk Regiment, 1914–1927*, 104.
193. Atkinson, *The Regimental History of the Royal Hampshire Regiment, Vol. II, 1914–1918*, 102–103.
194. Initials stand for "Territorial Decoration," awarded upon completion of 13 years service with the Territorial Army (12 Annual Training Camps).
195. Murphy, *The History of the Suffolk Regiment, 1914–1927*, 104–105.
196. Gibbons, *With the 1/5th Essex in the East*, 10–11.
197. *Ibid.*
198. *Ibid.*, 13.
199. Bush, *Gallipoli*, 273.
200. Hamilton, *Gallipoli Diary*, vol. 2, 89–90.
201. Bush, *Gallipoli*, 271.
202. Hamilton, *Gallipoli Diary*, vol. 2, 103.
203. *Ibid.*
204. *Ibid.*, 116–17.
205. Churchill, *The World Crisis*, vol. 2, 1915, 476.

Chapter 4

1. Alan Clark, *The Donkeys* (London:

Hutchinson, 1961), and others, including Private Mortlock, considered very, very few, if any, of the British generals "vibrant," though the latter had great respect, even admiration, for Field-Marshal Sir Edmund Allenby, Commander-in-Chief of the Egyptian Expeditionary Force, 1917–19.

2. Hamilton, *Gallipoli Diary*, vol. 2, 104.
3. *Ibid.*, 106.
4. *Ibid.*, 122.
5. *Ibid.* Ironically, after the war General Lindley took up residence in Wamil Hall, an Elizabethan manor house just across the River Lark, which separated it from the farm Private Jake Mortlock returned to work on. After marrying, Mortlock and his wife actually lived in the hamlet of Wamil for the first year.
6. It is worthy of note that not one volume of either *Who's Who* or *Who Was Who* mentions General Hammersley's Great War service.
7. Moorehead, *Gallipoli*, 296.
8. *Ibid.*
9. Barry Pitt, *Unfit to Command: Military Blunders Throughout History* (New York: W.W. Norton & Company, Inc., 1999), 29–30.
10. Hargrave, *The Suvla Bay Landing*, 237.
11. Bush, *Gallipoli*, 276.
12. Hargrave, *The Suvla Bay Landing*, 230.
13. Hamilton, *Gallipoli Diary*, vol. 2, 107.
14. Aspinall-Oglander, *The Official History of the War: Military Operations; Gallipoli*, vol. 2, 320–21.
15. *Ibid.*, 320.
16. *Ibid.*, 322. Also Lt.-Col. Russell Gurney, *History of the Northamptonshire Regiment*, vol. 1, *1742–1934* (Aldershot, U.K.: Gale & Polden, Ltd., 1935), 327: "On 30th July, 1915, they sailed for the East under the command of Lieutenant-Colonel E. G. Curtis, and on 15th August were landed on the Gallipoli peninsula, moving up to the trenches two days later. After a period of trench warfare the army was withdrawn from Gallipoli, and on 8th December proceeded to Mudros and thence to Egypt.
17. *Ibid.*, 322–23.
18. Moorehead, *Gallipoli*, 295.
19. Sanders, *Five Years in Turkey*, 67.
20. In fact Sir Ian Hamilton suggested that General Mahon acted upon his own initiative. Hamilton, *Gallipoli Diary*, vol. 2, 97–98.
21. All the principal primary sources, i.e., Cooper, Hanna, Hargrave, "Juvenis," and *The Official History*, agree on this episode.
22. Shrapnel, invented by General H. Shrapnel (1761–1842) during the Peninsular War, comprised a hollow canister containing lead pellets, which were scattered in a shower by a bursting charge set off by a time fuse.... High explosive shells relied on impact blast, as well as fragmentation, to destroy troops in the open. Some shells at Gallipoli incorporated a fuse that delayed explosion; others could be discharged like shrapnel, in an overhead burst, violently expelling a cone of bullets. Bombardier Thomas Carter, of the 25th Field Regiment Royal Artillery, Malayan Counter-Terrorist Emergency, 1952–54, explained that the O.P. [Observation Post] Officer directed the adjusting of the fuse-settings until the desired accuracy was achieved. Interview, December 29, 1975.
23. Private Mortlock. Interview, 10 August 1965.
24. Hargrave, *The Suvla Bay Landing*, 226; and Hargrave, *At Suvla Bay*, 64–65.
25. Hargrave, *At Suvla Bay*, 163.
26. Henry W. Nevinson, *The Dardanelles Campaign*, 329.
27. Private Mortlock. Interview, 10 August 1965.
28. "Juvenis," *Suvla Bay and After*, 54.
29. Hanna, *The Pals at Suvla Bay*, 329.
30. Hamilton, *Gallipoli Diary*, vol. 2, 62.
31. Hanna, *The Pals at Suvla Bay*, 113.
32. *Ibid.*, 104–105.
33. Cooper, *The Tenth (Irish) Division in Gallipoli*, 161–80.
34. Hargrave, *The Suvla Bay Landing*, 233–234.
35. *Ibid.*, 220–232.
36. *Ibid.*
37. *Ibid.*, 236–37.
38. Hamilton, *Gallipoli Diary*, vol. 2, 117.
39. Minutes of the Dardanelles Committee, held at 10 Downing Street, 19 August 1915 (London: Committee of Imperial Defence, 1916), 5.
40. Hankey, *The Supreme Command, 1914–1918*, vol. 1, 390–402.
41. *The Times* (London), 12 August 1915, 2.
42. *Ibid.*
43. Aspinall-Oglander, *The Official History of the War: Military Operations: Gallipoli*, vol. 2, 128, 134, and 143.
44. Hamilton, *Gallipoli Diary*, vol. 2, 120.
45. Hargrave, *The Suvla Bay Landing*, 235–236.
46. *Ibid.*, 123.
47. Private Mortlock stated that it was considered the height of ignominy to surrender, or allow oneself to be captured. Interview, 25 September 1965.

Notes — Chapter 4

48. Minutes of the Meetings of the Dardanelles Committee held at 10 Downing Street, 19 and 20 August 1915 (London: Committee of Imperial Defence, 1916), 1, 4.
49. One would have thought that a Commander-in-Chief would want to at least be within hailing distance of General de Lisle while this crucial battle was fought.
50. Hamilton, *Gallipoli Diary*, vol. 2, 126–28.
51. *Ibid.*
52. Sir Ian Hamilton, *The Tragic Story of the Dardanelles: Ian Hamilton's Final Despatch* (London: George Newnes, 1916), 114.
53. Gillam, *Gallipoli Diary*, 206.
54. Jones, *The Diary of a Padre at Suvla Bay*, 66.
55. Denham, *Dardanelles: A Midshipman's Diary, 1915–1916*, 154. The figures 7 and 27 refer to the shell's time of flight — to impact or aerial detonation — in seconds.
56. Nevinson, *The Dardanelles Campaign*, 341.
57. Hargrave, *The Suvla Bay Landing*, 244.
58. Jones, *The Diary of a Padre at Suvla Bay*, 66.
59. Hargrave, *The Suvla Bay Landing*, 245.
60. Hamilton, *Gallipoli Diary*, vol. 2, 128.
61. *Ibid.*
62. Jones, *The Diary of a Padre at Suvla Bay*, 66–67.
63. Gillam, *Gallipoli Diary*, 206–207.
64. Bush, *Gallipoli*, 283. Quoted from Major A.P. Herbert, M.P., *Mons, Anzac and Kut* (London: Hutchinson, 1919).
65. Norman Wilkinson, *The Dardanelles: Colour Sketches from Gallipoli* (London: Longmans, Green & Company, 1915), 17.
66. Teichman, *The Diary of a Yeomanry M.O.: Egypt, Gallipoli, Palestine and Italy*, 27–30.
67. Ashmead-Bartlett, *The Uncensored Dardanelles*, 236–237.
68. William Harmon, ed., *The Top 500 Poems: A Columbia Anthology* (New York: Columbia University Press, 1992), 651.
69. Cecil Woodham-Smith, *The Reason Why* (New York: McGraw-Hill Book Company), 233–34.
70. John Selby, *Balaclava: Gentlemen's Battle* (New York: Atheneum, 1970), 10.
71. Harmon, *The Top 500 Poems: A Columbia Anthology*, 651–53.
72. Captain Quintin Kennedy, Royal Field Artillery, 1911–33, of Riverside Cottage, Wamil, Suffolk, stated that his mother-in-law, the Honourable Mrs. Bamfylde, at that time living in Worlington, claimed to be a direct descendant of Captain Edward Nolan. Interview, 5 November 1961.
73. Harmon, *The Top 500 Poems: A Columbia Anthology*, 651–53.
74. Hargrave, *The Suvla Bay Landing*, 247.
75. *Ibid.*, 246–47.
76. Jones, *The Diary of a Padre at Suvla Bay*, 67.
77. Harmon, *The Top 500 Poems: A Columbia Anthology*, 651–52.
78. Atkinson, *The Regimental History of the Royal Hampshire Regiment*, vol. 2, *1914–1918*, 104.
79. Hamilton, *The Tragic Story of the Dardanelles: Ian Hamilton's Final Despatch*, 116.
80. Woodham-Smith, *The Reason Why*, 238.
81. Private Jake Mortlock also referred to this feature as "Burnt Hill." Interview 21 August 1965.
82. Gillam, *Gallipoli Diary*, 210–11.
83. Hamilton, *The Tragic Story of the Dardanelles: Ian Hamilton's Final Despatch*, 117.
84. Jones, *The Diary of a Padre at Suvla Bay*, 67.
85. Snelling, *VCs of the First World War: Gallipoli*, 213.
86. Sir John Hammerton, ed., *I Was There: Personal Narratives of the Great War* (London: Amalgamated Press, 1916–1921), 814.
87. Teichman, *The Diary of a Yeomanry M.O.: Egypt, Gallipoli, Palestine and Italy*, 31.
88. Hammerton, *I Was There: Personal Narratives of the Great War*, 814–816.
89. Snelling, *VCs of the First World War: Gallipoli*, 217.
90. Atkinson, *The Regimental History of the Royal Hampshire Regiment*, vol. 2, *1914–1918*, 106.
91. Teichman, *The Diary of a Yeomanry M.O.: Egypt, Gallipoli, Palestine and Italy*, 32–34.
92. *Ibid.*, 36.
93. *Ibid.*, 37.
94. *Ibid.*, 38.
95. *New York Times*, 30 August 1915, 1–2.
96. Sanders, *Five Years in Turkey*, 93–4.
97. Minutes of a Meeting of the Dardanelles Committee, held at 10 Downing Street, 19 August 1915, 1–7.
98. *Ibid.*, 30 August 1915. VERY SECRET appendix, Part IV, paragraphs 99–108.
99. See Map M.
100. Gibbons, *With the 1/5th Essex in the East*, 17.
101. Moorehead, *Gallipoli*, 297.

102. Williams, *Anzacs, the Media and the Great War*, 95.
103. Ibid.
104. Possibly this was the well Captains Fair and Wolton, the Suffolk Regimental historians, referred to in the following chapter.
105. Hargrave, *The Suvla Bay Landing*, 228.
106. Fair and Wolton, *The History of the 1/5th Battalion "The Suffolk Regiment,"* 20.
107. Private Mortlock's "Letter from Hill 60/Anzac," 3. See facsimile in Illustrations.
108. Ashmead-Bartlett, *The Uncensored Dardanelles*, 237.
109. Vera Brittain, *Letters of a Lost Generation: The First World War Letters of Vera Brittain and Four Friends: Roland Leighton, Edward Brittain, Victor Richardson, and Geoffrey Thurlow* (Boston: Northwestern University Press, 1999), 158.

Chapter 5

1. Hankey, *The Supreme Command, 1914–1918*, vol. 1, 337.
2. Basil Liddell Hart, "Gallipoli Judgement," *Purnell's History of the First World War*, March 9 (1971), 1140.
3. Attlee, *As It Happened*, 60–1.
4. Atkinson, *The Regimental History of the Royal Hampshire Regiment*, vol. 2, 1914–1918, 107.
5. *The Parliamentary Debates (Official Report). Fifth Series—Volume XIX. Fifth Session of the Thirteenth Parliament of the United Kingdom of Great Britain & Ireland. 5 and 6 George V. House Lords. Second Volume of Session 1914–15, comprising period from Thursday, 3rd June, 1915, to Wednesday, 20th October, 1915* (London: Printed under the authority of H.M.S.O. by Harrison & Sons, 1915), 810, 811,815.
6. Fair and Wolton, *The History of the 1st/5th Battalion "The Suffolk Regiment,"* 24.
7. Nepalese mercenaries who enlisted in the British Army in exclusively Gurkha (apart from commissioned officers) regiments. These fine soldiers were, and still are, mercifully, extremely pro–British.
8. Private Mortlock. Interview, 25 September 1965.
9. "General Hamilton had his secretary write to the colonel of the 6th Gurkha Rifles: 'It is Sir Ian Hamilton's most cherished conviction that had he been given more Gurkhas in the Dardanelles then he would never have been held up by the Turks.'" Byron Farwell, *The Gurkhas* (New York: W.W. Norton & Company, 1984,) 104.
10. Private Mortlock. Interview, 25 September 1965.
11. Lady Diana Cooper, *The Rainbow Comes and Goes* (London: Rupert Hart-Davis, 1958), 146.
12. Masefield, *Gallipoli*, 213.
13. Private Mortlock. Excerpt from "Letter from Hill 60, Suvla/Anzac." Dated 25 September 1915.
14. John Ellis, *Eye-Deep In Hell: Trench Warfare in World War*, 33.
15. Gillam, *Gallipoli Diary*, 233.
16. Commanding Officer of the 54th (East Anglian) Division.
17. Hamilton, *Gallipoli Diary*, vol. 2, 208. (With reference to the Indian troops, Private Jake Mortlock related that they smoked their cigarettes by drawing the smoke through cupped palms rather than in direct contact with their lips. Private Mortlock. Interview, 25 September 1965.)
18. Murphy, *The History of the Suffolk Regiment, 1914–1927*, 213–14.
19. Private Mortlock. Interview, 25 September 1965.
20. A Verey-pistol was one of the several souvenirs Private Mortlock brought home.
21. Ibid. Fair and Wolton, in their *History of the 1st/5th Battalion "The Suffolk Regiment,"* suggested that these men belonged to the Welsh Horse Imperial Yeomanry.
22. Private Mortlock told his daughter Patricia Anne that "we never had enough ammunition." P. Anne Cobbold, recounted in a letter dated 8 March 1994.
23. Fair and Wolton, *The History of the 1st/5th Battalion "The Suffolk Regiment,"* 25.
24. Possibly the one the Indian troops captured at Kabak Kuyu.
25. Fair and Wolton, *The History of the 1st/5th Battalion "The Suffolk Regiment,"* 25. C.E.W. Bean, *Gallipoli Correspondent: The Frontline Diary of C.E.W. Bean* (Sydney: George Allen & Unwin, 1922), 114.
26. Lance-Corporal Albert Collen, C Company, the 2nd Battalion, the Royal Fusiliers, stated that "whizz-bangs" were the most feared projectiles at Salonika. Interview, 6 July 1963. Col. Gibbons, in his *With the 1/5th Essex in the East*, 20, also describes the uncomfortable attentions of enfilading "75s."
27. Fair and Wolton, *The History of the 1st/5th Battalion "The Suffolk Regiment,"* 25.
28. Ibid., 23–24. Quotation, previously cited, is from A.P. Herbert's "Half-hours at Helles," in James, *Gallipoli*, 209. Also, Gibbons, *With the 1/5th Essex in the East*, 17.
29. The intense heat often caused the fat

content in the tins (cans) to melt so the substance was virtually liquid. Private Mortlock. Interview, 25 September 1965. The extremely saline nature of this product coupled with the water shortage made it unpopular. Accounts state that occasionally soldiers, particularly Australians, disgustedly threw the tins of corned beef into the Turkish trenches, sometimes to have them likewise returned, once with a note attached which suggested a more acceptable alternative. Moorehead, *Gallipoli*, 298, and elsewhere.

30. Private Mortlock. Interview, 25 September 1965.

31. *Ibid.*

32. "Juvenis," *Suvla Bay and After*, 271.

33. Private Mortlock. Interview, 25 September 1965.

34. Moorehead, *Gallipoli*, 297.

35. Minutes of the War Council and Dardanelles' Committee Meeting of October 6th, 1915, 3.

36. *Ibid.*

37. Ashmead-Bartlett, *The Uncensored Dardanelles*, 240.

38. Moorehead, *Gallipoli*, 309–10.

39. *Ibid.*, 310.

40. Private Mortlock's personal first ingredient of a recipe for a more effective British war effort in the Great War. Interview, 25 September 1965.

41. Moorehead, *Gallipoli*, 304.

42. Hamilton, *Gallipoli Diary*, vol. 2, 209–11.

43. Atkinson, *The Regimental History of the Royal Hampshire Regiment*, vol. 2, 1914–1918, 107–108.

44. Churchill, *The World Crisis*, vol. 2, 476.

45. Hamilton, *Gallipoli Diary*, vol. 2, 237.

46. *Ibid.*

47. Moorehead, *Gallipoli*, 298.

48. Private Mortlock. Interview, 25 September 1965.

49. The questionable water from the captured well at Kabak Kuyu?

50. The Reverend Chaplain Oswin Creighton was diagnosed with the same complaint at the time of the first Suvla landings. He, however, received much more compassionate treatment. Creighton, *With the Twenty-Ninth Division in Gallipoli*, 166–69.

51. "A hospital ship is a very wonderful thing, but when I saw the swinging iron cots and realised the stuffiness of the lower decks even when empty, I was thankful that fate had not ordered me to serve on a hospital ship." Vera Brittain, *Chronicle of Youth: The War Diary 1913–1917*, edited by Alan Bishop with Terry Smart (New York: William Morrow & Company, Inc., 1982), 328.

52. Those under-aged soldiers who had given false ages in order to enlist could gain their discharges if they reported the fact to their Commanding Officers. Sixteen-year-old Private Fincham, of D Company, 1/5th Suffolks, was too manly and proud to do so, and endured Gallipoli plus other theatres for the duration of the war. Private Mortlock. Interview, 5 November 1965. In the same brigade, the Sandringham Company of the 1/5th Norfolks had a fifteen-year old boy, who was wounded soon after landing, and later disappeared with the rest of his company in the attack on Anafarta Ova. *All The King's Men*. Television dramatization of Nigel McCrery's novel, February 20, 2000, and PBS Exxon/Mobil Masterpiece Theatre, Monday, 18th March, 2002, 9 P.M.

53. Murphy, *The History of the Suffolk Regiment, 1914–1927*, 214–15.

54. Macdonald, *1915: The Death of Innocence*, 566.

55. *Ibid.*

56. *Ibid.*, 567.

57. Hamilton, *Gallipoli Diary*, vol. 2, 272.

58. *Ibid.*, 273.

59. Churchill, *The World Crisis*, vol. 2, 516.

60. Hamilton, *Gallipoli Diary*, vol. 2, 189, 206.

61. Sanders, *Five Years in Turkey*, 188.

62. *Hansard Record of Parliamentary Debates*, vol. 5, Debate on the Naval and Military Situation, 564–565.

63. Lloyd George, *War Memoirs of David Lloyd George*, vol. 1, 1914–1915, 446–447.

64. Arthur, *Life of Lord Kitchener*, vol. 3, 186.

65. *Ibid.*, 188–189.

66. On 2 November Prime Minister Asquith reconstituted the War Council or Dardanelles Committee as it had been hitherto styled. In its new more compact form it was limited to the Prime Minister, Balfour, Kitchener, Grey, and Lloyd George. Bonar Law was added ten days later under Conservative pressure. Churchill was excluded. Churchill, *The World Crisis*, vol. 2, 522.

67. Arthur, *Life of Lord Kitchener*, vol. 3, 205–206. Attlee, *As It Happened*, 58.

68. Lloyd George, *War Memoirs of David Lloyd George*, vol. 1, 1914–1915, 441.

69. Murphy, *The History of the Suffolk Regiment, 1914–1927*, 108.

70. Gibbons, *With the 1/5th Essex in the East*, 23–24.

71. Fair and Wolton, *The History of the 1st/5th Battalion "The Suffolk Regiment,"* 33. Also, the then Corporal Reginald Lane. Interview, 20 November 1965.
72. Gibbons, *With the 1/5th Essex in the East*, 20.
73. A wooden frame to which barbed wire was attached, criss-crossed, and wound around.
74. Corporal Reginald E.S. Lane. Interview, 20 November 1965.
75. Fair and Wolton, *The History of the 1st/5th Battalion "The Suffolk Regiment,"* 34.
76. *Ibid.*
77. Lt.-Colonel F.W.D. Bendall, "The Flood at Suvla Bay," in *Everyman at War: Sixty Personal Narratives of the War*, edited by C.B. Purdom (London: J. M. Dent & Sons, Limited, 1930), 190–94.
78. Fair and Wolton, *The History of the 1st/5th Battalion "The Suffolk Regiment,"* 34.
79. *Ibid.*, and Gibbons, *With the 1/5th Essex in the East*, 28, footnote (both sources are quoting journalist G. Ward Price's graphic account in the press).
80. Attlee, *As It Happened*, 60.
81. Macdonald, *1915: The Death of Innocence*, 583.
82. Knyvett, *"Over There" with the Australians*, 131.
83. Bean, *The Official History of Australia in the War: The Story of Anzac: From 4 May, 1915 to the Evacuation of the Gallipoli Peninsula*, 383–384.
84. Fair and Wolton, *The History of the 1st/5th Battalion "The Suffolk Regiment,"* 35.
85. Atkinson, *The Regimental History of the Royal Hampshire Regiment*, vol. 2, *1914–1918*, 109. "After the flood had subsided, the Hampshire found many corpses in the trenches—some Turks as well as British, washed down from their lines—men who had been drowned or frozen, with any amount of material to be salvaged."
86. Farwell, *The Gurkhas*, 102.
87. *Ibid.*, 102.
88. Private Jake Mortlock. Interview, 30 November, 1965.
89. Atkinson, *The Regimental History of the Royal Hampshire Regiment*, vol. 2, *1914–1918*, 114.
90. Murphy, *The History of the Suffolk Regiment, 1914–1927*, 215.
91. Atkinson, *The Regimental History of the Royal Hampshire Regiment*, vol. 2, *1914–1918*, 114.
92. Fair and Wolton, *The History of the 1st/5th Battalion "The Suffolk Regiment,"* 35, 37.
93. Gibbons, *With the 1/5th Essex in the East*, 29–30.
94. Lloyd George, *War Memoirs of David Lloyd George*, vol. 1, *1914–1915*, 454.
95. Hamilton, *Gallipoli Diary*, vol. 1, 3.
96. Sanders, *Five Years in Turkey*, 98.
97. Private Mortlock. Interview, 7 December 1965.
98. Sanders, *Five Years in Turkey*, 99.
99. *Ibid.*, 103.
100. Nevinson, *The Dardanelles Campaign*, 406.
101. Private Mortlock. Interview, 21 March 1968.
102. Rupert Brooke, "The Soldier," from *The Collected Works of Rupert Brooke* (London: Macmillans, 1977), 34.
103. Wells, *The Outline of History*, 1,091.
104. Macdonald, *1914–1918; Voices and Images of the Great War*, 95.
105. James, *Winston S. Churchill: His Complete Speeches, 1897–1963*, vol. 3, 332–33.
106. Nevinson, *The Dardanelles Campaign*, 406.
107. Aspinall-Oglander, *The Official History of the War: Military Operations: Gallipoli*, vol. 2, 484.
108. *Ibid.*, 483–84.
109. Sanders, *Five Years in Turkey*, 104.
110. Farwell, *The Gurkhas*, 102–03.
111. Authoress, poetess, and wartime nurse, Vera Brittain nursed at St. George's Hospital in Malta after spending roughly a month at this isolation hospital as a patient. Bishop and Bostridge, eds. *Letters from a Lost Generation: The First World War Letters of Vera Brittain and Four Friends; Roland Leighton, Edward Brittain, Victor Richardson, Geoffrey Thurlow*, 278–80.
112. Private Mortlock. Interview, 11 November 1970.
113. Sara Mayfield, *Exiles from Paradise: Zelda and Scott Fitzgerald* (New York: Delacorte Press, 1971), 256–57.
114. East, ed., *The Diary of Sergeant Lawrence of the Australian Engineers*, 220.
115. Lance-Corporal Collen, Private Mortlock, and Sapper Phillips, the three soldiers from the West Suffolk hamlet of Worlington (population not more than 250) featured in this work, returned home safely. Twelve other fellow village lads did not.
116. George Herbert Clarke, ed., *A Treasury of War Poetry* (Boston: Houghton Mifflin Company, 1917), 223.
117. Niyazi Berkes, *The Development of Secularism in Turkey* (New York: Routledge, 1998), 483–84, 486–89, 494–95.
118. With the exception of the above, these thumbnail sketches are taken from the

following: *The Concise Dictionary of National Biography: Part II, 1901–1970* (Oxford: Oxford University Press, 1982), Holger H. Herwig & Neil M. Heyman, *Biographical Dictionary of World War I* (Westport, CT: Greenwood Press, 1982), & *Who Was Who*, vol. 3: *1929–1940* (London: Adam & Charles Black, 1941).

Chapter 6

1. Attlee, *As It Happened,* 60–1. Later to become the first post–Second World War British Prime Minister, Attlee was a company commander with the 6th South Lancashires (13th [Western] Division) at Suvla, and throughout his life remained convinced that the campaign had the potential for success.
2. Atkinson, *The Regimental History of the Royal Hampshire Regiment,* vol. 2, *1914–1918,* 101.
3. Andrew Green, *Writing the Great War: Sir John Edmonds and the Official Histories 1915–1948.* Cass Series: Military History and Policy (London: Frank Cass, 2003), 99.
4. Lloyd George, *The War Memoirs of David Lloyd George,* vol. 4, *1915,* 334.
5. H.A.L. Fisher, *A History of Europe,* vol. 3: *The Liberal Experiment* (Cambridge, MA: The Riverside Press, 1936), 1162.
6. "That's what we were there for!" was Jake Mortlock's comment when learning of Stopford's excuse. Interview, 20 August 1957.
7. *The Times* (London), 7 January 1916. Quoted in Williams, *Anzacs, the Media and the Great War,* 97.
8. Ashmead-Bartlett, *The Uncensored Dardanelles,* 230.
9. *The Times* (London), 7 January 1916. Quoted in Williams, *Anzacs, the Media and the Great War,* 98.
10. Lyn MacDonald, *1915: A Loss of Innocence,* 231.
11. Leonard Moseley, *Curzon: The End of an Epoch* (London: Readers Union, Longmans, Green & Company, 1961), 161.
12. Vivian Ogilvie, *The English Public School* (New York: The Macmillan Company, 1957), 195.
13. *Ibid.,* 180–197. Also T.B. Bottomore, *Classes in Modern Society* (New York: Pantheon Books, 1966), 36–42.
14. T.B. Bottomore, *Classes in Modern Society* (New York: Pantheon Books, 1966), 40.
15. *Ibid.,* 182.
16. Jack Pitman, *England Ebbing* (New York: Stein & Day, Inc., 1987), 53, 59, et al. In Robert Graves' *But It Still Goes On: An Accumulation* (New York: Jonathan Cape & Harrison Smith, Inc., 1931), 8, and endnote 2, he relates how his parents felt obliged to go and apologize to the Headmaster of Charterhouse for the disparaging remarks their son made about his old school in *Goodbye to All That.*
17. Jonathan Gathorne-Hardy, *The Old School Tie: The Phenomenon of the English Public School* (New York: The Viking Press, 1978), 203.
18. Mackenzie, *Gallipoli Memories,* 360–61.
19. Gathorne-Hardy, *The Old School Tie: The Phenomenon of the English Public School,* 204.
20. Hargrave, *The Suvla Bay Landing,* 236–237.
21. Ashmead-Bartlett, *The Uncensored Dardanelles,* 230.
22. *The Sunday Times* (London), 1 June 1997. Extract of a letter written by Winston Churchill to his younger brother, Jack, in 1915, quoted in an article by Stephen McGinty, entitled: "Revealed: Churchill's suicidal 1914 despair." *News,* 11. (The title of this article is most misleading as it implies a focus on the outbreak of the War.)
23. Green, *Writing the Great War: Sir John Edmonds and the Official Histories 1915–1948,* 99–100.

Appendix E

1. Succeeded Br.-Gen. S. H. Winter, 7th August.
2. Replaced Major-Gen. W. Douglas, in temporary command, 8th August.
3. Resumed command from Br.-Gen. W.R. Marshall, 8th August.
4. 4th Bty. and 1 section of 6th Bty. did not arrive from Egypt until September.
5. In Egypt.
6. 19th & 20th Btys. did not arrive from Egypt until September.
7. Attached 52nd Division till 28th August.
8. Attached A. & N.Z. Army Corps.
9. At Helles.
10. In Egypt. Eventually went to Salonika.
11. In Egypt. Eventually went to Salonika.
12. At Anzac.
13. On beach duty at Suvla.
14. Attached A. & N.Z. Army Corps.
15. Did not come further than Mudros. Eventually went to Salonika.
16. A & C Btys. did not arrive from Egypt until September.

17. At Helles, A & B Btys. did not arrive from Egypt until October.
18. In Egypt. Eventually went to Salonika.
19. Succeeded by Br.-Gen. Hon. H. A. Lawrence 19th August. Br.-Gen. W. R. Marshall took command 25th August.
20. Dismounted.
21. Attached.
22. Attached.
23. Dismounted.
24. H.Q. 2nd Bde and 6th (How.) Bty. did not arrive from Egypt until October. N.Z. artillery was then organized in 2 brigades.
25. *Ibid.*
26. Dismounted.
27. Only 5th Australian Bde. Present on the peninsula in August. Remainder arrived from Egypt early in September.
28. Dismounted.
29. 21st (Kohat) Bty and 26th (Jacob's) Bty.
30. In Egypt.

Bibliography

Primary Sources

Autobiographies, Collected Works, Diaries, Histories, Letters, Memoirs, Personal Narratives, Family Papers and Accounts of Participants and Other Eyewitnesses.

Aitken, Alexander. *From Gallipoli to the Somme: Recollections of a New Zealand Infantryman.* London: Oxford University Press, 1963.
Anonymous. *The Dardanelles.* London: Macmillan & Company, 1917.
Arthur, Sir George. *Life of Lord Kitchener.* 3 vols. New York: The Macmillan Company, 1920.
Ashmead-Bartlett, E. *Despatches from the Dardanelles.* London: George Newnes, 1915.
_____. "The Failure at Suvla," in *The Times History of the War.* Vol. 3. London: Times Publishing Company, 1919.
_____. *The Uncensored Dardanelles.* London: Hutchinson & Company, 1928.
Aspinall-Oglander, Brigadier-General C.F. *The Official History of the War: Military Operations: Gallipoli.* 2 vols. London: Heinemann, 1929 and 1932.
Asquith, H.H. [Herbert Henry]. *Memories and Reflections, 1852–1928, by the Earl of Oxford and Asquith, K.B.* Boston: Little, Brown, & Company, 1928.
Ataturk, Moustafa Kemal. *Souvenirs du Gazi Mustafa Kemal Pacha, version Française remaniée d'après l'original turc* [Memoirs of Mustafa Kemal, French Version taken from the original Turkish], trans. Jean Deny. Paris: Paul Geuthner, 1927. Taken from a Turkish government journal, *Milliyet* (March–April 1926).
Atkinson, C.T. *The Royal Hampshire Regiment.* Vol. 1, *To 1914.* Glasgow: Robert Maclehose & Company, Limited, 1950.
_____. *The Royal Hampshire Regiment.* Vol. 2, *1914–1918.* Glasgow: Robert Maclehose & Company, Limited, 1952.
Attlee, Clement R. *As It Happened.* New York: The Viking Press, 1954.
Austin, Walter F., and Charles F. Horne, eds. *Source Records of the Great War.* 7 vols. Washington, DC: National Alumni, 1923. All primary source materials.
Bean, C.E.W. *Anzac to Amiens.* Canberra: Australian War Memorial, 1928.
_____. *Gallipoli Correspondent: The Frontline Diary of C.E.W. Bean.* Sydney: George Allen & Unwin, 1922.
_____. *Gallipoli Mission.* Sydney: Angus & Robertson, 1924.
_____. *The Official History of the War: The Story of Anzac: From 4 May, 1915, to the Evacuation of the Gallipoli Peninsula.* Sydney: Angus & Robertson, 1924.

Bentley, James, ed. *Some Corner of a Foreign Field: Poetry of the Great War*. Boston: Little, Brown & Company, 1992.
Blackwell, Edwin, and Edwin C. Axe. *Romford to Beirut, via France, Egypt and Jericho: An Outline of the War Record of "B" Battery, 271st Brigade, R.F.A. (1/2nd Essex Battery, R.F.A.) with Many Digressions*. Clacton-on-Sea, Essex, England: R.W. Humphris, 1926.
Blake, George. *The Path of Glory*. New York: Harper & Brothers, 1926.
Brittain, Vera. *Chronicle of Youth: The War Diary 1913–1917*. Ed. Alan Bishop with Terry Smart. New York: William Morrow & Company, Inc., 1982.
_____. *Letters from a Lost Generation: The First World War Letters of Vera Brittain and Four Friends; Roland Leighton, Edward Brittain, Victor Richardson, and Geoffrrey Thurlow*. Ed. Alan Bishop and Mark Bostridge. Boston: Northeastern University Press, 1999.
_____. *Testament of Youth*. New York: Seaview Books, 1980.
Brooke, Rupert. *The Collected Works of Rupert Brooke*. London: Macmillan, 1977.
Brown, Malcolm, ed. *T.E. Lawrence: The Selected Letters*. New York: W.W. Norton & Company, Inc., 1989.
Bush, Captain Eric Wheler. *Gallipoli*. New York: St. Martin's Press, 1917.
Callwell, Major-General Sir C.E., K.C.B. *The Dardanelles*. Boston: Houghton Mifflin Company, 1919.
Churchill, Winston S. *The World Crisis*. Vol. 2, *1915*. New York: Charles Scribner's Sons, 1923.
Clarke, George Herbert, ed. *A Treasury of War Poetry*. Boston: Houghton Mifflin Company, 1917.
Cooper, Major Bryan. *The Tenth (Irish) Division in Gallipoli*. London: Herbert Jenkins, 1918.
Cooper, Lady Diana. *The Rainbow Comes and Goes*. London: Rupert Hart-Davis, 1958.
Creighton, The Reverend O. *With the Twenty-Ninth Division in Gallipoli: A Chaplain's Experiences*. London: Longmans, Green & Company, 1916.
Cutlack, F.M., ed. *War Letters of General Monash*. Sydney: Angus & Robertson, 1935.
Daniell, David Scott. *The Royal Hampshire Regiment, Vol. III: 1918–1954*. Aldershot: Gale & Polden, Limited, 1955.
Denham, H.M. *Dardanelles: A Midshipman's Diary 1915-16*. London: John Murray, 1919.
Dixon, W. MacNeile. *The British Navy at War*. Boston: Houghton Mifflin Company, 1917.
Djemal Pasha. *Memories of a Turkish Statesman, 1913–1919*. London: Hutchinson & Company, 1921.
East, Sir Ronald, ed. *The Gallipoli Diary of Sergeant Lawrence of the Australian Engineers, A.I.F*. Melbourne: Melbourne University Press, 1981.
Facey, Albert B. *A Fortunate Life*. Ringwood, Victoria: Penguin Books Australia, 1981.
Fair, Captain A., M.C., and Captain E. D. Wolton. *The History of the 1st/5th Battalion "The Suffolk Regiment."* London: Eyre & Spottiswoode, 1923.
From Dartmouth to the Dardanelles: A Midshipman's Log. Edited "By His Mother." London: William Heinemann, 1916.
Gibbon, Lt.-Col. Thomas, D.S.O. *With the 1/5th Essex in the East*. Colchester: Benham & Sons, Ltd., 1921.
Gillam, Major John, D.S.O. *Gallipoli Diary*. Stevenage: The Strong Oak Press/Tom Donovan Publishing, 1989.
Graves, Robert. *But It Still Goes On: An Accumulation*. New York: Jonathan Cape & Harrison Smith, Inc., 1931.
_____. *Good-bye to All That*. New York: Doubleday, Doran, & Company, 1957.
Great Britain. Cabinet. War Council. *[Papers of The War Council, Dardanelles Committee, and War Committee] (Cab. 42): 1915 & 1916*. London: Public Records Office, 1969. Microfilm. OCLC: 5218773.
Grey, Sir Edward (Edward, Viscount Grey of Fallodon). *Twenty-Five Years, 1892–1916*. 2 vols. New York: Frederick A. Stokes Company, 1925.

Gurney, Lt.-Colonel Russell. *History of the Northamptonshire Regiment.* Vol. 2, *1742–1934.* Aldershot (U.K.): Gale & Polden, Ltd., 1935.
Hafkesbrink, Hanna, and Rosemary Park, eds. *Deutsche erleben die Zeit (1914–1945).* Cambridge, Massachusetts: The Riverside Press, 1949.
Haldane, R.B. *Richard Burdon Haldane (Viscount Haldane): An Autobiography.* New York: Doubleday, Doran, & Company, 1929.
Hall, James Norman. *Kitchener's Mob: The Adventures of an American in the British Army.* London: Constable & Company, 1916.
Halsey, Francis Whiting. *The Literary Digest History of the World War: Compiled from Original and Contemporary Sources: American, British, French, German, and Other. In Ten Volumes Illustrated.* Vol. 8, *Turkey and the Balkans, August 1914–October 1918.* New York & London: Funk & Wagnalls Company, 1920.
Hamilton, Sir Ian. *Gallipoli Diary.* 2 Vols. New York: George H. Doran Company, 1920.
_____. *The Tragic Story of the Dardanelles: Ian Hamilton's Final Despatch.* London: George Newnes, 1916.
_____. *Supplement to Final Despatch.* London: H.M.S.O., 1916.
Hammerton, J.A., and H.W. Wilson, eds. *The Great War.* Originally published in serialized weekly installments. London: The Amalgamated Press, Ltd., 1916–1920.
Hammerton, Sir John, ed. *I Was There: Personal Narratives of the Great War.* Originally published in serialized weekly installments. London: The Harmsworth Press, Ltd., 1915–1919.
Hankey, Lord Maurice. *The Supreme Command, 1914–1918.* 2 vols. London: George Allen & Unwin, 1961.
Hanna, H[enry]. *The Pals at Suvla Bay: Being the Record of "D" Company, of the 7th Battalion the Royal Dublin Fusiliers.* Dublin: E. Ponsonby, 1917.
Harding, Samuel B. *The Study of the Great War: A Topical Outline, with Copious Quotations and Reading References.* Philadelphia: McKinley Publishing Company, 1918.
Hardy, Florence Emily. *The Life of Thomas Hardy.* Vol. 2. London: Macmillan & Company, 1933.
Hargrave, John. *At Suvla Bay.* London: Constable & Company, 1916.
_____. *Sketches from Suvla.* London: Cassell & Company, 1916.
_____. *The Suvla Bay Landing.* London: Constable & Company, 1964.
Herbert, Captain the Hon. Aubrey P. *The Secret Battle.* London: Methuen, 1919.
_____. *Mons, Anzac, and Kut.* London: Hutchinson, 1919.
James, Robert Rhodes, ed. *Winston S. Churchill: His Complete Speeches, 1897–1963.* 8 vols. New York: Chelsea House, 1974.
Jones, The Reverend Dennis, C.F. *Diary of a Padre at Suvla Bay.* Manchester: Faith Press, 1917.
"Juvenis." *Suvla Bay and After.* London: Hodder & Stoughton, 1916.
Kannengiesser, Major-General Hans. *The Campaign in Gallipoli.* Trans. Major C.J.P. Ball. London: Hutchinsons, 1927.
Keyes, Admiral Sir Roger. *The Naval Memoirs of Admiral of the Fleet Sir Roger Keyes.* Vol. 1, *The Narrow Seas to the Dardanelles, 1910–1915.* New York: E.P. Dutton & Company, 1934.
Knyvett, Captain R. Hugh. *"Over There" with the Australians.* New York: Charles Scribner's Sons, 1918.
Lloyd George, David. *War Memoirs of David Lloyd George.* 6 vols. Boston: Little, Brown & Company, 1933–37.
Macdonald, Lyn. *1914–1918: Voices and Images of the Great War.* London: Michael Joseph, Limited, 1988.
_____. *1915: The Death of Innocence.* New York: Henry Holt and Company, Inc., 1995.
Mackenzie, Compton. *Gallipoli Memories.* London: Cassells, 1929.
March, Francis A. *History of the World War: An Authentic Narrative of the World's Greatest War.* Vol. 2. New York: Leslie-Judge Company, 1919.

Marks, Thomas Penrose. *The Laughter Goes from Life*. London: William Kinder, 1922.
Marlow, Joyce, ed. *The Virago Book of Women and the Great War, 1914–1918*. London: Virago Press, 1998.
Martin-Harvey, Sir John. *The Autobiography of Sir John Martin-Harvey*. London: Sampson Low, Marston & Company, 1933.
Marwick, Arthur, and Wendy Simpson, eds. *War, Peace and Social Change: Europe 1900–1955. Documents 1: 1900–1929*. Open University Press, 1990.
Masefield, John. *Gallipoli*. London: Heinemann, 1916.
Miller, Francis Trevelyan, ed. *True Stories of the Great War: Tales of Adventure— Heroic Deeds— Exploits— Told by the Soldiers, Officers, Nurse, Diplomats, and Eye Witnesses*. Vol. 4. New York: Review of Reviews Company, 1918.
Morgenthau, Henry. *All in a Life-Time*. Garden City, NY: Doubleday, Page, 1922.
_____. *Ambassador Morgenthau's Story*. Garden City, NY: Doubleday, Page, 1918.
_____. *Secrets of the Bosphorus*. London: Hutchinson & Company, 1918.
Muir, Ramsay. *The Character of the British Empire*. London: Constable & Company, Limited, 1917.
Murphy, Lt.-Colonel C.C.R. (late The Suffolk Regiment). *The History of the Suffolk Regiment, 1914–1927*. London: Hutchinson & Company, Ltd., 1928.
Nevinson, Henry W. *The Dardanelles Campaign*. London: Nesbit & Company, 1918.
Part, T.R. *The Diary of Thomas Reginald Reginald Part: An Australian Soldier Who Fought in World War I.* (Diary on Active Service, No. 77 Lance-Corporal Part, T. R., H.Q.D., 24th Battalion, 6th Infantry Brigade, 2nd Division, Australian Imperial Forces— Period covered March 17, 1915 to April 25, 1916.) Ed. by Pauline Carter (L/Cpl. Part's niece), and David Jones, who jointly transcribed the exact diary into digital form. Cumberland Park, South Australia: Carter-Jones Computer Publishing, 1997.
Patterson, J.H. *With the Zionists in Gallipoli*. London: Hutchinson & Company, 1916.
Pen Pictures of British Battles: Painted by Author and Artist. London: Eyre & Spottiswoode, Limited, 1917.
Petre, F. Loraine, O.B.E. *The History of the Norfolk Regiment, 1685–1918*. Vol. 2, *4th August, 1914 to 31st December, 1918*. Norwich: The Empire Press/Jarrold & Sons, Ltd., 1953.
Pomiatowski, Joseph. *Der Zusammenbruch des Ottomanischen*. Zurich: Amalthea-Verlag, 1928.
Priestman, E.Y. *With a B. P. Scout in Gallipoli: A Record of the Belton Bulldogs*. 2nd ed. London: George Routledge & Sons, 1917.
Prigge, Major E.R. *Der Kampf um die Dardanellen*. Berlin: Kiepenhaver, 1916.
Purdom, C.B., ed. *Everyman at War: Sixty Personal Narratives of the War*. London: J.M. Dent & Sons, Ltd., 1930.
Rawlinson, Lt.-Colonel Anthony. *Travels in the East, 1918–1922*. London: Jonathan Cape, 1930.
Raymond, Ernest. *The Story of My Days*. London: Cassell & Company, 1968.
_____. *Tell England: A Study in a Generation*. London: Cassell & Company, 1922.
Sanders, Marshal Otto Liman von. *Five Years in Turkey*. Annapolis: U.S. Naval Institute Press, 1927.
Sazonov, Serge. *Fateful Years, 1909–1916: The Reminiscences of Serge Sazonov, G.C.B., G.C.V.O., Russian Minister for Foreign Affairs 1914*. New York: Frederick A. Stokes Company, 1928.
A Short History of Turkish Operations in the Great War. Vol. 1. Constantinople: Historical Section, General Staff, 1920.
Stevenson, David, ed. *British Documents on Foreign Affairs: Reports and Papers from the Foreign Office Confidential Print: Series H: The First World War, 1914–1918*. Vol. 1, *The Allied and Neutral Powers: Diplomacy and War Aims, I: August 1914–July 1915*. New York: University Publications of America, 1989.
Stuermer, Dr. Harry. *Two Years at Constantinople*. New York: Doubleday, Doran, & Company, 1918.

Teichman, Captain Oskar, D.S.O., M.C. *The Diary of a Yeomanry M.O.: Egypt, Gallipoli, Palestine and Italy*. London: T. Fisher Unwin, Ltd., 1921.
Tirpitz, Grand Admiral Baron Alfred von. *My Memoirs*. Trans. by Georg Hans Krefeld. 2 vols. New York: Dodd, Mead & Company, 1919.
Wallace, Edgar. *Kitchener's Army and the Territorial Force: The Full Story of a Great Achievement*. London: George Newnes, 1915.
War Poetry. London: Pocket Books, 2001.
Wedgwood, the Hon. J.C. *Essays and Adventures*. London: Allen & Unwin, 1924.
Wilkinson, Norman. *The Dardanelles: Colour Sketches from Gallipoli*. London: Longmans, Green & Company, 1915.
The World's Work: A History of Our Time. Vol. 29 (May, 1915 to October, 1915); vol. 30 (November, 1915 to April, 1916); vol. 31 (May, 1916 to October 1916). Garden City, New York: Doubleday, Page & Company, 1915, 1916.

Journals

Bolton, Jake. "Gallipoli." *Century* 95, no. 3 (March 1918): 625–34.
British War Office. "Final Official Reports on Gallipoli." *New York Times Current History Magazine* 6 (June 1917): 508–11.
Fagan, M.M. "Cheap at a Thousand Dollars a Drop." *American Magazine* 86, no. 10 (October 1918): 32–37.
Gallinshaw, A.J. "Gallipoli: the Adventures of a Survivor." *Century* 92, no. 7 (July 1917): 371–82.
Moseley, S.A. "End of a Great Adventure." *Living Age* 288, no. 2 (February 1916): 557–59.
_____. "Evacuation of Gallipoli." *Fortune* 105, no. 2 (February 1916): 354–59.
_____. "Pictures from Gallipoli." *Fortune* 104, no. 12 (December 1915): 1058–66.

Newspapers

The Daily Mail (London.) "The Tragedy of the Shells," 21 May 1915.
The New York Times. Various issues August-September 1915. Reports from war correspondents and news agencies; official releases. Specific Issues dealing with Suvla Bay/Anzac: 12, 22, and 25 August; 1 and 18 September; 30 November; 2, 3, and 30 December. Of particular interest is a lengthy Associated Press report featuring authenticated excerpts from the diaries, letters, and notebooks of dead British soldiers buried by the Turks, dateline Gallipoli Peninsula, June 19, 1915. Permission to cite portions of these documents was granted by the High Command of the Turkish Army. Published in the Sunday, August 8, 1915, edition, p.2, column 6. In the adjacent column (7) is a detailed report by Weber Pasha, the German Commanding Officer.
The Times (London.) Various issues from February until late December 1915. War correspondents' coverage; official releases; published communiqués; and news agencies' reports. Specific issues reporting on the Suvla Bay theater: 11, 12, 27, 28, and 30 August; 7, 14, 15, and 21 September; 8 November; 2, 4, and 28 December.

Minutes, Reports, Replies and Communiqués

Communiqués issued by the Commander of the Turkish Army of Gallipoli, Marshal Otto Liman von Sanders. Ditto from the Ministry of War in Constantinople. Reports from Colonel and General Hans Kannengieser, Colonel and General Mustapha Kemal, and Major Fritz Willmer.
First Report of the Dardanelles Commission. London: H.M.S.O., 1917, and *Supplement to First Report*. London: H.M.S.O., 1917.

Great Britain: War Office. *Army: Arrangements Made for Water Supply to the Troops During Landing at Suvla Bay.* London: H.M.S.O./Harrison & Sons, 1915.

Parliament. Hansard's records of *The Parliamentary Debates, Fifth Series.* Vols.18–82 *(Official Report), Commons & Lords,* George V. London: H.M.S.O., 1915–16. Comprising Ministerial replies, verbal and written, to Members' questions, debates on the floor of the Houses of Parliament, comments and observations by Members and Ministers. Also: microfilmed *Great Britain. Parliament. House of Commons. Parliamentary Debates (Hansard) Official Report.* Vols. 75–76, *1914/15.* London: H.M.S.O., 1915–16.

War Council and Dardanelles Committee: Minutes, Memoranda, and Reports. Telegraphic correspondence from and to Earl Kitchener and Generals Hamilton, Birdwood, and Munro. Secret deliberations with regard to all aspects and implications of the Mediterranean Expeditionary Force. Communiqués issued by General Sir Ian Hamilton, et al. Reports and communications from and to the Admiralty, Rear-Admirals, Vice-Admirals of the Royal Navy, and from French military and naval commanders.

Letters

Cobbold, P. Anne (*née* Mortlock), daughter of Private S. Jacob P. Mortlock, D Company, 1/5th Battalion, the Suffolk Regiment, twice mentioned under Primary Sources. A written record of her recollections of her father's narrations of his war experiences on various occasions. Dated 3 October 1993.

Halliday, Owen A., apropos of interviews of 29 and 30 March 1994, in which he recounted the experiences of his aunt, Nurse Amy Halliday, detailed below. Dated 20 April 1994.

Mortlock, Desmond Peter, 2nd Lieutenant and Lieutenant in A Company of the 1st Battalion, the Punjabi Light Infantry Regiment, Indian Army, Dehra Dun, 1945–47, and Sergeant in Q Battery, 358 Medium (the Suffolk Yeomanry) Regiment, R.A., Territorial Army, 1948–52, nephew of Private Mortlock (below mentioned). Written reminiscences of conversations with the latter. Dated 25 January 1994.

Mortlock, Richard Joseph, son of Private Mortlock (next entry). Anecdotes regarding the latter contained in a letter. Dated 12 September 1993.

Mortlock, S. Jacob P., 175671 Private, D Company, 5th & 1/5th Battalions, the Suffolk Regiment, 163rd Brigade, 54th (East Anglian) Territorial Division, attached 9th Army Corps, Mediterranean Expeditionary Force, 1915–16, and Egyptian Expeditionary Force, 1916–19. Letter from Hill 60, Suvla Bay/Anzac, dated 25 September 1915. Also postcard sent from Imtarfa Isolation Hospital, Malta, dated 12th December, 1915.

Family Papers and Photographs

Drackett-Case Family Papers: contemporary postcard.
Mortlock Family Papers: contemporary photographs, postcards, and letters.

Interviews

Aldous, William S., Trooper, D Troop, Omdurman Squadron, the Sherwood Rangers, 1913–19. Interview, 21 August 1965.

Bendall, Lt.-Colonel F. W. D., 2/3rd Battalion, the London Regiment, 1914–1916. Personal narrative.

Bolton, Charles L., Private, B Company, 4th Battalion, & D Company, 1/5th Battalion, the Suffolk Regiment, 1914–19; and Corporal-Farrier, Royal Horse Artillery, India, 1920–1927. Interviews, 24, 25, 26, and 27 December 1956.

Bibliography

Burlham, Timothy, Private, D Company, 1/5th Battalion, the Suffolk Regiment, 1914–19. Interview, 1 June 1955.
Collen, Albert E., Private, Lance-Corporal, C Company, 2nd Battalion, the Royal Fusiliers, 1915–23. Interview, 6 July 1963.
Drackett-Case, Frederick P., Private, Corporal, and Sergeant, B Company, 1st Battalion, the King's Liverpool Regiment, 1914–19. Interviews, 28 April 1969 and 28 April 1970.
Drackett-Case, Marjorie (*née* Rumbelow), wife of above, and sister of Private Vincent Rumbelow, D Company, 5th and 1/5th Battalions, the Suffolk Regiment, survivor of Gallipoli, but who died of wounds sustained on Mansura Ridge in front of Gaza, April 1917. Interviews, 28 April 1969 and 28 April 1970.
Goodrum, Harold, cousin of Private Mortlock, and nephew of Kate Goodrum, whose parcel proved such a disappointment to certain soldiers. Reminiscences. Interview, 6 July 1963.
Halliday, Owen A., nephew of Nurse Amy Halliday, who served on a hospital ship during the Gallipoli campaign. The vessel was hit by Turkish shellfire and a fragment of shrapnel actually pierced her blanket. Nurse Halliday was decorated for her services in the Dardanelles. Interviews, 29 and 30 March 1994.
Hemsley, Arthur, Private, Lance-Corporal, Corporal, B Company, 2/4th Battalion, Queen's Royal West Surrey Regiment. Recorded interview.
How, George, Private, Lance-Corporal, Corporal, Sergeant, D Company, 5th & 1/5th Battalions, the Suffolk Regiment, 1912–19. Interview, 10 August 1965.
Kennedy, Quintin B., 2nd Lieutenant, Lieutenant and Captain in various Batteries, Royal Field Artillery, 1911–33. Interview, 5 November 1961.
Kent, Harold S., Trooper, F Troop, Q Squadron, the Suffolk Yeomanry, South African War, 1899–1901. Interviews, 26 and 31 December 1945.
Lane, Reginald E.S., Private, 2nd Battalion, the Cambridgeshire Regiment, 1914; Private, Lance-Corporal, Corporal, D Company, 1/5th Battalion, the Suffolk Regiment, 1914–17; later 2nd Lieutenant, Lieutenant, and finally Captain, Egyptian Labour Corps, 1917–19. Interviews, 5 November and 10 December 1965.
Leverington, John S., Private, A Company, 1/8th Battalion, the Hampshire Regiment, 1915–1919. Interviews, 21 August 1965 and 25 April 1975.
Mortlock, Chrissie (*née* Ward). Information re: 2nd Lieutenant Bernard Powers, the Middlesex Regiment — seconded to the Royal Flying Corps, and reported missing.
Mortlock, Gwendoline May, sister of Private Mortlock (next entry), and fiancée of Private W. Vincent Rumbelow, above mentioned. Interview, 21 August 1942.
Mortlock, S. Jacob P., 175671 Private, D Company, 5th, & 1/5th Battalions, the Suffolk Regiment, 1912–19. Interviews, 10 August, 25 September, 5 November 1965; 4 December 1970; 13 February and 14 December 1971.
Parker, Jack, cousin of Private Mortlock (see above.) Responsible for saving all the letters Private Mortlock wrote him while on active service. Interview, 25 December 1972.
Parker, Spencer F., 2nd Lieutenant, Flying Officer, Royal Flying Corps, 1914–16. Interview, 26 December 1965.
Phillips, H. Gordon, later Sapper Phillips, 66th Field Company, the Royal Engineers, Western Front, 1916–19. Quoted prediction of 5 August 1914, while carrying Private Mortlock to the station to entrain upon mobilization. The incident recounted by the latter during an interview on 10 August 1965. Interviewed in person, 6 July 1966.
Rolfe, Frank, Sapper, 31st Field Company, Royal Engineers, 1915–19. Interview, 25 April 1965.
Scaley, William A., Private, Lance-Corporal, B Company, 2/4th Battalion, the Queen's Royal West Surrey Regiment, 1914–17. Interview, 18 September 1975.
Utteridge, Henry G.S., Gunner, Lance-Bombardier, D Troop, Seringapatam Battery, 49th Brigade, Royal Field Artillery, 1914–19. Interview, 21 August 1965.
Watts, Trooper Walter, 17/21st Lancers. Zulu and South African Wars 1880–1901. Interviews, various dates, 1943–1945.

Williams, Maurice, Private — Sergeant, D Company, 5th and 1/5th Battalions, the Suffolk Regiment, 1913–16, and 2nd Lieutenant, 15th (Suffolk Yeomanry) Battalion, the Suffolk Regiment, and Lieutenant, Captain, B Company, 4th Battalion, South Staffordshire Regiment, 1916–19. Later Scoutmaster, 1st Mildenhall (Suffolk) Troop 1938–64. Interview, 6 July 1963.

Other

The Imperial War Museum, Lambeth Road, London. Research assistance 29 September, 15 October 1993.
The Public Records Office, St. Mary's Square, Bury St. Edmunds, Suffolk. Research facilities.
The Suffolk Regimental Museum, housed in the Keep at Gibraltar Barracks, Out Risbygate, Bury St. Edmunds, Suffolk, and the Suffolk Yeomanry Museum, formerly at the old cavalry barracks in King's Road, Bury St. Edmunds, later moved to the TAVR Centre, Out Risbygate, Bury St. Edmunds. Various research assistance over several years.

SECONDARY SOURCES

Published Books

Adams, R.J.Q. *Bonar Law.* Stanford, CA: Stanford University Press, 1999.
Albion, Robert G., and Walter Phelps Hall. *A History of England and the British Empire.* 3rd edition. Boston: Ginn and Company, 1953.
Alexander, Bevin. *How Great Generals Win.* New York: W.W. Norton & Company, Inc., 1993.
Andrews, E.M. *The Anzac Illusion: Anglo-Australian Relations During World War I.* Cambridge: Cambridge University Press, 1993.
Armstrong, H.C. *Gray Wolf: The Life of Kemal Ataturk.* New York: Capricorn Books, 1961.
Asher, Michael. *Lawrence: The Uncrowned King of Arabia.* Woodstock, New York: The Overlook Press, 1999.
Asprey, Robert B. *The German High Command at War: Hindenburg and Ludendorff Conduct World War I.* New York: William Morrow and Company, Inc., 1991.
Ball, Stuart. *Winston Churchill.* British Library Historic Lives Series. New York: New York University Press, 2003.
Banks, Arthur. *A Military Atlas of the First World War.* New York: Taplinger Publishing Company, 1985.
Barnett, Corelli. *The Great War.* New York: G.P. Putnam's Sons, 1980.
Batchelor, John, and Ian Hogg. *The Naval Gun.* Blandford, Dorset: Blandford Press, 1978.
Beckett, Ian, and Keith Simpson. *A Nation in Arms: A Social Study of the British Army in the First World War.* Manchester: Manchester University Press, 1985.
Benns, F. Lee. *Europe Since 1914.* 4th ed. New York: F.S. Crofts & Company, 1939.
Bentley, Geoffrey, and Maurice Conly, eds. *The History of the New Zealand Army.* Auckland, NZ: Grantham House, 1989.
Berkes, Niyazi. *The Development of Secularism in Turkey.* New York: Routledge, 1998.
Bidwell, Shelford. *Gunners at War: A Tactical Study of the Royal Artillery in the Twentieth Century.* London: Arms and Armour Press, 1970.
Blythe, Ronald. *Akenfield: Portrait of an English Village.* New York: Pantheon, 1969.
Bond, Brian. "The First World War" in *The Shifting Balance of World Forces, 1898–1945.* Cambridge University Press, 1968, 171–207, in *The New Cambridge Modern History.* 2nd ed. Vol. 12. Cambridge: Cambridge University Press, 1968.
Bottomore, T.B. *Classes in Modern Society.* New York: Pantheon Books, 1966.
Bourne, J.M. *Britain and the Great War, 1914–1918.* London: Edward Arnold, 1989.

Brodie, Bernard and Fawn. *From Crossbow to H-Bomb: The Evolution of the Weapons and Tactics of Warfare.* Revised and enlarged edition. Bloomington: Indiana University Press, 1973.
Brown, Judith M., and William Roger Louis, eds. *The Oxford History of the British Empire.* Vol. 4, *The Twentieth Century.* Oxford: Oxford University Press, 1999.
Bruce, Anthony, and William Cogar. *An Encyclopedia of Naval History.* New York: Facts on File, Inc., 1998.
Bryson, Thomas A. *Tars, Turks, and Tankers: The Role of the United States Navy in the Middle East, 1800–1979.* Metuchen, NJ, & London: The Scarecrow Press, 1980.
Burg, David F., and L. Edward Purcell. *Almanac of World War I.* Lexington, KY: The University Press of Kentucky, 1998.
Carver, Field Marshal Lord. *The Seven Ages of the British Army.* New York: Beaufort Books, 1984.
Childs, David. *Germany in the Twentieth Century.* London: B.T. Batsford, Ltd., 1991.
Clark, Alan. *The Donkeys.* London: Hutchinsons, 1961.
D'Artagnan, Jack (pseud.). *Sentimental Journey.* Richmond, VA: Minden Rose Publishers, 1984.
David, Saul. *Military Blunders: The How and Why of Military Failure.* New York: Carroll & Graf, Publishers, Inc., 1998.
Davis, Paul K. *100 Decisive Battles: From Ancient Times to the Present.* Oxford: Oxford University Press, 1999.
Delbrück, Hans. *Delbrück's Modern Military History.* Ed. And trans. Arden Bucholz. Lincoln: University of Nebraska Press, 1997.
Dickinson, Frederick R. *War and National Reinvention: Japan in the Great War, 1914–1919.* Cambridge (Massachusetts): Harvard University Asia Center, 1999.
Dictionary of National Biography: The Concise Dictionary, Part II, 1901–1970. Oxford: Oxford University Press, 1982.
Dupuy, R. Ernest, and Trevor N. Dupuy. *The Encyclopedia of Military History.* Rev. ed. New York: Harper & Row, 1977.
Edwards, Major T.J., M.B.E., F.R. Hist. Soc. *Regimental Badges.* 4th rev. ed. Revised by Arthur L. Kipling. Aldershot: Gale & Polden, 1966.
Eggenberger, David. *A Dictionary of Battles.* New York: Thomas Y. Crowell & Company, 1967.
Ellis, John. *Eye-deep in Hell: Trench Warfare in World War I.* New York: Pantheon Books, 1976.
Enser, A.G.S. *A Subject Bibliography of the First World War: Books in English, 1914–1987.* Aldershot: Gower Publishing Company, Limited, 1990.
Esher, Viscount Reginald. *The Tragedy of Lord Kitchener.* New York: E.P. Dutton & Company, 1921.
Esposito, Brigadier-General Vincent J., ed. *A Concise History of World War I.* New York: Frederick A. Praeger, 1964.
Fair, Charles. *From the Jaws of Victory.* New York: Simon & Schuster, 1971.
Falls, Cyril. *Great Battles of the Modern World.* London: Macmillans, 1970.
Farwell, Byron. *The Gurkhas.* New York: W.W. Norton & Company, 1984.
Fisher, H.A.L. *A History of Europe.* Vol. 3, *The Liberal Experiment.* Cambridge, MA: The Riverside Press, 1936.
Fisher, Sydney Nettleton. *The Middle East: A History.* 2nd ed. New York: Alfred Knopf, 1968.
Frame, T.R., and G.J. Swinden. *First In, Last Out: The Navy at Gallipoli.* Melbourne: Kangaroo Press, 1978.
Fuller, Major-General J.F.C. *The Conduct of War, 1789–1961.* New Brunswick: Rutgers University Press, 1961.
_____. *A Military History of the Western World.* Vol. 3. New York: Funk & Wagnalls, 1954.

Gardiner, Juliet, and Neil Wenborn, eds. *The History Today Companion to British History*. London: Collins & Brown, Ltd., 1995.
Gardiner, Robert, ed. *Conway's History of the Ship. The Eclipse of the Big Gun: The Warship 1906–45*. Consultant editor: David K. Brown, R.C.N.C. Annapolis: Naval Institute Press, 1992.
Gathorne-Hardy, Jonathan. *The Old School Tie: The Phenomenon of the English Public School*. New York: The Viking Press, 1978.
Gilbert, Martin. *Winston S. Churchill*. Vol. 3, *1914–1916: The Challenge of War*. Boston: Houghton Mifflin Company, 1971.
Gilbert, Sandra, and Susan Gubar. *No Man's Land: The Place of the Woman Writer in the Twentieth Century*. Vol. 2. New Haven, Connecticut: Yale University Press, 1989.
Gooch, G.P. *History of Modern Europe, 1878–1919*. New York: Henry Holt & Company, 1922.
Goodspeed, Lt.-Colonel D.J. *The German Wars, 1914–1945*. Boston: Houghton Mifflin Company, 1977.
Gray, Randall, with Christopher Argyle. *Chronicle of the First World War*. Vol. 1, *1914–1916*. New York: Facts on File, 1990.
Green, Andrew. *Writing the Great War: Sir James Edmonds and the Official Histories 1915–1948*. Cass Series: Military History and Policy. London & Portland, Oregon: Frank Cass Publishers, 2003.
Green, Lieutenant-Colonel Howard, M.C. *The British Army in The First World War: The Regulars, the Territorials, and Kitchener's Army*. London: William Clowes, 1968.
Grey, Jeffrey. *A Military History of Australia*. Cambridge: Cambridge University Press, 1990.
_____. *A Military History of Australia*. Revised edition. Cambridge: Cambridge University Press, 1999.
Hallows, Ian S. *Regiments and Corps of the British Army*. London: Arms and Armour Press, 1991.
Halsey, Francis Whiting. *The Literary Digest History of the World War: Compiled from Original and Contemporary Sources: American, British, French, German, and Other*. 10 vols. New York: Funk & Wagnalls Company, 1920.
Harding, David. *Weapons: An International Encyclopedia from 5,000 B.C. to 2,000 A.D.* New York: St. Martin's Press, 1980.
Harding, Samuel B. *The Study of the Great War: A Topical Outline with Copious Quotations and Reading References*. Philadelphia: McKinley Publishing Company, 1918.
Harmon, William. *The Top 500 Poems: A Columbia Anthology*. New York: Columbia University Press, 1992.
Hart, Peter, and Nigel Steel. *Defeat at Gallipoli*. London: Macmillan, 1994.
Hassall, Christopher. *Rupert Brooke*. New York: Harcourt, Brace & World, 1964.
Haythornthwaite, Philip J. *A Photohistory of World War One*. London: Arms and Armour Press, 1993.
_____. *The World War One Source Book*. London: Arms and Armour Press, 1996.
Herwig, Holger H., and Neil M. Heyman. *Biographical Dictionary of World War I*. Westport, Connecticut: Greenwood Press, 1982.
Higgonet, Margaret R., ed. *Lines of Fire: Women Writers of World War I*. New York: Plume Books, 1999.
Hilditch, Neville. *In Praise of the British: An Anthology for the Present Times*. London: Hines & Company, 1931.
Hogg, Ian V. *Historical Dictionary of World War I: Historical Dictionaries of War, Revolution, and Civil Unrest*, No. 3. Lanham, Maryland: The Scarecrow Press, 1998.
Hough, Richard. *The Great War at Sea, 1914–1918*. Oxford: Oxford University Press, 1983.
Howard, Harry N. *Turkey, the Straits and U.S. Policy*. Baltimore: The Johns Hopkins University Press, 1974.

Hoyt, E.P. *Disaster at the Dardanelles.* London: Barker Publishing, 1976.
The Hutchinson Illustrated Encyclopedia of British History. Chicago: Fitzroy Dearborn Publishers, 1999.
Hynes, Samuel. *The Soldier's Tale: Bearing Witness to Modern War.* New York: Penguin Books, 1997.
Ireland, Bernard. *Jane's Battleships of the 20th Century.* Illustrated by Tony Gibbons. New York: Harper Collins Publishers, 1996.
James, Robert Rhodes. *Gallipoli.* London: B.T. Batsford, 1965.
Jones, Archer. *The Art of War in the Western World.* Urbana and Chicago: University of Illinois Press, 1987.
Judge, Harry, ed. *Oxford Illustrated Encyclopedia.* Vol. 3, *World History from Earliest Times to 1800.* Oxford: Oxford University Press, 1988.
Karatay, Baha Vefa. *Mehmetcik ve Anzaklar.* Ankara: Kapak Duzeni, 1987.
Kemp, Peter, ed. *The Oxford Companion to Ships and the Sea.* London: Oxford University Press, 1976.
Kinross, John Patrick Balfour, Baron. *Ataturk: A Biography of Mustapha Kemal, Father of Modern Turkey.* New York: William Morrow & Company, 1965.
Kinzer, Stephen. *Crescent and Star: Turkey Between Two Worlds.* New York: Farrar, Straus & Giroux, 2001.
Kipling, Arthur L., and Hugh L. King. *Head-dress Badges of the British Army.* London: Frederick Muller, 1972.
Knightley, Phillip. *The First Casualty. From Crimea to Vietnam: The War Correspondent as Hero, Propagandist, and Myth Maker.* New York: Harcourt, Brace, Jovanovich, 1975.
Koss, Stephen E. *Lord Haldane: Scapegoat for Liberalism.* New York: Columbia University Press, 1969.
Laffin, John. *Damn the Dardanelles: The Story of Gallipoli.* London: Osprey Publishing, 1980.
Latham, B. *A Territorial Soldier's War.* Aldershot: Gale & Polden, 1967.
Liddell Hart, B.H. *History of the First World War.* London: Pan Books, 1970.
_____. *Strategy.* New York: Frederick A. Praeger, 1954.
Liddle, Peter. *Men of Gallipoli.* London: Allen Lane, 1976.
Lincoln, W. Bruce. *Passage Through Armageddon: The Russians in War and Revolution, 1914–1918.* New York: Simon & Schuster, 1986.
Lohrke, Eugene. *Armageddon: the World War in Literature.* New York: Jonathan Cape and Harrison Smith, 1971.
Lucas, James. *Experiences of War: The British Soldier.* London: Arms and Armour Press, 1989.
Macdonald, John. *Great Battlefields of the World.* New York: Macmillan, 1984.
Marder, Arthur J. *From the Dreadnought to Scapa Flow: The Royal Navy in the Fisher Era, 1904–1919.* Vol. 2, *The War Years, to the Eve of Jutland.* London: Oxford University Press, 1965.
Mayfield, Sara. *Exiles from Paradise: Zelda and Scott Fitzgerald.* New York: Delacorte Press, 1971.
McLeod, Godfrey. *Anzacs.* North Ryde, N.S.W.: Methuen Australia, 1985.
Moir, Guthrie. *The Suffolk Regiment.* Famous Regiments Series, ed. Lieutenant-General Sir Brian Horrocks. London: Leo Cooper, 1969.
Mollo, Boris. *The Indian Army.* Poole, Dorset, England: Blandford Press, 1981.
Moorehead, Alan. *Gallipoli.* London: William Heinemann, 1956.
Moorhouse, Geoffrey. *Hell's Foundations: A Town, Its Myths and Gallipoli.* London: Hodder & Stoughton, 1992.
Moseley, Leonard. *Curzon: The End of an Epoch.* London: Readers Union; Longmans, Green & Company, 1961.
Mowat, C.L., ed. *The New Cambridge Modern History: The Shifting Balance of World Forces, 1898–1945.* 2nd ed. Vol. 12. Cambridge: Cambridge University Press, 1968.

Moyer, Laurence V. *Victory Must Be Ours: Germany in the Great War, 1916–1918*. New York: Hippocrene Books, 1995.
Nekrasov, George. *North of Gallipoli: The Black Sea Fleet at War, 1914–1917*. Boulder, CO: East European Monographs, 1992.
The New Encyclopedia Britannica. 15th ed. "Turkey and Ancient Anatolia," by M.E. Yapp.
The New York Times History of the War. Vol. 3. New York: New York Times Press, 1920.
Nicolson, Harold. *Some People*. London: Constable & Company, 1946.
Niven, David. *The Moon Is a Balloon*. New York: G.P. Putnam's Sons, 1972.
North, John. *Gallipoli: The Fading Vision*. London: Faber & Faber, 1936.
Ogilvie, Vivian. *The English Public School*. New York: The Macmillan Company, 1957.
Oxford English Dictionary. 2nd ed. Vol. 4. Oxford: Clarendon Press, 1989.
Paget, General Lord George, K.C.B. *The Light Cavalry in the Crimea*. London: John Murray, 1881.
Palmer, Alan. *Victory 1918*. New York: Atlantic Monthly Press, 1998.
Palmer, A.W. *A Dictionary of Modern History, 1789–1945*. Baltimore: Penguin Books, 1964.
Palmer, R.R., ed. *Historical Atlas of the World*. Chicago: Rand McNally & Company, 1961.
Parker, Gilbert. *The World in the Crucible: An Account of the Origins and Conduct of the Great War*. New York: Dodd, Mead & Company, 1915.
Partington, Angela, ed. *The Oxford Dictionary of Quotations*. 4th ed. Oxford: Oxford University Press, 1992.
Pavlovich, Rear Admiral (Retired) Prof. N.B., ed. *The Fleet in the First World War*. Vol. 1, *Operations of the Russian Fleet*. Translated from the Russian. New Delhi: Amerind Publishing Company, Pvt. Ltd., 1979.
Pemsel, Helmut. *A History of War at Sea*. Trans. Major G.D.G. Smith. Annapolis: Naval Institute Press, 1979.
Pitman, Jack. *England Ebbing*. New York: Stein & Day, Inc., 1987.
Pitt, Barrie. *1918: The Last Act*. New York: W.W. Norton & Company, Inc., 1963.
Poolman, Kenneth. *The Winning Edge: Naval Technology in Action, 1939–1945*. Annapolis: Naval Institute Press, 1997.
Potter, E.B. *Sea Power: A Naval History*. 2nd ed. Annapolis: Naval Institute Press, 1981.
Potter, Roy, ed. *Myths of the English*. Cambridge: Polity Press, 1993.
Pugsley, Christopher. *Gallipoli: The New Zealand Story*. Auckland: Hodder & Stoughton, 1976.
Ragsdale, Hugh, and Valerii N. Ponomarev, eds. *Imperial Russian Foreign Policy*. Cambridge: Cambridge University Press, 1993.
Regan, Geoffrey. *The Brassey's Book of Naval Blunders*. Washington, DC: Brassey's, Inc., 2000.
Riasanovsky, Nicholas V. *A History of Russia*. New York: Oxford University Press, 1963.
Robbins, Keith. *A Bibliography of British History, 1914–1989*. Oxford: Clarendon Press, 1996.
Roshwald, Aviel, and Richard Stites, eds. *European Culture in the Great War: The Arts, Entertainment, and Propaganda, 1914–1918*. Cambridge: Cambridge University Press, 1999.
Rosignoli, Guido. *Army Badges and Insignia*. New York: The Macmillan Company, 1972.
Rutherford, W. *The Russian Army in World War I*. London: Gordon & Cremonesi, 1975.
Schaefer, Christina K. *The Great War: A Guide to the Service Records of All The World's Fighting Men and Volunteers*. Baltimore: Genealogical Publishing Company, Inc., 1998.
Schulze, Hagen. *Germany: A New History*. Trans. Deborah Lucas Schneider. New Haven, Connecticut: Harvard University Press, 1998.
Selby, John. *Balaclava: Gentlemen's Battle*. New York: Athenaeum, 1970.
Sellwood, A.V. *The Saturday Night Soldiers: The Stirring Story of the Territorial Army*. London: Wolfe Publishing, 1966.
Shepherd, William R., ed. *Shepherd's Historical Atlas*. 9th ed., rev. and updated. New York: Barnes & Noble Books, 1976.

Sheppard, Lieutenant-Colonel Alan. "Gallipoli: The Generals." In Vol. 3 of *The Illustrated Encyclopedia of World War I*, ed. Edward Young. 12 vols. New York: Marshall Cavendish, 1984.
Shores, Christopher, Norman Franks, and Russell Guest. *Above the Trenches*. New York: Fortress Publications, 1990.
Snelling, Stephen. *VCs of the First World War: Gallipoli*. Burton-on-Trent (U.K.): Wren's Park Publishing, Ltd., 1999.
Steel, Nigel. *The Battlefields of Gallipoli — Then and Now*. London: Lee Cooper, 1990.
Strachan, Hew, ed. *World War I: A History*. Oxford: Oxford University Press, 1998.
Strawson, John. *Churchill and Hitler: In Victory and Defeat*. New York: Fromm International, 1998.
Street, Edna, and Steve Burke. *Gallipoli Illustrated*. Adelaide: Kangaroo Press, 1985.
Taylor, Phil, and Pam Cupper. *Gallipoli: A Battlefield Guide*. Melbourne: The Kangaroo Press, 1987.
Terraine, John. *The Great War, 1914–1918: A Pictorial History*. London: Hutchinson, 1965.
Thomson, Alistair. *Anzac Memories: Living with the Legend*. Melbourne: Oxford University Press, 1994.
Timechart of Military History, The: 3000 B.C. to the Present. Foreword by David G. Chandler. Rickmansworth, Hertfordshire: TTC. The Timechart Company, 1999.
The Times History of the War. 10 vols. London: Times Publishing Company, 1919.
Tuchman, Barbara W. *The Guns of August*. New York: Macmillan Publishing Company, 1962.
Tucker, Spencer C. *The Great War, 1914–18*. Bloomington: Indiana University Press, 1998.
Turner, John, ed. *Britain and the First World War*. London: Unwin Hyman, 1988.
Van Creveld, Martin. *Supplying War: Logistics from Wallenstein to Patton*. Cambridge: Cambridge University Press, 1980.
Van Hartesveldt. *The Dardanelles Campaign, 1915: Historiography and Annotated Bibliography*. Westport, Connecticut: Greenwood Press, 1997.
Venzon, Anne Cipriano. *The United States in the First World War: An Encyclopedia*. New York: Garland Publishing, Inc., 1995.
Wallin, Jeffrey D. *By Ships Alone: Churchill and the Dardanelles*. Durham, N.C.: Carolina Academic Press, 1981.
Ward, Barbara. *Turkey*. London: Oxford University Press, 1942.
Weigall, David. *Britain & The World, 1815–1986: A Dictionary of International Relations*. New York: Oxford University Press, 1987.
Wells, H.G. *The Outline of History*. New York: Garden City Books, 1931.
Who Was Who. Vol. 3, 1929–1940. London: Adam & Charles Black, 1941.
Who's Who 1920: An Annual Biographical Dictionary with Which Is Incorporated "Men and Women of the Time." London: A.& C. Black, 1920.
Wilkinson, Frederick. *Militaria*. New York: Hawthorn Books, 1969.
Williams, John F. *Anzacs, The Media and the Great War*. Sydney: University of New South Wales Press Limited, 1999.
Winter, Denis. *25 April 1915: The Inevitable Tragedy*. Brisbane: University of Queensland Press, 1994.
Winter, Jay, and Blaine Baggett. *The Great War and the Shaping of the 20th Century*. New York: Penguin Studio, 1996.
Wintle, Justin, ed. *The Dictionary of War Quotations*. New York: The Free Press, 1989.
Woodham-Smith, Cecil. *The Reason Why*. New York: McGraw-Hill Book Company, 1954.
Woodward, David R. *Lloyd George and the Generals*. Newark: University of Delaware Press, 1983.
_____. *Field Marshal Sir William Robertson, Chief of the Imperial General Staff in the Great War*. Westport, Connecticut: Praeger, 1998.
Woodward, Sir Llewellyn. *Great Britain and the War of 1914–1918*. London: Methuen & Company, Ltd., 1967.

Wright, Richard, "Gallipoli: The Second Stage." In Vol. 3 of *The Illustrated Encyclopedia of World War I*. 12 vols. New York: Marshall Cavendish, 1984.
Yardley, Michael. *A Biography: T. E. Lawrence*. New York: Stein & Day (Publishers), 1987.
Younger, R.M. *Australia and the Australians: A New Concise History*. Adelaide: Rigby, Limited, 1974.

Television Documentaries

Barnett, Corelli, and John Terraine. *The Great War, 1914–1918*. London: British Broadcasting Corporation — Television. Twenty-six part series, broadcast 1965–66. An adaptation of John Terraine's *The Great War, 1914–1918: A Pictorial History*. London: Hutchinson, 1965. Terraine was the principal scriptwriter of the series, and also the commentator/narrator.
Gilbert, Martin. *The Complete Churchill: The Definitive Story of a Legendary Statesman: An Epic Lifetime in Four Parts*. Vol. I, *The Maverick Politician: A & E Collectors' Edition Biography*. London & New York: B.B.C. Lionheart Television/Arts & Entertainment Network-Hearst/ABC/NBC, 1992.
Nufus/Martin. *Mysteries and Myths of the Twentieth Century: Gallipoli*. London: Nufus/Martin Productions Studios, 1995.

Television Plays

All the King's Men. A dramatization of the story of The Lost Company of the Norfolk Regiment, raised exclusively from the estate workers at Sandringham (one of the royal residences), which disappeared in an attack at Suvla Bay on the 15th August, 1915. London: B.B.C. TV, 1999. Shown on PBS Exxon/Mobil Masterpiece Theatre, 18th March, 2002.
Sherriff, R.C. *Journey's End*. London: B.B.C. Television, 1968.

Service Reviews

Gallipoli Studies at the U.S. Marine Corps School. Quantico, VA: U.S. Naval College, 1932. Lectures, theses, reports, and papers on 5 reels of microfilm, one of which was an introduction. These sources are listed below by author, with one exception.
Gallipoli: The Origin of Modern Amphibious Doctrine. Annapolis: National Defense College Press, 1915.
Khulak, V.H., ed. *Manual for Naval Overseas Landing Operations*. Quantico, VA: U.S. Naval College, 1934.
Townsend, Commander L.W., U.S. Navy. "The Dardanelles Campaign." Lecture delivered at Marine Corps Schools, Quantico, VA: Marine Corps Schools Detachment, 1922.
Van Orden, Lieutenant George O., U.S. Marine Corps, "The Gallipoli Landings: Suvla Bay 6 August–20 December, 1915." Thesis, U.S. Naval College, Quantico, VA, 1935.

Periodicals and Journals

James, Robert R. "Gallipoli: the History of a Noble Blunder," a Review, by E. Weeks. *Atlantic Monthly* 216, no. 10 (October 1965): 1099–2001.
Liddell Hart, B.H., "Gallipoli Judgement." *Purnell's History of the First World War* 3, no. 9 (March 1971): 1140.

Marshall, Brigadier-General S.L.A., U.S. Army Reserve, Retired. "Suvla Bay." *Military Review* 43, no. 11 (November 1963): 60–68.
Okse, Necati. "Ataturk in the Dardanelles Campaign." *Revue Internationale d'Histoire* 50, no. 1 (January 1978): 8–15.
Smith, C.J., Jr. "Great Britain and the 1914–1915 Straits Agreement with Russia: the British promise of November 1914." *American Historical Review* 70, no. 7 (July 1965): 1015–34.
Thomson, Alastair. "History and 'Betrayal': The Anzac Controversy." *History Today* 43, no. 1 (January 1993): 8–11.
Walker, James. "Anzac: The Myths and the Realities." *History Today* 52, no. 1 (February 1993): 34–39.

Newspapers

The Bury Free Press (Bury St. Edmunds, Suffolk). 27 July 2001. Article on the Suffolk Regiment (Twelfth of Foot). Mainly about the Regiment's involvement in the Battle of Minden, August 1759.
The New York Times. 50th Anniversary Retrospective, 25 April 1965.
The New York Times. Catharine Reynolds, "Gallipoli: Landscape of Sacrifice," in the Travel Supplement (Section) of Sunday, 13 April 1997, devoted to Turkey, pp. 10 and 28.
The Observer (London). Commemorative article in the Colour Supplement. Sunday 25 April 1965.
The Sunday Times (London). Hugh McManners, Defence Correspondent, article on "the lost Company of the 1/5th Norfolks," 3 May 1998, p.12.
The Sunday Times (London). Hugh McManners, Defence Correspondent, "Bad Maps Led to Carnage of Gallipoli," 21 March 1999, p. 11.
The Sunday Times (London). Stephen McGinty, "Revealed: Churchill's suicidal 1914 despair," 1 June 1997. (The year cited is very misleading as the piece deals with letters Churchill wrote to his younger brother, Jack, during the first part of the war 1914–1915.)
The Times (London). 50th and 75th Anniversary Retrospectives, 26 and 27 April 1965, and 27 and 26 April 1990, respectively.
The Washington Post. 50th and 75th Anniversary Retrospectives, 25 April 1965, and 25 April 1990.

Letters

Condell, Diana, Curator, Department of Exhibits and Firearms, Imperial War Museum, London. A reply to query regarding the change of siting of insignias of rank from sleeve to shoulder on the dress of commissioned officers in the British Army during 1915. Dated 13 October 1993.
Phillips, Victor G. (see below), Hon. Secretary of the Suffolk Regiment's Old Comrades' Association, Mildenhall (Suffolk) Branch. A reply to various queries dated 18 May 1994.

Interviews

Agnew, Major, Battery Commander, Q Battery 358 Medium (Suffolk Yeomanry) Regiment, R.A., T.A., 1956–1957.
Aves, Arthur, Trooper, Lance-Bombardier, Mercer's Troop, Waterloo Battery, 2nd Regiment, Royal Horse Artillery, Suez Canal Zone & Cyprus, 1952–1954. Interviews, 21, 22, and 30 October, 1976.

Bibliography

Carter, John, Gunner, Lance-Bombardier, Bombardier, and Sergeant, 58 Medium Regiment, Royal Artillery, 1938–45; and Sergeant, Q Battery, the 358 Medium (the Suffolk Yeomanry) Regiment, R.A., Territorial Army, 1945–65. Interviews, 10 and 11 November, 1976.

Carter, Thomas, Gunner, Lance-Bombardier, and Bombardier, Badajoz Battery, 25th Field Regiment, Royal Artillery, Malaya and Singapore, 1953–1956. Interviews over an extended period, 1972–1982.

Champness, Peter, Major, and Lieutenant-Colonel, T.D., Battery Commander of Q Battery, 358 Medium (the Suffolk Yeomanry) Regiment, R.A., Territorial Army, 1952–56; and Commanding Officer of the 358 Medium (the Suffolk Yeomanry) Regiment, R.A., Territorial Army, 1956–60. Interview, 8 June 1955.

Clark, Trooper Nigel ("Nobby"), 2nd Regiment, Royal Horse Artillery, England and Canal Zone Egypt, 1951–1953. Also Q Battery, 358 Medium (the Suffolk Yeomanry) Regiment, R.A., Territorial Army, 1954–55. Interview, 22 November 1954.

Cudmore, Derek, Gunner, Lance-Bombardier, 18th Medium Regiment, Royal Artillery, 1951–1953, and 202 (Suffolk & Norfolk Yeomanry) Battery, 100 Medium Regiment, R.A., Territorial Army, 1954–1984. Interview, 1 April 1980.

Eck, Barbara-Jean W. (née Walters). Interviews March 2001. Her father's accounts of his experiences with Gurkha soldiers given.

Francis, Major R.C., P.S.O. (Permanent Staff Officer), 202 (Suffolk & Norfolk Yeomanry) Battery, 100 Medium Regiment, R.A., T.A. Interviews, 1975–1981.

Grieveson, Private Alan, 1st Battalion, the Green Howards—att.1st Battalion, the Northumberland Fusiliers, Korea 1950–1951. Interviews, November 1953.

Halls, Gunner Walter "Hotlegs," 46 Colenso Battery, 20th Field Regiment, Royal Artillery, British Commonwealth Division, Korea, 1952–53, and Q Battery, 358 (the Suffolk Yeomanry) Regiment, R.A., Territorial Army, 1953–56. Interviews, 18 September 1953, and 11 June 1955.

Houghton, Private Vivian, C Company, 2nd Battalion, the Suffolk Regiment. North Africa, N.W. Europe, and Palestine, 1942–1948. Interview, 10th December 1981.

Hubbard, John Arthur, Gunner, Lance-Bombardier, and Bombardier, 37th Heavy Ack Ack Regiment, R.A., 1950–52.

Jenkinson, Major Nicholas C., T.D., Battery Commander of 202 (the Suffolk & Norfolk Yeomanry) Battery, 100 Medium/Field Regiment, R.A. (V), Territorial Army, 1976–81. Interviews, 14 and 15 July, and 2 November 1977.

Lawley-Yorke, William Lanchester, Gunner, Lance-Bombardier, and 2nd Lieutenant, 22 Gibraltar Battery, 52 Locating Regiment; and 33 Dettingen Battery, 86 Heavy Anti-Aircraft Regiment, Royal Artillery, 1952–54. Interviews, 8 March 1952, and 21 December 1953.

Long, Captain Nigel St. J., T.D., Battery Captain, 202 (Norfolk & Suffolk Yeomanry) Battery, 100 Medium/Field Regiment, Royal Artillery (V), Territorial Army, 1975–1983. Interviews, July14–17, 1977, and April 19–21, 1980.

Mackenzie, Andrew. Supplied E-mailed material regarding his great-uncle, Rifleman David Anderson Mackenzie, of the 1st/5th (The Edinburgh Rifles) the Royal Scots, who was killed at Gallipoli on 3 May,1915. Communication dated 27 October, 1999.

Moore, Anthony E., Lance-Corporal (Acting/Unpaid) through to Company Quartermaster-Sergeant, the Royal Corps of Military Police, 1934–46, 1949–56. Sergeant, the Palestine Police, 1946–48. Interviews, 11, 21, and 22 December 1953.

Mortlock, Desmond Peter, 2nd Lieutenant, Lieutenant, A Company, 1st Battalion, the Punjabi Light Infantry, Indian Army. Dehra Dun, 1945–1947. Sergeant, Q Battery, 358 (Suffolk Yeomanry) Medium Regiment, R.A., T.A., 1948–1952.

Orchard-Lisle, Paul D., Lieutenant-Colonel, Colonel, and Brigadier-General, T.D., Commanding Officer of the 100 Medium Regiment, Royal Artillery, Territorial Army, 1974–79. Subsequently Adjutant-General of the Territorial Army and Volunteer Reserve, U.K. Interview, 15 June 1976.

Parker, Flying Officer Ronald Rhodes, Bomber Command, Royal Air Force, 1940–1946.
Peachey, Keith, Sapper, Lance-Corporal, Corporal, Royal Engineers, The Gambia, 1941–1945. Interviews, December 14 and 23, 1972.
Phillips, Victor G., Private, and Lance-Corporal (son of Sapper H. Gordon Phillips, above mentioned). A Company, the 5th Battalion, the Suffolk Regiment. P.O.W. Singapore, 1942–45. Honorary Secretary, the Suffolk Regiment's Old Comrades' Association 1948–93. Interview, 21 July 1968.
Rochester, Gunner Nigel. Incomplete personal information on army service 1950–1972.
Rose, Rifleman Stanley, B Company, the 2nd Battalion, The Green Jackets. Known locally as "Tall Story Stan." Served in the Suez Canal Zone, 1952–1953.
Rudd-Clarke, Lieutenant-Colonel the Honourable Lionel Le Mesurier, Commanding Officer of 52 Locating Regiment, Royal Artillery, 1951–56; and Commandant H.M. Military Prison, Shepton Mallett, Dorset, 1956–1960. Parade address, 21 December 1953.
Sheridan, Lance-Corporal Widnes, Royal Military Police. Provost Corporal, Trieste, 1950–51; British Zone, Austria, 1953–1955. Interviews, 1952–1953.
Smith, Rifleman Frederick B.S., D Company, 5th Battalion, the King's Royal Rifle Corps. Personal anecdotes, December 1953–May 1984.
Smith, Battery Sergeant-Major Terence E.M., 202 (Suffolk & Norfolk Yeomanry) Battery, the 100 Medium/Field Regiment, R.A.(V), Territorial Army, 1977–82. Interviews, 29 July 1978, 11 November 1979, and 12 April 1980.
Tillbrook, Gunner Herbert, Q Battery 358 (Suffolk Yeomanry) Regiment, R.A., T.A., Royal Artillery, Tripoli, 1951–1953. Interviews over extended period, 1954–1956.
Treble, Private through to Regimental Sergeant-Major H. Livingstone, A Company, 1st Battalion, the Somerset Light Infantry, 1932–51; and Captain, General Staff, G.H.Q., British Commonwealth Division, Korea, 1951–53. Interviews, 16 and 17 December 1983.
Walters, 33631268 Corporal Herman Edwin, C Coy., 133rd Infantry Regiment, 34th Infantry Division, United States Army. North Africa and Italy, 1943–44. Wounded. Awarded Purple Heart. Personal experiences with Gurkhas recounted.

Other

Condell, Diana, Curator, Department of Exhibits and Firearms, The Imperial War Museum, Lambeth, London. Supplied helpful information re: change of location of British Army Officers' rank distinctions, and an excerpt from a forthcoming book on Gallipoli by two of her colleagues; plus a quotation from a sound recording of a combatant's recollections of the campaign. Letter/enclosures, 13 October 1993.
Imperial War Museum, Duxford, Cambridgeshire. Research assistance, September, 2001.
Imperial War Museum, Lambeth, London. Research assistance. Regimental Museums in Bury St. Edmunds: The Suffolk Regimental Museum, at Gibraltar Barracks, and the Suffolk Yeomanry Museum, the TAVR Centre, secondary research assistance over an extended period.
The Suffolk Records Office, St. Mary's Square, Bury St. Edmunds, Suffolk. Research facilities over an extended period.

Index

An *n* following a page number indicates the item is found in a note referenced on that page. Numbers in ***bold italics*** indicate pages with photographs, illustrations or maps.

A Beach, Suvla Bay 48, 73, 80; 5/Suffolk and 5/Essex land at ***48***, ***62***, ***83***, 86
Achi Baba: "rises bare and rounded" 16; the eminence of 16, ***16***, ***24***, 25; Braithwaite urges Hamilton to order the R.N.D. to dash to the heights of 30; within their reach 31; the sullen hill of 32; becomes objective of the Helles armies 33; unattained objective of the "Battle of the Landing" 50–51; frowning fortress 55; key to the Narrows 59; Naval Nurse Edith Campbell "saw flashes from" 59; "one mass of bursting shells" 60; miles of trenches which run zigzag from Cape Helles to Achi Baba 135, 155
Aegean Sea ***16***, 19, 22, 23, ***24***, 40, 66
Agamemnon, H.M.S. 16, 53
Airplanes 60, 64
Airship 128
Aitken, Private Alexander, New Zealander: brings violin ashore 149; estimated the steepness of the gradients at Anzac Cove 34, 34*n*; enters academia 149
Akenfield, book about Suffolk quoted *see* Bibliography
Alexandretta ***11***
Alexandria: ships carrying 29th Division's equipment diverted to 23; motorized transport remained at 32; Black Ace Gang members transfer their attention to the bazaars of 42; filled with dysentery cases 144; 1/8 Hampshire sailed for 42; 1/5 Suffolk disembark at 144; Private Charlesworth, 1/8 Manchester, described 165; Captain Lynch *en route* for 167
Alston, 2nd Lt. G. K., 1/5th Suffolk: killed in action 93
Anafarta Biyuk, village of 59, 67, 68, 85
Anafarta Hills: Suvla Plan envisaged link up with the ANZAC attackers in the 49, 86, 104; failure of the 9th Corps to seize 131; 9th Corps failed to take the 155

Anafarta Ova (Kuchuk Anafarta Ova): trifling advance made in region of 84; General Lindley "could not undertake to clear of snipers" 89
Anafarta Plain: delay the dispatch of Turkish reinforcements to 44; Major Willmer entrusted with the defense of 47; three ridges which encircle 45; positions which dominated the 57; August Plan entailed occupation of all high ground which encompassed the 67
The Anafarta Ridge: number of warships with their guns trained on 84; a swift and vigorous advance might have given Stopford's troops this 148
Anafarta Sagir Valley 153
Anafarta Sagir, village of 67, 68, 79, 153–154
Anafarta Spur 45, 80, 92, 105, 107, ***107***, 116–117, 131
Anatolia 5*n*, 8*n*
A.N.Z.A.C. (Australian and New Zealand Army Corps): form part of Hamilton's command Mediterranean Expeditionary Force 21; Kitchener informed colleagues of ANZAC allocation 24–25; landed at the wrong location 29; steep gradients in their sector 34; ANZAC Commander Birdwood proposed what next phase should consist of 39; when large reinforcements would be acceptable at 39; Suvla support for ANZAC breakout 44–45; offensive strategy agreed upon by ANZAC Commander Birdwood and Hamilton 45; in conjunction with ANZAC breakout, Hamilton planned a new landing which was intended to link up with the ANZAC attackers in the Anafarta Hills 45; when ANZAC left Australia 48; 13th (Western) Division sent to bolster ANZAC offensive 49; Turkish defenses opposed to ANZAC offensive

219

Index

strengthened 54–55; mystique surrounding the ANZAC epic 55; reinforcements for 55; a barrage seen and heard by ferried Suvla troops 56; heights which dominated the ANZAC positions 58; already under intense pressure 67; ANZAC Commander Birdwood preferred that extra pressure be at Suvla 67; ANZAC had fought themselves to a standstill 96; Hamilton borrowed snipers from ANZAC 98; ANZAC and Indian Brigade push forward towards Hill 60 120; casualties suffered by ANZAC in effecting the Suvla/ANZAC juncture 120; after blizzard, Turks and ANZAC stood exposed to each other 142–143; popular conception of the Turk by ANZAC 143–144; ANZAC casualties of the Gallipoli Campaign 147; Birdwood and ANZAC on the Western Front 150

Anzac Cove: retrospective newspaper reports describe the landing at as a victory 20; Australian Trooper Morton described what conditions at ANZAC Cove were like 29; Suvla Bay only one mile further from Mudros than ANZAC Cove 34; same old tedium of trench warfare continued at 39; Mustapha Kemal's role at 65; possible alternative landing place was between Cape Helles and ANZAC Cove 54; the Suvla Bay operations intended to relieve and support the constricted struggle in the ANZAC Cove enclave 54; boatload of Australians just out of 55; off Cape Helles and ANZAC Cove flashes of gunfire illuminated the night sky 56; heavy fighting raged at 57; juncture of Suvla Bay and ANZAC Cove achieved 83

Aquitania, H.M.T.: 37; 1/5 Suffolk embark on 44; "life on board consisted of" 50; steamed majestically into Mudros harbor 56; 1/5 Suffolk remained aboard for three days 86

Apricot jam 129

Archduke Francis Ferdinand 1, 6

"Archies" (anti-aircraft guns): Turks tried to shoot geese down with 138

Ari Burnu, ANZAC area: **48**, **94**, 145

Ark Royal, H.M.S.: had float-shod seaplanes 53

Armes, Lt.-Colonel W. M., C.O. 1/5th Suffolk, 1911–1915: killed at Kuchuk Anafarta Ova, August 12, 1915 93

Army Service Corps (later Royal Army Service Corps) 27

Ashmead-Bartlett, Ellis, war correspondent 21n, 27–28n, 29, 99n, 112, 122, 131, 132, 155n, 156, 158n, 159, 159n, 198, 201

Ashton, Lt. E. M., 1/5th Suffolk: wounded 93

"Asiatic Annie": Reg Lane's descriptive name of heavy gun on Asiatic side 139

Askold, lone Russian cruiser in action at Dardanelles: only Russian warship present 23, *23*; strains of the Russian National Anthem float from 27; nicknamed the "Packet o' Woodbines" by British troops and sailors 28; eye-witness description of *Askold*'s bombardment of Cape Helles 28

Aspinall-Oglander, Brigadier-General Cecil F., military historian. author of *The Official History of the War: Military Operations; Gallipoli, Vol.'s I & II*. Lt.-Col. Aspinall not only co-conceived the ill-fated operations but served on the General Staff throughout the Campaign ix, 12n, 20n, 37n, 39n, 49n, 58, 68, 70n, 73, 78, 78n, 80, 81, 83n, 84n, 87n, 91, 91–92n, 94n, 100–101n, 106, 147, 153

Asquith, Herbert Henry, British Prime Minister 1, 33–34n, 45n; voices his annoyance 90, 99, 104, 131, 136

Attlee, Captain Clement, 6th South Lancashires, 13th (Western) Division 55, 123, 142, 154, 159n

The August Plan: described 57; falling into place 58; very much behind schedule 67; in serious jeopardy 72; is a failure 76, 77, 79, 87, 96, 153, 155

Australia Gully West: where Jake Mortlock wrote letter 122n

Axe, Edwin. Co-author of *Romford to Beirut via France, Egypt and Jericho* and a serving gunner and N.C.O. with the unit concerned 23n, 28n

B Beach, Suvla Bay **48**, **62**, 69, 73, 77, **83**

Bacchante, H.M.S.: Shell's Ridge 77

Baghdad 8

Baillard, General, Commander of the French Corps 182

Balaclava 112–114

Balaclava, Battle of 112–114

Balaclava Helmet 140

Balfour, Arthur 33n, 182n

The Balkans 1, **2**, 8, 35

Balloons 53

Basic British Army Structure 21

Bathing 75–76

Battleship Hill 65

Beauchamp, Lt.-Colonel Sir Horace, C.O. 5/Norfolk: placed in local command of 163rd Brigade 89; leads storming parties into oblivion, and perishes 91–92

Bean, Captain C. E. W. Australian war correspondent and author of books on Gal-

Index

lipoli as well as the *Official Australian History of the War* 34n, 55, 70n, 84n, 100, 143
Beck, Captain. company commander, Sandringham Company, 1/5th Norfolks. "Lost Company" at the action at Kuchuk Anafarta Ova 91–92
Beech, L/Corporal, inventor of the periscopic rifle (formerly a Sydney builders' foreman) 34, 34n
Bedfordshire Regiment, 1/5th Battalion, 162nd Brigade, 54th (East Anglian) Division 100–101
"Beetles," landing-craft used at Suvla 61, 71
"Belton Bulldogs" 63
Bendall, Lt.-Col., of the 2/3rd Battalion, the London Regiment: penned a vivid account of the Flood at Suvla, November 1915 ix, 139, 149n, 153, 155, 156
Berkshire Yeomanry 110, 116–117
Berlin 8
Birdwood, Lt.-General Sir William, General Officer Commanding ANZAC Forces: friend of Hamilton's 13; told by Hamilton to dig in 29; proposes first phase of new operations 39; Hamilton adopts Birdwood's plan 39; set to launch an offensive 39; launches a savage assault 44, 55; 9th Corps to assist Birdwood's attack 46, 57, 59, 85, 96; comes upon an Australian shaving 129, **130**, 137; life after Great War 150
Biscuits 129
Bismarck 5
Biyuk Anafarta Valley 155
The Black Ace Gang 42
Black Sea 2, 10, 15, 25
Blackwell, Edwin. Co-author with Axe (see above) 23n, 28n
Blizzard at Suvla 142–143
Bolton, Private Charles, of Denham, posted to D Coy, 1/5th Suffolk from another battalion of the same regiment in France *see* Bibliography
Bombard, medieval artillery piece used against Admiral Duckworth's squadron 1807 10
Bonar Law, Andrew 33n, 34n, 104, 120
Bosphorus 25
Bouvet, French battleship sunk with all hands in the Dardanelles 17
Braithwaite, Major-General Walter Pipon, (Hamilton's chief of staff) **17**, 30, 58, 106, 122, 132, 150
Breslau 9
Brigades *see* Appendix E
Brighton Beach, ANZAC 29
Brittain, Vera. Oxford undergraduate. Wartime nurse. Authoress. *Testament of Youth* and other works; also a patient in Imtarfa (Mtarfa) Isolation Hospital 122; nursed in Malta, 1916 122
Brodrick, Captain: the Hon. George St. John. Low esteem of General Staff in letter to his father, Lord Midleton 76
Brooke, Sub-Lieutenant, Royal Naval Division. Lionized Georgian poet who participated at Antwerp, and in the early part of the Dardanelles Campaign, but died of blood poisoning just prior to the commencement of the landings at Gallipoli 16, 21, 44, 149
Brown, Albert Joseph, ordinary telegraphist "mentioned in dispatches," with the sinking of H.M.S. *Irresistible* 17, 17n, 182
Brulard, General, French Commander of 1st Division 178
Brunswick, Prince Ferdinand, Duke of, Commander of Allied Army at Minden 175, 215
Buckinghamshire Yeomanry 110
Buffs *see* Appendix E
Bulair **16**, 54
Bulair, Isthmus of **16**, 47
Bulford — Salisbury Plain 29
Bulgaria: enters the War on the side of the Central Powers 146
Bully beef (corned beef) 6n, 55, 129, 123n, 195
Burlham, Private Timothy, of Newmarket, D Company, 5th & 1/5th Suffolks, 1913–1919, Black Ace Gang 42, 207
Burnt Hill 80, *83, 107*, 113, 158; *see also* Hill 170; Scimitar Hill
The Bury Free Press 215
Bush, Lt.-Commander Eric Wheeler 10, 10n, 15n, 99–100

C Beach, Suvla Bay **24**, **38**, **40**, **48**, 76
Cairo 42
Camoufleches 34
Campbell, Nurse Edith 59, 75
Cape Helles<en.20n, 24, 24, 25, 33, 45, 54, 56, 58, 59, 60, 69, 145
Cardiff 48
Cardigan, Brig.-Gen. James Thomas Brudenell, Earl of: in the Crimea; at Balaclava 112
Carson, Sir Edward 120, 123
Casualties 147–148
Caucasus 10
The Central Powers 2, 146
"The Charge of the Light Brigade," epic poem by Tennyson, Alfred Lord, cited 112–114

222   Index

Charlesworth, Private R., 8/Manchester: excerpts from diary of 164
Charterhouse (public school): Robert Graves compelled to apologize for remark 148
Chocolate Hill 16, 48, 56, 62, 66, 68, 77, 79, 81, *83*, *107*, 113, 116, 153
Chunuk Bair 37, 58, 68, 83, 96, 105, 129
Churchill, Winston Spencer 1, 2, 3, 10, 13, 19n, 35n, 96–97, 130, 133, 135, 160
City of London Yeomanry 112–117
Colchester. Garrison town in Essex 8, 42–43
Collen, Private, Lance-Corporal Albert, of Worlington, A Company, 2nd Battalion, the Royal Fusiliers. Served in France, Flanders, Salonika, and Russia, 1915–1921 44, 44n, 132, 149, 186, 207
Colvin, 2nd Lieutenant, 1/5 Essex 93
Compton, Mackenzie<en 51, 59, 62, 70, 84, 158
Constantinople 2, 9, *10*, 19, 20, 25–26, 31, 70, 146
Corned beef ("bully beef") 55, 129, 123n, 195
Connaught Rangers, 8th Battalion: jointly capture Hill 60 119–120
Corps *see* Appendix E
Cory, 2nd Lieutenant C. W., 1/5th Suffolk: killed in action Kuchuk Anafarta Ova 93
County of London Yeomanry *see* Appendix E
Creighton, Reverend Oswin, Chaplain, 29th Division 26–27n, 49n, 133n
Crewe, Marquis of 130
Cricket 158
Crimea, Ukraine *2*
Crimean War 112–114, 120, 186
Curzon 130

D Beach, Suvla Bay *83*
d'Amade, French General commanding the French Corps, "chivalrous" 13
Dardanelles Committee 10, 13, 22, 32, 35, 37, 119, 122, 135
Davies, Lt.-Gen. Sir F.J. *see* Appendix E
Davis, Major G. F. M., 1/11th Battalion, the London Regiment, 54th (East Anglian) Division: killed in action on Kiretch Tepe Ridge 101
Dawnay, Lt.-Col. Guy Payan 78, 106, 132
De Lisle, Major-General H. Beauvoir 44, 80–81, 100, 105, 143, 114, 158
Denham, Midshipman Harry 53, 60, 76–77, 80, 99, 100n, 106, 106n, 108, 147, 147n, 206
Denton, Company Captain 91; killed in action 93
Derbyshire Yeomanry 110

De Totts Battery, Helles *24*, 49
de Winton, Brig.-General C., Commanding Officer, 162nd Brigade, 54th (East Anglian) Division: leads attack on Kidney Hill. Badly wounded 100–101
Diarrhea 125
Diet 52, 55, 123n, 129
Diphtheria 125
Divisions composition of 39; Appendix E
Dixon's Gully: group of Suffolk officers photographed in 130
Doris, H.M.S., destroyer: escorts hospital ship from Imbros to Cape Helles 57
Dorset Yeomanry 110
Duckworth, Admiral Sir John Thomas: fateful exploit in 1807 10
Dysentery 69, 125

East Yorkshire Regiment, 6th battalion: entrenched on Scimitar Hill 91; recalled to attack 91; patrol of successfully probed Tekke Tepe 82, 83, *83*
Edwards, Rev. C. Pierrepont, Chaplain 163rd Brigade, 54th (East Anglian) Division: awarded Military Cross for bravery while leading a volunteer stretcher-party, Kuchuk Anafarta Ova, August 12th, 1915 92–93
Egypt 21, 45–46, 48, 51, 92, 144, 146, 148–149, 144, 149, 151
Ejelmer Bay<en.68, 123
Elandslaagte, Battle of, 1899<en.59
Ellison, Major-Gen. G.F. *see* Appendix E
Endymion, H.M.S., destroyer present and assisting the Suvla landings 71, 128
Entente Powers 5
Essex Regiment 27, 39, 44, 49, 86, 90, 92, 93, 138, 151
Eton 70, 157
Euryalus, H.M.S.: Harry Denham observed from 108
Evacuation 144–146
Everett, Lieutenant H. F., Royal Army Medical Corps: wounded at Kuchuk Anafarta Ova 93
Ezbekiah Gardens. A pleasure-park in central Cairo frequented by Allied troops 42

Fair, Captain A., Military Cross, co-author of *The History of the 1st/5th Battalion "The Suffolk Regiment"* 202
Fauvette, vessel to which 5/Suffolk transferred for passage Mudros to Suvla Bay 86
Fedourine Heights, Crimean War 112
Feizi Bey, Colonel 66, 67, 80
The Fens 49

Ferdinand, Archduke Francis: assassination of 6
Ferdinand, Prince, Duke of Brunswick. Commander of Allied Army at Minden 215
Fisherman's Hut, ANZAC area, planned landing spot *24*
Fitzgerald, F. Scott; affair with Sheila Graham (see below) 148–149
Flash-spotters 139
Flies 31, 33, 69; swarms of 93; pestilential plague of 94; black plague of 96; almost intolerable 96, 129
Flood at Suvla 139–142
Foreign Legion, French 22, 30, 48
Foxhound, H.M.S., destroyer: supports advance on Kiretch Tepe Ridge 117
Freckenham, Suffolk 149
French Foreign Legion 22, 30, 48
French naval forces 17
Frostbite 144, 148
Fuses: *13*, 101; incorrect setting of 108; length erred on the side of caution 35; observation Post Officer adjusts for shrapnel bursts 102, 102*n*, Chapter 3 endnotes

Gaba Tepe *16*, *24*
Geese: migration of 138–139
Ghazi Baba, Hill 10, *40*, *48*
Gibbons, Lt.-Col. Thomas, D.S.O., of the 1st/5th Battalion, the Essex Regiment. and its historian ix, 45, 46*n*, 53*n*, 115*n*, 116, 116*n*, 120*n*, 121, 124–126*n*, 126, 127*n*, 128, 160*n*, 170*n*, 171*n*, 181*n*, 186*n*, 190*n*, 201
Gibraltar 145
Gillam, Major John, D.S.O., Army Service Corps. Service at Helles and Suvla recorded in his *Gallipoli Diary* 14*n*, 19, 22, 22*n*, 48, 48*n*, 53*n*, 58–59, 59*n*, 66, 66*n*, 87*n*, 146, 146*n*, 150*n*, 154, 155*n*, 168, 168*n*, 198, 211
Gloucestershire Yeomanry 110
Godley, Major-General Alexander 75; unhappy that Suvla units "are idling while his men are fighting like tigers 120; "sssessment of the August gains as "five hundred acres of bad grazing ground" 144
Goeblen 9
The Golden Horn 10
Graham, Sheila: married Major Gillam 148
Grampian: carried 5/Essex from Mudros to Suvla Bay 86
Grampus, H.M.S.: destroyer supports advance 117
Granby, General the Marquis of. At the Battles of Minden and Warburg 215

Grand Duke Nicholas 10
Graves, Robert 158–159
Greeks 45
Green Hill 85
Grey, Sir Edward, British Foreign Secretary 6
Guépratte, Admiral, commander of French naval squadron 17
Guildford: rowing on the Thames at 27
Gulf of Saros/Xeros *16*, 54, 102
Gully Beach, Helles *16*
Gurkhas 30, 58, 72, 125, 144
Gurkhas: 1/5th Battalion Gurkha Rifles 72; 1/6th Battalion Gurkha Rifles 72

"Half Hours at Helles" 33–34, 129
Halliday, Nurse Amy: shrapnel pierced her hospital-ship cabin 207
Hamilton, General Sir Ian Monteith, Commander-in-Chief of the Mediterranean Expeditionary Force ix; appointed by Lord Kitchener 13, *17*; appraises the situation from aboard H.M.S. *Phaeton*, 2, 10; forces allocated him, 20–21; Hamilton's estimate of enemy troops strengths, 11*n* Early frustration re: 29th Division 22; evolves a strategy 24; expects Russian divisions to be assigned 26; Russian contribution anticipated 26; reportedly "anxious" 20; observes the landings 21–22; Birdwood dismayed — Hamilton tells him to "dig, dig, dig . . . ," 29; fails to exploit unopposed Y Beach landing 30; begs and pleads for reinforcements and replacements 31; cause of failure 31–35; note on Sir Ian's early career — re: Suffolk Regiment 36*n*; plans a new offensive 37–39; strategy for new offensive 38–40, *38*, *40*; meets General Sir Frederick Stopford, designated commander of the new Army Corps 50; who bears a message from Lord Kitchener 54, 55, 58; Sari Bair and August Plan 58; Stopford's instructions (from Braithwaite) 58; orders to Stopford fatally amended 59*n*; Hamilton's rallying speech to his troops on the eve of the Battle of Elaandslaagte, 1899 59*n*; welcomes news of the successful landings at Suvla Bay 62; Liman von Sanders' realization of Hamilton's intentions 67; one objective of Hamilton's "to secure a safe haven . . ." 67–69; the Salt Lake's surface tested 68–69; bound by the Old School Tie mentality 70; inspects departing troops at Mudros harbor 70–71; waits for news of progress at Suvla and frets 73; telegraphs Stopford urging action, spends a second night "on tenter

hooks" 77; Aspinall sends H. a despairing telegram 78; patience exhausted H. confronts Stopford aboard the *Jonquil* 78; hastens to Suvla and orders Hammersley to launch an attack 79; patience exhausted over-rules Hammersley's excuses and insists that the one Brigade ready should advance forthwith 79; experts' opinions re: Hamilton's last-minute intervention 79–80; Hamilton's ignorance of the tragic abandonment of Scimitar (Burnt) Hill 82–83, **83**; driven to distraction Hamilton does the rounds again 84–85; orders the 53rd (Welsh) Division to land at Suvla Bay with a view of storming the Tekke Tepe heights 85; orders last reserves (54th [East Anglian] Division) to land at Suvla Bay 86; visits Suvla Bay, August 9 86; and sees Stopford 87; *The Official History's* version of Hamilton's orders to the 54th Division 91*n*; plans for the 54th Division to storm the Tekke Tepe Ridge 93; receives cable from Kitchener 89; sends Kitchener a "complete *résumé*" and a list of requirements 97; replacement generals meet with Hamilton's approval 97; upbraids Stopford 97; Hamilton's *aide-de-camp* sums up Stopford and his General Staff in a derogatory manner 98; Hamilton sums up the landings in retrospect 98; condemned by his own words 99; hopes the dismissed Stopford might wish to see him 99; Hamilton stresses that General Mahon acted on his own initiative 100*n*, 140; Bonar Law's sarcastic reference to Hamilton 104; prepares for another Suvla offensive 105–107; describes the plan for the 21st August assault 105; watches the attack and gives his account of it 106–107; his observation position 106; Bonar Law and Prime Minister Asquith speak in uncomplimentary terms of Hamilton 120; General Mahon's opinion of Hamilton and Braithwaite 122; his support eroded further in the corridors of power. The Dardanelles Committee refuses Hamilton more troops 122–123; Hamilton instructs his secretary to write a letter of commendation to the Colonel of the 6th Gurkhas 128*n*; Hamilton visits the 54th Division, lunches with its commander, compliments his men, and mentions the Indian Brigade 128; Hamilton, a sublime optimist 133; his arch-critics combine in disparaging Hamilton 131–135; sands of time trickle out for Hamilton 135; Dardanelles Committee severely restricts Hamilton's freedom of action 134–135; Stopford's attack on Hamilton 134–135; dismissal and recall of Sir Ian Hamilton 135; later life 150

Hammersley, Major-General Frederic, Commanding Officer 11th (Northern Division): alleged mental instability of 52; absence of at the sailing of invasion fleet 59, 73; at Suvla Bay 71; congratulated by Stopford 73–74; Stopford goes to see Hammersley at Suvla 78; Hamilton visits, prevails over Hammersley reluctance 79; ordered to launch an attack 82–83, 84; "energy and dash alien to" 89; Kitchener suggests replacement of 95; Hammersley relieves Brigadier Sitwell 99; "taken off peninsula in a state of collapse" 99; overlooked by *Who's Who* 150; described as "dilatory and incompetent" 155, 158

Hampshire, H.M.S.: Lord Kitchener amongst those who perished when she went down 160

Hampshire Regiment, 2nd Battalion: up from Helles advance across Salt Lake under shellfire 112–114

Hampshire Regiment, 8th Battalion (163rd Brigade) 39, 44; arrive at Mudros 88; disembark at Suvla Bay 89; in front line 90; role in attack 90; suffered almost 50% casualties 93; move to Rhododendron Spur, ANZAC 95; left Gallipoli for Mudros 144; sailed for Alexandria 144

Hampshire Regiment, 10th Battalion, at Rhododendron Spur, ANZAC 95

Hankey, Lt.-Col. Maurice, secretary to the Dardanelles Committee and War Council: recounted Kitchener appointment of Hamilton to lead M.E. F. 13; details expected Russian contribution to the Dardanelles operations 25, 25*n*; is sent to Gallipoli 25; reports on the use of the periscopic rifle 34; one of those who sounded the alarm with regard to the inertia at Suvla Bay 71; comments on the smallness of the area in British hands 73–74; is appalled by Bank Holiday atmosphere at Suvla 75–76; is sent to investigate the holdup at Suvla 78; predicts development of trench warfare if Turks seize the Anafarta Ridge 78; relates how Hamilton overcame Hammersley's reluctance 79; is distressed by the attitude of the Suvla Staff 104; comments on the lack of enemy shellfire and the absence of any bellicose action by the British army 81, 85; shows Hamilton a cable from the Prime Minister's secretary, Bonham Carter 90. Dardanelles Committee in possession of Hankey's detailed report on the Suvla fiasco 104; takes his leave of Sir Ian Hamilton 106; leaves with the King's Messenger 106; delivers his *Memorandum on the Situation, August 30, 1915* 120, 159

Hanna, Henry: recorded the exploits of the 7th Battalion, the Royal Dublin Fusiliers ix; at Mytilene 47; night voyage to Suvla Bay 60–61; landing 62; on the Kiretch Tepe Ridge 102; and the fighting at the Pimple 103; on Chocolate Hill 116; leaves for Salonika 132; is named as one of many who vouched for the enthusiasm and patriotism of the new troops 159; described landings as orderly and not a shambles 159

Hansen, Captain Percy H., V.C., 6th Battalion, the Lincolnshire Regiment: on the slopes of Scimitar Hill, 9th August 81; rescues many wounded from encroaching flames 81–82; is awarded the Victoria Cross for "conspicuous bravery" 83

Hare, Brig.-Gen, Maj.-Gen.: rallying speech before Helles landings 26

Hargrave, Sergeant John, 32nd Field Ambulance, Royal Army Medical Corps, 10th (Irish) Division. Author of three works on the Suvla Bay Landing. Served Gallipoli and Salonika 1915–1916 ix; unfavorable impressions of Lemnos 49; lack of maps and information recounted 53; fatal phrase, "if possible" inserted into Stopford's orders alluded to 104*n*; sails for the New Landing 59; recalls seeing men blown up by hidden devices as they went ashore, falling-in "in fours" 63; scoutmaster, and author of three books on the Suvla Bay Landing 63–64; incredulity at parade-like posture 63; observed few enemy entrenchments 64. witnessed German airplane dropping bombs 64; eulogizes General von Sanders 65; alleged Hamilton upset by warship dropping shell into Salt Lake 68–69; sketched semaphore signalers 71; explanation for bathing scene at Suvla Bay 76; water shortage 80; August 8th—"Sunday—day of rest" 81; shrapnel bursts, graphically described together with their lethal effect 102, 102*n*; "chaos in command" 103; reason for loss of direction in advance given 108–109; "tornado of shrapnel and machine-gun fire" 110; observes advance of the Yeomanry 113; temperatures of "over 100 degrees" described 121; sails for Salonika 132; serves in Salonika 148; invalided out 148; founds Boys' Movement after the war 148; new troops' enthusiasm and patriotism vouched for by 159; maintained that the landings at Suvla Bay were orderly 159

The Haricot. Fortified Turkish position in the Kereches Dere on the Helles front for which the French suffered heavy casualties attempting to take 33

Harrods, the elite London store from whence the celebrated "Harrods' hampers" emanated 129; Lt. *'Juvenis'* receives one 129

Havelock, H.M.S., Royal Navy monitor: bombards at Suvla 76–77

Hawke, Private. Royal Army Medical Corps orderly at Suvla Bay with the 10th (Irish) Division. Companion of Sargeant Hargrave (see above): described troops forming and falling-in "in fours" as "sheer murder" 63

Hay, Major Stuart, Brigade Major, 162nd Brigade, 54th (East Anglian) Division: led attack on Kidney Hill 103

Hayes, Private, 6/Manchester: excerpts from diary of 216–217

Helen of Troy 23

Hell's Spit, ANZAC shoreline **24**

Herbert, Captain and Major the Hon. Aubrey P. British intelligence officer and author of *The Secret Battle*: pens epitaph to Third Battle of Krithia (Battle of the Fourth of June), "Half Hours at Helles" 33–34; acts as interpreter at the arranged truce to bury the dead 56; describes the "unforgettable sight" of the Yeomanry's advance under fire 109–110; paints a depressing scene of a night relief of infantry unit 125–126; final lines of "Half Hours at Helles" quoted: . . . The corpses on the parapet. The maggots in the floor 129

Herefordshire Regiment *see* Appendix E

Hertfordshire Yeomanry 110

Hill, Brig.-Gen. Felix Frederic. commanding officer of the 34th Brigade, 10th (Irish) Division, during the Suvla Bay Landings: demonstrated clear credentials of competence in command 52; said to have been ignorant as to where he was when he landed and did not possess a map of the area 53; ordered to land 53; suffered under the organized chaos 71; he and his brigade victims of the beach redesignation and deployed on the wrong flank 74; invalided off with acute dysentery 99; nominated to succeed Mahon as Commanding Officer of the 10th (Irish) Division 103

Hill 10 (aka Ghazi Baba.): two whole brigades advance against 73; evacuated

by the Turks 73; troops lying behind for protection prior to the 21st August attack 113
Hill 60 83, **94**, 106, *121*, 122, 128; ANZAC and Indian Brigade to push towards 120; vicious engagement in the Hill 60-Kaiajik salient 120; Turks still occupy the crestline of 120; letter written by Private Mortlock to cousin Jack Parker after a tour of duty on 122; 54th (East Anglian Division) took over line from Aghyl Dere to Hill 60 128; 1/5th Suffolks garrisoned Hill 60 for nine days casualties and ammunition expenditure given for the period 128
Hill 170 82, **83**, **94**, 107, 113, 158; *see also* Burnt Hill; Scimitar Hill
Hinnell, 2nd Lieutenant T.S.: killed in action Kuchuk Anafarta Ova 93
Homer 16, 23
Horsford, Private William, 6/Lincolns and Reconnaissance Corps: in Maltese hospital with Private Jake Mortlock, also convalesced at the same establishments in England. Was most certainly involved in "the Last Battle" 207
Hospital ships 75, 133
Hospitals: Lemnos, Malta (Imtarfa) 148, London (St. Bartholomew's) 148, Alexandria
House of Commons 135–136
How, Sergeant George, D Company, 1/5th Battalion, the Suffolk Regiment: as Corporal, chronically seasick on voyage out 44–45, **45**; obliged to stay behind in Egypt because of rioting 149; resumes civilian life as miller, and later as landlord of the *Golden Boar* public house — in both instances in his native village of Freckenham 149; cited as a primary source 207
Hume, Private W., 5/Suffolk: killed in action 137
Hunter-Weston, Major-General Sir Aylmer. Commander of the 29th Division and subsequently the 8th Corps: described by Hamilton as "a slashing man of action 13; submits an "appreciation" of the problems 22; said to be "full of pluck and confidence" 27; "blotted his copybook" 30; launches bludgeoning frontal assaults at Helles 33; instance of folly of 36*n*; leaves peninsula; his successor named 44–45; Hamilton said to have "tried his best" 50; conditions Stopford might expect to face said by Hamilton to be easier than those faced by Hunter-Weston 51; alleged callous remark about casualties 56; bully-boy approach 156.

Hamilton did not question Hunter-Weston's judgment 158

The Iliad 16, 23
Ilium *11*, 16, *16*, 23
Imbros, island of *11*; Greek government allowed Allies to use Lemnos, Imbros, and Mitylene as bases 21*n*; described as "peaceful and beautiful" on the morning of the 25th April 29, 56, 60–61, 69–70, 73, 104; airship from Imbros sailed overhead to Anafarta 128
Imperial Yeomanry 110
Imtarfa Isolation Hospital, Malta 122*n*, 148
Indian Brigade, the 29th: objective of 120. Brigade visited by Sir Ian Hamilton 128; Indian troops' manner of smoking cigarettes 17*n*, 128*n*, 195
Indian Mule Corps: "showed the greatest contempt for enemy fire" 111
Inferno on Scimitar Hill 82–83
Inflexible, H.M.S. badly damaged in the Dardanelles
Inglefield, Major-General Francis, G.O.C. 54th (East Anglian) Division: is keen to attack 89, 150; lunches with Hamilton 128, 160, 176
Inniskillings — 10th (Irish) Division: "Juvenis," a subaltern describes landing at Suvla Bay 72–73
Inniskillings — 87th Brigade, 29th Division: suffer severely storming Scimitar Hill 108; "severely cut up, only 250 men and two officers left" 114
Irresistible, H.M.S.: founders in the Dardanelles 17; author's uncle served aboard 1913–1915 17*n*
Ismail Oglu Tepe (W Hills): General Staff Orders state its capture to be accomplished "*coup de main* before daylight" 58; topography described 68; failure to adhere to plan for seizure of 77; Turco-German resolution to secure this feature 79; 33rd Brigade (11th [Northern] Division) attempts to seize 82–83; 6/Lincolns begin their advance 82; attack of 53rd (Welsh) Division, supported by 11th (Northern) 83; Hamilton assembles a strong force to storm 105; featured in Hamilton's plan to wrest victory from defeat 108; 87th Brigade, 29th Division "constantly compelled to retire from" 109; Hamilton took back seat at crucial battle for 158
Isthmus of Bulair *16*, 25, 65

Jaggard, Private Bob, D Company, 5th & 1/5th Battalions, the Suffolk Regiment: "Bob Jaggard is all right, wishes to be remembered to you." letter from Hill 60 *42*, Appendix D

"Jam Tin" Bombs: local manufacture of 35, Private Mortlock's opinion of 35*n*

Jephson's Post, a strongpoint on the Kiretch Tepe Ridge scene of bitter fighting 90

Jonquil, H.M.S.: General Stopford establishes his HQ upon 71; Aspinall boards to alert Stopford to the lack of progress ashore 78; Hamilton confronts Stopford aboard, and races away from 78–80

"Juvenis," nom de plume of an officer in the Inniskillings. Author of *Suvla Bay and After*: was sure that beer was obtainable on the battleships below 102; wounded on the Kiretch Tepe Ridge 132–133; unable to accompany his battalion to Salonika — bound for Britain on a hospital ship 132; vouched for enthusiasm and patriotism of the new troops 159; gave account of the orderliness of the Suvla Bay Landing 159

Kaiajik Dere, a dry watercourse adjacent to Hill 60, scene of a vicious engagement in late August 120

Kaiser Wilhelm II: invariably referred to as "Kaiser Bill" by British and antipodean troops 6; visits Suvla 135

Kannengiesser, Col., Brig.-Gen., and Maj.-Gen. Hans ix; awaits developments, tries to sleep on wolf skin spread on table-"bed" 65; looks down on Suvla Bay and the invasion force 65–66; his account substantiated Hamilton's estimates of Turkish troop strengths in the Suvla Bay sector 67; Spartan accommodation of and daily rides around his troops units 70; supervises defense of a Sari Bair sector 70; wounded and invalided off the peninsula 70; his eyewitness account verifies the good order and discipline of the British invasion force at Suvla Bay 159; primary source reports of cited 203

Karakol Dagh *48*, 87

Kate, Aunt (Katharine Booty [née Parker]): Private Jake Mortlock's aunt sends a parcel of *Little Gleaners* 129–130, Harold Goodrum, nephew of 207

Kemal, Mustapha, Lt.-Col., Brig.-General, General: commands successful counterattack at Anzac Cove and Sari Bair 29; Colonel Kemal's 19th Division garrisons Gaba Tepe 54; adjudged British would select Suvla Bay for new landing 65; substantiated that the garrison at in the Suvla Bay area was small 57; rallied dispirited defense on Sari Bair 80; cleared Chunuk Bair 96; Clement Attlee pays tribute to 123; "rugged determination" cited 151; "the greatest Ottoman military hero to emerge from the war" 152; saved the situation at Suvla 153–155; adjudged British success at Suvla was initially possible 155

Kendle, Major R. H. 1/5th Suffolk: killed in action Kuchuk Anafarta Ova 93

Kereches Dere. Ravine in the Cape Helles sector: French fight bloody battles in 33; suffer heavy casualties in 33

Keyes, Commodore Roger, R.N.: *17*; early enthusiasm for the Dardanelles operation 18; urges persistence; advocates renewed assaults 18; civilian minesweepers viewed as ineffectual 18; shares concern about Suvla inaction 73; following land debacle, K. attempts unsuccessfully to have the original naval strategy revived 150–152

Khilid Bahr Plateau: dominates the Narrows *24*, 25, *38*, 45

Kidney Hill — Kiretch Tepe Ridge: attack on by 162nd Brigade 100–101

King George V's Sandringham Company, "Lost Company" *94*

Kingsley, General. Commander of the British infantry regiments at Minden 215

Kipling, Rudyard 70

Kiretch Tepe Sirt/Kiretch Tepe Ridge: 9th Corps to seize 40; shelling of described 78; reported still in Turkish hands 80; topography of *40*, *62*; Small Turkish outpost on 68; 10th (Irish) Division was to have deployed 74; Irish infantry advance along 75; main objective achieved only on Kiretch Tepe 77; shelling of 79; 1/Suffolk deployed on 87; 10th (Irish) advance observed 90; enfilade fire from 92; 54th (East Anglian) Division support 10th Division on 100; General von Sanders' opinion of importance of 101; artillery support for advance along 102; Lt. "Juvenis" wounded on 103; withdrawal from ordered 103; further thrust contemplated 104; from Kiretch Tepe to Sulajik 54th and 53rd holding the line 107; General Hamilton watches last battle from 109; Private Mortlock celebrates 20th birthday on 120–121; Lt. "Juvenis" wounded on 132–133; 54th Division replaces 10th on 133; Lt. Priestman killed on 146–149; General Stopford's preposterous excuse for not advancing along Kiretch Tepe 155

Kitchener, Lord Horatio, British Secretary

228

Index

of State for War 1914–1916: revokes decision re: 29th Division for Mediterranean Expeditionary Force (M.E.F.) 13; appoints General Sir Ian Hamilton to command expeditionary force 13; details composition of M.E.F. 13; enemy granted grace period by Kitchener's vacillation 20; relents over committing 29th Division 20; expected strong supporting demonstration by Russians 25–26; referred to Russian promise of support 26; advocates "prosecution of the Dardanelles Campaign with the utmost vigour" 35; Kitchener and Churchill did what they could to assist Hamilton and relieve his plight 35; Hamilton's candor in his cable to 36–37; Western Front failures weigh heavily with 37; on casualties (Western Front) 37; Kitchener's Army composed the vast majority of the new divisions assigned to Gallipoli 39; the renowned recruitment poster 40–41; Private Mortlock and comrades "thought we were better than Kitchener's Army [personnel]" 44; message from to Hamilton expounded by latter to General Stopford 50; and Kitchener's "key to success" enumerated 50–51; fundamental grasp of situation Kitchener had 51; cables disappointment over Suvla fiasco 89; Hamilton cables Kitchener hinting at relief of incompetent generals 97; Kitchener's response 99; tells Dardanelles Committee members that if at fault the Suvla High Command must be replaced 99; extricates H. from "the skein of chivalry in which he was enmeshed" 99; H. tells K. that de Lisle is the only general who can pull the Suvla forces together 100; is advised by Hamilton of the need for vast replacements and reinforcements 104; Dardanelles Committee plan that Kitchener should make personal visit to Gallipoli 122; cables Hamilton re: Salonika commitment will deplete Gallipoli troop strengths 122; cables Hamilton that Dardenelles Committee expects him to adopt "only a defensive attitude" 133; has already made up his mind about evacuation 135; arrives Gallipoli 137; advises evacuation 137; originally designated task force as "Constantinople Expeditionary Force" 145; Hamilton continually stressed chronic shortage of troops and ordnance to 153; emphasized the element of surprise prior to the Suvla débâcle 153; the mettle of Kitchener's New Army volunteers vouched for 159

Kitchener's Army 21, 39; Private Jake Mortlock and comrades "thought we were better than Kitchener's Army [personnel]" 44; the mettle of Kitchener's New Army volunteers vouched for 159

Knife-rests 138–139

Knyvett, Capt. R. Hugh, Australian intelligence officer describes blizzard 142, 143*n*

Koja Chemen Tepe, peak in the Sari Bair Range **40**, 54, 58, 80

Krithia, small town at Cape Helles which the British attempted to take 33, 54

Kukris Gurkhas draw blood if unsheathed 125; Captain Lane acquired a pair 125; depicted **23**, 126

Kum Kale: Asiatic landing made by French troops 24, 25

Lacy Scott, Capt./Major G., 1/5th Suffolks 93

Laindon Hill, ANZAC, 1/5th Essex: admire view and mules 138

Lala Baba, hillock on edge of Suvla Bay **94**; seen for first time by Lt. "Juvenis" 60; men digging in behind crest of 60; Lt. Priestman's experiences on 63; Colonel Kannengieser sees "English troops on" 66; physical features described 68; small outposts on 71; Turks abandon 73; General Hamilton hurries to 78; Colonel Rettie arrives at 81; Yeomanry shelter behind 106; Yeomanry moves out from behind 113

Lancashire Fusiliers 55, 87

Lanchard, Lieutenant, Army Service Corps 128

Lane, Corporal Reginald **88**; D Company, 1/5th Battalion, Suffolk Regiment. First forward patrol 88; gains weight on Gallipoli 125; acquired a pair of kukris 125

Latrines **121**

Lawrence, Sergeant Cyril, Australian Engineers: he and his compatriots burrowing deep in hillsides 34; observes Suvla Bay landing 72; bitter about the way "the Tommies are letting our boys down" 46; on Western Front decorated for bravery and granted a commission; changes opinion about Tommies 149; rises to eminence as a civil engineer 149

Lawrence, T.E. describes lack of adequate maps 28

Ledward, Captain G.W., 1/5th Suffolk killed in action Kuchuk Anafarta Ova 93

Lemnos, Aegean island **11**, 13; 29th Division to be dispatched to 22; 29th Division's ships redirected to Alexandria 46; one destination of sick and wounded

45–46; perfect natural harbor 47, 47*n*; Sergeant Hargrave disembarked at— impressions 49; Chaplain Creighton found "enchanting" 49; tent cities emptied 56; batteries of 4.5 inch howitzers waiting at 105

Leon floating mines 22

The Light Horse: Australian, attempt to storm the Nek 100

Lincolnshire Regiment, 6th Battalion, 33rd Brigade, 11th (Northern) Division: attempted to seize Ismail Oglu Tepe 80–82; Captain Hansen, of, rescued, wounded under fire 83

Lindley, Maj.-Gen., the Honorable John Edward, 13th (Welsh) Division: lacked reputation 52; unimpressive record of 84; lands at Suvla Bay 85; throws in the towel 89; confessed to General Hamilton that he could not control his division 89; lack of "energy and dash" 89; could not undertake to clear the Anafarta Ova of snipers 89; resigns and is rewarded with a base command at Mudros 99; dilatory and incompetent 155; pathetic excuses 160

Listening posts 128

Little Gleaner 129–130

Liverpool 48; 1/5 Suffolk entrained for 44, embarked at 45, 51; Suffolk Yeomanry embarked at 128

Lloyd George, David 2, 120, 136, 137, 144, 145, 154–155

London Regiment, unspecified battalion at Suvla. Joined Major Gillam's brigade 128

London Regiment, 1/10th Battalion, 162nd Brigade, 54th Division 39; takes part in the action on the Kiretch Tepe Ridge 100–101

London Regiment, 1/11th Battalion, 162nd Brigade, 54th Division 39; takes part in the action on the Kiretch Tepe Ridge 100–101

London Regiment, 2/3rd Battalion: mentioned in relation to its C.O., Lt.-Col. F. Bendall ix; C.O. of describes awfulness of the floods and blizzard at Suvla 142–143

Lone Pine Ridge: General Birdwood to launch a strong attack on 44; immortalized as a blood-tinged chapter in Australian history 55; heavy fighting raged at 67; seven Victoria Crosses gained at 75

Lord Nelson, H.M.S. 16, 53

"Lost Company" of the Norfolks (1/5th) 91, 92*n*

Lucan, Lt.-Gen. George Charles Bingham, Earl of Lucan: in Crimea. The Charge of the Light Brigade 112

Lynch, Captain F.: excerpts from diary of 165–166

Machine guns: ammunition 128; siting of, Hill 60 **121**; Turkish 103, 114

Mackenzie, Private Andrew Anderson, 5th (Edinburgh Rifles) Battalion, the Royal Scots ix; public school sportsman and university medical undergraduate, volunteers; killed at Cape Helles 19*n*; on board the *Dongola* 22

Mackenzie, Captain Compton: British intelligence officer at GHQ Imbros. Lunches with newly arrived General Stopford whom he describes 51, 51*n*; eve of Suvla operation described 62; "dark night of the Suvla landing" 62; waxes pessimistic over Suvla prospects 70; is bitter over squandered chance at Suvla 84; distrust of British caste system 85, 158

Mackenzie, Taylor, Lieutenant, 5/Essex 93

Mahon, Lt.-Gen. Sir Bryan: Officer Commanding 10th (Irish) Division. Demonstrated clear credentials of competence in command 52; has one of his brigades commandeered 71; his 31st Brigade is separated completely from his command 74; now possessed an emasculated division 74; even so his depleted division penetrated furthest on the first day at Suvla 75; his infantrymen on the Kiretch Tepe Ridge suffer from raging thirst as they strive to hold the positions gained 80; only general to respond with anything like enthusiasm 84; seemed motivated by offensive spirit and was "keen" 89; Kitchener erroneously assumed that Hamilton included him on the replacement list 99; ordered by General Stopford to advance along the Kiretch Tepe Ridge; seized "the Pimple" 100; his gallant Irishmen captured "the Pimple" at bayonet-point, and desperately held out against repeated counter-attacks 103; refused to waive seniority, and departed for Mudros 103; Ashmead-Bartlett interviewed. "He complained bitterly" 122; sailed from Suvla Bay 132; disembarked at Salonika 132; appointed commander of the British Salonika Force 132; one of the few Suvla generals to show any enterprise 150

Maidos **16**, **24**, **38**, 47

Malta 17, 46, 133, 144

Manchester Regiment 164

Manor Farm, Suffolk, England : Private Mortlock called from the harvest field at 6

Maps: woefully inadequate 32; Hargrave's disgust 60; depicted another part of the

Peninsula 51; Stopford alleged to have lost vital ones on train! 53; Those of Cromer, Sheringham and Kings Lynn issued! 91; depicted another part of the peninsula 91

Maris, Lieutenant, 1/5th Suffolk 91

Marmora, Sea of 2, 9–10, *11*, 153

Mauretania, H.M.T.: Cunard liner converted to troopship. Contingents of the 13th (Welsh) Division sail on, and stay cooped up aboard 85

McMahon, Sir Henry. High Commissioner to Egypt: General Hamilton sends a bluntly worded letter to complaining of the Egyptian Press' betrayal of the projected Gallipoli landings 28

Mediterranean Sea 9, 10, 146, 148

Middlesex Yeomanry 110, 112–113

Miers, Lt.-Col. H. J.: Monmouthshire Regt , becomes Commanding Officer 1/5th Suffolks, October, 1915 129*n*

Minden. The silent toast to "those who fell at Minden" 215

Minden, Battle of article which appeared in *The Bury Free Press* (Suffolk), August 1, 2001, giving origin of Minden rose, *et cetera* 215; Sellwood's account 217–219

The Minden Rose. Public house in Bury St. Edmunds, Suffolk 215

Minefields 15, 16, *16*, 17, 18

Mines 16, *16*, 17, 18, 34

Monitor, *H. M. S. Havelock*: shells ridges at Suvla 76–77

Moon: phases of at landings, crescent new moon 58

Morto Bay, Helles *16*, *24*

Mortlock, Hannah (née Parker), Private Mortlock's mother — to whom his postcard was addressed, illustration 9

Mortlock, Private S. Jacob P., D Company, 1/5th Battalion, the Suffolk Regiment, 163rd Brigade, 54th (East Anglian) Division: called up from harvest field 6*n*, 8*n*, *8*, 12; reverse of card 9; opinion of "jamtin" bombs 35*n*; on snipers 34*n*, 35*n*, 38*n*; bloated corpses punctured by bullets 33; possibly saved lives of sleeping comrades 42–43; goes AWOL Christmas, 1914, *41*, *42*, *43*, 43, 43*n*; thought, "We were better than Kitchener's Army" 44, 44*n*; bedbug experience 43*n*, 45*n*, 51*n*; "Moaning Minnies" 52*n*; never bathed, snipers active 76; wistfully viewed Anafarta village 85*n*; account of landing at A Beach, Suvla Bay 86–87; vowed never to waste water 87*n*; in group *97*; on shrapnel 102, 102*n*; viewed life on warships as "a picnic" 102; ignominious to surrender 106*n*; "Burnt Hill" 114*n*; celebrated 20th birthday on Kiretch Tepe Ridge 120–121; writes to his cousin, Jack Parker 122; water, flies 122*n*; on Gurkhas 125, 125*n*; on Corporal Lane's unique obesity 125, 125*n*; letter penned 127; way Indian troops smoked cigarettes 128*n*; said Suvla never given same publicity as ANZAC and Helles 128; "We never had enough ammunition" 128*n*;, Verey pistol souvenir 128*n*; ended spell on Hill 60, 129; graphically described the constant plague of flies 129; and the liquidity of tinned (canned) corned beef 129; received parcel from his Aunt Kate 130; distributed disappointing contents of 130; expressed his "All the generals ought to be shot" opinion 132;, the first ingredient of recipe for successful prosecution of war 132*n*; reported sick 133; received callous treatment 133; sent to front line 133; returned on stretcher and diagnosed as a severe case of diphtheria 133, 133*n*; invalided off peninsula 133; sixteen-year-old soldier mentioned by 133*n*; described frostbitten Gurkha ward-companions on a hospital ship 144, 144*n*; cynicism of successful evacuation 145, 145*n*; in Maltese hospital 148; paralyzed from waist down 148; rejoined his company in Palestine and Egypt 148; survives war 148; service in WWII 148; death of 148; interviews with 207; letter from Hill 60 Appendix D

Mounted Division, the 2nd: ordered to sail from Egypt 97–98; General Peyton, commander of interviewed by Ellis Ashmead-Bartlett 112; numbered 5,000 113; was one of the two chief sufferers at Scimitar Hill 132; *see also* Yeomanry, Yeomanry Division

Mudros, town and harbor: Sir Ian Hamilton observed in 49, 22; large natural harbor of 23, 140; transport and war vessels assemble at 23; fine sight at night 27; Suvla troops assembled at 48; 1/5 Suffolk 86; *Aquitania*, H.M.T., steamed into 56; pith helmeted soldiers throng the wharves at 59; General Lindleys's reward, "a base command at" 99; General Mahon departed to 103; hospitals at filled with dysentery cases 125; 54th (East Anglian) Division ordered to proceed to 139; 1/8 Hampshire left for 144

Mules 112, 138, 143

Murdoch, Keith, Australian journalist: dispatched critical cable 142; granted conditional permission to visit the battlefields 131; meets up with Ashmead-Bartlett 131; celebrated letter to

Australian Prime Minister 132; shared a low esteem for generals with Jake Mortlock 132; virulent letter 135
Musk, Private, 1/5th Suffolks, author of the limerick featured in Illustration 134
Mytilene/Mitylene (Lesbos): Hamilton assembled some troops at 49; some Royal Dublin Fusiliers enjoyed a brief respite at 52; and were in complete ignorance of their destination when they departed 60; tent city rapidly emptied 60; one brigade from to enforce 69; received its orders 70

Napoleon 52, 146
The Narrows 15, *24*, 32
Nebrunesi Point 1, *16*, *24*, 38
The Nek: Australian Light Horse attempt to take 67
Nelson, Lord 19, 59
Nevinson, Henry. war correspondent: views battlefield from Chocolate Hill 108; makes sober observation 146; gives comprehensive list of casualties, 147; eye-witness account of cited 159
New Zealand Mounted Rifle Brigade *see* Appendix E
New Zealanders 13, 21, 30, 58, 91
Newfoundlanders 30
Nicol, Brig.-General L. L., Commanding 30th Brigade, 10th (Irish) Division: his battalions achieved definite success; seizure of "he Pimple" 100–101
Nolan, Captain Edward: carries orders for the Light Brigade to charge at Balaclava; is killed 112
Norfolk Regiment, 1/4th Battalion, 163rd Brigade, 54th (East Anglian) Division 39; in action at Suvla Bay 123; relieved by 1/5 Suffolk on Hill 60 126
Norfolk Regiment, 1/5th Battalion, 163rd Brigade 39; in action at Suvla Bay, two companies lost on Kuchuk Anafarta Ova 91–92; discovery of the "Lost Company" bodies after the War 92*n*; 1/5 Suffolk reach line occupied by 127; fifteen year-old boy in Sandringham Company of 176*n*
Northamptonshire Regiment, 1/4th Battalion, 162nd Brigade, 54th (East Anglian) Division 39; last of Brigade to come ashore at Suvla 100
Nottinghamshire Yeomanry 110
Notts & Derbyshire Yeomanry 110
Number 2 Outpost, West ANZAC *48*
Nurses 59, 75, 122

Ocean, H.M.S. 16
Ocean Beach, ANZAC *16*, 24

Official History of the War: Military Operations; Gallipoli 58, 68, 81, 91, 147, 153
Oliver, 2nd Lieutenant G. G., 5/Suffolk: narrow escape of 133
Olympic: White Star liner requisitioned by the British government as a troopship 137; Suffolk Yeomanry sail from Liverpool aboard; hazards of the voyage described 144
Osmanieh, H.M.T.: troopship 1/5 Suffolk leave peninsula on, bound for Lemnos 144
Ottoman Empire 8
Outpost, Number 2, West ANZAC *48*

Paget, Lord George: Commander of the Light Brigade at Balaclava. His cigar lasted until he reached the Russian guns 112–113
"The Pals," D Company, the 7th Battalion, the Royal Dublin Fusiliers: enjoy a brief spell of acclimatization on the island of Mitylene/Lesbos 48, 48*n*; played a notable part in an action on Kiretch Tepe Ridge 100–103; are unsupported and unsupplied 103. Private Wilkin's fearlessness, and death 103; Lieutenant Hamilton only officer left 103
Parker, Lieutenant A.S., 1/5th Suffolk: wounded at Kuchuk Anafarta Ova 93
Parker, Jack, Private Mortlock's cousin, with whom he corresponded: *see* Appendix D
Periscopic rifles: Hankey reports use of 31; inventor of 32*n*
Peyton, General, C.-C. 2nd Mounted (Yeomanry) Division 112
Phelps, Lt.-Col. M., C.O. 6/Lincolns, on the slopes of Scimitar Hill 82
"The Pimple," feature on the Kiretch Tepe Ridge: vicious fighting at 100–103
Pinard, French wine 24
Pitman, Jack, author of *England Ebbing* 157
Plain of Maidos: push through to accomplish a strategy 26
Playing fields 70
Plymouth 48
Poilu, French soldier 24
Pomiankowski, Major Joseph: provided catalogue of Dardanelles' ordnance 19, 19*n*
Portiano Rest Camp, Mudros, Island of Lemnos, 1/5th Suffolk marched to, and remained there eight days 145
Potts, Trooper (later L/Cpl.) Frederick W. O., V.C., B Squadron, the Berkshire Yeomanry: badly wounded during storming of Scimitar Hill, after coming unscathed

across Salt Lake 114; ordered to "fix bayonets!" 114; his account of his ordeal when after being wounded he dragged a badly wounded comrade, Trooper Andrews, down on a shovel 115–116; awarded Victoria Cross for Gallantry of Potts on Hill 70 (Scimitar or Burnt Hill), 21st-23rd August 116, 148
Powers, 2nd Lieutenant, Bernard Alexander, Middlesex Regiment, and Lieutenant, Royal Flying Corps: Private Jake Mortlock goes AWOL to attend celebration in B. Power's honor 9, *12*, 208
Priestman, 2nd Lieutenant Edmund Y., 6th Battalion, the York and Lancaster Regiment. Author of posthumously published *With a B.P. Scout in Gallipoli: The Belton Bulldogs at Suvla Bay* ix; observed an American taking motion pictures of the embarking troops at Imbros 61; account refutes Hamilton's "silent army" contention 51*n*; gives detailed account of voyage to Suvla Bay including the issue of maps 62; gives graphic account of his unit's landing at Suvla Bay 63–64; sketching scoutmaster and author 63–64; orderliness of the landing emphasized 63–64; depicts swarms of flies in a humorous sketch 64; killed in action Kiretch Tepe Ridge and buried threat 103; gallant death of 146; patriotism and enthusiasm of volunteers verified by 159; knew what objectives were, 159
Prigge, Major Erich, German commanding officer on the Gallipoli peninsula: his account substantiated the British assessment of the troop strength of the Suvla garrison 84
Princip, Gavrilo: assassinates the Arch Duke Francis Ferdinand and the Arch Duchess Sophia in Sarajevo, Serbia 6
Public schools 70–71, 148, 158–159

Queen Alexandra 93
Queen Elizabeth, H.M.S.: calibrates her mighty 15-inch guns by firing over the peninsula to pound the Narrows' forts 15, 15*n*; is one of Admiral de Robeck's hardest hitters 16; is one of the vast conglomeration the world had ever known 28; approached Y Beach on 25 April 29; is recalled by the Admiralty 53

Rabbit Island in Aegean Sea off coast of Asia Minor: where crippled warship was towed *11*
Raglan, Field Marshal Fitzroy James Henry Somerset, Baron: made Gallipoli his Crimean War headquarters 149; at Balaclava the order he gave the Light Brigade to charge "perhaps unclear" 112–114
Ramadan 55
Reed, Major- General H.L.: exerted a bad influence on General Stopford 52
Rettie, Lt.-Col. W. J. K., R.F.A.: observation upon arrival at Suvla 81
Rhododendron Spur: Anzacs gain a V.C. at 75; 8/Hampshire (54th [East Anglian] Division), deployed 95
River (Lark), "oh, for a row on. . . ." 171; Private Mortlock's letter from Hill 60.
Romania *2*
River Clyde, converted freighter used as landing-craft at Helles—V Beach 27, 28
Rooke, Lieutenant N., 1/5th Suffolk: wounded Kuchuk Anafarta Ova 93
Royal Buckinghamshire Hussars *see* Appendix E
Royal Dublin Fusiliers, 6th Battalion: land at Suvla Bay 73; *see also* Appendix E
Royal Dublin Fusiliers, D "The Pals" Company, 7th Battalion: enjoyed a brief period of acclimatization on the Aegean island of Mitylene (Lesbos) 52; ignorant of their destination when embarking for Suvla Bay 60; desperate plight of on the Kiretch Tepe Ridge 75
Royal Dublin Fusiliers, 7th Battalion: land at Suvla Bay 73; interrogated Turkish prisoners 102–103; Private Wilkins killed 103; foolhardy heroism of Private Wilkins 103
Royal Engineers: engaged in constructing a splinter-proof dug-out for General Stopford and his staff 81, 86; could have been digging wells, or constructing roads 81
Royal Fusiliers, 2nd Battalion *see* Appendix E
Royal Gloucestershire Hussars 110, Appendix E
Royal Inniskilling Fusiliers, 5th Battalion (10th [Irish] Division): "Juvenis" a subaltern with 73, 103
Royal Inniskilling Fusiliers, 6th Battalion (10th [Irish] Division) 73, 103
Royal Inniskilling Fusiliers, (87th Brigade, 29th Division): "suffered severely" in the 21st August attack (Scimitar Hill, Ismail Oglu Tepe, and the Anafarta Spur) 108; "severely cut up . . . only 250 men and two officers left" 108
Royal Munster Fusiliers: severely shot up leaving the *River Clyde* 28
Royal Nottinghamshire Hussars 110
Royal Scots 28
Rum 91; rations, 5/Suffolk were to have been issued with 91

Index 233

Rumbelow, Private W. Vincent, D Company, the 1st /5th Battalion, the Suffolk Regiment. Freckenham, Suffolk *42*, *43*

S Beach, Helles *16*
Sackville, Lord George: incompetent British Commander at Minden and elsewhere 112–114, 215
St. Bartholomew's Hospital Convalescent Centre, Swanage, Kent 148
St. Bartholomew's Hospital, London 148
Salisbury Plain, a very large military training area in southern England 29*n*
Salonika: report from betrayed Allies' intentions 44
Salonika Anglo-French Expeditionary Force: largely emasculated by King Constantine's pro–German stance 20; L/Corporal Albert Collen served in 132, 148; planned dispatch of British and French force to 132; commitment at 132; Greece asked Allies to send force to 132; 10th (Irish) Division disembarked at 132; General Sir Bryan Mahon appointed commander of Anglo-French Army of 132; Sgt. John Hargrave invalided from 148; L/Corporal Collen fought at 148; some of those who survived Gallipoli saw service at 148; after arrival of French General Sarrail General Mahon commanded British Expeditionary Force at 132; effect of Salonika commitment on Gallipoli Campaign 137
Salt Lake: shell screamed over 63; Turks retreated over 68; silvery expanse of 72; fire from small Turkish post between Salt Lake and Nebrunesi Point 87; no forward movement of attempted 96; General de Lisle testified there was an abundance of underground water between Salt Lake and the Kiretch Tepe Ridge 80–81; 1/5 Suffolk deployed to fill gap between 9/Lancashire Fusiliers and N.E. corner of Salt Lake 88; Yeomen march in extended order over 109; "splendid advance of Yeomanry Brigade" 109; Yeomanry marched steadily in open order across 110; dismounted Yeomanry attacked Turks across 113; troops brought across in broad daylight 113; unit moved across in open formation 115; B Squadron, Berkshire Yeomanry crossed unscathed 117; November floods swept down into 139–140
Samothrace, one of the large islands in the Aegean off the Gallipoli Peninsula *11*
Samson, Commander: aerial reconnaissance of 60; Hamilton delighted with Samson's report 60

Sanders, General Otto Liman von: ix; approved the Porte's precautionary measures 18; head of German Military Mission to Turkey 20; Ottoman Government offered command of Gallipoli Army Corps 20; Enver Pasha appointed him Commander in Chief of Turkish Fifth Army 20*n*; expressed confidence in ability to hold back Anglo-French invaders 33; feared that new invasion would be in Bulair region 47, 54, 55; caught off guard by Suvla Bay Landing 62; stated that success of new landings "would be a severe blow to us" 65; ended speculation as to site of potential landing 65; Major Willmer reports new landings to 65; realized significance of new offensives 65; makes up mind as to Hamilton's intentions 66–67; austere habits of 70; consulted with subordinates as to how to combat new threat 79–80; all his reinforcements now arrived 87; opinion of potential seriousness of Kiretch Tepe Ridge advance 101–102; *Communiqué* published in the *New York Times* describes the Suvla venture as a complete failure 119; confessed ignorance of British evacuation plans 145; catalogued booty left behind after evacuation 145–146; gives casualty figures 147–148; Post-Gallipoli, post-war life of 151; detained for six months at Malta 151; advanced view that success was within the grasp of the Anglo-French invaders 154
Sandringham Company, 5/Norfolk 92–93
Sarajevo 6
Sari Bair. One of the three commanding heights of the Gallipoli Peninsula *16*, 25; planned occupation of 39; plan to storm 44; after achieving original objectives Suvla forces would press in upon 45, 54; assault on about to begin 57; assault on to coincide with the landing at Suvla Bay 58; storming parties move upwards towards 58; highest peak of 58; landing at compared with prospects at Suvla Bay 59; Colonel Kannengeisser supervised critical battle for this feature 70; General Birdwood's gallant troops fought desperate and bloody battles to fulfill their part of Suvla Bay strategy 76; Turks needed to expel units lodged on 79–80; 54th (East Anglian) Division originally intended for action at 85; the heights of overlooked the whole Suvla beach 87; Sari Bair cleared of allied lodgments 96
Saros, Gulf of 54
Sarrail, French General at Salonika 132

Scimitar Hill **83**, **94**, *107*; *see also* Burnt Hill; Hill 170
Sea of Marmora 10–11, *11*, 153
Sedd-el-Bahr: one planned landing site in area of 16; landing at Sedd-el-Bahr, one of *Pen Pictures of Battles* 21*n*; landing at Sedd-el-Bahr compared with prospects at Suvla Bay 95
Sharpshooters 127
Shaw, Major-General Frederick, G.O.C. 13th (Western) Division 47
Shellfire 60–61
Shells 118, **118**
Sherwood Rangers 110, 113
Shrapnel: "Beetle" landing barges included shrapnel-proof protection 61, 71; "tommies charging across plain under bursting shells and shrapnel" 84; General Stopford supervising construction of shrapnel-proof shelter close to the shore 85–86; 5/Essex under heavy shrapnel-fire 101; elucidated **13**, 101; Private Jake Mortlock describes 102; Sergeant John Hargrave describes 102; inventor of 102*n*; wound caused by a shrapnel ball 102; wasted shrapnel on own troops 108; "tornado of shrapnel and machine gun fire" 109; "enemy turned a baddish shrapnel firer on [attacking troops]" Hamilton 109; curtain of; white puff of 109; burst over them continually 110; brought across Salt Lake under heavy shrapnel fire 112; began to thin them out 113; 5/Suffolk "were continuously under shrapnel and sniper fire" 122
Sickness, 800 per day evacuated 133
Sing, Private, Australian sharpshooter 27
Sitwell, Brig.-General William, 34th Brigade, 11th (Northern) Division: unimpressive campaign record of 52; Hammersley failed to ensure that Sitwell's brigade secured its objectives 89; "energy and dash" alien to 89; relieved of command 99; departure of 103; dilatory and incompetent 155
Sixty-pounders: firing at Suvla **18**, 117
Small arms ammunition 128
Snipers 34; to the beach 76
Sound-rangers 139
South African Wars 20, 51, 70–71, 158
South Nottinghamshire Hussars 110
South Wales Borderers, 2nd Battalion (29th Division): just back from successful siege of Tsing Tao 20–21; under shrapnel fire on Kiretch Tepe Ridge 102
South Wales Borderers, 4th Battalion (13th [Western]Division) *see* Appendix E
South Wales Borderers' Gully 102*n*
Southampton 48

Stopford, Lieutenant-General the Honorable Sir Frederick, Commander-in-Chief 9th Army Corps: arrived at GHQ Imbros 50; lectured by General Hamilton on basic concepts of warfare 50; faced with an easier task than Hunter-Weston's in April, 0–51. Compton Mackenzie's negative assessment of 51; succeeded Hunter-Weston for a short time as 8th Corps Commander at Helles 51; allegation that he lost important maps 51; left crucial documents on a train in England 51*n*; comes under the pessimistic influence of General Reed, later to become his chief of staff 52; kept in ignorance of date and place of new landing 53; specific instructions issued to 58–59; absent at embarkation of invasion forces 59; aboard the *Jonquil* 71; established his headquarters aboard the *Jonquil* 71; poor communicator 73; informed Hamilton that he has been able to advance "little beyond the beach" 73; "dawdling on his command ship" 73; urged to "grasp the Kiretch nettle" 75; S. and his staff summed up as "a lifeless crew" 76; mishandled the 9th Corps 100; suffered from a sprained knee 87; deigned to reply 77; confronted by Aspinall 78; confronted by Hamilton 78; goes ashore 78; supervises construction of personal bunker 85; relieved of command 99; villifies Hamilton 132; later life 150; assessment of 155
Street, Major-General Lyster, V.C.: advocate of intense artillery preparation 55; in that respect exerted a pessimistic influence on General Stopford 55–56; becomes Stopford's chief of staff 57; goes back to the Western Front 210
The Sublime Porte 8
Submarine nets at Suvla Bay 139
Submarines active in Aegean, Marmora and Mediterranean Seas 53
Suffolk (West, administrative region)<en.6
Suffolk Regiment, 5th Battalion 35; those 72% who volunteered for overseas' service 41; became the 1/5th Battalion 42; trained full-time after mobilization August 5, 1914 41–42; at Colchester 42–43
Suffolk Regiment, 1/5th Battalion, 163rd Brigade, 54th (East Anglian) Division: "Jam-tin" bombs 35, 35*n*; became part of Colchester garrison 43–44; embarked for eastern destination 44; confined on board at Mudros 86; transferred to another vessel 86; landed at Suvla Bay 86; accounts of landing 86–87; battalion

headquarters mentioned 87; ordered to move into the firing line 88; moved to a more forward position 89; ordered to attack; attack described 91; relieved; casualties incurred 92; tainted well 12*n*; D Company Soldiers **97**; Hill 60 **121**; awful conditions enumerated 122; depleted battalion on Hill 60 121; flies 122*n*; under-age soldiers of 133*n*; firing at migrating geese 138–139; knife-rest tug-o'-war 138–139; sailed from Peninsula 144; in Egypt 144; Egypt, Sinai, Palestine, and Syria 148; two officers and a non-commissioned officer of Suffolk Regiment mentioned 148–149

Suffolk Yeomanry, Suffolk Regiment, 15th (Suffolk Yeomanry) Battalion: embarked for Gallipoli 128; arrived Gallipoli October 10th, 1915 133; landed at Anzac Cove 133; experiences in the line 134; some of the last to leave Suvla/Anzac 144; sailed for Egypt 144

Suvla: the flood at 139, 140*n*, 141, 142; withdrawal from. Dardanelles Committee considers a withdrawal to be advisable 132; Lord Kitchener recommended that Suvla and ANZAC should be evacuated 137; evacuation of discussed 137

Suvla Bay 53, 55, 66, 69, 71–72, 74; generals squandered opportunity at 147, 149, **149**; a judgment on the failure 153–161

The Suvla Plan 39, **40**

Suvla Point 25, 35, **38**, 62, 86, 94, **94**, 120

Swiftsure, H.M.S.: shells heights at Suvla 128; Major Gillam witnesses *Swiftsure*, H.M.S. fire at Sari Bair 128

Swimming 75–76; *see also* Bathing

Taube, German airplane 79

Teichman, Capt. Oskar, R.A.M.C. ix; arrival of 49; advance across Salt Lake described in detail 110–113; casualties and conflagrations 115–119; Post-Gallipoli Service 151

Tekke Tepe: complex of ridges 47; running south between Ejelmer Bay and the village of Anafarta Sagir is nearly 900 feet high 68; unoccupied (prior to August 6th) 68; Turks needed to secure 80; Turks drew ever closer to 80; General Hamilton insisted that a brigade should seize 82; offensive aimed at 82; still unoccupied (August 8th) 82; 53rd Division to storm the 85; most probably the 87; first view of by Private Jake Mortlock 87; 54th (East Anglian) Division to seize at dawn 90; Company of 5/Norfolk swallowed up on the scrubby slopes of 91–92;

the Turkish forces occupy in strength on 10th August 93

Tennant, the Honorable, under-secretary for war 169–170

Tennyson, Lord Alfred: the Light Brigade's Charge immortalized 112–114

Theseus, H.M.S., destroyer present in assisting the Suvla landings 76

Thirst 88–89

The Times (London) 51, 92

Tirpitz, Grand Admiral Baron Alfred von: observation on the Dardanelles fighting 68–69

Trench 13 Helles sector. Bitterly contested earthworks; Essex soldier's cynical account 45*n*

Triad, Vice-Admiral de Robeck's yacht: top level meeting on 15, 17, **78**, 97

Troy 16, 23, 27, 53

Tsar Nicholas II 14

Tug o' war 138–139

Turkey 1, 8, 9, 10

"Turkey Trot" trench, Hill 60. Turks explode mine beneath 121–122

Turkish: ruling faction 8, 9; connivance 9; Army handbook 2; capital 8, 15, 19, 20, 130; ministry of war 8, 19; Army 12; authorities 18; General Weber Pasha, commander of Cape Helles garrison 15*n*, 167; Army of Gallipoli 20; Army of Gallipoli 20; Counterparts, 20, 22, 33. Army divisions 22; Troop dispositions, 22, 25; forces 22; defenders 22; Enver Pasha, Turkish minister of war 18; appointed General von Sanders Commander of Turkish Fifth Army 20, 47, 53; sniper's 34*n*, counter-attacks 34; to pin down as many T. troops 44; turn T. right flank 45; undermine T. frontline trenches 48; Army of Gallipoli 51, 53; Ninth Division (Kannengieser) 54; Army of Gallipoli 54; artillery possessed batteries of *minenwerfers* 54*n*; troops defending Helles front 54; Ninth Division 54; Commander in Chief Fifth Army von Sanders 54; commanders 54; defenses 54; observation of Ramadan 58; Picquet driven in by the (British unit) 63; positions on the Sari Bair range 63; four batteries on the Kislar Dagh 64; Chocolate Hill firmly in T. hands 65; bombardment still blanketed the Turkish positions 65; accounts 65; Nineteenth Division 65; battalions just starting off 66; 3,000 men comprised T. troop dispositions in Suvla area 67; primary sources 67; force 67, **83**; small T. post on Lala Baba 68*n*; Gendarmerie 75; reserves were miles away 76; military hierarchy 79; divisional commander

(Kemal) 80; counter-attacks 80; lines 80; weary T. reinforcements 82; artillery shelling Chocolate Hill 82; forces overwhelmed 84; seasoned T. troops 85; infiltrators 93–94; front line 92; grenades 103; sniping menace 105; positions overlooked entire Suvla Plain 105; gunners and O.P. officers 105; heavy bombardment of T. positions 108; T. bombardment 108; Burnt (Scimitar) Hill remained T. 114; troopers wounded to rear of T. frontline trenches 114; trench captured 115; official T. government announcement 119; officers 119; Army 119; divisions 119; battery puts a shell over 128; Hill 60 formed a salient in both British and T. lines 129; Army; positions . . . series of impassable mountains and valleys; counter-attacks 131; minister of war (Enver Pasha) 132; trenches on the flank 138; Holm-oak line 139; lines 142; booty of war material used for other T. armies 145–146; soldiers; artillery 145–146; casualties 147–148; official count 147–148; records, authorities, infantry regiments 147–148; sniper 148; front in Palestine 148; nation 152; Young T. officer (Kemal) 151–152

Ukraine, Crimea 2
Undermining 34, 128, 130

V Beach, Helles 16
Valetta Harbor, Malta: General von Sanders detained at 149
Verey lights, "garish glare of" 128
Vermin, presence of 124
Victorian, H.M.T.: 5/Suffolk and remainder of 163rd Brigade leave Lemnos for Egypt on 146

W Beach, "Lancashire Landing," Helles: eye-witness account by Major Gillam 18, 19, 20
War Cabinet/War Council 10, 13, 22, 32, 35, 37, 119, 122, 133, 135
War office document Re: Army arrangements for water survey to troops at Suvla 52
Warburg, Battle of Marquis of Granby distinguished himself at 215
Warnes, Lieutenant G. G., 1/5th Suffolk: wounded Kuchuk Anafarta Ova 93
Warwickshire Yeomanry: Major Gillam served in prior to the war, witnesses his old regiment in action 109
Water: desperate crisis 88; sources which could be tapped 88–89
Watford 43; 8/Hampshire joined rest of 54th (East Anglian) Division at 44; 5/Suffolk training at 92
Watson, Sergeant J.: 8/Northumberland Fusiliers, lands at Suvla 64
Weevils 129
Wellington, Duke of 70, 158
Welsh Horse 128
Welsh Imperial Yeomanry 128
Wemyss, Rear-Admiral Rosslyn: states view on complacency at GHQ 79
Westminster Dragoons 110
"Whizz-bangs." Most feared projectile at Salonika 129n
Wilkins, Private, 6th Royal Dublin Fusiliers: killed by grenade 103
Willmer, Major Fritz, German officer i/c Anafarta detachment: "circumspect and energetic," entrusted with defense of the Anafarta Plain encircling Suvla Bay 47; forces at his disposal 47; asserted his artillery had not suffered from British naval gunfire 64–65; unlikely to have deployed all ordnance on Kiretch Tepe 64n; reported Suvla Bay landings to General von Sanders 65; his detachment put up spirited resistance 65; Colonel Kannengiesser detected Willmer's companies deployed 66; inadequate forces blocking Suvla threat 67; sends further report to Sanders; urges dispatch of reinforcements post haste 72; anxiety eased somewhat 77; reported continuing landing of hostile forces 79; Ninth Corps held up by his Anafarta detachment 79; account of Suvla landings acknowledged good order of British troops 159
Wiltshire Regiment: overwhelmed and decimated on the Sari Bair Ridge 129
Wine 24, 169–170
Wolfe, General James, of Quebec fame 58
Woodward, Brig.-Gen. E.M. *see* Appendix E
Wolton, Captain E. D., co-author of *The History of the 1st/5th Battalion "The Suffolk Regiment"* ix; "Jam-tin" bombs and catapult 35; 5th to 1st/5th and 2nd/5th Suffolk 41; lack of adequate maps 51; listening-post personnel identified 128n; capture of well related 129; migrating geese described by 138–139; cited shortages of artillery ammunition as precipitating the knife-rest incident 138–139; floods and blizzard 139–143; returns to civilian profession 149; testified to good order and military discipline of the landings 160
Wolton, Lieutenant H. Cœur de. D Company, 1/5th Suffolk Detailed: Corporal Lane to take detachment to man an out-

post 88; replies rather regally to Lane's concerned query 88; instrumental in obtaining Corporal Lane a commission 88*n*

Wolton, Lieutenant O.B., 1/5th Suffolk: killed in action Kuchuk Anafarta Ova 120

Worcestershire Yeomanry 110

Worlington, Suffolk 6, 44, 148–149

X Beach, Helles *16*

Y Beach, Helles: unopposed landing, opportunity not exploited *16*, 29–30

Yeomanry: brought over from Egypt 98; advance of first operation of the war 109; shelter below Chocolate Hill 112; storming assault on Scimitar Hill 113; made good progress and ordered to "fix bayonets!" 114; 2nd Mounted (Yeomanry) Division "were the chief sufferers" of unsuccessful 21st August attack 132; exemplary discipline of 159

Yeomanry: specific regiments (in the newly created Territorial and Reserve Forces cavalry brigades were largely made up of Yeomanry units) 1/1st Berkshire storm Scimitar Hill, Trooper Potts' (B Squadron) gallantry earned him a Victoria Cross 110, 112, 115–116, 128; Imperial 128; Suffolk 128*n*; Middlesex 109; Sherwood Rangers 109; Warwickshire 109; Welsh Imperial (former miners later manned "listening-post") 128*n*; 2nd Mounted (Yeomanry) Division ordered to sail from Egypt 97–98; 2nd Mounted (Yeomanry) Division brought up from Egypt — minus horses, 105; corps reserve at Lala Baba 106; advance under shrapnel made by 109; marched steadily across the Salt Lake 109; Capt. Teichman advances with them and extols their velour 110–112; dismounted Yeomanry attacked the Turks across the Salt Lake and never faltered in their advance 110; General Peyton, Commander of 2nd Mounted Division of Yeomanry, talked with Ellis Ashmead-Bartlett after battle 112; said some Y. regiments had no idea of their objective 112; magnificent view of 113; advanced splendidly under a curtain of shrapnel 113; unable to get to grips with the enemy 114; were the chief sufferers on 21st August 132; exemplary discipline of 159

The Young Turks 8–9

Zeppelins 128

Zero Hour 148

Zion Mule Corps 204

www.ingramcontent.com/pod-product-compliance
Ingram Content Group UK Ltd.
Pitfield, Milton Keynes, MK11 3LW, UK
UKHW041940140426
5217IPUK00014B/583